# MONEY
# BOOK

## *MONEY MATTERS USA*

350 N. Guadalupe St., Suite 140-288
San Marcos, TX 78666

E-mail: afwes@msn.com

## Acknowledgements

*To all Airmen, Soldiers, Sailors, and Marines, whose gallant Sacrifices will always keep America the land of the free.*

I would like to express my thanks and deep appreciation to all who have generously assisted me in one way or another to write this book:

To Elaine Squires, Bruce Gallop, Mickey Howard, Bryan Dopp, Ed Davis, Tom Breazeale, Jim Vasile, Gail Van Akin and to all the unnamed others, my gratitude is great.

---

## Dedication

To: Mom, Dad, Geneva; my Children Jackie, Bobby, Cherrie, Amber, Jayson, Marlena and Grandchildren Chris, Deevena, Kyra, Jackie Jr. & Elsabeth.
I love you all.

---

## Forward

*Money Book* is for the Consumer who craves financial knowledge to bring forth vast financial opportunities that are readably available, but have eluded them thus far.
   Therefore, the hope is that in providing this valuable book of insight, each Consumer will experience rewards and fullness life has to offer.
   Dear Consumer, your journey has just begun. Your fight for financial survival is now in written format, full of creative illustrations for easy reading and comprehension. Now, go and fight the good fight—you have the tools.

Sincerely,

J. Burch

---

## Disclaimer

# MONEY BOOK CONTENTS:

## UNITED STATES ARMY

The first US Army, the Continental was created in 1775 by the Continental Congress as a unified army for the statesto fight Great Britain.

### CORE VALUES OF THE ARMY

- ➤ Loyalty
- ➤ Duty
- ➤ Respect
- ➤ Courage
- ➤ Honor
- ➤ Integrity
- ➤ Selfless Service

### IMPORTANT ARMY SITES

**Official site of the United States Army:** www.army.mil
**Army Knowledge Online (AKO):** www.us.army.mil
**US Army & Army Reserve Recruiting:** www.goarmy.com
**Army ROTC:** www.goarmy.com/rotc
**Army Reserves Site:** www.armyreserve.army.mil/ARWEB
**Army National Guard Site:** www.arng.army.mil
**Army Links:** www.army.mil/info/a-z
**Army Insider:** www.armyinsider.com
**U.S. Armed Forces Legal Services:**
http://legalassistance.law.af.mil/index.php
**Army Personnel Center:** www.hqda.army.mil/MPSC
**Army Education Link:**
www.hrc.army.mil/site/education/Related_Links.html
**Army Healthcare (Tricare):** www.tricare.mil
**Army Benefits:** www.militarybenefits.com/military_active.html
**DoD Library:** www.dod.mil/other_info/libraries.html
**Army/Civilian Employment Center (CPOL):** www.cpol.army.mil
**Operation Home Front:** www.operationhomefront.org
**Army Emergency Relief:** www.aerhq.org
**Army Wikipedia:** http://en.wikipedia.org/wiki/US_Army
**Association of the United States Army (AUSA):**
www.ausa.org/webpub/DeptHome.nsf/byid/DeptHome.nsfhome
**Army Veterans Associations:**
www.army.mil/veteransorganizations
**Army Retirement Services:** www.armyg1.army.mil/rso
**Military Benefit Association (MBA):** www.militarybenefit.org

## UNITED STATES AIR FORCE

The National Security Act of 1947 became law on July 26, 1947. It created the Department of the Air Force. On September 18, 1947, W. Stuart Symington became Secretary of the Air Force.

### CORE VALUES OF THE AIR FORCE

- ➤ Integrity First
- ➤ Service Before Self
- ➤ Excellence In All We Do

### IMPORTANT AIR FORCE SITES

**Official Website of the Air Force:** www.af.mil
**Air Force Portal Splash Page (AFKO):** https://www.my.af.mil
**Air Force Recruiting:** www.airforce.com
**Air Force ROTC:** www.afrotc.com
**Air Force Reserves Site:** www.afrc.af.mil
**Air Force National Guard Site:** www.ang.af.mil
**Air Force Links:** www.airforce.com/af-links
**Air Force Insider:** www.airforceinsider.com
**U.S. Armed Forces Legal Services:**
http://legalassistance.law.af.mil/index.php
**Air Force Personnel Center:** http://ask.afpc.randolph.af.mil
**Air Force Education Link:**
www.au.af.mil/au/awc/awcgate/awcgate.htm
**Air Force Healthcare (Tricare):** www.tricare.mil
**Air Force Benefits:**
www.militarybenefits.com/military_active.html
**DoD Library:** www.dod.mil/other_info/libraries.html
**Air Force/Civilian Employment Center:**
https://ww2.afpc.randolph.af.mil/resweb
**Operation Home Front:** www.operationhomefront.org
**Air Force Aid Society:** www.afas.org/index.cfm
**AF Wikipedia:** http://en.wikipedia.org./wiki/US_Air_Force
**Air Force Association:** www.afa.org
**Air Force Sergeants Association:** www.afsahq.org
**Air Force Retiree Services:** www.retirees.af.mil
**Military Benefit Association (MBA):** www.militarybenefit.org

I WANT YOU FOR U.S. ARMY
NEAREST RECRUITING STATION

# UNITED STATES NAVY

The United States Navy traces its origins to the Continental Navy, which the Continental Congress established on October 13, 1775.

## CORE VALUES OF THE NAVY

- ➤ Honor
- ➤ Courage
- ➤ Commitment

## IMPORTANT NAVY SITES

**Official site of the United States Navy:** www.navy.mil
**Navy Knowledge Online:** wwwa.nko.navy.mil/portal/home
**Navy Recruiting:** www.navy.com
**Navy ROTC:** www.navy.com/careers/nrotc
**Naval Reserves Site:** www.npc.navy.mil/Channels
**Navy Links:** www.navy.mil/links/alpha.asp
**Navy Insider:** www.navyinsider.com
**U.S. Armed Forces Legal Services:**
http://legalassistance.law.af.mil/index.php
**Navy Personnel Command:** www.npc.navy.mil/channels
**Navy Education Link:** www.navycollege.navy.mil
**Navy Healthcare (Tricare):** www.tricare.mil
**Navy Benefits:** www.navy.com/benefits
**DoD Library:** www.dod.mil/other_info/libraries.html
**Navy Civilian Employment Center:** https://chart.donhr.navy.mil
**Operation Home Front:** www.operationhomefront.org
**Navy-Marine Corps Society:** www.nmcrs.org
**Navy Wikipedia:**
http://en.wikipedia.org/wiki/The_United_States_Navy
**Navy Family Disaster Assistance:**
http://taskforcenavyfamily.navy.mil/NavyFamilies
**Navy Retired Activities Homepage:**
www.npc.navy.mil/commandsupport/retiredactivities
**Military Benefit Association (MBA):** www.militarybenefit.org

# UNITED STATES MARINE CORPS

On November 10th, 1775, the Second Continental Congress agreed to raise two battalions of Continental Marines, which created the birth of our United States Marine Corps.

## CORE VALUES OF THE MARINE CORPS

- ➤ Honor
- ➤ Courage
- ➤ Commitment

## IMPORTANT MARINE CORPS SITES

**Official site of the United States Marine Corps:** www.usmc.mil
**Marine Knowledge Online:** wwwa.nko.navy.mil/portal/home
**Marine Corps Recruiting:** www.marines.com
**Marine JROTC:** www.mcjrotc.org
**Marine Corps Reserves Site:** www.marforres.usmc.mil
**Marine Corps Links:** www.operationmom.org/resources.html
**Marine Corps Insider:** www.marinecorpsinsider.com
**U.S. Armed Forces Legal Services:**
http://legalassistance.law.af.mil/index.php
**Marine Corps Combat Command:** www.mccdc.usmc.mil
**Marine Corps Education Link:** www.tecom.usmc.mil
**Marine Corps Healthcare (Tricare):** www.tricare.mil
**Marine Corps Benefits:** www.marines.com/main/index/quality_citizens/benefit_of_services
**DoD Library:** www.dod.mil/other_info/libraries.html
**MCCS Employment Center:** www.usmc-mccs.org/employ
**Operation Home Front:** www.operationhomefront.org
**Navy-Marine Corps Society:** www.nmcrs.org
**USMC Wikipedia:**
http://en.wikipedia.org/wiki/United_States_Marine_Corps
**Marine Corps League:** www.mcleague.com/mdp/index.php
**Marine Corps Heritage Foundation:** www.marineheritage.org
**Marine Corps Association:** www.mca-marines.org
**Marine Corps Retiree Life:** www.usmc-mccs.org/retiree
**Military Benefit Association (MBA):** www.militarybenefit.org

Today's military personnel and their families face many challenges, as well as the additional stress associated with frequent separation. To assist with such difficulties, Family Centers, along with other agency programs, veteran centers and state veteran benefit programs provide much needed help and support.

## U.S. Military Family Centers

Located on most military installations, Family Centers provide information, life skills education, and support services to military members and their families. "Family Centers" is a generic term that includes similar offices in each of the separate military branches. These centers provide community service programs that enhance the quality of life for military personnel and their families. One key function of a Family Center is to link customers with appropriate services available in the local community and/or through state and federal assistance programs. To properly fulfill this role, the Family Center director develops partnerships with organizations, such as those related to health and human services, school systems, employment assistance, law enforcement and recreation. If you cannot locate a Family Center, please contact your respective military branch's headquarters office listed below. The designation "DSN," preceding some of the phone numbers, refers to the military phone system and does not apply to the civilian sector.

### MILITARY FAMILY CENTERS DIRECTORY

Access to a directory of Family Centers by Service and by State is available through the Military Family Resource Center (MFRC) website at www.mfrc.dodqol.org/progDir. If you have questions on other services of MFRC, visit their site or e-mail them at **mfrc.request@caliber.com**.

### Air Force Community Readiness and Family Support

AF/A1SF 4E235
Force Sustainment Division
1040 Air Force Pentagon
Washington DC 20330-1040
(703) 697-0067
Website: **www.afcrossroads.com**

Air Force Crossroads is a comprehensive resource for Air Force members and their families with support, advice and contacts relating to nearly every aspect of personal and professional life. Along with topics that range from health and wellness, finances, family matters and recreation, the network includes access to the Air Force Spouse Forum, chat rooms, an employment forum, a flea market and links to news sources.

### Marine Corps Community Services

3280 Russell Rd. Quantico, VA 22134-5103
703-784-0275
DSN: 278-0275
Toll free: 1-800-MARINES
Fax: 703-784-9816
Website: **www.usmc-mccs.org**

The Personal and Family Readiness Division (MR) provides a number of Marine Corps personnel service programs, such as: Casualty Assistance, DEERS Dependency Determination, Voting Assistance, Postal Services, and Personal Claims.
MCCS delivers goods and services at over 2,250 facilities and has a staff of more than 12,000 employees worldwide.

### Fleet and Family Support Programs

Commander, Navy Installations Command
2713 Mitscher Road, SW, Suite 300
Washington, DC 20373-5802
Ph: 1-800-FSC-LINE (800-372-5463)
Website: **www.nffsp.org**

The Fleet and Family Support Program delivered by Commander, Navy Installations Command, provides support, references, information and a wide range of assistance for members of the Navy and their immediate families to meet the unique challenges of the military lifestyle. Up-to-date news, messages, links and resources are provided, including assistance with relocation, employment, career and benefits, healthy lifestyles, casualties, domestic violence, and retirement. Family and Morale, Welfare and Recreation Command (FMWRC).

### Family Programs Directorate, Army Community Service

4700 King Street
Alexandria, VA 22302
703-681-5375 / DSN: 761-5375
Fax: 703-681-7236
Website: **www.myArmyLifeToo.com**

My Army Life Too portal is the single gateway to comprehensive information on the support available to Army personnel and families, including resources to strengthen home and family life, Army basic training, lifelong learning, finances, employment, relevant news, along with links to key resources.

### U.S. Coast Guard

2100 Second St., SW, Room 6320
Washington, DC 20593
202-267-6160
Toll free: 1-800-368-5647 (Safety)
Toll free: 1-877-NOW-USCG (Recruiting)
Fax: 202-267-4798
Website: **www.uscg.mil**

The U.S. Coast Guard can provide key resources, including core publications, career information and related news, as well as a comprehensive background about its mission, community services, history, photos and reports.

### Military HomeFront
**www.militaryhomefront.dod.mil**
Military HomeFront is the official Department of Defense website for relevant information to assist and improve the quality of life for troops and their families. Members of all branches of the military service and their immediate families will find reliable, up-to-date details and advice on such topics as education, housing, legal matters, parenting, personal finances, pay and benefits, relocation and healthcare. Military Home Front also makes it easier for leaders to locate official quality of life program information and resources for their troops and families. In addition, service providers can access desk guides, policies, forms and other resources.

### Military OneSource
**www.militaryonesource.com** or **1-800-342-9674**
Military OneSource is an excellent hub of information and assistance for military personnel and their families. This comprehensive, 24/7 resource offers a wide variety of helpful services and tools dedicated to meeting the special needs and improving the lives of service men and women, both personally and professionally. In addition to in-person counseling and direct links to all of the armed services home sites, Military OneSource offers advice and who-to contact information on matters such as health, education, training, moving, shopping, and legal issues and finances. Podcasts, webinars, discussion boards and news feeds cover special topics and provide answers to help resolve problems.

### Better Business Bureau Military Line
The BBB Military Line (**www.military.bbb.org**) offers consumer education and advocacy to service members and their families. Five service-specific sites contain current military-related consumer news, as well as links to local BBBs and other sites with useful consumer information:
- **www.army.bbb.org**
- **www.navy.bbb.org**
- **www.airforce.bbb.org**
- **www.marinecorps.bbb.org**
- **www.coastguard.bbb.org**

Users may request reports, file complaints, and sign up for a custom consumer newsletter. On a local level, area BBBs provides educational briefings for military personnel and their families, and work with local businesses to promote ethical treatment of military consumers.

### Commissaries and Exchanges
Consumers who shop at military commissaries and exchanges, and who have a question or problem should contact the local manager before contacting the regional offices. If your problem is not resolved at the local level, then write or call the regional office nearest you. Be sure to discuss the problem with the local and regional offices of a commissary or exchange before contacting the national headquarters.

### Department Of Veteran Affairs
Toll free: 1-800-827-1000
TTY: 1-800-829-4833 (Toll free)
Fax: 202-273-5716
**www.va.gov**
For information about VA medical care or benefits, write, call or visit your nearest VA facility.

### National Cemetery Administration
810 Vermont Ave., NW
Washington, DC 20420
202-273-5221
Fax: 202-273-6698
**www.va.gov**
Contact the National Cemetery Administration for information about burials, headstones or markers, the State cemetery grants program, and presidential memorial certificates.

### Veterans Benefits Administration
810 Vermont Ave., NW
Washington, DC 20420
202-273-7588 (Publications Only)
Toll free: 1-800-827-1000
**www.va.gov**

### Veterans Health Administration
810 Vermont Ave., NW
Washington, DC 20420
Toll free: 1-877-222-8387
Fax: 202-273-9609
**www1.va.gov/health/index.asp**

### Veteran's Employment and Training Service
Department of Labor
Room S1325
200 Constitution Ave., NW
Washington, DC 20210
Toll free: 1-866-4-USA-DOL (487-2365)
TTY: 1-877-889-5627 (Toll free)
**www.dol.gov/vets**

**Veterans' State Benefits Websites:**
www.va.gov/statedva.htm or
www.military.com/benefits/veteran-benefits/state-veterans-benefits-directory

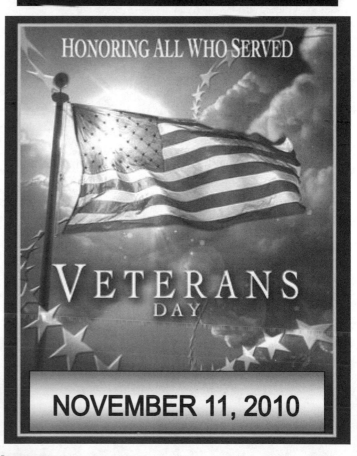
HONORING ALL WHO SERVED
VETERANS DAY
NOVEMBER 11, 2010

## PART I: MILITARY SERVICE COMPENSATION

■ **Military Pay Raises:** This main component of military pay is based on grade and time in service. It is computed using your "pay date". Since 2007, pay raises are now equal to the increase in the Employment Cost Index (ECI). Pay raises may exceed these automatic levels if authorized and funded by Congress.
**www.dfas.mil/militarypay/militarypaytables.html**

■ **Basic Allowance for Subsistence (BAS):** BAS is a non-taxable allowance used to offset the cost of the service member's meals. Members assigned to single-type Government quarters at their permanent duty station are required to eat in government dining facilities, receive BAS and are charged discounted meal rate which is deducted from their pay. These members are allowed to claim missed meals when a Government meal is not reasonably available for consumption. Regular 2009 BAS rates for enlisted members is $323.87 and for officers is $223.04.
**www.defenselink.mil/militarypay/pay/bas/index.html**

■ **Annual Leave:** Annual leave is accrued at a rate of 2.5 days of leave for each month of active duty service for a total of 30 days of leave each fiscal year. Members who are unable to use leave due to military necessity may accumulate a maximum of 60 days by the end of a fiscal year. In the event service members are unable to use their excess accrued leave before 30 September as a result of mission requirements, approval may be requested to carryover the excess leave days (Special Leave Accrual).
**www.dfas.mil/airforce2/militarypay/militaryleave.html**

■ **Federal Tax Advantage:** While all pay is taxable, most allowances are tax-exempt. The primary allowances for most individuals are Basic Allowance for Subsistence (BAS), Basic Allowance for Housing (BAH) or Overseas Housing Allowance (OHA), and Family Separation Allowance (FSA). Tax savings can be significant as BAS and BAH averages over 30% of a member's total regular cash pay. In addition to being tax-exempt from Federal and State taxes, these allowances are also excluded from Social Security taxes.
**www.defenselink.mil/militarypay/pay/tax/index.html**

■ **Regular Military Compensation Calculator:**
**www.defenselink.mil/militarypay/pay/calc/index.html**

■ **Family Subsistence Supplemental Allowance (FSSA):** FSSA is a monthly entitlement paid in whole dollars; equal to amount needed to bring military families household income to 130% of the Federal poverty line but not to exceed $500 for large families or households. All active duty members' stationed in or outside the United States are eligible to apply for and participate in the FSSA.
**www.dmdc.osd.mil/fssa**

■ **Family Separation Allowance (FSA):** The purpose of FSA is to compensate qualified members serving inside or outside the United States for added expenses incurred due to an enforced family separation. FSA has three different categories: FSA-R, FSA-S, and FSA-T. Members are eligible for FSA-R if transportation of dependents, including dependents acquired after the effective date of orders, is not authorized at Government expense and dependents do not live in the vicinity of the member's permanent duty station. FSA-S applies to members serving on ships away

from the homeport continuously for more than 30 days. A member is eligible for FSA-T if member is on TDY away from permanent station continuously for more than 30 days and member's dependents are not residing at or near TDY station. This includes members required to perform a period of the TDY before reporting to their initial station of assignment. Family Separation Allowance is $250 per month.
**www.dfas.mil/militarypay/woundedwarriorpay/familyse parationallowancefsa.html**

■ **Hardship Duty Pay (HDP):** HDP is payable to members entitled to basic pay, at a monthly rate not to exceed $300, while performing duty designated by Secretary of Defense as hardship duty. Secretary of Defense has established that HDP shall be paid to members for performing a designated mission, when assigned to a designated location and/or, when serving a designated involuntary extension of duty.
**www.dfas.mil/militarypay/woundedwarriorpay/hardship dutypay.html**

■ **Combat Zone Tax Exclusion (CTZE):** Presidential Executive Order determines combat zones and applicable dates. Earnings received while performing duties in, or in direct support of areas designated as a combat zone are excluded from taxable income. This exclusion is unlimited for enlisted members and warrant officers, but is limited to $6,867.60 per month for officers. **www.dfas.mil/navy2/ taxinformation/combatzonetaxexclusion.html**

■ **Imminent Danger Pay (IDP)/Hostile Fire Pay (HFP):** Both are covered under Title 37 USC Section 310 and are used synonymously; they are commonly referred to as IDP. IDP is a "threat based" pay meaning it is payable for any month the member performs duty in an IDP area (designated by USD P&R). These are areas where members are the subject to threat of physical harm because of civil insurrection, civil war, terrorism, etc. HFP is an "event based" pay, meaning if member is exposed to an actual occurrence of hostile fire or an explosion of hostile mine, member is entitled to HFP for the month in which hostile fire happened, and up to 3 months afterwards while hospitalized. IDP/HFP rate is $225 per month. Designated areas are listed in DOD FMR, Vol. 7a, and Ch 10.
**www.dfas.mil/army2/specialpay/hostilefireimminentdan gerpay.html**

■ **Savings Deposit Program (SDP):** Military members may be authorized to participate in the SDP during assignments and deployments to specified locations. The program provides an interest rate of 10%, provides service members to contribute any portion of their unallotted current pay, and allowances up to a maximum amount of $10,000. Interest paid on the amounts deposited into the SDP is taxable.
**www.dfas.mil/army2/investmentoptions/savingsdeposit programsdp.html**

■ **Travel Entitlements:** Members may be eligible for a wide variety of travel entitlements for themselves and their authorized dependents when ordered to perform official travel for TDY and/or PCS. Members should seek counseling from their MPF, FSO, and TMO. For more information visit: **www.military.com/benefits/ tricare/prime-travel-entitlement**

## PART II: HOUSING ALLOWANCES

■ **Basic Allowance for Housing (BAH):** The intent of BAH is to provide service members accurate and equitable housing compensation based on housing costs in local civilian housing markets and is payable when Government quarters are not provided. BAH is a paid allowance to assignments to a Permanent Duty Station (PDS) in the United States and is based not on actual expense, but on median rental costs, utilities, and renter's insurance. BAH rate calculations do not include mortgage costs. Members residing in family-type Government quarters are not entitled to BAH. Many installations are privatizing their quarters, meaning that private contractors are taking over previously owned and operated family housing. Members in these privatized quarters are entitled to BAH and the rental agreement requires a rent amount equal to the BAH entitlement paid via allotment. The Leave and Earning Statement (LES) displays the BAH rate below the heading ENTITLEMENTS, listed as BAH. The PAY DATA portion of the LES shows the BAH type and BAH dependents, as well as other housing-related data. **http://perdiem.hqda.pentagon.mil/perdiem**

■ **BAH Differential (BAH-DIFF):** This is the housing allowance amount for a member who is assigned to single-type quarters and who is authorized a basic allowance for housing solely by reason of the members payment of child support. A member is not authorized BAH-DIFF if child support payment is less than applicable pay grade BAH-DIFF amount. BAH-Diff is published annually and is determined by increasing the previous year's table by the percentage growth of the military pay raise. **www.defenselink.mil/militarypay/pay/bah/02_types.html**

■ **BAH-Partial:** Members without dependents who are not authorized to receive full BAH or OHA and are residing in Government single-type quarters, are entitled to partial BAH if they meet certain conditions.

■ **Overseas Housing Allowance (OHA):** OHA is a cost reimbursement based allowance to help defray housing costs incident to assignments to a PDS outside the United States. Members are reimbursed actual rental costs not to exceed the maximum OHA rate for each locality and grade. There are two types of allowances paid under OHA, Move-In Housing Allowance (MIHA) and monthly OHA including a utility/recurring maintenance allowance. The location MIHA (for those who qualify) is based on the average "move-in" costs for members. The monthly OHA is the rent, up to the rental allowance at a PDS, plus the utility/recurring maintenance allowance. **www.defensetravel.dod.mil/perdiem/allooha.html**

■ **Family Separation for Housing (FSH):** The purpose of FSH is to pay a member for added housing expenses resulting from enforced separation from dependents (more than 30 consecutive days). It is not payable under any condition to a member permanently assigned to a duty station in Hawaii or any duty station under permissive orders. FSH is payable to each member with dependents who is on permanent duty outside the United States or in Alaska who meets all of the required conditions. **www.dfas.mil/more/legislativeaffairs/fy05legislation/section603.pdf**

■ **Station Allowances:** Members may be authorized certain station allowances for themselves and their command-sponsored dependents when assigned OCONUS. They include Cost of Living Allowance and Temporary Living Allowance. **http://www.defensetravel.dod.mil/perdiem**

■ **CONUS COLA:** CONUS Cost-of-Living Allowance (CONUS COLA) provides compensation for variations in non-housing costs in the continental United States. Members and authorized dependents may be entitled to CONUS COLA when assigned or residing in a high-cost area. CONUS COLA should not be confused with BAH which considers median rental costs, rental insurance and utilities. CONUS COLA varies by pay grade, years of service (YOS), and whether or not the member has dependents. For information about CONUS COLA visit: **www.defensetravel.dod.mil/perdiem/ccform.html**

## PART III: RETIREMENT PAY & TSP BENEFITS

■ **Retirement Pay:** One of the most attractive incentives of a military career is the retirement system that provides a monthly retirement income for those who serve a minimum of twenty years. Your retirement represents a considerable value over your life expectancy. While many civilian employees must contribute to their retirement, yours is provided at no cost to you. Currently, there are three retirement plans in effect based upon your Date of Initial Entry to Uniformed Service (DIEUS) -- Final Pay, High-3, and Choice of High-3 or Redux with $30K Career Status Bonus. For more information, visit: **www.dfas.mil/retiredpay.html**

■ **Thrift Savings Plan (TSP):** The TSP provides military members a 401(k)-like savings plan, which allows members to contribute pre-tax dollars thereby reducing current taxes, and to accumulate long-term, tax-deferred savings and earnings, which can supplement future retirement income. Participation is painless through payroll deduction, and account management is easy via worldwide web interface. The open seasons are eliminated and members can accomplish any action at any time. The Internal Revenue Code places an annual limit on elective deferrals, e.g., tax-deferred employee contributions to the TSP. For 2009, the elective deferral limit is $16,500. Useful information can be found at the following Website: **www.tsp.gov**

## PART IV: DEATH AND SURVIVOR BENEFITS

■ **Servicemember's Group Life Insurance (SGLI):** If you elect to participate in SGLI and subsequently die on active duty, your survivors will be eligible for life insurance payments. You may purchase life insurance coverage in $50,000 increments up to $400,000 at a very low cost. Additionally, family member coverage of up to $100,000 for the member's spouse (spouse coverage is limited to no more than the member's current coverage) and $10,000 per child became effective 1 Nov 2001, and was automatic for all members participating in SGLI. The spouse cover-rage premium is an additional monthly premium of $6-$54 for maximum coverage based the spouse's age; coverage for children is free. You have the option to reduce or decline spouse coverage and the associated premium. **www.insurance.va.gov/sgliSite/SGLI/SGLI.htm**

■ **Dependency and Indemnity Compensation (DIC):** Surviving dependents may also be eligible to receive monthly DIC payments (nontaxable) in the amount of $1033 for the surviving spouse and an additional $257 for each surviving child. DIC is adjusted annually for inflation. **www.vba.va.gov/bln/21/Rates/comp03b.htm**

■ **Death Gratuity:** The death gratuity is a lump sum payment for beneficiaries of a member who dies on active duty, active duty for training, or inactive duty for training, or full-time National Guard duty. Its purpose is to assist the survivors in their readjustment and to aid them in meeting immediate expenses incurred. Currently, the death gratuity is $100,000, and normally payment is made within 24 hours of member's untimely expiry to beneficiaries. **www.dfas.mil/airforce2/deathandburialbenefits.html**

■ **Survivor Benefit Plan (SBP):** Your regular pay stops when you die. However, if you die on active duty with 20 or more years of service, or in the line of duty with less than 20 years of service, your surviving spouse and children are automatically protected by SBP--at no cost to you. The surviving spouse will get an annuity equal to the difference between the DIC payment and the maximum SBP payment that would be paid if you had been retired on the date of your death. The SBP survivor annuity is adjusted each year by the same percentage increase given to military retired pay. For AD deaths in the line of duty the annuity is 55% of what retired pay would have been if retired for total disability. For a retiree the annuity is 55% of the elected retired base pay amount. Survivors of members who retired on or after 28 Oct 04 who participated at the maximum level are not subject to any offset at age 62, when Social Security starts. For those surviving spouses age 62 and older already drawing the SBP annuity, reduction will be eliminated by 5% a year. Since Apr 08, the full 55% is paid to all annuitants. **www.vba.va.gov/survivors/index.htm**

■ **Other substantial benefits:** Surviving dependents may be eligible to receive additional benefits upon the death of a member. They include mortuary entitlements to reimburse the costs of burial, housing for 365 days, active duty transitional health and dental care for 3 years, commissary and exchange privileges, and various Veteran's Affairs and Social Security benefits. For more information: **https://iris.va.gov/scripts/iris.cfg/php.exe/enduser/home.php or call 1-800-827-1000**

■ **Federal Long Term Care Insurance Program:** Members may be eligible to obtain coverage from the FLTCIP at premiums estimated to be 15-20% less than standard premiums for comparable coverage. The Federal Long Term Care Insurance Program was designed specifically for members of the Federal Family. It is sponsored by the Federal Government and backed by two of the country's top insurance companies. The Federal Program is designed to help protect enrollees against the high costs of long term care. Personal access to registered nurse care coordinators, and home care provisions are just a few of the reasons why the Federal Program may be the smart choice for you. To learn more, visit: **www.ltcfeds.com**

## PART V: SUPPORTING BENEFITS

■ **Base Exchange:** "We Go Where You Go" is the motto of AAFES. For more than 105 years, the exchange service has remained true to its commitment to Value, Service, and Support for the military customer and their families worldwide. Independent price surveys indicate that AAFES' customers save an average of 11% over the competition. AAFES helps in two principal ways. First is its guarantee to "meet or beat" any retailer's price on the same item (under $5, no questions asked, or over $5, within 30 days of the retailers advertisement). Second, profits are used to support the Services' Morale, Welfare, and Recreation programs. AAFES now offers 24/7 conveniences through its new website: **www.aafes.com**

■ **Base Services:** Installation services provide conveniently located, low-cost, well managed activities and entertainment. Programs include the golf course, child development center, skills development center, auto skills, Aero Club, community centers, swimming pool(s), Enlisted Club, intramural sports, bowling center, library, chapel, youth center, outdoor recreation, and discounts on special events/off-base recreation areas through Information, Ticket and Tours and base fitness center in conjunction with SG-run health and wellness center.

■ **Career Broadening Opportunities:** Assignments, Special Duty Assignments, Retraining, Overseas Duty, etc. **http://ask.afpc.randolph.af.mil/main_content.asp?prods1=1&prods2=14&prods3=186&prods4=606**

■ **Child Care/Youth Programs:** Child Development Centers (CDC) offer care on a space available basis for children 0-5 years of age. Licensed family childcare is available at most installations. Centers are certified by the Department of Defense and accredited by the National Association for the Education of Young Children. Fees are based on total family income. Before and after school programs are also offered as part of our Youth Programs. Youth Centers are affiliated with the Boys & Girls Clubs of America and offer a variety of character and leadership development, education and career development, health and life skills, arts, and sports, fitness and recreation programs. Extended duty childcare is offered for members required to work late or who have regular childcare arrangements, temporarily not available.

■ **Commissary:** (the cornerstone of Military Quality of Life): Items are sold at cost plus a 5% surcharge, which covers the construction of new commissaries and modernization of existing stores. Customers save an average of 30%, approximately $2,400 per year for a family of four, compared to commercial prices. Military members and retirees consistently indicate commissaries are one of the most important benefits. **www.commissaries.com**

## PART VI: EDUCATION

■ **Montgomery GI Bill (MGIB):** Individuals entering Service after 1 Jul 85 are automatically enrolled in the MGIB, unless they disenroll in basic training. The MGIB program provides up to 36 months of education benefits. The MGIB requires $100 a month nontaxable pay reduction for the first full 12 months of active duty. Generally, benefits are payable for 10 years following your release from active duty. For more information and how to increase your monthly benefit visit: **www.gibill.va.gov**

■ **Post-9/11 GI Bill:** Provides financial support for education and housing to individuals with at least 90 days of aggregate service on or after 9/11/ 2001, or discharged with a service-connected disability after 30 days. Honorable discharge is required to be eligible. For more information visit: **www.gibill.va.gov/GI_Bill_Info/CH33/Post-911.htm**

■ **Transferability of GI Bill to Dependents:** Eligible soldiers may transfer their GI Bill to spouses or children. For more information visit: **www.gibill.va.gov/GI_Bill_Info/CH33/Transfer.htm** or **www.defenselink.mil/home/features/2009/0409_gibill** To apply, start here: **www.dmdc.osd.mil/TEB**

- **Montgomery G.I. Bill "Kicker":** The **"Kicker"** is an additional educational GI Bill benefit, which can increase your monthly GI Bill payment rate by as much as **$950 a month**. An individual's branch of service may offer the **"Kicker"** as part of an enlistment or reenlistment contract, or other reasons. Ask your recruiter what the requirements are to be eligible, and how to get the most from of the program. To learn more visit: **www.todaysmilitary.com/benefits/tuition-support www.military.com/money-for-school/gi-bill/gi-bill-kicker**

- **G.I. Bill "Buy Up" Program:** The "Buy-Up" Program can help individuals get up to an extra **$150** a month added to their standard MGIB "pay rate" (if eligible). The program allows additional contributions in $20 increments up to $600. Each $20 contribution results in a $180 total increase to your GI Bill benefit. For more information: **www.military. com/money-for-school/gi-bill/gi-bill-buy-up-program**

- **Tuition Assistance:** The Armed Services currently pays 100% of tuition up to $250 per credit hour ($4,500 annually) in off-duty courses with accredited schools. To learn more visit: **www.todaysmilitary.com/benefits/tuition-support**

- **Loan Repayment Programs:** If member is full-time duty in the Armed Forces, they can qualify for the **"Loan Repayment Program"** that can help them out of debt. To learn more visit: **www.todaysmilitary.com/benefits/tuition-support**

- **Commissioning Opportunities:** Education and Commission Programs offered by the Armed Forces is an excellent way for enlisted members to earn a college degree and commission. To learn more, please visit:
Army: **www.goarmy.com/rotc/enlisted_soldiers.jsp**
Air Force: **www.afoats.af.mil**
Navy: **www.navy.com/careers/officerplanner/ enlistedtoofficer**
Marines: **www.marines.usmc.mil/RS/CRSC/CPCs/ CRSC%2029.doc**

- **Scholarships:** Many scholarships are available for both military members and their families who are pursuing a bachelor's degree. **http://aid.military.com/scholarship/ search-for-scholarships.do**
Spouse: **www.milspouse.org/Educ/Fund/MilFScholar**
For children: **www.ourmilitary.mil/scholar_mil_ children.shtml**

- **Yellow Ribbon Program:** If you are enrolled at a Yellow Ribbon participating institution and the tuition and fees exceed the highest public in-state undergraduate tuition or fees, additional funds may be available for your education program without an additional charge to your entitlement. To learn more visit: **www.gibill.va.gov/GI_Bill_info/ch33/yellow_ribbon.htm**

## PART VII: OTHER SUPPORT & BENEFITS

- **Family Readiness Centers (FRC):** Several programs are offered through installations to promote a positive family and community environment. Centers offer Transition Assistance Program for those separating/retiring from the Service, an extensive Relocation Assistance Program that includes a Smooth Move program to prepare those who will PCS and a base newcomer's tour. The family services program offers a loan locker, which includes pots, pans, cribs, and other household items available for checkout to relocating members and their families. The volunteer resource office maintains a list of agencies accepting volunteers and a list of those wishing to volunteer. The family life program offers classes in parenting, couples communication, stress management, and a host of other family-related courses. The family readiness program prepares families for the stress of deployments, NEOs, and repatriations. Emergency financial assistance programs and the Personal Financial Management Program offer information, education, and personal financial counseling on the full range of financial issues. To learn more visit: **www.military.com/benefits/ resources/family-support/ family-support-services**

- **IDEA & Suggestion Programs:** Eligible service members may participate in IDEA & Suggestion Programs offered by the Armed Forces where they can receive monetary recognition. Service members may receive money for each approved idea that results in validated tangible savings, and approved ideas resulting in intangible benefits. For more information visit:
ARMY: **http://asp.hqda.pentagon.mil/public/default.htm**
AIR FORCE: **www.vandenberg.af.mil/library/factsheets/ factsheet.asp?id=10854**
NAVY & MARINES: Submit your suggestion in writing, either on a suggestion form or in a letter format, to your local MILCAP administrator.

- **Legal Assistance:** The installation Legal Assistance Office assists members with preparing wills, powers of attorney, notary service, and provides advice on domestic relations problems, contracts, civil law matters, and income tax assistance.

- **Space Available Travel:** Active duty members are eligible for travel aboard military aircraft worldwide while family members are eligible for space available travel outside the CONUS. Click on **www.military.com/Travel/ TravelPrivileges/0,13396,,00.html**

- **VA Home Loans:** AF members may be eligible for home loans through the Veterans Administration. **www.homeloans.va.gov**

- **Vocational Training Opportunity:** Service members have training opportunities for both formal training and with various classes related to personal enhancement (PME, computer classes, management training, etc.).

- **Programs for documented personal difficulties:** Emergency leave with priority on military aircraft, Humanitarian reassignment, Permissive reassignment, Exceptional Family Member Program (EFMP), Air Force Aid Society **www.afas.org**

- **Military.com site map:** Wealth of information about education, news, blogs, recruiting tips, benefits, finance, careers, military network & more: **www.military.com/sitemap**

- **Medical and Dental:** TRICARE is the name of the DOD's regional managed health care program. Under TRICARE, there are three health plan options: TRICARE Prime (all active duty are automatically in Prime, but family members have other options); TRICARE Standard, a fee for service plan; TRICARE Extra, a Preferred Provider Organization plan. The personal costs experienced are determined by the plan selected. To learn more, contact the Beneficiary Counseling and Assistance Coordinator at the nearest military treatment facility. **www.tricare.osd.mil**

For dental care: **www.tricare.osd.mil/dental/Pro_High.cfm**

All states and American territories offer veterans benefits. These benefits may include educational grants and scholarships, special exemptions or discounts on fees and taxes, home and land loans, veteran's homes, free hunting and fishing privileges, and more.

The following is a list of phone numbers and links to websites for each of the individual states and American territories that offer veterans benefits. Be sure to take advantage of the benefits you have earned.

**ALABAMA:** 334.242.5077 / www.va.state.al.us

**ALASKA:** 907.428.6016 / http://veterans.alaska.gov

**ARKANSAS:** 501.370.3820/ www.veterans.arkansas.gov

**ARIZONA:** 602.255.3373 / www.azdvs.gov

**CALIFORNIA:** 800.952.5626 (in state) / 800.221.8998 (outside CA) / www.cdva.ca.gov

**COLORADO:** 303.343.1268 / www.coworkforce.com/vet/default.asp

**CONNECTICUT:** 860.529.2571 / 800.550.0000 / www.ct.gov/ctva

**DELAWARE:** 302.739.2792 / .800.344.9900 (in state) / http://veteransaffairs.delaware.gov

**DISTRICT OF COLUMBIA:** 202.724.5454 / http://ova.dc.gov/ova/site/default.asp

**FLORIDA:** 727.319.7400 / www.floridavets.org/index.asp

**GEORGIA:** 404.656.2300 / http://sdvs.georgia.gov

**HAWAII:** 808.433.0420 / http://hawaii.gov/dod/ovs

**IDAHO:** 208.334.3513 / www.veterans.idaho.gov

**ILLINOIS:** 800.437.9824 / 217.782.6641 (outside IL) / www.veterans.illinois.gov

**INDIANA:** 317.232.3910 / 800.400.4520 (in state) / www.in.gov/dva

**IOWA:** 800.838.4692 / www.iowava.org

**KANSAS:** 785.296.3976 / www.kcva.org

**KENTUCKY:** 502.564.9203 / 800.572.6245 / http://veterans.ky.gov

**LOUISIANA:** 225.922.0500 / www.vetaffairs.com

**MAINE:** 207.941.3005 / www.maine.gov/dvem/bvs

**MARYLAND:** 410.260.3838 / www.mdva.state.md.us

**MASSACHUSETTS:** 781.982.0056 / www.sec.state.ma.us/cis/cisvet/vetidx.htm

**MICHIGAN:** 517.335.6523 / www.michigan.gov/dmva

**MINNESOTA:** 888.546.5838 / www.mdva.state.mn.us

**MISSISSIPPI:** 601.576.4850 / www.vab.state.ms.us

**MISSOURI:** 573.751.3779 / http://mvc.dps.mo.gov

**MONTANA:** 406.248.8579 / http://dma.mt.gov/mvad

**NEBRASKA:** 402.471.2458 / www.vets.state.ne.us

**NEVADA:** 775.688.1653 / www.veterans.nv.gov

**NEW HAMPSHIRE:** 603.624.9230 / 800.622.9230 (in state) / www.nh.gov/nhveterans

**NEW JERSEY:** 888.865.8387 / www.state.nj.us/military

**NEW MEXICO:** 866.433.8387 / www.dvs.state.nm.us

**NEW YORK:** 888.838.7697 / http://veterans.ny.gov

**NORTH CAROLINA:** 919.733.3851 / www.doa.state.nc.us/vets/index.htm

**NORTH DAKOTA:** 701.239.7165 / 866.834.8387 www.nd.gov/veterans

**OHIO:** 614.644.0898 / 888.387.6446 / http://dvs.ohio.gov

**OKLAHOMA:** 405.521.3684 / www.ok.gov/ODVA

**OREGON:** 503.373.2000 / 800.828.8801 / www.odva.state.or.us

**PENNSYLVANIA:** 717.861.2000 / www.milvet.state.pa.us/DMVA/index.htm

**RHODE ISLAND:** 401.253.8000 ext. 495 / www.dhs.ri.gov/dhs/dvetaff.htm

**SOUTH CAROLINA:** 803.734.0200 / www.govoepp.state.sc.us/va

**SOUTH DAKOTA:** 605.773.3269 www.state.sd.us/military/vetaffairs/sdbenefit.htm

**TENNESSEE:** 615.741.2931 / www.state.tn.us/veteran

**TEXAS:** 800.252.8387 / www.tvc.state.tx.us

**UTAH:** 801.326.2372 / 800.894.9497 / http://veterans.utah.gov

**VERMONT:** 802.828.3379 / www.va.state.vt.us

**VIRGINIA:** 804.786.0286 / www.dvs.virginia.gov

**WASHINGTON:** 800.562.2308 / www.dva.wa.gov

**WEST VIRGINIA:** .304.558.3661 / 866.984.8387 (in state) / www.wvs.state.wv.us/va

**WISCONSIN:** 608.266.1311 / 800.947.8387 / http://dva.state.wi.us

**WYOMING:** 307.772.5016 / www.nasdva.net/group/wyoming

## U.S. TERRITORIES

**To see American Samoa, Guam, Puerto Rico and U.S. Virgin Islands, visit** www.va.gov/statedva.htm or www.nasdva.net (National Association of State Directors of Veterans Affairs [NASDVA]).

The road to seemingly mythical "financial freedom" is riddled with potholes, speed bumps, and dangerous intersections. We make decisions every day without considering what tomorrow will bring, but when it comes to spending, having a financial plan is essential to ensure that tomorrow holds all the potential of today and much more.

Now, in this time of nationwide economic difficulty, the value of being financially prepared for the future is clear, and we can no longer afford to put off until tomorrow a plan that can be put into action today.

Even though Americans live in the wealthiest country on the planet, most of them struggle to earn enough money to provide the proper amount of comfort and security necessary to safeguard themselves, their loved ones, and their way of living.

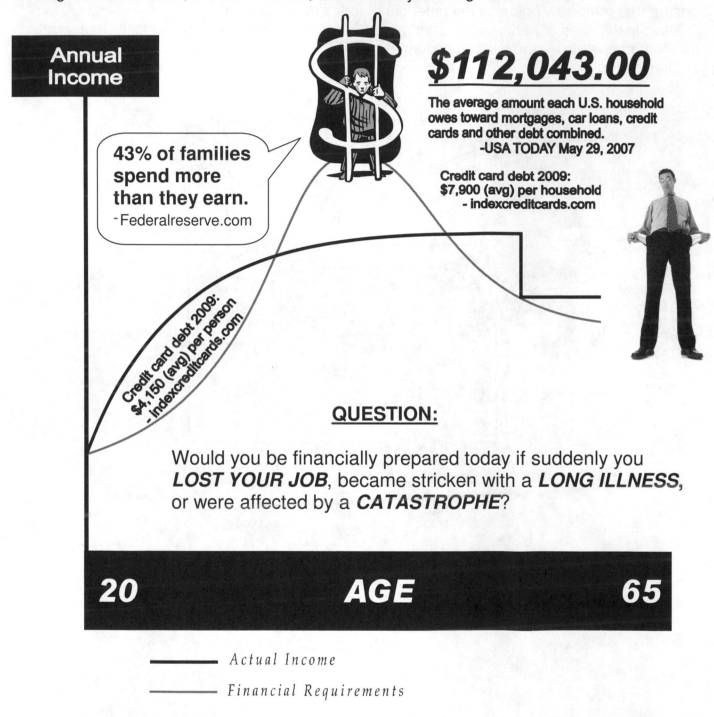

**Annual Income**

**43% of families spend more than they earn.**
-Federalreserve.com

**$112,043.00**

The average amount each U.S. household owes toward mortgages, car loans, credit cards and other debt combined.
-USA TODAY May 29, 2007

Credit card debt 2009:
$7,900 (avg) per household
- indexcreditcards.com

Credit card debt 2009:
$4,150 (avg) per person
- indexcreditcards.com

**QUESTION:**

Would you be financially prepared today if suddenly you *LOST YOUR JOB*, became stricken with a *LONG ILLNESS*, or were affected by a *CATASTROPHE*?

**20**  **AGE**  **65**

———— *Actual Income*

———— *Financial Requirements*

Statistics show that more and more Americans are accumulating mountains of debt while living well beyond their means. Some of them will incur enough debt to follow them for the rest of their lives.

The fiscal fact of life is that excessive debt often proves the path to ruin, threatening to shortchange dreams, stifle careers, delay retirement, and place a strain on marriage and family life, all from the stress of financial difficulties.

*"Individuals need to know the financial cost of not starting to save today can have a serious impact on their financial well-being 10, 20 or 30 years down the line."*

— Don Blandin, President American Saving Education Council

*Only 16% of the population who qualify for an IRA has one.*

— New York Times

*"More than half of us are not putting aside enough to maintain anything like our present standard of living upon retirement. One in three has no retirement savings"*

— Senator Paul Sarbanes, Maryland, Chairman of the Senate Banking, Housing and Urban Affairs Committee

*Pension plans for federal employees paid out in separate accounts, are underfunded by more than $1 trillion.*

*Hundreds of US companies are underfunded.*

— New York Times

*"Today's average fifty year old has only $2,300 saved towards retirement."*

*Only 5% of the population in America can put their hands on $10,000 when they're 65-years old."*

— J. Arthor Urcivoll, Sr. V.P. Merrill Lynch

## STOCK MARKET HISTORIC ANNUALIZED RETURN:

## 10.4%

However, once you subtract the effects of inflation, brokerage charges, investors' tendency to buy high, sell low and taxes, then the historic 10.4% past returns on stocks was less than:

## 2.4%

— James Garland, Journal of Investing; Ibbotson Associates; Money Research

*"Americans' #1 fear is running out of money during retirement."*

— USA Today Survey

"Looking for work? We're in need of a *'Fry-Cook'* on nightshift. Want an application?"

*"Many of the boomers, especially those in their early 50s, believe that they will be able to afford retirement by continuing to work. And often put off the sacrifice of saving money today. People who are betting on working longer to compensate for a lack of current savings are setting themselves up for a rude awakening and significantly poorer standard of living in retirement."*

— David Hunt, McKinsey & Co., LA Times

*4 out of 10 retired workers left their jobs sooner than expected. The reasons why:*

47% cited health reasons
44% pointed to job loss
9% to care for an ailing family member

*Workers with less than $50,000 in assets were most likely forced out of their careers because of health problems.*

— McKinsey & Company, LA Times

*"We know that people who lose jobs in their 50s and early 60s have a very difficult time finding new employment."*

— John Rother, AARP Executive Officer, LA Times

*Women are twice as likely as men during retirement to receive income below the poverty level.*

— "A Financial Warm up," U.S. Department of Labor

## Companies finding ways to trim pension plans

"If your pension has changed in the 1990's, it probably changed for the worse."
-The Wall Street Journal

## Don't bank 401k on employer's stock
*If company hits bad spot, retirement plan can tank*

## Employees can lose more than jobs
*When firms fold, pensions and benefits can crumple too*

## 401k losses dim retirement picture
*The biggest lesson: Be sure to diversify*
-USA TODAY

"If you manage to get a job with a company that has a private pension plan, if you stay with that same company for 30 years without being laid off or discharged, if you survive to age 65, if the company does not go out of business and if the pension fund does not suffer losses in its investments-you may be lucky enough to get an adequate pension."
- Senator Harrison Jr. Dem. - NJ

*U.S. Senate Labor Committee did an investigation*, which found that **73%** to **92%** of workers covered today by a pension plan, would never receive a penny. The reasons why:

- ❑ **Your job situation:**
  - A. You may get sick or hurt
  - B. Laid off, terminated or quit

- ❑ **Your company's situation:**
  - A. Your company merges
  - B. Files bankruptcy
  - C. Goes out of business

- ❑ **More importantly, the average person changes jobs a minimum of 5 to 9 times in their lifetime.**

## GI fights to keep job until retirement
**Army seeks to oust 17-year veteran over year-old bad mark. Others face same fate**

By DAVID LAMB
LA TIMES STAFF WRITER

COLORADO SPRINGS, Colorado-Like thousands of other soldiers, Staff Sgt James B., age 41, is a victim of the *peace dividend* and has, in effect, been fired, less than three years short of completing the 20 years needed for retirement. Instead of the $863-a-month lifetime pension and medical benefits he and his wife Daisy, had counted on to start a second career in a small business back home in Pennsylvania, James will leave the Army with nothing, but his separation papers.

## The next great bailout: Social Security

In 1983, the system was projected to be "solvent" until the 2050s. This year it's only until 2037.
-Fortune, Gary Sloan: July 2009

## MOUNTAIN OF DEBT: Social Security crisis looms

Trustees of the system recently said that in 2016, a year earlier than previously forecast, money paid out in benefits will start exceeding the tax dollars flowing in. With no changes, Social Security will be completely depleted in 2037, the trustees said.

Medicare, government health care that now covers 45 million elderly and disabled people, is in even worse shape. It's been paying out more than it takes in since last year and is projected to go insolvent in 2017.

- Tom Raum: Townhall.com

Factors that contribute to the falling ratio of people paying taxes compared to people receiving benefits:

1. Increase in life expectancy without a comparable increase in the retirement age.
2. The higher birthrate of the baby boom generation compared to the birthrates of succeeding generations.
3. The increasing number of people receiving disability benefits.
-Source: www.justfacts.com/socialsecurity.asp

**Fewer paying:** Social Security is a ***supplemental*** retirement program for Americans that currently has obligations it cannot meet for current workers and retirees at current Social Security tax rate. How did Social Security become a huge problem? Social Security typically has run a surplus because there were more workers paying taxes than people receiving benefits. The surplus is expected to disappear as the number of Americans age 65 and older increases much faster than the number of working-age people. Example:

**2006: 13 billion (surplus) in Social Security Funds**
**2007: 7 billion (surplus) in Social Security Funds**
**2008: 5 billion (surplus) in Social Security Funds**
**2009: -(6) billion (DEFICIT) in Social Security as of August close**

- Zero Hedge

| YEAR | Ratio of people paying taxes to people receiving Social Security Fund benefits | | | | |
|------|------|------|------|------|------|
| 1945 | 41.9 people support 1 individual | | | | |
| 1950 | 16.5 | " | " | 1 | " |
| 1960 | 5.1 | " | " | 1 | " |
| 1970 | 3.7 | " | " | 1 | " |
| 1980 | 3.2 | " | " | 1 | " |
| 1990 | 3.4 | " | " | 1 | " |
| 2000 | 3.4 | " | " | 1 | " |
| 2007 | 3.3 | " | " | 1 | " |
| 2030 | 2.2 | " | " | 1 | " |

-Source www.justfacts.com/socialsecurity.asp

Few people will satisfy their total needs at retirement, according to a recent government study, it shows that for every 100 Americans at age 65:

**25** Die before making it to age 65

**20** Have annual incomes under $6,000 (below poverty level)

**51** Have annual incomes between $6,000 and $35,000 ($12,000 average), but must reduce their standard of living at retirement

**4** Have annual incomes over $35,000 (financially secure)

*- U.S. Department of Health and Human Services, SSA Pub. #13-11871*

**BEATDOWN GOES ON:** About 1% of men 65 to 74 years of age, their annual income ranges from $155,000 to over $500,000. Excluding men with the top 1% of earnings, average earnings for all men aged 65 to 74 plunges to $7,630 (below poverty level). *- Social Security Administration*

**BAD NEWS:** In 2004, income from assets (stocks, bonds, funds, real estate, etc.) declined for all senior age groups:

Age 65-69: Average income from assets went from 20% in '87 to 12%
Age 70-74: Average income from assets went from 26% in '87 to 12%
Age 75-79: Average income from assets went from 28% in '87 to 14%
Age 80-84: Average income from assets went from 31% in '87 to 15%
Age 85+: Average income from assets went from 32% in '87 to 14%

**WORST NEWS:** In 2004, seniors over age 70 relied (and still does today) enormously upon pensions and Social Security for their income sources as the research shows below:

Age 70-74: Social Security plus pensions represented 62% of their income
Age 75-79: Social Security plus pensions represented 70% of their income
Age 80-84: Social Security plus pensions represented 75% of their income
Age 85+: Social Security plus pensions represented 80% of their income

If pensions and Social Security became extinct (it might happen), today's labor force would have to rely on income from assets or earnings. That is why it is important for today's workforce to invest in 401ks, IRAs, SIRPs, etc.

*IF YOU ARE NOT INVESTING FOR RETIREMENT, YOU MAY NEVER HAVE ONE! - Distribution of Older Population's Average Annual Income – EBRI*

**THE AVERAGE 100 AMERICANS AT AGE 65:**

57 are dead or broke

27 are dependent upon others

8 are still working (see above)

7 have some income

1 is considered well off

*- U.S. Department of Labor and Commerce*

■ *93% OF MEN AT AGE 65 WHO FAILED FINANCIALLY SAID IT WAS DUE TO LACK OF A PLAN.*
*- Liama Co-operative Research*

■ *85 OUT OF 100 PEOPLE REACHING 65 DO NOT EVEN HAVE A PALTRY $250.*
*- Social Security Administration*

■ *ONLY 3 OUT OF 10 IN THE TOP INCOME BRACKET ($50,000 up) CAN QUIT THEIR JOB AT 65.*
*- National Underwritter Association*

■ *OF THE 3 MILLION RECIPIENTS OF THE MINIMUM $122 MONTHLY SOCIAL SECURITY BENEFIT, 85% ARE WOMEN.*
*- Social Security Administration*

■ *OF THE ELDERLY WITH INCOMES BELOW $5,000 A YEAR, 78% ARE WOMEN.*
*- Ralph Nader consumer advocate*

■ *A NEW STUDY SHOWS SENIOR CITIZENS ARE THE FASTEST GROWING AGE GROUP HEADED INTO BANKRUPTCY COURT, PRIMARILY BASED ON THEIR GROWING CREDIT CARD DEBT, AN INCREASE OF 217% IN THE LAST 10 YEARS. THE SITUATION WORSENS WITH THE SHRINKING WEALTH OF SENIORS.*
*- Retiring In the Red: A New Reality for Older Americans*

C-1

Take a sobering look at the financial statistics provided by the program **"JumpStart,"** which show that American adults are creating a financial nightmare, not only for themselves, but possibly their children and children's children.

**2008 JumpStart Personal Financial Literacy's Survey of High School Students** found that high school seniors correctly answered only **48.3%** (**failing score**) of the questions. This mean score is a decrease from those posted by the senior class of **2006**, which correctly answered **52.4%** (also, a **failing score**) of the questions.

**87%** of college students and **90%** of high school students **rely on their parents for financial guidance.**

Nearly **72%** of parents surveyed acknowledged that they are their **children's primary source of personal finance education**, although **44%** admit to needing more guidance on how to teach their children the financial skills necessary to become responsible and successful adults.
  - 2008 survey by The Hartford Financial Services Group, Inc

More than **2/3** of parents (**69%**) admit to feeling **less prepared** to give their teen's **advice and guidance** about investing than they do the "birds and the bees."
  - Charles Schwab's 2008 "Parents & Money"

**Almost half** of all parents said they **don't set a good example** when it comes to handling their own money and are **not capable** of properly teaching their children.

**41%** of parents say they **never learned** how to manage money properly.

**75%** of credit card holders have **maxed-out at least one credit card** during the past year.

**41%** of the young adults in Generation Y (ages18-29) **do not pay** their bills each month.
  - 2008 Financial Literacy Survey of adults, conducted on behalf of the National Foundation for Credit Counseling, Inc. and MSN Money

**64%** of consumers' ages **18 to 24 do not know** the interest rates, they pay on their credit cards.

**31%** of students polled **do not worry about debt**, believing they can pay it back once, they are out of school and earning a paycheck.
  - 2008 study of college students sponsored by the National Association of Retail Collection Attorneys (NARCA)

More than **25%** think it is reasonable to **run up debt** to splurge on a special celebration with friends at a restaurant or to use a credit card as a way to **"raise cash."**
  - 2008 study of college students sponsored by the National Association of Retail Collection Attorneys (NARCA

An average of **23%** chooses to **ignore overdraft penalties** and the prospect of months or years of paying off a debt incurred for a moment of fun.
  - 2008 study of college students NARCA sponsored

**1 in every 10 Americans** with a mortgage reports being **late or missing a mortgage payment** in the last year.
  - 2008 Financial Literacy Survey of adults, conducted on behalf of the National Foundation for Credit Counseling, Inc. and MSN Money

The **fastest growing group declaring bankruptcy** today is young adults age **20** to **24.**

Before new bankruptcy laws in were in place: In 2005 over **2 million Americans filed for bankruptcy**. With new laws in place: Bankruptcies have steadily **increased** from nearly 600,000 in 2006 to over 1.4 million in 2008.
  - Source: www.bankruptcyaction.com/USbankstats.htm

**80%** of Americans were **not confident** about making good investment decisions.

More than **1/3** of adults say they **do not have any non-retirement savings**. Though a majority is currently saving for their retirement, more than one-quarter are not.
  - 2008 Financial Literacy Survey of adults, conducted on behalf of the National Foundation for Credit Counseling, Inc. and MSN Money

Nearly **2/3** of American adults and students didn't know that in times of inflation **money loses its value.**

**44** million (**39.4%**) U.S. families are either **unbanked** or **underbanked.**

**60%** of adults are more likely to **turn to family members for advice** rather than a **financial professional.**

**Bottom Line:** America's financial troubles can be best summed up with these words of wisdom:
*"He, who understands interest, __earns it__.*
*He, who does not understand interest, __pays it__."*

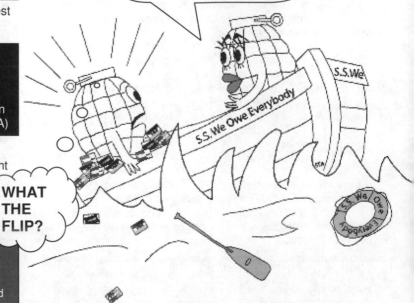

I got us another credit card, Sweetie. Let's go out and have some FUN!

WHAT THE FLIP?

## GOOD NEWS: WE'RE LIVING LONGER

Records show that of 100 senior citizens reaching age 65:

45 may live to be 80
24 may live to be 85
10 may live to be 90

### CENTENARIAN BOOM

"Estimates are that the centenarian population is doubling every 10 years," said John Wilmoth, a research demographer and professor at the University of California, Berkeley. "That's a much faster rate of growth than any other segment of the population.

"This doesn't mean that everyone's going to live to be 100 years old, but rate of growth seems large because so few survived to the age before."

According to the U.S. Census Bureau

Americans 100 and older:
1960: 4,000
1996: 57,000
Future Projections:
2015: 170,000
2050: 834,000

CHESTER'S BURGERS

## BAD NEWS: WE'LL NEED MORE MONEY

Increased income needed, caused by inflation:

Hypothetical income throughout the years, based on 4.7% inflation rate from 1973 to 2009:

Income at age 30: $  30,000
Income at age 40: $  47,488
Income at age 50: $  75,172
Income at age 60: $118,993
Retired at age 65: $149,711
Retired at age 70: $188,360

Possible nightmare scenario:

Working again at age 75: $236,986

I love that I'll probably have to work for the rest of my life, just because, I didn't prepare adequately for retirement!

## YOUR LIFE EXPECTANCY!

| People who are this age today | Are expected to live to this age | |
|---|---|---|
| Age 20 – 21 | Male 72 | Female 77 |
| Age 22 – 27 | Male 73 | Female 77 |
| Age 28 – 33 | Male 73 | Female 78 |
| Age 34 – 41 | Male 74 | Female 78 |
| Age 42 – 43 | Male 74 | Female 79 |
| Age 44 – 49 | Male 75 | Female 79 |
| Age 50 – 51 | Male 75 | Female 80 |
| Age 56 – 57 | Male 77 | Female 80 |
| Age 50 – 59 | Male 77 | Female 81 |
| Age 60 – 63 | Male 78 | Female 81 |
| Age 64 – 65 | Male 79 | Female 82 |
| Age 70 | Male 81 | Female 84 |
| Age 80 | Male 86 | Female 87 |
| Age 90 | Male 93 | Female 93 |
| Age 100 | Male? | Female? |

## INFLATION & FUTURE PAYCHECK:

Inflation withers your wherewithal and balloons expenses. Inflation has averaged around 4.70% since 1973. Check out the chart below to see how your paycheck needs to grow to keep up with inflation.

| Rank | 2009 | 2015 | 2020 | 2025 |
|---|---|---|---|---|
| E-2 | 1,569 | 2,067 | 2,600 | 3,272 |
| E-3 | 1,650 | 2,174 | 2,735 | 3,441 |
| E-4 | 1,921 | 2,531 | 3,184 | 4,006 |
| E-5 | 2,230 | 2,938 | 3,696 | 4,650 |
| E-6 | 2,602 | 3,428 | 4,312 | 5,426 |
| E-7 | 3,099 | 4,082 | 5,136 | 6,462 |
| E-8 | 3,878 | 5,100 | 6,427 | 8,086 |
| E-9 | 4,796 | 6,318 | 7,949 | 10,001 |
| O-2 | 4,589 | 6,045 | 7,606 | 9,569 |
| O-3 | 4,732 | 6,233 | 7,843 | 9,867 |
| O-4 | 5,640 | 7,429 | 9,347 | 11,761 |

To learn more (inflation), visit: **http://inflationdata.com**

C-1

Have you ever had a conversation with a senior citizen about money? It seems as if they all say, *"I wish I had started saving when I was your age."* Why? Because they realize in hindsight that they would have been financially better off in their older age. Moreover, they could have benefited more from compound interest.

The illustration below shows what the power of time and money can do, based on a yearly deposit of $2,000 starting on January 1 of each New Year at a compounded rate of 10%.

## SAVER
### Investing at age 18
### Total investment: $16,000

## EXCUSE MAKER
### Investing at age 26
### Total investment: $78,000

## PROCRASTINATOR
### Investing at age 40
### Total investment: $250,000

| Age | Investment | Total Value | Age | Investment | Total Value | Age | Investment | Total Value |
|---|---|---|---|---|---|---|---|---|
| 18 | 2,000 | 2,200 | 18 | 0 | 0 | 18 | 0 | 0 |
| 19 | 2,000 | 4,620 | 19 | 0 | 0 | 19 | 0 | 0 |
| 20 | 2,000 | 7,282 | 20 | 0 | 0 | 20 | 0 | 0 |
| 21 | 2,000 | 10,210 | 21 | 0 | 0 | 21 | 0 | 0 |
| 22 | 2,000 | 13,431 | 22 | 0 | 0 | 22 | 0 | 0 |
| 23 | 2,000 | 16,974 | 23 | 0 | 0 | 23 | 0 | 0 |
| 24 | 2,000 | 20,871 | 24 | 0 | 0 | 24 | 0 | 0 |
| 25 | 2,000 | 25,158 | 25 | 0 | 0 | 25 | 0 | 0 |
| 26 | 0 | 27,674 | 26 | 2,000 | 2,200 | 26 | 0 | 0 |
| 27 | 0 | 30,442 | 27 | 2,000 | 4,620 | 27 | 0 | 0 |
| 28 | 0 | 33,486 | 28 | 2,000 | 7,282 | 28 | 0 | 0 |
| 29 | 0 | 36,834 | 29 | 2,000 | 10,210 | 29 | 0 | 0 |
| 30 | 0 | 40,518 | 30 | 2,000 | 13,431 | 30 | 0 | 0 |
| 31 | 0 | 44,570 | 31 | 2,000 | 16,974 | 31 | 0 | 0 |
| 32 | 0 | 48,027 | 32 | 2,000 | 20,871 | 32 | 0 | 0 |
| 33 | 0 | 53,929 | 33 | 2,000 | 25,158 | 33 | 0 | 0 |
| 34 | 0 | 59,322 | 34 | 2,000 | 29,874 | 34 | 0 | 0 |
| 35 | 0 | 65,256 | 35 | 2,000 | 35,072 | 35 | 0 | 0 |
| 36 | 0 | 71,780 | 36 | 2,000 | 40,768 | 36 | 0 | 0 |
| 37 | 0 | 78,958 | 37 | 2,000 | 47,045 | 37 | 0 | 0 |
| 38 | 0 | 86,854 | 38 | 2,000 | 53,949 | 38 | 0 | 0 |
| 39 | 0 | 95,540 | 39 | 2,000 | 61,544 | 39 | 0 | 0 |
| 40 | 0 | 105,094 | 40 | 2,000 | 69,899 | 40 | 10,000 | 11,000 |
| 41 | 0 | 115,603 | 41 | 2,000 | 79,089 | 41 | 10,000 | 23,100 |
| 42 | 0 | 127,163 | 42 | 2,000 | 89,198 | 42 | 10,000 | 36,410 |
| 43 | 0 | 130,880 | 43 | 2,000 | 100,318 | 43 | 10,000 | 51,051 |
| 44 | 0 | 153,868 | 44 | 2,000 | 112,550 | 44 | 10,000 | 67,156 |
| 45 | 0 | 169,255 | 45 | 2,000 | 126,005 | 45 | 10,000 | 84,872 |
| 46 | 0 | 188,180 | 46 | 2,000 | 140,805 | 46 | 10,000 | 104,359 |
| 47 | 0 | 204,798 | 47 | 2,000 | 157,086 | 47 | 10,000 | 125,795 |
| 48 | 0 | 226,278 | 48 | 2,000 | 174,094 | 48 | 10,000 | 149,374 |
| 49 | 0 | 247,806 | 49 | 2,000 | 194,694 | 49 | 10,000 | 175,312 |
| 50 | 0 | 272,586 | 50 | 2,000 | 216,363 | 50 | 10,000 | 203,843 |
| 51 | 0 | 299,845 | 51 | 2,000 | 240,199 | 51 | 10,000 | 235,227 |
| 52 | 0 | 329,830 | 52 | 2,000 | 266,419 | 52 | 10,000 | 269,750 |
| 53 | 0 | 362,813 | 53 | 2,000 | 295,261 | 53 | 10,000 | 307,725 |
| 54 | 0 | 399,094 | 54 | 2,000 | 326,988 | 54 | 10,000 | 349,429 |
| 55 | 0 | 439,003 | 55 | 2,000 | 361,886 | 55 | 10,000 | 395,447 |
| 56 | 0 | 482,904 | 56 | 2,000 | 400,275 | 56 | 10,000 | 445,992 |
| 57 | 0 | 531,194 | 57 | 2,000 | 442,503 | 57 | 10,000 | 501,591 |
| 58 | 0 | 584,314 | 58 | 2,000 | 488,953 | 58 | 10,000 | 562,750 |
| 59 | 0 | 642,745 | 59 | 2,000 | 540,048 | 59 | 10,000 | 630,025 |
| 60 | 0 | 707,020 | 60 | 2,000 | 596,253 | 60 | 10,000 | 704,027 |
| 61 | 0 | 777,722 | 61 | 2,000 | 658,078 | 61 | 10,000 | 785,430 |
| 62 | 0 | 855,494 | 62 | 2,000 | 726,086 | 62 | 10,000 | 874,973 |
| 63 | 0 | 941,043 | 63 | 2,000 | 800,895 | 63 | 10,000 | 973,471 |
| 64 | 0 | $1,035,148 | 64 | 2,000 | $883,185 | 64 | 10,000 | $1,080,818 |

YOUR LIFE IS TICKING

## THE ODDS:

To win the California Lottery "Pick 6" game......................................1 in 23 million
Fatally struck by lightning in any given year...................................1 in 3 million
Picking 14 out of 14 winners on a football parlay card....................1 in 16,384
Killed in a car accident in a given year.........................................1 in 5000
Throwing snake eyes at dice in a Las Vegas casino.............................1 in 36
Winning a pro basketball bet against the Las Vegas point spread....................1 in 2

The statistics above prove that there is no easy way to get rich.

Over the years, I've aided young and old alike to free up money, so they could keep a portion for their future and not have to play the odds. I'm then stunned when they give me these excuses as to why they cannot save any of it:

"I _need a car_, so I can't save right now."

"I can't save. _My car broke down_ and I have to save money to fix it."

"I'll save when my _GI Bill payment_ stops."

"When I get my _next promotion_, I'll start saving."

"Save now? _I need to think about it_."

"I need to talk to my _parents (spouse, friends, supervisor, boy/girlfriend, etc.) before I can save._"

"Save? _I love spending money_ too much."

"I'm _transferring to another installation_," so I'd better hold off and not save at the moment."

Keep blowing your money. You'll be here before you know it, dead broke like me!

"I'm _getting out of the service._ When I get a job I'll start saving."

"I'm getting out of the service and going to _college_, so I really can't save now."

"We can't save, because _we're getting married_, and we need to buy things."

"We're _having a baby_, and we can't save."

"When we _pay off our bills_, then we'll save."

"_Consumer Credit Counselors_ are helping us to get out of debt, so we can't save now."

"We're _filing for bankruptcy_, so when this is over, we'll start saving."

"I don't need to save. I have my _military pension_."

"I'm _getting divorced_, so I can't save right now."

"Save? Due to my _child support_ and _alimony payments_, I barely have enough left over to live on."

"I'm looking for a _second job_, just to make ends meet, so I can't save."

_As you age, the excuses don't stop, but eventually, you will run out of them:_

"Why didn't you come see me when I was younger? I wish someone had told me to save earlier in life."

"My _military pension doesn't pay enough_ to let me retire. I'm going to have to work the rest of my life."

"The '_lottery_' is my retirement plan."

**Most famous, "Day of Infamy," last excuse used, when a procrastinator is confronted to save money: "I need to think about it."**

C-1

Throughout the years, I have witnessed several kinds of spending habits. I have known individuals, who had a five pack-a-day cigarette habit, or others that needed several cups of coffee to get through the day, but purchased from high priced coffee shops. Typically, I cringe when standing in line to pay for gas in a convenience store and I hear the person in front ask for $20 worth of lottery tickets. Sometimes, I want to blurt out that they have a better chance of being struck and killed by lightning, than winning anything (see **page 9** for odds winning the lottery). Furthermore, I have a good friend that purchases two to four expensive **energy drinks** daily from convenience stores. One day he confessed to me that it did absolutely nothing for him; just enjoyed the taste despite the cost.

Bad spending habits can be costly. The examples provided below will give you an idea just how steep a cost, even when spending small sums of money ($1 to $5 per day). **NOTE:** If you're living from paycheck to paycheck and not saving one penny of your money, you definitely need to start budgeting, and change your spending habits.

**Bottom line:** Are you willing to change your habit(s) for the betterment of your future?

I love ATMs!

## Chart reflects money lost to various habits or breaking habits and saving difference. Projections are based on yearly deposits into a 10% account up to age 65

| Age & Years | Lottery Ticket 1-ticket a day habit $1 = $365 a year | Energy Drink 1-Can a day habit $2 = $730 a year | Cigarettes 1-pack a day habit $3 = $1,095 a year | Specialty Coffee 1-Cup a day habit $4 = $1,460 a year | Fast Food 1-lunch a day habit $5 = $1,825 a year |
|---|---|---|---|---|---|
| 18 / 47 | $347,484 | $694,967 | $1,042,337 | $1,389,821 | $1,737,190 |
| 19 / 46 | 315,352 | 631,064 | 946,492 | 1,262,024 | 1,577,453 |
| 20 / 45 | 286,485 | 572,970 | 859,361 | 1,145,846 | 1,432,237 |
| 21 / 44 | 260,079 | 520,157 | 780,150 | 1,040,229 | 1,300,222 |
| 22 / 43 | 236,073 | 472,146 | 708,141 | 944,214 | 1,180,209 |
| 23 / 42 | 214,249 | 428,499 | 642,678 | 856,927 | 1,071,106 |
| 24 / 41 | 194,410 | 388,820 | 583,166 | 777,576 | 971,922 |
| 25 / 40 | 176,374 | 352,784 | 529,064 | 705,438 | 881,754 |
| 26 / 39 | 159,978 | 319,955 | 479,881 | 639,858 | 799,784 |
| 27 / 38 | 145,072 | 290,144 | 435,168 | 580,240 | 725,265 |
| 28 / 37 | 131,521 | 263,043 | 394,521 | 526,042 | 657,521 |
| 29 / 36 | 119,203 | 238,405 | 357,569 | 476,771 | 595,935 |
| 30 / 35 | 108,004 | 216,008 | 323,976 | 431,980 | 539,948 |
| 31 / 34 | 97,823 | 195,646 | 293,437 | 391,260 | 489,050 |
| 32 / 33 | 88,568 | 177,135 | 265,674 | 354,242 | 442,780 |
| 33 / 32 | 80,154 | 160,308 | 240,435 | 320,589 | 400,716 |
| 34 / 31 | 72,505 | 145,010 | 217,491 | 289,995 | 362,476 |
| 35 / 30 | 65,551 | 131,102 | 196,632 | 262,183 | 327,713 |
| 36 / 29 | 59,230 | 118,459 | 177,670 | 236,899 | 296,110 |
| 37 / 28 | 53,483 | 106,966 | 160,431 | 213,914 | 267,379 |
| 38 / 27 | 48,259 | 96,517 | 144,760 | 193,018 | 241,261 |
| 39 / 26 | 43,509 | 87,018 | 130,513 | 174,022 | 217,517 |
| 40 / 25 | 39,192 | 78,383 | 117,562 | 156,753 | 195,932 |

I have a hobby collecting movies on DVD, which would be costly if I bought them new, so I spend some of my free time rummaging through stores that offer them used at a cheap price. In addition, DVDs no longer wanted, are sold, or traded, which then allows me to afford the hobby.

Make a chart like the one below; list your bad habit(s) and enter the amount that you spend daily for one month. After you determine how much money you are losing, try to break the habit or develop a less costly solution (brown bag your lunch, for example). Once your habit(s) are under control, save and invest the money before creating a new habit(s) or bill(s).

| List bad habits | Mon | Tue | Wed | Thu | Fri | Sat | Sun | Total |
|---|---|---|---|---|---|---|---|---|
|  |  |  |  |  |  |  |  |  |
|  |  |  |  |  |  |  |  |  |
|  |  |  |  |  |  |  |  |  |
|  |  |  |  |  |  |  |  |  |
| Total |  |  |  |  |  |  |  |  |

You see and hear it while walking or driving. Family, friends, co-workers and strangers hawk it free on their clothing. Through television, newspapers, Internet, etc., It is hyped during your leisure time. From the moment you wake up in the morning, it starts to bombard you from all sides. Even while you sleep, it might creep into your subconscious mind and interact with your dreams. It's everywhere, and there's little chance of escaping it. Therefore, what am I talking about? It's called **advertising**. Not surprisingly, advertising is a trillion dollar (booming) industry with 2 million brands fighting for your attention, affection, loyalty, and ultimately, your money. Competition is fierce in the advertising world, which is on account of 700 new products being showcased to consumers every day. If you're looking for a break from ads, it's not going to happen. Matter of fact, it is going to accelerate, and have all of us reaching ever deeper into our pockets to spend money more than ever. Accelerate? Yes, on account of advertisers wanting more bang for their advertising dollars. Today, scientists, researchers, psychologists and economists are developing and garnering new funding to understand why biologically and consciously the human brain seeks out certain brand products, or what induces consumers to buy. In the process, they are gathering information as to how our minds might be manipulated to boost sales, generate fads and win product loyalty.

Check out the eye popping data below that will help you to understand why and how advertisers continually work on building an edge.

- In order for businesses to net profits, especially with so many similar products to choose from, marketers try to brand a product on a consumer's mind. The average American adult is hit with as many as _3,000 ads daily_, five times more than two decades ago.
- Sadly, children are exposed to _40,000 commercials every year_. By the time babies are _18 months old_, they can recognize logos and by 10, they've _memorized 300 to 400 brands_.
                                                                                          - USA TODAY 2005

Gee, it'll be a year round **holiday shopping bonanza**, when advertisers finally get their wish, to have the ability to literally zap all our brains with ads sent through impulses that will have us all joining the latest fad or craze, and ultimately, have us waiting in long lines to pay for things we don't even need.

The financial results below reflect the power of advertising that have left American consumers in a financial quandary (P.S. Enjoy the 3,000 or more ads you will see or hear today):

- _44%_ of American consumers can't wait to blow their paychecks.
- _28%_ claim to have NO spare cash left over each month after paying essential living expenses.
- Adults under _age 25_ make an average income of _$20,773_, but manage to spend _$24,229_ yearly.
- The average American consumer has 8 to 10 credit cards, not counting their bank cards.
- The average American family has over _$26,000_ in credit debt and _22-29_-year olds over _$23,000._
- Average credit card debt for _22-29_-year olds _$5,781._
- Average installment loans for 22-29-year olds _$17,208._
- _65%_ of consumers can only make the minimum payment on their credit cards.
- _49%_ between ages _22 and 29_ have stopped paying a debt, forcing lenders to _"Charge-Off"_ debt and sell it to a collection agency, or had cars repossessed.
- Before new bankruptcy laws in place, over _2 million_ Americans filed bankruptcy in 2005. With new laws in place, bankruptcies have steadily risen to over _1.4 million_ in 2008.
- The fastest rising group filing for bankruptcy today is between ages _20 and 24_ and the biggest group is between the ages of _55 and 65._
- _57%_ of marriages that led to a divorce were due to financial matters.
- _64%_ of American consumers feel they are falling behind on their retirement savings goals, and fear that they may have to work the rest of their lives.

**Americans work 8 Hours Per Day, Just To Pay Bills**
- Tax Foundation

C-1

**11**

Have you ever wondered how much money you will earn by the time you reach age 65? To find out, match your age with your current monthly income from the chart below.

**Example: 24-year-old earning $2,500 monthly, will earn $1,230,000 by age 65.**

| Age | $1,000 | $1,500 | $2,000 | $2,500 | $3,000 | $4,000 | $5,000 | $6,000 |
|-----|--------|--------|--------|--------|--------|--------|--------|--------|
| 18 | $564,000 | 846,000 | 1,128,000 | 1,410,000 | 1,692,000 | 2,256,000 | 2,820,000 | 3,384,000 |
| 19 | $552,000 | 828,000 | 1,104,000 | 1,380,000 | 1,656,000 | 2,208,000 | 2,760,000 | 3,312,000 |
| 20 | $540,000 | 810,000 | 1,080,000 | 1,350,000 | 1,620,000 | 2,160,000 | 2,700,000 | 3,240,000 |
| 21 | $528,000 | 792,000 | 1,056,000 | 1,320,000 | 1,584,000 | 2,112,000 | 2,640,000 | 3,168,000 |
| 22 | $516,000 | 774,000 | 1,032,000 | 1,290,000 | 1,548,000 | 2,064,000 | 2,580,000 | 3,096,000 |
| 23 | $504,000 | 756,000 | 1,008,000 | 1,260,000 | 1,512,000 | 2,016,000 | 2,520,000 | 3,024,000 |
| 24 | $492,000 | 738,000 | 984,000 | 1,230,000 | 1,476,000 | 1,968,000 | 2,460,000 | 2,952,000 |
| 25 | $480,000 | 720,000 | 960,000 | 1,200,000 | 1,440,000 | 1,920,000 | 2,400,000 | 2,880,000 |
| 26 | $468,000 | 702,000 | 936,000 | 1,170,000 | 1,404,000 | 1,872,000 | 2,340,000 | 2,808,000 |
| 27 | $456,000 | 684,000 | 912,000 | 1,140,000 | 1,368,000 | 1,824,000 | 2,280,000 | 2,736,000 |
| 28 | $444,000 | 666,000 | 888,000 | 1,110,000 | 1,332,000 | 1,776,000 | 2,220,000 | 2,664,000 |
| 29 | $432,000 | 648,000 | 864,000 | 1,080,000 | 1,296,000 | 1,728,000 | 2,160,000 | 2,592,000 |
| 30 | $420,000 | 630,000 | 840,000 | 1,050,000 | 1,260,000 | 1,680,000 | 2,100,000 | 2,520,000 |
| 31 | $408,000 | 612,000 | 816,000 | 1,020,000 | 1,224,000 | 1,632,000 | 2,040,000 | 2,448,000 |
| 32 | $396,000 | 594,000 | 792,000 | 990,000 | 1,188,000 | 1,584,000 | 1,980,000 | 2,376,000 |
| 33 | $384,000 | 576,000 | 768,000 | 960,000 | 1,152,000 | 1,536,000 | 1,920,000 | 2,304,000 |
| 34 | $372,000 | 558,000 | 744,000 | 930,000 | 1,116,000 | 1,488,000 | 1,860,000 | 2,232,000 |
| 35 | $360,000 | 540,000 | 720,000 | 900,000 | 1,080,000 | 1,440,000 | 1,800,000 | 2,160,000 |

Keep in mind; you will probably receive pay increases along the way, so there is a good chance that you will earn more. However, the chart below illustrates how many days it took in one year or hours and minutes (per 8 hours) Americans worked to pay in major spending categories in 2007 (Source: www.taxfoundation.org/files/sr152.pdf).

*NOTE: U.S. personal savings rate declined from 10.8% in 1984 to zero in 2005. (Bureau of Economic Analysis, 2006)*

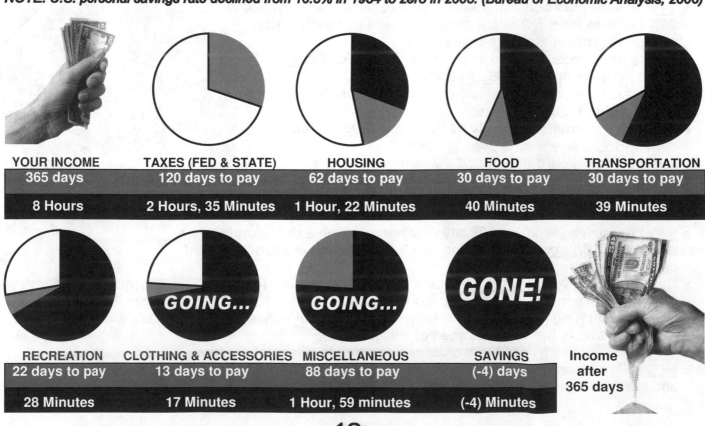

| YOUR INCOME | TAXES (FED & STATE) | HOUSING | FOOD | TRANSPORTATION |
|-------------|---------------------|---------|------|----------------|
| 365 days | 120 days to pay | 62 days to pay | 30 days to pay | 30 days to pay |
| 8 Hours | 2 Hours, 35 Minutes | 1 Hour, 22 Minutes | 40 Minutes | 39 Minutes |

| RECREATION | CLOTHING & ACCESSORIES | MISCELLANEOUS | SAVINGS | Income after 365 days |
|------------|------------------------|---------------|---------|----------------------|
| 22 days to pay | 13 days to pay | 88 days to pay | (-4) days | |
| 28 Minutes | 17 Minutes | 1 Hour, 59 minutes | (-4) Minutes | |

GOING... GOING... GONE!

Who's in control of your money? For one thing, it sure isn't you. With banks handing out a measly 2% or less on regular savings accounts; then federal and state taxes applied against that interest you earned, and finally, the _"Erosion of Worth"_ by inflation during the year, what's left? You'll find yourself with almost nothing or less like most Americans who do not understand how outside influences such as banks, taxes, government and inflation can affect your daily finances and have you forever spinning out of control in the _"Financial Cycle of Pain and Suffering,"_ shown below.

**BEGIN**

**FINANCIAL CYCLE OF PAIN & SUFFERING**

**PAY FEDERAL & STATE TAXES**

**MONEY PUT INTO SAVINGS ACCOUNT**

**INFLATION: 4.70% SINCE 1973**

**BANK PAYS 2% ON SAVINGS ACCOUNT**

yearly inflation rate

**U.S. GOVERMENT PRINTS & HAWKS 4% SAVINGS BONDS**

**BANK UTILIZES YOUR MONEY TO ISSUE LOANS OF 7% - 21% OR HIGHER**

**U.S. GOVERNMENT ISSUE LOANS TO FOREIGN COUNTRIES**

C-1

## DO YOU SEE ANY REALISTIC CHANCE OF MAKING MONEY IN THIS SYSTEM?

ALMOST HALF OF ALL PARENTS SAY THEY DON'T SET A GOOD EXAMPLE, WHEN IT COMES TO HANDLING THEIR OWN MONEY, AND ARE NOT CAPABLE OF PROPERLY TEACHING THEIR CHILDREN.

80% OF AMERICAN ADULTS ARE NOT CONFIDENT ABOUT MAKING GOOD INVESTMENT DECISIONS.

60% OF AMERICAN ADULTS ARE MORE LIKELY TO TURN TO FAMILY MEMBERS FOR FINANCIAL ADVICE...RATHER THAN A FINANCIAL PROFESSIONAL.

PEOPLE WHO ARE SUCCESSFUL DON'T SINK INTO FINANCIAL QUICKSAND. WHY YOU ASK? BECAUSE THEY HAVE GUIDANCE FROM PROFESSIONALS.
HAVE YOU EVER HEARD OF A PROFESSIONAL ATHLETE THAT DOESN'T HAVE A COACH? OF COURSE NOT!

A COACH IS CRITICAL TO GETTING THAT ATHLETE TO PERFORM AT THEIR PEAK LEVEL. THEREFORE, THAT'S WHY IT'S IMPORTANT TO SEEK FINANCIAL GUIDANCE FROM PROFESSIONAL PLANNERS.

ESPECIALLY, IF IT'S YOUR MONEY!

COACH SAVER'S TIP #1: "SEEK A PROFESSIONAL COACH TO HELP YOU DEVELOP A SUCCESSFUL FINANCIAL GAME PLAN."

"Hi! I'm Coach Saver, and YOU LOOK FINANCIALLY LAZY AND WEAK! DROP AND GIVE ME 100, FRUIT CUP!"

"WHEN YOU'RE DONE, MAGGOT, I want to have a word with you, in private, about the possibility of me being your financial coach."

"WELL, WHAT ARE YOU DOING JUST STANDING THERE WITH YOUR PIEHOLE OPEN? GIVE ME MY 100, CREAMPUFF!"

LATER:

"I'M YOUR COACH, TULIP!"

"ARE YOU WITH ME ON THAT, SUGAR?"

"FINANCIAL BOOT CAMP STARTS NOW! I'M GOING TO POUND SO MUCH FINANCIAL INFORMATION DOWN YOUR THROAT THAT YOU'LL BREAK OUT IN HIVES JUST THINKING ABOUT SPENDING MONEY, MEAT."

TIP #2: "STARTING WITH YOUR AGE TODAY, IF YOU PUT $1 INTO 10% TAX DEFERRED SAVINGS, BY AGE 65 YOU'D EARN:"

EXAMPLE: $1 saved at age 23 = $54.76 (age 65)

|  | |  | |  | |
|---|---|---|---|---|---|
| Age 1 = | 445.79 | Age 23 = | 54.76 | Age 45 = | 6.73 |
| Age 2 = | 405.27 | Age 24 = | 49.79 | Age 46 = | 6.12 |
| Age 3 = | 368.42 | Age 25 = | 45.26 | Age 47 = | 5.56 |
| Age 4 = | 334.93 | Age 26 = | 41.14 | Age 48 = | 5.05 |
| Age 5 = | 304.48 | Age 27 = | 37.40 | Age 49 = | 4.60 |
| Age 6 = | 276.80 | Age 28 = | 34.00 | Age 50 = | 4.18 |
| Age 7 = | 251.64 | Age 29 = | 30.91 | Age 51 = | 3.80 |
| Age 8 = | 228.76 | Age 30 = | 28.10 | Age 52 = | 3.45 |
| Age 9 = | 207.97 | Age 31 = | 25.55 | Age 53 = | 3.14 |
| Age 10 = | 189.06 | Age 32 = | 23.23 | Age 54 = | 2.85 |
| Age 11 = | 171.87 | Age 33 = | 21.11 | Age 55 = | 2.59 |
| Age 12 = | 156.25 | Age 34 = | 19.19 | Age 56 = | 2.36 |
| Age 13 = | 142.04 | Age 35 = | 17.45 | Age 57 = | 2.14 |
| Age 14 = | 129.13 | Age 36 = | 15.86 | Age 58 = | 1.95 |
| Age 15 = | 117.39 | Age 37 = | 14.42 | Age 59 = | 1.77 |
| Age 16 = | 106.72 | Age 38 = | 13.11 | Age 60 = | 1.61 |
| Age 17 = | 97.02 | Age 39 = | 11.92 | Age 61 = | 1.46 |
| Age 18 = | 88.20 | Age 40 = | 10.83 | Age 62 = | 1.33 |
| Age 19 = | 80.18 | Age 41 = | 9.85 | Age 63 = | 1.21 |
| Age 20 = | 72.89 | Age 42 = | 8.95 | Age 64 = | 1.10 |
| Age 21 = | 66.26 | Age 43 = | 8.14 | Age 65 = | 1.00 |
| Age 22 = | 60.24 | Age 44 = | 7.40 | | |

The chart below will assist you in determining at what age you would become a millionaire, if you cleverly save a fixed amount of money each month.

**Example: 20-year-old depositing $200 a month into 10% tax-deferred savings for 38 years would become a millionaire by age 58.**

To accomplish this feat, budget monthly, start investing, and avoid bills with high payments that could derail your plans.

## Goal: Deposit Money Monthly into a 10% Tax-Deferred Account

| AGE | $1000 | $750 | $500 | $250 | $200 | $150 | $125 | $100 | $75 |
|---|---|---|---|---|---|---|---|---|---|
| 18 | 41 | 44 | 47 | 54 | 56 | 59 | 61 | 63 | 66 |
| 19 | 42 | 45 | 48 | 55 | 57 | 60 | 62 | 64 | 67 |
| 20 | 43 | 46 | 49 | 56 | 58 | 61 | 63 | 65 | 68 |
| 21 | 44 | 47 | 50 | 57 | 59 | 62 | 64 | 66 | 69 |
| 22 | 45 | 48 | 51 | 58 | 60 | 63 | 65 | 67 | 70 |
| 23 | 46 | 49 | 52 | 59 | 61 | 64 | 66 | 68 | 71 |
| 24 | 47 | 50 | 53 | 60 | 62 | 65 | 67 | 69 | 72 |
| 25 | 48 | 51 | 54 | 61 | 63 | 66 | 68 | 70 | 73 |
| 26 | 49 | 52 | 55 | 62 | 64 | 67 | 69 | 71 | 74 |
| 27 | 50 | 53 | 56 | 63 | 65 | 68 | 70 | 72 | 75 |
| 28 | 51 | 54 | 57 | 64 | 66 | 69 | 71 | 73 | 76 |
| 29 | 52 | 55 | 58 | 65 | 67 | 70 | 72 | 74 | 77 |
| 30 | 53 | 56 | 59 | 66 | 68 | 71 | 73 | 75 | 78 |
| 31 | 54 | 57 | 60 | 67 | 69 | 72 | 74 | 76 | 79 |
| 32 | 55 | 58 | 61 | 68 | 70 | 73 | 75 | 77 | 80 |
| 33 | 56 | 59 | 62 | 69 | 71 | 74 | 76 | 78 | 81 |
| 34 | 57 | 60 | 63 | 70 | 72 | 75 | 77 | 79 | 82 |
| 35 | 58 | 61 | 64 | 71 | 73 | 76 | 78 | 80 | 83 |
| 36 | 59 | 62 | 65 | 72 | 74 | 77 | 79 | 81 | 84 |
| 37 | 60 | 63 | 66 | 73 | 75 | 78 | 80 | 82 | 85 |
| 38 | 61 | 64 | 67 | 74 | 76 | 79 | 81 | 83 | 86 |
| 39 | 62 | 65 | 68 | 75 | 77 | 80 | 82 | 84 | 87 |
| 40 | 63 | 66 | 69 | 76 | 78 | 81 | 83 | 85 | 88 |
| 41 | 64 | 67 | 70 | 77 | 79 | 82 | 84 | 86 | 89 |
| 42 | 65 | 68 | 71 | 78 | 80 | 83 | 85 | 87 | 90 |
| 43 | 66 | 69 | 72 | 79 | 81 | 84 | 86 | 88 | 91 |
| 44 | 67 | 70 | 73 | 80 | 82 | 85 | 87 | 89 | 92 |
| 45 | 68 | 71 | 74 | 81 | 83 | 86 | 88 | 90 | 93 |
| 46 | 69 | 72 | 75 | 82 | 84 | 87 | 89 | 91 | 94 |
| 47 | 70 | 73 | 76 | 83 | 85 | 88 | 90 | 92 | 95 |
| 48 | 71 | 74 | 77 | 84 | 86 | 89 | 91 | 93 | 96 |
| 49 | 72 | 75 | 78 | 85 | 87 | 90 | 92 | 94 | 97 |
| 50 | 73 | 76 | 79 | 86 | 88 | 91 | 93 | 95 | 98 |

**TIP #3: PAY BILLS WITH 70% OF YOUR PAYCHECK**   **SAVE 10%-20%**   **SAVE 10%-20%**

TIP #4: Pay yourself first! *NO ONE* is more important than you.

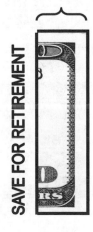

SAVE FOR EMERGENCIES

SAVE FOR RETIREMENT

C-1

1. **FINANCIALLY ILLITERATE:**
   See **page 06**

2. **WASTE MONEY DAILY:**
   See **pages 2, 6, 10, 11, 12** and **13**

3. **SPEND IMPULSIVELY:**
   See **pages 2, 6, 10, 11, 12** and **13**

4. **USE CREDIT POORLY:**
   See **pages 2, 6,** and **11**

Before new bankruptcy laws in place: In 2005, over **2 million** Americans filed for bankruptcy (record). With new laws in place: Bankruptcies have steadily increased from nearly 600,000 in 2006 to over **1.4 million** in 2008. -Source: www.bankruptcyaction.com/USbankstats.htm

5. **DO NOT PROTECT ASSETS AND INCOME:**

**68 million** adult Americans have no life insurance and those with insurance have considerably less than most experts recommend. **81%** of Americans say they need life insurance. -Source: Life and Health Insurance Foundation for Education (LIFE); New York Life, Life and Health Insurance Foundation for Education; LIMRA International

6. **USE TAX LAWS IMPROPERLY:**
   See **pages 121, 122, 123,** and **124**

Income tax returns or **"forced savings"** are literally a free loan to the federal government. In 2009, the average U.S. income tax refund was **$2,675**. That amounts to **$222.92 monthly** that people could be using to pay down debt or earn interest.

7. **FAIL TO PLAN OR SET GOALS:** See **page 5**

8. **DO NOT KNOW HOW TO START OR WHERE TO INVEST:** See **pages 3** and **6**

9. **DO NOT DIVERSIFY SAVINGS AND INVESTMENTS:** See **page 4**

10. **DO NOT UNDERSTAND INFLATION:**
    See **pages 6** and **7**

**Nearly 2/3** of American adults and students didn't know that in times of inflation **money loses its value.**

11. **SEEK ADVICE FROM NON-PROFESSIONALS:** See **pages 6** and **14**

12. **MAKE EXCUSES NOT TO SAVE OR PROGRASTINATE:** See **pages 8** and **9**

"Learn it! Know it! Burn all to memory, the reasons why people fail financially, so you'll never forget them. Then live the exact opposite lifestyle, so you'll be a financial success in life."

"Why do you have that look, I need a break or nap? Read my lips, **'BREAKS ARE FOR FINISHERS'** So, since you haven't finished squat, let's continue."

"I'm going to start issuing my **10 Commandments of Personal Finance**, one within each chapter. Therefore, since this is Chapter One, my **First Commandment**:

**THOU SHALL NOT SPEND MORE MONEY THAN EARNED.**

It is amazing to me that I even have to mention this commandment, but see reasons why people fail #2, #3 and #4 on this page."

"Below, are a few tips of mine that, if implemented, can help begin the process of getting you into financial shape. See you in Chapter Two."

## Coach Saver's quick stick and move, 2-minute financial drill:

■ Track your spending habits (see **page 33**).
■ Budget monthly (see **page 153**).
■ Suspend the use of your credit cards. Drop them in a glass of water and freeze them in your refrigerator. In case of emergency, break glass!
■ Spend cash! Nothing affects the brain like cash.
■ Put your pocket change into a piggy bank each day. In a year's time, you should accumulate $500-$750 in change.
■ Time your purchases and ask for cash discounts.
■ Do things yourself that you would normally pay professionals to do (please try to use common sense, Pea Brain).
■ Start savings account at a credit union.

We'd be in great financial shape if it wasn't for all your hobbies and other interests.

Don't nitpick, Dick. We need coach Saver's help. Our bills are out of control. He's our only hope.

Jane, explain how we're suppose to eat new clothing, shoes, etc. that you buy weekly from siphoning our food budget?

If we follow his orders, he'll get us in financial shape.

"This is your next big lesson and it's an important one, so listen up! It's estimated that two-thirds of all service members who contribute to the Montgomery G.I. Bill don't use benefits of the program. That's nice! However, that's not going to happen to you, right? Let me give you a clue as to what you can earn with a college degree, Poindexter. According to the Census Bureau, this is the value of a college education:

- Bachelor's degree $2.1 million
- Associates degree $1.6 million

Okay Einstein, all you need to know about higher education is in this chapter. If you've got what it takes to earn an degree, I can help you through the process. If together we succeed; the world is your oyster, if not, oh well, the world needs ditch diggers too. The early bird catches the worm, so start digging, Professor Dimwit!"

**Second Commandment:
"THOU SHALL SPEND MONEY
THINKING OF YOUR FUTURE"**

HOLLYWOOD

**UNIVERSITY OF CALIFORNIA
LOS ANGELES (U.C.L.A.)
THIS EXIT**

SCHOOL OF HARD KNOCKS

HIGHER LEARNING

WELCOME TO SUNNY CALIFORNIA

C-2

*CHOOSE*

## PRE-HIGH SCHOOL

■ Take challenging classes in English, mathematics, science, history, geography, the arts, and a foreign language.

■ Develop strong study skills.

■ Start genuinely thinking about which high school classes will best prepare you for college.

■ If you have an opportunity to choose among high schools, or among different programs within one high school, investigate options and determine which ones will help you:

1. Further your academic and career interests
2. Open doors to many future options

■ Start saving for college if you haven't already. Investigate different ways to save such as:

1. Buy a U.S. Savings Bond
2. Open savings account in a bank
3. Invest in mutual funds

## HIGH SCHOOL: 9th GRADE

■ Take challenging classes in English, mathematics, science, history, geography, a foreign language, government, civics, economics, and the arts.

■ Get to know your career counselor or guidance counselor as well as other college resources available in your school.

■ Talk to adults in a variety of professions to determine what they like and dislike about their jobs and what kind of education is needed for each kind of job.

■ Continue saving for college.

## HIGH SCHOOL: 10th GRADE

■ Continue taking challenging classes in English, mathematics, science, history, geography, a foreign language, government, civics, economics, and the arts.

■ Continue having discussions with adults in a variety of professions to determine what they like and dislike about their jobs and what kind of education is needed for each kind of job.

■ Become involved in school or community-based extracurricular (before or after school) activities that interest you and/or enable you to explore career interests.

■ Meet with your career counselor or guidance counselor to discuss colleges and their requirements.

■ Take the Preliminary SAT/National Merit Scholarship Qualifying Test (PSAT/NMSQT). You must register early. If you have difficulty paying the registration fee, see your guidance counselor about getting a fee waiver.

■ Take advantage of opportunities to visit colleges and talk to students.

■ Continue saving for college.

## HIGH SCHOOL: 11th GRADE

■ Continue taking challenging classes in English, mathematics, science, history, geography, a foreign language, government, civics, economics and the arts.

■ Have further meetings with your career or guidance counselor to discuss colleges and their requirements.

■ Continue involvement in school or community-based extracurricular activities.

■ Decide which colleges most interest you. Contact them to request information and an application for admission. Ask about special admissions requirements, financial aid and deadlines.

■ Talk to college representatives at college fairs.

■ Visit colleges and talk to students.

■ Consider people to ask for recommendations – teachers, counselors, employers, etc.

■ Investigate the availability of financial aid from federal, state, local, and private sources. Talk to your guidance counselor for more information.

■ Find out more about the domestic Peace Corps, called AmeriCorps, by calling **1-800-942-2677 (TTY 1-800-833-3722)**, or visiting **www.americorps.org.**

■ Investigate the availability of scholarships provided by organizations such as corporations, labor unions, professional associations, religious organizations, and credit unions (see **page 20**).

■ If applicable, go to the library and look for directories of scholarships for women, minorities, and disabled students (see **page 20**).

■ Register for and take SAT I, ACT, SAT II Subject Tests or any other exams required for admission to the colleges you might want to attend. If you have difficulty paying the registration fee, see your guidance counselor about getting a fee waiver.

■ Continue to save for college.

## HIGH SCHOOL: 12th GRADE

■ Take challenging classes in English, mathematics, science, history, geography, a foreign language, government, civics, economics, the arts, and advanced technologies.

■ Meet with your counselor early in the year to discuss your plans.

■ Complete all necessary financial aid forms, especially the *Free Application for Federal Student Aid* (FAFSA). Apply online at **www.fafsa.ed.gov.**

■ Write colleges to request information and applications for admission. Ask about financial aid, admissions requirements, and deadlines.

■ If possible, visit the colleges that most interest you.

■ Register for and take the SAT I, ACT Assessment, SAT II Subject Tests or any other exams required for admission to the colleges to which you are applying. If you have difficulty paying the registration fee, see your guidance counselor about getting a fee waiver.

■ Prepare your application carefully. Follow instructions, and PAY CLOSE ATTENTION TO DEADLINES! Be sure to ask your counselor and teachers at least two weeks before your application deadlines to submit the necessary documents to colleges (your transcript, letters of recommendation, etc.)

**NOTE: Excerpted from *Preparing Your Child for College,* available at www.ed.gov/pubs/Prepare.**

## USEFUL WEBSITES

**Federal Student Aid home page:**
**www.studentaid.ed.gov**

1. *The Student Guide* (12th grade and beyond)
2. *Funding Your Education* (before 12th grade) available at this site.

FAFSA on the Web:
**www.fafsa.ed.gov**
Personal Identification Number (PIN):
**www.pin.ed.gov**
Federal government resources for education:
**www.students.gov**

## GENERAL INFORMATION

Information about federal student aid programs, assistance with the application process and how to obtain federal student aid publications.

**1-800-4-FED-AID (1-800-433-3243)**
TTY for the hearing-impaired **1-800-730-8913.**

The Department of Veterans Affairs administers the following education benefit programs:

**Post-9/11 GI Bill:** Provides financial support for education and housing to individuals with at least 90 days of aggregate service on or after 9/11/ 2001, or discharged with a service-connected disability after 30 days. Honorable discharge is required to be eligible. For more information visit: **www.gibill.va.gov/GI_Bill_Info/CH33/Post-911.htm**

**Transferability of GI Bill to Dependents:** Eligible soldiers may transfer their GI Bill to spouses or children. For more information visit: **www.gibill.va.gov/GI_Bill_Info/CH33/Transfer.htm** or **www.defenselink.mil/home/features/2009/0409_gibill** To apply, start here: **www.dmdc.osd.mil/TEB**

**Montgomery GI Bill (Active Duty):** The MGIB program provides up to 36 months of education benefits. Generally, benefits are payable for 10-years following your release from active duty.

**Montgomery GI Bill (Selected Reserve):** This benefit may be used for a degree and certificate programs, flight training, apprenticeship/on-the-job training and correspondence courses.

**Reserve Education Assistance Program (REAP):** This program is designed to provide educational assistance to members of the Reserve components called or ordered to active duty in response to a war or national emergency.

**Veterans Educational Assistance Program (VEAP):** This program is available if you elected to make contributions that are matched on a $2 for $1 basis by the government from your military pay.

**Summary of Benefits Under the Educational Assistance Test Program:** Program was created by the DOD to encourage enlistment and reenlistment in the Armed Forces.

**Survivors' and Dependents' Educational Assistance Program (DEA):** DEA provides education and training opportunities to eligible dependents of veterans who are permanently and totally disabled due to a service-related condition, those who died while on active duty or as a result of a service related condition.

**National Call to Service:** This program expects a participant to perform a period of national service to be eligible for benefits. The VA manages this Department of Defense program.

**Accelerated Payment for the MGIB-AD:** Lump sum payment of 60% of tuition and fees are given for certain high cost, high tech programs. To qualify, you must be enrolled in a high tech program, and you must certify that you intend to seek employment in a high tech industry as defined by VA.

**Tuition Assistance Top-Up Program:** An education program that permits the VA to pay a Tuition Assistance Top-Up benefit that can be equal to the difference between the total cost of a college course and the amount of Tuition Assistance, which is paid by the military for the course.

**National Call to Service:** This program allows the VA to reimburse claimants for the fee charged for national tests for admission to institutions of higher learning and national tests providing an opportunity for course credit at institutions of higher learning.

**VA reimburses for licensing & certification tests:** You can receive reimbursement for licensing and certification tests that must be approved for the GI Bill, but does not include other fees connected with obtaining a license or certification.

**Entrepreneurship Training:** As a service member or veteran you now have an opportunity to use your education benefits to learn how to start or enhance a small business.

**Work-Study Program:** Students under this program are paid at either the state or federal minimum that work at the school veterans' office, VA Regional Office, VA Medical Facilities, or State employment offices.

**Tutorial Assistance Program:** This program is available if you are receiving VA educational assistance at half-time or more rates and have a deficiency in a subject making tutoring a necessity.

**Education forms:** Forms are available for print through: **www.gibill.va.gov/GI_Bill_Info/education_forms.htm** or contact the VA toll free at **888-442-4551**

**Other sources for financial education assistance:** Check with the Financial Aid office at your school and with the State office that handles Veterans Affairs for the state where your training facility is located. Your State may offer other education benefits based on military service or being a dependent of a veteran. To locate, visit: **www.va.gov/statedva.htm**

**Other useful web sites: Dantes** provides a wealth of information about educational benefits and programs. The site also links to each state of the Voluntary Education for the Reserve Components and the Army National Guard Institute: **www.dantes.doded.mil**

The Department of Education: **www.ed.gov**

The Coalition of America's Colleges and Universities: **www.collegeispossible.org**

The Department of Labor's Employment and training Administration (ETA) site: **www.doleta.gov**

**Special state education programs of interest:**

**Illinois:** The Illinois Veteran Grant (IVG) Program pays tuition and certain fees at all Illinois state-supported institutions of higher learning for eligible veterans. For more information: **www.collegezone.com** or call **800-899-ISAC**

**Texas:** Tuition for eligible Texas veterans at state-supported schools (Hazelwood Act). To learn more call **800-252-8387** or **www.tvc.state.tx.us/Hazlewood.html**

**For more Information about education benefits:** Visit the Department of Veterans Affairs website at **www.gibill.va.gov** or **www.gibill.va.gov/GI_Bill_Info/benefits.htm** or speak with a VA benefit counselor by calling (toll free): **888-442-4551**

GO UCLA! BEAT USC!

C-2

# INTERNET: HIGHER EDUCATION RESOURCES

Below is a checklist of Internet addresses to assist you in identifying schools that match your interests, application to schools, answering questions, searching for financial aid and more.

## Career

**All College Courses**
www.allcollegecourses.com
**CareerBuilder**
www.careermosaic.com
**Career Network**
http://careernet.4jobs.com
**Occupational Outlook Handbook**
www.bls.gov/oco/home.htm
**Princeton Review**
www.princetonreview.com
**US News Colleges & Career**
www.usnews.com/sections/business/careers/index.html

## Federal & State Government

**Chronicle of Higher Education**
www.chronicle.com
**FAFSA on the Web**
www.fafsa.ed.gov
**Federal Student Aid: application**
www.studentaid.ed.gov
**The Student Guide**
www.studentaid.ed.gov/PORTALSWebApp/students/english/publications.jsp
**U.S. Department of Education**
www.ed.gov

## Schools

**Colleges and Universities**
www.universities.com
**CollegeView**
www.collegeview.com
**CollegeXpress**
www.collegexpress.com
**Community College Web**
www.mcli.dist.maricopa.edu/cc
**United States Two-year Colleges**
http://cset.sp.utoledo.edu/twoyrcol.html
**U.S. News Colleges & Career**
www.usnews.com/sections/education/index.html
**Vocational Information Center**
www.khake.com/page50.html

## College Applications

**CollegeApps**
www.collegeapps.com
**CollegeLink**
http://collegelink.org
**CollegeNet**
www.collegenet.com

## Testing & Admissions

**American College Testing (ACT)**
www.act.org
**College Board Online**
www.collegeboard.org
**Dear Admissions Guru**
www.jayi.com/ACG/ques.html
**Educational Testing Organization**
www.ets.org
**Kaplin Educational Centers**
www.kaplan.com
**Princeton Review**
www.princetonreview.com

## Scholarship Search

**CollegeBoard**
www.collegeboard.org
**FastAid**
www.fastaid.com
**Fastweb—Scholarship Search**
www.fastweb.com
**FinAid**
www.finaid.org
**Nat. Assoc. of Stu. Fin. Aid Adm.**
www.NASFAA.org
**Ref. Ser. Press Funding Focus**
www.rspfunding.com/index.html
**Lane Disabilities Service**
www.lanecc.edu/foundation/scholarships.htm
**American Student Assistance**
www.amsa.com/index.cfm
**U.S. Department of Education**
www.ed.gov
**U.S. Dept. of Ed., Project EASI**
http://people.rit.edu/easi
**Wired Scholar: SallieMae**
www.wiredscholar.com
**FreSch!**
www.freschinfo.com
**National Merit Scholarship Corp.**
www.nationalmerit.org
**Xap.com**
www.xap.com/getmoney

## Financial Aid Information

**College Aid**
www.collegeaid.com
**CollegeNet**
www.collegenet.com
**FastWeb**
www.fastweb.com
**Minority Online Info. Ser. (MOLIS)**
www.molis.us
**Petersons Education Center**
www.petersons.com

**Princeton Review**
www.princetonreview.com
**Texas Guar. Student Loan Corp.**
www.tgslc.org
**The Fin. Aid Information Page**
www.finaid.org
**U.S. Department of Education**
http://studentaid.ed.gov/PORTALSWebApp/students/english/index.jsp

## Private Lenders

**Crestar Student Loans**
www.student-loans.com
**Wachovia Education Loans**
www.wachovia.com/personal/page/0,,325_496,00.html
**KeyBank USA Educat. Resour.**
www.key.com/html/H-1.3.html
**Sallie Mae**
www.salliemae.com

## Military Related

**American Legion**
www.legion.org
**DOD Voluntary Education**
www.voled.doded.mil/voled_web/voledhome.asp
**DANTES**
www.dantes.doded.mil/dantes_web/DantesHome.asp
**eArmyU Program**
www.earmyu.com
**Enlisted Education Programs:**
www.airforce.com/education/enlisted/index.php
**Officer Education Programs:**
www.airforce.com/education/officer/index.php
**Transition Assistance**
www.taonline.com
**Troops to teachers**
www.ed.gov/programs/troops/index.html
**Tuition Assistance (TA) Program**
www.military.com/money-for-school/tuition-assistance/tuition-assistance-ta-program-overview

## Miscellaneous

**Search Engines**
www.yahoo.com/Education
**Study Abroad**
www.studyabroad.com

"Back for more, Smarty Pants? Take a knee. Next lesson. Credit can be your friend or your worst enemy. Credit is valuable because you can buy things you might not be able to afford right away and pay over time. However, credit also means you're borrowing against **uncertain** future income, without an ability to predict what will happen tomorrow. *Dun & Bradstreet* defines credit as, *"Man's Confidence in Man."* Right now, I don't have much confidence in you, as matter-of-fact, I wouldn't loan you a wooden nickel. Pay attention! Credit is a privilege; don't start collecting credit cards as if they were baseball cards. I'll teach you how to establish or re-establish credit without purchasing anything. I'll show you how to choose the right credit card(s), and not over-extend yourself (credit). Oh, and one more thing, **I'M YOUR COACH!** So, what are you waiting for? Start reading, Slacker!"

**Third Commandment:**
**"THOU SHALL NOT COLLECT CREDIT CARDS, NOR USE THEM CARELESSLY"**

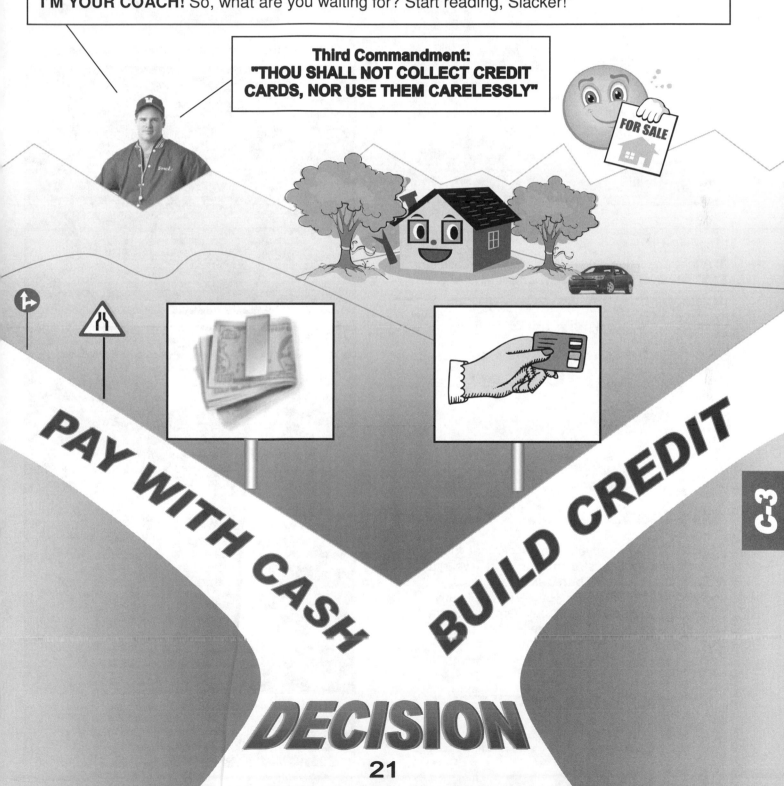

PAY WITH CASH

BUILD CREDIT

DECISION

As stated earlier, credit can be a valuable financial tool that allows you to purchase items, while promising to pay with future income. However, in order to use credit, you must first establish a credit history that ensures that you are capable of paying current or future obligations.

There are several ways to establish credit (some very costly). The three examples below are by far the easiest and least expensive to establish or even re-establish credit.

## How to establish a credit history

**1.** Establish savings account through a *credit union*.

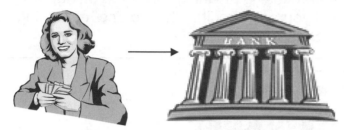

**2.** Deposit $100 into new savings account.

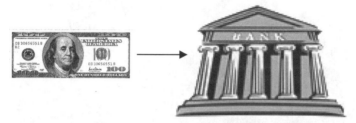

**3.** After transaction, find a *loan officer* and ask for a $100 *secured loan against your savings account*.

"I'd like to secure a $100 loan against my savings."

"Sounds great, but I'm a lawyer. Bank's next door."

**IMPORTANT:** Inform your loan officer that you want the loan payments to stretch for at least 1-year, and **reported to the credit bureaus**. If loan goes unreported to the bureaus, you will not build any credit history. **WARNING:** Repayment plan of small loan may vary depending on credit union policy.

**4.** When loan officer hands you a check for $100, deposit it into your savings account.

 =

**5.** One year later: Loan is paid-off; you have *established* or *re-established credit,* and $200 with interest in savings account.

 +

## Other methods of establishing a credit history

■ **Secured Credit Cards:**
Secured credit cards help build or re-establish credit; yet can pay for goods and services much like any credit card. However, a secured card requires a deposit that may range from a few hundred or thousand dollars. Usually, a bank will pay interest on your deposit, but you may have to pay application and processing fees, sometimes totaling hundreds of dollars. Before applying, ask what the total fees are, and whether they will be refundable if denied credit card. Typically, a secured card has a higher interest rate than an unsecured card.
**NOTE:** If you are a credit union member, inquire about a secured card there. Almost half of all credit unions offer secured cards to their members. Some credit unions offer lower interest rates and waive annual fees. For more information visit:
**www.bankrate.com/brm/news/cc/19990823.asp**

■ **Establish your own credit history:**
Approximately 100 million Americans have little or no credit history with the "big three" credit bureaus. While millions of these consumers earn steady incomes, and meet regular payment obligations, there has been no easy way for mainstream lenders to evaluate them as potential borrowers...until now.
PRBC (Payment Reporting Builds Credit) is a national credit bureau that captures consumers' history of paying rent, utility, and other recurring bills not reported to traditional bureaus. They enable business partners to help their consumers and small business customers to build a credit file automatically as they pay their bills, or by verifying self-reported payments they have made in the past. Their service bridges the gap between consumers seeking credit and lenders seeking to qualify them.
**Patented Innovation:** PRBC has been qualified as a "Community Development Service" for Financial Institutions, by the Federal Reserve Board, Office of the Comptroller of the Currency, Office of Thrift Supervision, Federal Deposit Insurance Corporation, and by the State of New York Banking Department. The FHA (see **http://prbc.com/popup/fha-letter.php**) and Sallie Mae (see **http://prbc.com/popup/fannie-quote.php**) accept PRBC reports. To learn more, visit: **http://prbc.com** or call **877.772.2123.**

To learn more about establishing credit, visit:
■ **www.frbsf.org/publications/consumer/credit. html#establish**
■ **www.bankrate.com/brm/news/debt/20021108a.asp**

The average American household is buried in personal debt of over $112,000, with a staggering 65% making only minimum payments that could possibly last a lifetime. So, how can one avoid being buried in high interest debt, when charging for goods and services, especially with zero or bad credit? To begin with, join a credit union; sign up to a savings account and start depositing money. Another method is to get in touch with a financial group or firm, and set up savings or investment plan that can be used as collateral. When it's time to purchase a big ticket item or something you can't live without, secure or collateralize a loan against your account(s) at very reasonable interest rates.

**Example:** Five consumers purchase a computer in different ways.

SALE
$1,500

| Categories: | Consumer 1 | Consumer 2 | Consumer 3 | Consumer 4 | Consumer 5 |
|---|---|---|---|---|---|
| Price of computer | $1,500 | $1,500 | $1,500 | $1,500 | $1,500 |
| Balance in savings | 0 | $1,500 | $1,500 | $1,500 | $1,500 |
| Savings interest rate | 0% | 1% | 1% | 5% | 5% |
| Type of loan | Credit card | Pay with cash | Secured | Collateral | From self |
| Monthly installments | 105 Months | 0 Months | 30 Months | 30 months | 30 months |
| Loan interest rate | 18.9% | 0% | 4% | 4% | 0% |
| Payments | $60 | 0 | $52.62 | $52.62 | $50 |
| Monthly interest paid | $8.40 | 0 | $2.62 | $2.62 | 0 |
| Total interest paid | $882.14 | 0 | $78.60 | $78.60 | 0 |
| Total payoff | $2,382.14 | $1,500 | $1,578.60 | $1,578.60 | $1,500 |
| Interest earned / savings | 0 | 0 | $37.80 | $195.09 | $195.09 |
| In savings, with interest | $0 | $0 | $1,537.80 | $1,695.09 | $1,695.09 |
| After taxes (15% bracket) | $0 | $0 | $1,532.09 | *$1,695.09 | *$1,695.09 |
| Type : Passbook savings, supplemental fund and insurance cash value | None | Bank Savings Account | Credit union savings account | SIRP *(tax-deferred) | Universal Life *(tax-deferred) |

## Other benefits using secured or collateral loans:

- Money in your savings account continues to grow and earn interest.
- Payments applied to your loan can be re-borrowed.

   **Example:** Loan payments of $200 x 3 months – $600
   You would then be able to secure other loans up to $600

- You can pay-off loan at anytime, because your principle is still secured in savings account.
- Even with bad credit, you still qualify for a low interest (**2%-3%**) secured loan.

This little piggy is heading to the market!

C-3

Before rushing to apply for several credit cards, let's take a short stroll through *"Credit Card-land."* The information provided below will help make you aware what type of financial roller coaster ride that you might be thinking about getting on.

**In 2004, American consumers carried and juggled:**

- **657 million bank credit cards**
- **228 million debit cards**
- **550 million retail credit cards**

**Based on cards per household:**

- **6.3 bank credit cards**
- **2.2 debit cards, and**
- **6.4 retail credit card**

**All payment cards combined:**

- **14.9 cards per household!**

(Source: CardData)

■ The average number of credit cards per consumer is **4**. **1 in 7** Americans carry **10 or more credit cards**.
(Source: Experian's "National Score Index")

**The top 10 credit card issuers controlled approximately 88% of the credit card market at the end of 2006, based on credit card receivables outstanding.**
(Source: FDIC)

■ Top **10** issuers of general-purpose credit cards:

1. **Bank of America**
2. **JPMorgan Chase**
3. **Citigroup**
4. **American Express**
5. **Capital One**
6. **Discover Card**
7. **HSBC**
8. **Wash. Mutual**
9. **Wells Fargo**
10. **US Bancorp**

(Source: Cardweb)

**Market share ranked by major card type:**

1. **Visa – 54%**
2. **MasterCard – 29%**
3. **American Express – 13%**
4. **Discover Card – 4%**

(Source: Cardweb)

■ A recent study shows that the safest card issuers are:

1. **Bank of America**
2. **American Express**
3. **Discover & First National Bank Omaha**
4. **Citibank**
5. **Navy Federal Credit Union**

The research study also revealed that in fraud prevention, Citibank ranked top and American Express ranked #1 in fraud detection.
(Source: Javelin Strategy & Research)

**U.S. households will receive approximately 5.3 billion offers for new credit cards in 2007.**
(Source: Synovate, mailmonitor.synovate.com)

■ The average interest rate across all existing credit card accounts were **13.46%** as of May 2007.
(Source: Federal Reserve)

**The average interest rate for standard bank credit cards topped 19% in March 2007.**
(Source: **www.cardtrak.com**)

■ More than **4 out of 10** consumers between ages **18 and 21** who surf the Web now own a credit card, and **65%** of these young surfers used the Web to apply for a card.
(Source: Forrester Research)

**23.8% of American households have no credit, bank or retail cards.**
(Source: Liz Pulliam Weston, www.asklizweston.com)

■ **31.2%** of households pay-off their most recent credit card debt in full.
(Source: Liz Pulliam Weston, www.asklizweston.com)

**Almost 50% of credit card holders don't pay the full amount of credit charges each month. About 11% say they usually pay only the minimum monthly payment.**
(Source: Experian-Gallup Personal Credit Index)

■ Only **one household in 50** carries more than **$20,000** in credit card debt. However, that figure represents more than **2 million** American homes.
(Source: Liz Pulliam Weston, www.asklizweston.com)

**In 2007, U.S. consumers charged nearly $63 billion worth of fast food on their personal credit and debit cards. The average credit card ticket is about $12.65. Americans spend about $170 billion per year at quick service restaurants.**
(Source: VISA USA)

■ **40%** of American families spend more than they earn.
(Source: www.federalreserve.gov)

Out of the 14 credit cards I own, let's see if this one works, today.

A credit card can be more convenient to use than carrying cash, and under federal law, offers valuable consumer protections. However, a credit card is a big responsibility. If you don't use it carefully, you may owe more than you can repay, damage your credit rating and create financial problems for yourself that may last years. Use the following tips to find a great credit card, and remember to use it responsibly.

**Qualifying for a credit card:** If you're 18-years old and have regular income, you may qualify for a card. Despite the invitations from card issuers, you still have to prove that you're worthy of risk before they grant you credit. If you've financed a car loan or paid something monthly, you probably have a history with one of the credit reporting bureaus. A credit history shows how responsible you are paying bills, and helps the credit card issuer decide how much credit to extend. Before you submit a credit application, get a free copy of your credit report from the five major credit bureaus listed below. More than one credit bureau may have a file on you, so make sure they are accurate.

> **EQUIFAX:** (800) 685-1111 / www.equifax.com
> **EXPERIAN:** (888) 397-3742 / www.experian.com
> **TRANS UNION:** (800) 888-4213 / www.tuc.com
> **INNOVIS:** www.innovis.com
> **PRBC:** (877) 772 2123 / http://prbc.com

**Getting first credit card:** If you haven't financed a car loan, a computer, or some other major purchase, you probably have very little credit established or none. So how do you get a credit card? Start with:

■ Banking and credit union institutions on some military installations, have programs set up for service members to help them get their first credit card. The Industrial Bank on Peterson AFB, CO has a *"First Time Credit"* program. Service members must attend an AFTEC class and credit counseling by bank manager before receiving a $300-500 line of credit.
■ Apply and qualify for a credit card issued by a local store. Make sure they report to a credit bureau. If you pay your bills on time, you'll establish a good credit history.
■ Qualifying for a secured credit card typically requires opening and maintaining a checking account at a bank or credit union to secure a line of credit. Your credit line will be a percentage of your deposit. Application and processing fees are common for secured credit cards. In addition, secured cards usually carry higher interest rates than non-secured cards (for more, see **page 22**).

**Denied:** If you are denied credit, it may signal that you haven't been at your current job or address long enough; income may not meet the issuer's criteria, or their standards. If several issuers' turn you down it may mean that you are not credit worthy. However, if you've been denied credit due to data supplied by a credit bureau, federal law requires the creditor to give you the name, address and telephone number of the bureau that supplied the data. If you contact that bureau within 60-days of receiving the denial, you are entitled to a free copy of your report. If your file contains accurate negative data, only time and good credit habits will restore your credit worthiness. If you find an error in your report, correct it ASAP through that credit bureau at no charge. You should dispute any inaccuracy in your report with

the credit bureau and also with the company that furnished the information to the credit bureau. A positive credit history is an asset, not only when you apply for a credit card, but also when you apply for a job, auto insurance, or want to finance a car or home.

> **Tips on how to get the best credit card:** Fees, charges, and benefits vary among credit card issuers. When choosing a credit card, shop around. Use the following pages as a checklist and compare important features. Begin your search with **"Consumer Actions 2009 Credit Card Survey"** for the latest news and trends in credit cards. Visit: **www.consumeraction.org/ news/articles/2009_credit_card_survey/#Topic_06**

**1. Check out the Annual percentage rate (APR):** The APR is a measure of the cost of credit, expressed as a yearly interest rate. Terms and conditions vary widely, so it is important to compare offers. Look for:

■ Regular (non-introductory) APRs
■ APRs near or below 15%
■ Cards that don't assess penalty APRs or if unavoidable, penalty no higher than 20% and for a limited period of time, such as, until two consecutive payments are made
■ "periodic rate," is the rate issuer applies to outstanding balance to figure finance charge for each billing period.
■ **"Universal Default"** clauses in the fine print (If found, avoid card)

**2. Maximum credit limit:** Based on a consumer's credit history, the credit line or limit is the amount of money a consumer may borrow from a credit card lender.

**3. Grace period:** The time between the date of purchase and the date interest starts being charged is called a *grace period*. If your card has a standard grace period, you can avoid finance charges by paying your current balance in full. Some issuers allow a grace period for new purchases even if you do not pay your balance fully each month. If no grace period, you'll owe interest from the day you make a purchase, even if you pay the bill promptly. Look for a card with a 25-day grace period.

**4. Annual fees:** Many card issuers charge an annual fee between $15 and $90 a year. If you plan to pay balance in full each month, and not interested in frequent flyer miles, etc., you should have no trouble finding a card with no annual fee. Although rare, issuers may waive annual fee for new customers or longtime cardholders. If you have an excellent credit history, or do significant business with the lender, ask for a fee waiver.

**5. Transaction fees/other charges:** Some issuers charge a transaction fee (at higher rate) if card is used for cash advances. Extra fees applied when failing to make payment on time or exceeds credit limit. Some charge a flat fee every month whether you use the card or not.

**6. Methods of computing balances:** If you plan to carry a balance from month to month, choose a card with low interest rate. Methods of computing balances vary widely and have a big effect on the cost of credit. There are three main methods:
■ **Adjusted balance** is the most consumer-friendly method of balance computation. Payments/credits received are subtracted from balance at the beginning of the billing cycle. New purchases are not included in the

25

C-3

calculations. Example, if cardholder's beginning balance was $2,000, and cardholder made a payment of $500 during the billing period, the cardholder would only be charged interest on the remaining balance of $1,500.

■ **Average daily balance** is the most common method of computation. Issuer credits your account the day your payment's received. To figure the balance due, the issuer totals the beginning balance for each day in the billing period and subtracts any credits made to your account that day. While new purchases may or may not be added to the balance, depending on your plan, cash advances typically are included. The resulting daily balances are added to the billing cycle and total is divided by the number of days in the billing period to get the average daily balance.

■ **Two-cycle balance** is the least friendly method of balance computation. To obtain balance, card issuers add the average daily balances for the current and previous billing cycles. The average daily balances for the current billing period may include new purchases.

**7. Interest Rates:** Sometimes you'll have a choice between two types of interest rates, variable or fixed:

■ **Variable rates** tend to be lower than fixed; they are usually tied to the bank's prime rate or the recent cost of T-bills. There is no way to know how much interest you will pay from month to month.

■ **Fixed rates** can be changed by banks with no warning.

**8. Beware of introductions:** Low introductory rates are a marketing device that can eventually zoom upward, becoming less than a bargain. If you do take advantage of low rate cards, watch for expiration date, and switch cards when the time comes.

**9. Less is better:** The fewer credit cards you own, the more impressive your credit rating looks. Lenders tend to interpret multiple credit cards as numerous ways to get into debt. Thus, find one or two cards that work well with your spending and payment patterns, and keeps your credit file attractively slim.

**10. Other benefits:** Issuers may offer additional benefits (some with a cost), such as insurance, credit card protection, discounts, rebates and special offers.

**11. Disclosure chart:** The disclosure chart contains the most important information of the offer. Read carefully before accepting a card. Many punitive fees are stated only in the fine print below the disclosure chart. By law, the disclosure chart must contain:
■ Actual APR, once the introductory period ends
■ Formula for the APR, if the rate is variable
■ Length of the grace period
■ Amount of the annual fee, if any
■ Minimum finance charge
■ Any transaction fees, such as cash advances, etc.
■ Method of computing the purchase balance for each billing period
■ Late payment fees and default or delinquency fees
■ Over-the-limit fees

**12. Customer service:** Make sure an issuer has a 24-hour, toll-free telephone number.

**Credit card traps:** Card issuers are reaping more profit from late fee income than ever before, using three tactics:
■ More than doubling late fees between 1992 and 2000.
■ Decreased the amount of time between when they mail a bill and when payment is due.

■ Nearly two-thirds of companies have eliminated leniency periods.

**1. Higher over-the-limit fees:** In 2000, only one card charged a fee of less than $20 to consumers who exceeded their credit limits. The highest fee was $35. In contrast, a 1995 survey found only one bank that charged a fee of $20 or more. Many companies assess this fee to cardholders that exceed their limits by as little as $1.

**2. Hidden transaction fees:** Fees for cash advances, balance transfers and quasi-cash transactions like the purchase of lottery tickets significantly raise the cost of these transactions. The terms of these transactions are buried in fine print, where it can easily be missed. Minimum fees (also in fine print), allow card issuers to guarantee themselves high fee income regardless of the transaction amount. Example: X-card has a transaction fee of 3% and minimum $10. This means that the cash advance fee will be 3% of the cash advance amount or $10 minimum, whichever is more.

**3. Punitive (APR) increases:** Average penalty APR (higher interest rate for missed or late payment), is 52% higher than the average regular (non-penalty, non-introductory) APR. In 1998, penalty APRs averaged 4.5 percentage points higher than regular APRs.

**4. Declining grace periods:** While grace periods historically were a full month long, they now average 23 days. Some cards have no grace periods at all.

**5. Introductory APRs:** 57% of card offers advertised a low introductory APR. The average introductory APR was 4.13% and lasted an average of 6.8 months. Card issuers use low, short-term introductory APRs to mask regular APRs that are an average of 264% higher (rate increases are not prominently disclosed).

**6. Minimum payments:** Minimum monthly payments are designed to sound attractive to consumers, but they encourage cardholders to pay more in finance charges as the length of time needed to pay off a balance increases significantly. Card issuers have decreased minimum payments in recent years from the historic industry standard of 5% to a new standard of 2% to 3%.

**7. "Fixed" APR:** So-called *"fixed"* interest rates (in the fine print) can be increased with as little as 15 days notice to cardholders.

**8. "Bait and Switch" credit card offers:** Direct mail credit card offers generally advertise the premium card the bank has to offer, yet the fine print includes the caveat that the company can substitute a lower-grade, non-premium card if the applicant does not qualify for the premium card. The lower-grade card costs more and offers less attractive terms, facts rarely mentioned in the official disclosure of the offer.

**9. Tiered pricing:** Tiered pricing is the new practice, which is catching on quickly with credit card companies. In an offer, the company quotes a wide range of possible APRs that are meaningless; for example, X-company quotes a range of 7.99% to 20.24%. Based on the applicant's credit history, X-company then assigns an APR to each applicant once card is issued. Thus, consumers are being denied the right to know the conditions of a credit card before they accept an offer.

**Kinds of credit accounts:** Credit card companies generally issue three types of accounts. The basic terms of these account agreements are:

- **Revolving agreement:** Consumer pays in full each month or chooses to make a partial payment based on the outstanding balance. Department stores, gas and oil companies and banks typically issue credit cards based on a revolving credit plan.
- **Charge agreement:** Consumer promises to pay the full balance each month, so the borrower does not have to pay interest charges. Charge cards (not credit cards) and charge accounts with local businesses often require repayment on this basis.
- **Installment agreement:** Consumer signs a contract to repay a fixed amount of credit in equal payments over a specific period. Cars, furniture, appliances and personal loans are usually financed using installments.

**The do's with credit cards:**

- Sign your cards as soon as you receive them.
- Papers that come with your credit card have information, such as how to contact customer service, in case your card is stolen or lost. File this information in a safe place.
- Keep records of your account numbers, expiration dates and address of each company.
- Call the card issuer or make account inquiry from ATM machine to activate card. Many issuers require this step to minimize fraud and to give you additional information.
- Keep your account information to yourself.
- Carry your cards separately from your wallet in a zippered compartment or a business card holder.
- Watch your card during the transaction and retrieve it as quickly as possible.
- Void incorrect receipts and destroy carbon receipts.
- Keep copies of sales slips and compare charges when your bill arrives. Promptly call or report in writing any questionable charges to the card issuer.
- Shred all unwanted credit card applications. Otherwise, organized *"Garbage Rings"* (that exist in many areas), may find an application(s); fill it out with a new address and get card(s) in your name.
- Notify card issuers in advance if you change address.
- Always keep ATM PIN a secret.
- Beware of the date your monthly statement usually arrives. If it doesn't show up within a few days of when it's supposed to, notify the issuer immediately to prevent *account takeover*. Someone could have stolen the statement from the mail and used the information to go on a buying spree at your expense.

**The don'ts with credit cards:**

- Don't lend your credit card to anyone, even to a friend.
- Never leave cards or receipts lying around.
- Don't leave personal information in your home or barracks, especially if you have roommates.
- Never sign blank receipts. Be sure to draw a line through any blank spaces.
- Do not write your account number on a postcard or the outside of an envelope.
- Never give out your credit card number or expiration date over the phone unless you know whom you're dealing with. A criminal can use this information to steal money from you, or even assume your credit identity.
- Don't use your address, birth date, phone number or social security number as a PIN number.
- Never keep your PIN number on a slip of paper in your purse or wallet.
- Don't charge more than you can afford.

**Transfer credit debt to a lower rate:** Credit card issuers want your business, and are willing to spend, on the average, $75 to $80 per customer persuading you to accept a new card. The credit card industry becomes more competitive each year, due to the credit card issuers need to maintain or increase their market share to support their foundation. Card issuers try to lure cardholders from one or more of the cards they already use. The most effective *"hook"* is the teaser rate, a single digit interest rate for the next 6 to 12 months. Even more tempting; transferring your unpaid balance from your present card to the new lower rate. Depending on what interest rate your current card charges, you can slash your minimum monthly payment in half.

**Teaser rates, good and bad:** Teaser rates provide a quicker way to get out of debt. Unpaid balance will shrink faster, because less payment goes to interest, and more to principal. Example: Credit card rate is 18%; balance $1,000, with $20 monthly payment. At this pace, it would take nearly 8-years to pay-off debt. However, if rate is reduced to 7% with same $20 monthly payment, debt will be wiped out in less than 5-years.

- **Problem:** The teaser is only temporary. To stay ahead, you must keep switching credit card companies just before each low rate expires.
- **Solution:** Shortly before the teaser period ends, call the card issuer and ask for an extension, or better rate. Explain that you will close your account and transfer the debt elsewhere if an extension is not possible. Make sure to have other new card offers, so that you are prepared to make good on your threat. Most lenders will extend the rate, if you have been a good customer. Some may ask that you transfer additional balances to the account, which may further your efforts to consolidate debt. If the card issuer will not extend the initial low rate, or if you can get a better teaser rate somewhere else, go ahead and make the switch.
- **Problem:** Not canceling, the old card as soon as you receive the new one could create a large available-credit line that will appear on your credit report and may signal *danger* to some lenders. As a result, future loans may be harder to get, or only obtain credit at a higher rate than others pay.

**Solution:** Notify the previous card issuer in writing and instruct the company to notify the credit reporting bureaus that you closed the account. Otherwise, someone might assume that the company closed the account because you were a poor credit risk.

**If you receive a better offer:** When you receive a teaser rate offer, pick up the phone and call your present credit card company, and explain that you are thinking about taking the new card. However, ask the current issuer if they would like to offer you a better deal to stay. You may not get the teaser rate, but the likelihood of them offering you a more favorable rate is high.

**Sky-high rates for high-risk borrowers:** If you are applying for credit in your name for the first time, or you had good credit but fell behind, there are plenty of lenders eager to do business with you. However, the costs are exorbitant. The good news is that even cards with high interest rates and fees can help you reach your financial goals, if you play them right.

The average APR for someone with decent credit is between 13% and 16%. Interest rates in the low-to-mid-20s are more typical for those with bad credit or none at all. In addition, fees for being late or over the limit tend to hover between $25 and $29.

Risk is one reason rates are high. The credit card business as a whole is a bigger gamble for financial institutions. Veribanc found that in 1998, the losses by U.S. banks for credit card debt were more than seven times higher than for other types of loans. When an issuer targets people with bad credit, risk increases. The key is to use the card as a charge card rather than a credit card. If you have a tremendous self-discipline, it's not a bad deal for restoring your credit.

**Rule of thumb for high-interest credit cards:**
■ Never carry a balance.  Use card to charge items that can be paid off in full before the grace period ends.
■ Mail your credit card payment one week early to avoid late payment, and default penalty interest rates.
■ After six months of on-time payments, check to make sure the lender is sending that information to the credit reporting agencies. Some issuers keep good information to themselves so you won't get other competitors offers.
■ After six months of on-time payments, ask issuer to give you a better interest rate.  Lenders won't make that offer, so it's up to the customer to request it.
■ If card issuer won't cut your rate after a year of good behavior, close the account and find another deal.
■ If you aren't sure you can handle a line of credit, obtain a secured card.
■ If you need quick access to cash for an emergency, consider short-term personal loan instead of a credit card.

**Federal protections for cardholders:** Federal law offers the following protections when you use credit cards:

**1. Prompt credit for payment:** When an issuer receives your payment, they must credit your account that day. The exceptions are if the payment is not made according to the creditor's requirements, or the delay in crediting your account won't result in a charge.

To avoid finance charges, follow the issuers mailing instructions. Payments sent to the wrong address could delay crediting your account for up to five days.  If you misplace your envelope, look for the payment address on your billing statement or call the issuer.

**2. Refunds of credit balances:** When you make a return or pay more than the total balance at present, you can keep the credit on your account or write your issuer for a refund, if it's more than a dollar. A refund must be issued within seven business days of receiving your request. If a credit stays on your account for more than six months, the issuer must make a good faith effort to send you a refund.

**3. Errors on bill:** If you discover an error on your bill, you must notify card issuer in writing within 60 days after the first mailed bill containing the error. In your letter, include:
■ Your name and account number
■ Why the bill contains an error
■ Date and amount of the error

In return, the card issuer must investigate the problem and either correct the error or explain to you why the bill is correct. This must occur within two billing cycles and not later than 90 days after the issuer receives your billing error notice. You do not have to pay the sum in question during the investigation.

**4. Unauthorized Charges:** If your credit card is used without your authorization, you can be held liable for up to $50 per card.  If you report the loss before the card is used, you can't be held responsible for any unauthorized charges. If unauthorized charges are made before you report your card missing, the most you will owe is $50.

To minimize your liability, report the loss as soon as possible. It's a good idea to follow-up with a letter to the issuer by sending:
■ Your name and your account number
■ The date you noticed your card missing
■ The date you reported the loss

**5. Disputes about merchandise or services:** You can dispute charges for unsatisfactory goods or services. To do so you must:
■ First make a good faith effort to resolve the dispute with the seller. No special methods are required to do so.
■ Have made a $50 or more purchase in your home state or within 100 miles of your current billing address. These limitations don't apply if the seller is the card issuer or if a special business relationship exists between the seller and the card issuer.

If these conditions don't apply, you may want to consider filing an action in small claims court.

**Using credit and charge cards wisely:**
■ **Never charge any item under $25:** Most unneeded debt stems from small purchases. Make it a policy of only paying cash for small purchases.
■ **Say NO to gold or platinum cards:** Unless a premium card offers special services you need, skip it. Most charge annual fees.
■ **Ask merchants for a cash discount:** Put away your credit card when merchant's give discounts of 5% to 10% or more on cash purchases.
■ **Know your rights:** The Government publishes booklets on consumer credit, the Fair Credit Reporting Act and other consumer topics. To get the full list of titles or to request copies, call or visit **Consumer Information Catalog Center 888.878.3256 or www.pueblo.gsa.gov**

The first thing you need to think about is how will you use a credit card? Do you expect to pay your monthly bill in full, carry over a balance from month to month, or get cash advances? Once you have decided, you can use the checklist below to compare cards. Information about most of the features on this checklist is given in the 'Disclosure Box' that must appear in all printed credit card solicitations and applications. **IMPORTANT:** Begin your search with **"Consumer Actions 2009 Credit Card Survey"** for the latest news and trends in credit cards. Please, visit **www.consumeraction.org/news/articles/2009_credit_card_survey/#Topic_06**

| FEATURES | CARD A | CARD B | CARD C |
|---|---|---|---|
| **What are APRs?** | | | |
| For purchases | | | |
| For cash advances | | | |
| For balance transfers | | | |
| If you pay late | | | |
| **What type of interest does card have?** | | | |
| Fixed, variable or tiered | | | |
| **How long is grace period?** | | | |
| If you carry over a balance | | | |
| If you pay off the balance each month | | | |
| For cash advances | | | |
| **How is the finance charge calculated?** | | | |
| One cycle or two | | | |
| Including or excluding new purchases | | | |
| Average or adjusted | | | |
| Minimum finance charge | | | |
| **What are the fees?** | | | |
| Annual | | | |
| Late-payment | | | |
| Over-the-credit-limit | | | |
| Set-up | | | |
| **What are the cash advance features?** | | | |
| Transaction fees | | | |
| Limits | | | |
| **How much is the credit limit?** | | | |
| **What kind of card is it?** | | | |
| Secured | | | |
| Regular | | | |
| Premium | | | |
| **Does the card offer other features?** | | | |
| Rebates | | | |
| Frequent flier miles | | | |
| Insurance | | | |
| Other | | | |
| **Does the credit card have a universal default clause embedded in fine print of the contract?** | | | |
| **Is credit card issuer based in a state that can charge any interest rate they choose as long as it is listed in the agreement and (you) the borrower agrees?** | | | |
| Other: | | | |

C-3

The websites below can ably assist you to find the best rates, transfer an existing account onto a lower rate, keep you posted on the latest credit law, fad, and scam or assist you to better understand credit.

**Bankrate:** www.bankrate.com is the Web's leading aggregator of financial rate information. Bankrate's rate data research offering is unique in its depth and breadth. Bankrate continually surveys approximately 4,800 financial institutions in all 50 states in order to provide clear, objective, and unbiased rates to consumers. Their Web site, Bankrate.com, provides free rate information to consumers on more than 300 financial products, including mortgages, credit cards, new and used automobile loans, money market accounts, certificates of deposit, checking and ATM fees, home equity loans and online banking fees.

**CardTrak:** www.cardtrak.com since 1986 has provided millions of consumers with timely information on credit cards and other payment cards via printed survey lists, newsletters, the national news media and the Internet. CardTrak and its Website are also renowned for fair and balanced reporting on credit card issues.

**ConsumerUnion.Org:** www.defendyourdollars.org/topic/credit_cards offers pros and cons of credit cards with 'Credit Card Tips For College Students.' Consumers Union (CU) is an expert, independent, nonprofit organization, whose mission is to work for a fair, just, and safe marketplace for all consumers. CU publishes Consumer Reports. Furthermore, Consumers Union has over 500,000 online activists who work willingly to bring about change in legislation and the marketplace in favor of the consumer interest (and several public education Web sites). Since its founding in 1936, Consumers Union has never taken any advertising or freebies of any kind.

**CardWeb.com:** www.cardweb.com is a leading online publisher of information pertaining to all types of payment cards, including, but not limited to, credit cards, debit cards, smart cards, prepaid cards, ATM cards, loyalty cards and phone cards. The firm uniquely serves all constituencies connected to the payment card business: consumers, institutions, merchants, acquirers, processors, manufacturers, consultants, news reporters and many others. The company is renowned for its independence, credibility and fairness.

**Credit.com:** www.credit.com serves as an educator, advocate and facilitator. *Credit.com* empowers consumers with easy-to-understand information about money, credit, loans and more. Credit.com is partnered with trusted financial experts and select companies in order to offer online consumers insightful tips, helpful tools and excellent deals.

**CreditCards.com:** www.creditcards.com is a leading online credit card marketplace, bringing consumers and card issuers together. Their site is a free online resource where consumers can compare hundreds of credit card offers by category, including low interest credit cards, credit cards with rewards programs, airline credit cards, and cash back credit cards, small business credit cards, student credit cards, instant approval credit cards as well as prepaid debit cards. Over one million users access their website each month.

**CreditorWeb:** www.creditorweb.com/aboutus.aspx provides articles on how to get the most out of credit cards and avoid common pitfalls. They also supply calculators and other tools to help consumers fully understand the cost of credit card debt, and a credit card search engine to make it easy to compare credit card offers from multiple issuers on a single page. They keep track of trends on which credit cards are frequently being applied for, and the percent of these applications that are approved to provide additional info on the popularity and odds of approval for each card. This is all done without collecting any personal information about individual visitors. Each card is carefully and objectively reviewed by industry experts to provide consumers with as much information as possible before applying for a card. They also provide links to the full terms and conditions for each card on the issuers website to ensure all data is fully disclosed. Finally, their experts rank each card with a five star rating system.

**The Federal Reserve:** www.federalreserve.gov/Pubs/shop http://www.federalreserve.gov/Pubs/shop/ offers an online booklet called '*Choosing a Credit Card*' that is packed with information that can assist consumers to find the right credit card(s), save money on interest, fees and more.

**Federal Trade Commission:** www.ftc.gov/bcp/edu/pubs/consumer/credit/cre05.shtm the FTC offering of '*Choosing and Using Credit Cards*' is a great source to help consumers understand terms and conditions, balance computation methods, protections, disputes and more.

**LowCards.com:** www.lowcards.com has been serving as a consumer resource for credit cards since July, 2000. It has been used by over one million people. They constantly analyze over 1000 different credit cards and write objective opinions for consumers. Due to this objectivity, LowCards.com has been rated as one of the best credit card comparison sites in the nation.

**Howstuffworks.com:** http://money.howstuffworks.com/credit-card.htm offers consumers several articles on how credit cards work. Do you know what the numbers mean on a credit card or how the magstripe on the backside of one works?

**MSN Money:** http://moneycentral.msn.com/banking/services/creditcard.asp offers '*Credit Card Analyzer*' to help consumers find credit cards based on the criteria you care about most.

**Truth About Credit:** www.truthaboutcredit.org is a project of the U.S. PIRG Education Fund and the Student PIRGs (Public Interest Research Groups). U.S. PIRG works to pursue a mission of standing up to powerful interests on behalf of the public. U.S. PIRG conducts research, education and advocacy on behalf of consumers.

**Consumer-action.org:** www.consumer-action.org/news/articles/2009_credit_card_survey/#Topic_06 explains in depth, their 2009 credit card survey (great read).

"Just smell that rocky mountain air, ahhh! So far, we've learned that credit can be a valuable and convenient financial tool. With a steady income and a budget, servicing reasonable credit debt is straightforward. On the other hand, if your income is disrupted due to job loss, serious illness, etc., there can be dire consequences. It can start with harassing notices, collection calls, and snowball into vehicle repossession(s), liens, evictions, bankruptcy, and even significant.

This chapter will give you the tools necessary to prevent, manage or eliminate debt turmoil and help keep you on financial course. Okay Magellan, set sail and steady as we go!"

**Fourth Commandment:**
**"THOU SHALL DEVELOP A BUDGET, AND STICK WITH IT"**

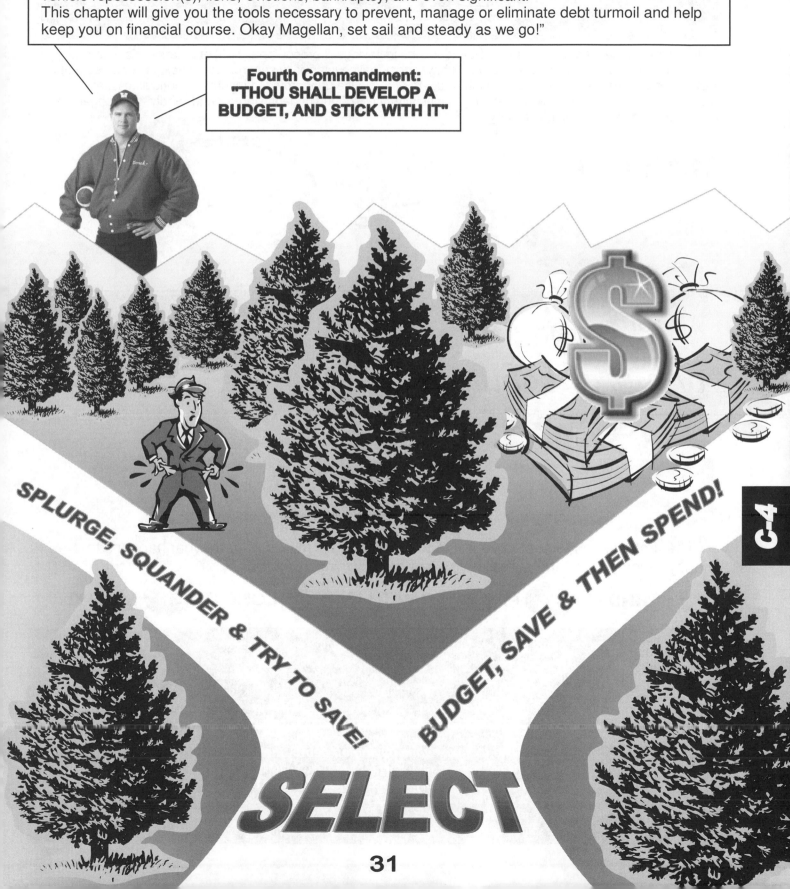

SPLURGE, SQUANDER & TRY TO SAVE!

BUDGET, SAVE & THEN SPEND!

C4

## SELECT

Looks like you have put on a few pounds lately. Let's do a financial checkup to see how much you weigh. Please step up to the scale and pile all your debt on the left side of the scale and on the right all your savings. Every $1,000 you have in debt or savings will equate to 1 lb.

| EXAMPLE: | | | | |
|---|---|---|---|---|
| Car | $19,000 = 19 lbs | | Bank savings | $2,000 = 2.0 lbs |
| Credit cards | $ 6,000 = 6 lbs | | Investment | $ 500 = 0.5 lbs |
| | $25,000 = 25 lbs | | | $2,500 = 2.5 lbs |

Using the model above, 25 lbs in debt and 2.5 lbs in savings is proportionally out of balance. For some consumers, having $2,500 in savings would have most feeling financially secure. Nevertheless, for those that have experienced divorce(s), loss of a job or death of a spouse (that provided income), a long illness, etc., they'd know that $2,500 wouldn't last long, especially with $25,000 of debt lying around. Sadly, the dangers I've described happen to people everyday.

## $1,000 = 1 lb

*"Are you in or out of balance?"*

The first lesson in keeping your finances balanced is to understand what happens to money, once you get it. As a rule, you can do four things with money:

**1. SPEND IT   2. PAY BILLS WITH IT   3. LOSE IT   4. SAVE IT**

Everyone is an expert at spending money. Most consumers are generally good at spending and paying bills. Then there are those who lose money by not taking advantage of tax laws or by other means. However, successful people manage to balance spending, paying bills, saving, and for the most part, avoid losing money (discussed throughout the book).

Let's use two examples of people with finances out of balance who want to get back in balance. Jack prefers the method of, *"I'd like to pay off all my bills before saving."* It might take him awhile, but eventually, he'd pay-off his debt (car, credit cards, etc.). However, if Jack has no money in savings and an unforeseen emergency were to surface, such as his car breaks down and needs another ASAP, what would happen? Jack would go back into debt, right? Now let's see how Jill does with using the method of, *"I'd like to save, while paying off debt."* If she experiences the same car emergency and period as Jack, Jill would have money to pay cash for her car and avoid going back into debt.

**Question: Whose method of getting financially balanced makes sense to you?**

To balance your finances, begin by starting a monthly budget (see **page 153**); track any bad spending habits, eliminate and save monthly into savings plans that are available to you. Saving now will pay huge dividends throughout your life and keep your financial foundation sound, even if you run into a few unexpected bumps or obstacles along the way.

# TURN WASTE INTO TOMORROW'S RICHES

*Where does all the money go? We put money in our account, and it evaporates into thin air.* I hear this from servicemembers and their families a lot, who battle each month trying to make ends meet. In most cases, they've been playing '*keep up with the Jones's*' or have gotten use to the good life and as a result, have developed some bad spending habits along the way. To correct their situation, I usually throw out some quick fix ideas like eat at home, rent movies instead of going out to see them, use cloth diapers instead of plastic diapers, etc. Most take my words to heart and decide to make changes, but a few, regardless of what I say, give me that pained look of, it's impossible or do we really have to change our lifestyle. Yes, change is hard, but the *payoff* can be huge.

Example: Gary Greenbucks, 21-year old married E-3, cuts back on spending and is now able to save $125 a month. If he places the $125 in a 10% tax-deferred account on a monthly basis, he would have:

- $1,076,982 by age 65, which is a *staggering* sum of money and well worth the sacrifice.

It doesn't take a lot of money to invest for your future, but it does require time to plan, research, break old habits and patience. Make a copy of the form below, or purchase a budget book, and if you're married, get one for your spouse too. Keep a weekly record of how you spend money daily. At the end of the month, tally up what you've spent. You won't believe how much you waste on little things. Once you've identified where your paycheck is going, try to curb your spending habits, by changing your daily routine. If someday, an unexpected emergency does arise, not only will you be better prepared, financially to absorb the shock and awe of the situation, but glad to have ridden past spending habits.

## TRACK YOUR DAILY SPENDING HABITS; THEN ELIMINATE AND SAVE

| HABIT | Day 1 | Day 2 | Day 3 | Day 4 | Day 5 | Day 6 | Day 7 | 7-Day Total |
|---|---|---|---|---|---|---|---|---|
| Alcohol | | | | | | | | |
| Cigarettes | | | | | | | | |
| Lottery | | | | | | | | |
| Soda | | | | | | | | |
| Snacks | | | | | | | | |
| Other: | | | | | | | | |
| **FAST FOOD** | | | | | | | | |
| Breakfast | | | | | | | | |
| Lunch | | | | | | | | |
| Dinner | | | | | | | | |
| Late Evenings | | | | | | | | |
| **RESTAURANTS** | | | | | | | | |
| Breakfast | | | | | | | | |
| Lunch | | | | | | | | |
| Dinner | | | | | | | | |
| Late Evenings | | | | | | | | |
| **ENTERTAINMENT** | | | | | | | | |
| Movies | | | | | | | | |
| Rentals | | | | | | | | |
| Music CD's | | | | | | | | |
| Video Games | | | | | | | | |
| Dance Clubs | | | | | | | | |
| Concerts/Events | | | | | | | | |
| Books | | | | | | | | |
| Magazines | | | | | | | | |
| Other: | | | | | | | | |
| **SHOPPING** | | | | | | | | |
| Groceries/ Shopette | | | | | | | | |
| Clothing | | | | | | | | |
| Hobbies | | | | | | | | |
| Other: | | | | | | | | |

C-4

The 1940 (amended 2004) Servicemembers' Civil Relief Act (**SCRA)** helps members manage their personal civil affairs, so they can devote attention to their duties. In addition, the **SCRA** recognizes the sacrifices members make to answer their country's call to serve, although it may include difficult financial obligations.

The **SCRA** helps Soldiers in many ways, however, for the sake of this article; I will focus on a scant section of the **SCRA** that limits interest charged to members at 6%. The **SCRA** allows this lower interest rate only on debt incurred *before* a servicemember enters the service. Therefore, credit debt incurred *after* entry is not covered.

However, over the years, countless service members have gotten their credit debt reduced as low as 0%, even though they acquired that debt *after* entry.

**How to use the SCRA after entry:** The easiest way to lower your interest rate is to talk to your creditor through their customer service department. Some companies will be more than glad to assist you with your request, even if you do not qualify through the **SCRA**.

**Example:** The Company may have a motto of, *"Keep customers happy. Give them what they want, and make them loyal customers."* Otherwise, get lucky, and find a helpful service rep that is willing to work with you.

Remember, even at lower rates, creditors still make millions of dollars. While companies may play along with you invoking the **SCRA**, the results may vary.

**Example A:** One customer service rep said her company had no special interest rates for the military; however, if their credit rating was in good standing, the company would lower its fixed rate and even drop to 6% if the member went to war.

**Example B**: Another service rep seemed well versed with the **SCRA**, at least on the behalf of the customer. When asked about military discounts, she replied, *"Have them send us a copy of their orders, and we'll lower their interest rate to 6% under the SCRA."* Furthermore, the fixed rate would continue until members left the service. In addition, when asked about debt accumulated *after* enlistment, she replied, *"That applies to all balances."*

Therefore, in both examples, the offers were more generous than the legal restrictions of the **SCRA**.

**What if creditors do not agree to lower rates:** Do not give up! Call another customer service rep. usually, there are several service reps within a company; therefore, you might find one that will work with you. However, if you are not making any headway, then ask for the manager. The manager may agree with your request to lower the interest rate. In addition, you will further your chances of a rate reduction, if you are courteous and not demanding over the phone, especially, since creditors are not obligated to lower debt that you accrued while *after* enlisting.

**What else can I do to lower interest rates with my creditors?** When re-enlisting, send a letter (on right) to your creditor that invokes the **SCRA,** including re-enlistment paperwork. As a public relations gesture, your creditor may lower your interest rate on debt accrued from your past enlistment, but expect to be billed at current rate of interest for any future transactions.

**Sample letter:** First, call your creditor to let them know that you will pay 6% while in the service, and cite the **SCRA** as your authority. However, if this does not work, send creditor this letter, and attach a copy of your proof of enlistment with it:

Customer Service Department/
Collections Department
Address: _____
_____

Date:_____

Name: _____
Address:_____
_____

Subject: Loan # / Account #_____

To whom it may concern:

This is to inform you that I am now in the Armed Forces of the United States. About my indebtedness or obligation to you, I am reserving any and all rights I have under Federal and State laws, and particularly the Servicemembers' Civil Relief Act of 1940, United States Code (50 U.S.C., Appendix, Sections 501-590), and amendments thereto. These laws apply to persons who voluntarily enlist or are called to active duty in the armed forces.

I entered the armed forces of the United States on:

**Month:** _____ **Day:____ Year:_____**

As the result of joining the Armed Forces, my income has been substantially reduced, and due to this reduction in income, my ability to meet obligations has been significantly affected.

Your attention is called to the fact that under the Act, interest on outstanding balances is to be reduced to **6 %** simple interest. Please compute the payoff amount of the loan as of the date I entered the Service and notify me of that amount. Then re-compute my monthly payments based on that payoff, with interest at **6%** simple interest effective when I became active duty. Notify me of that amount and I will resume payments and bring my account current as soon as possible.

Sincerely,

cc:

To learn more about the *SCRA*, visit:
- www.dmdc.osd.mil/scra/owa/info.help
- www.defenselink.mil/specials/Relief_Act_Revision/index.html
- www.military.com/benefits/legal-matters/scra/overview
- www.military.com/ benefits/legal matters/scra/frequently-asked-questions
- www.usafa.edu/superintendent/ja/Servicemen.cfm?catname=JA
- http://usmilitary.about.com/od/sscra/l/blscramenu.htm
- www.creditcards.com/credit-card-news/military-servicemembers-civil-relief-act-debt-burden-1282.php
- http://192.156.19.104/JAL_mess.nsf/c26d42f246f2c23d85256cb000675dd8/e5ce49deb49dbd1b85256e120050f9e4

## 1.) Universal Default (UD)

*"Universal Default"* is the term for a practice in the financial services industry for a particular lender to change normal terms of a loan to default terms, which include higher rates. So, when first lender is *"informed"* that their customer has defaulted with another lender (even if the customer has not defaulted with first lender), then *"Universal Default"* clause can be initiated.

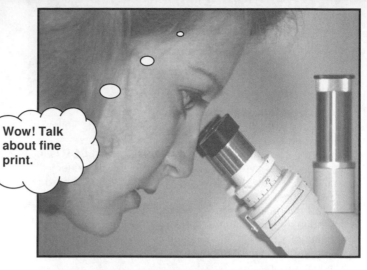

Wow! Talk about fine print.

### What triggers "Universal Default"?
A number of credit card companies evaluate credit reports monthly, some quarterly and few once a year, and if you've had a history of making late payments, then they'll review your files more often than those who always pay on time. Thus, if they see on your report:

- Lower credit score or inaccurate blemish **(90.48%)**
- Late payments **(85.71%)**
- Going over credit limit **(57.14%)**
- Bounced payment check **(52.38%)**
- High debt to income ratio **(42.86%)**
- Too much available credit **(33.33%)**
- Getting new credit card **(33.33%)**
- Inquiring about a car or mortgage loan **(23.81%)**
  - Source: Consumer Action survey

then they can let loose their **UD** clause on you. Therefore, whether you are applying for a new credit card or already have a few, it would be wise to check the contract fine print. Consumer Action (non-profit organization), reports that about 45% of all banks use universal default clauses and the clauses are in nearly all agreements issued by the nation's top 10 credit card issuers, who currently control 80% of the market.
To compound the problem, most major issuers of credit cards are located in states without interest rate caps. Banks and credit card issuers based in these states can charge any interest rate they choose as long as it is in the contract and borrower agrees. Incidentally, there is no federal limit on what interest rates credit card companies can charge.

### Things you can do to combat Universal Default:
**1.** Make your monthly payments at least a week ahead of the due date, or when they arrive.
**2.** If you have a large credit balance, transfer it to a low fixed rate card that does not have a **UD** clause.
**3.** Wean yourself off credit cards.
**4.** Monitor your accounts carefully and examine each bill when it arrives, especially its due date.
**5.** When disputing a bill, act without delay and work something out with the creditor. Once a negative remark hits your credit report; it's hard to remove.
**6.** Keep an accurate list of credit card payment due dates, along with balances, limits and interest rates.
**7.** Change your payment due date if it falls at an inconvenient time of the month.
**8.** Pay your bills automatically through your bank or electronically by computer each month.
**9.** When applying for credit, research all options, costs, benefits and especially, read all the fine print.
**10.** Remember, when you sign up for credit, you are entering into a legally binding agreement.

**Consumer Reports (CR) 10 most consumer-friendly credit cards: www.consumerreports.org**
None of the cards has a *"universal default"* clause, two-cycle billing, or balance transfer fees. All cards have a grace period of at least 25 days and have no annual fees.

To learn more about *"Universal Default"* and other credit related topics, visit the sites below:
- **www.bankrate.com/brm/news/credit-management/20040120a1.asp**
- **www.financial-education-icfe.org**

## 2.) Courtesy Overdraft Protection

*"Courtesy Overdraft Protection"* (**COP**) is where a bank, at their discretion, decides whether or not, to cover a check that a consumer writes, if their account is underfunded. **COP** covers a client from **$100** to **$1,000** in transactions, who unintentionally make purchases for which they have *no funds* in their checking account.

The FDIC did a 2006 study of *"Courtesy Overdraft Protection"* (**www.fdic.gov/bank/analytical/overdraft**). Here are some of the highlights:
**1.** Overdraft fees have APRs ranging from **1,067%** to **3,520%**.
**2.** Banks operating automated overdraft programs reported a median transaction of **$36**.
**3.** Young adults paid the most in overdraft fees and were responsible for the most NSF transactions.
**4.** Customers were automatically enrolled in overdraft-protection programs.
**5.** Banks process large debits first, which cause overdrafts more frequently.
**6.** Banks allow ATM and debit card overdrafts, but do not alert customers in advance.
**Bottom line:** *"Courtesy Overdraft Protection"* is big business. In 2006, banking institutions raked in over **$17 billion** in **COP** fees.

### Culprits that trigger COP:
**1.** Not having a budget in place.
**2.** Overuse of check writing, credit / debit card purchases or ATM withdrawals while checkbook is unbalanced.
**3.** Living from paycheck to paycheck and over extended with credit, etc.

**C-4**

> *"The fees and short time given to pay back the OVERDRAFT often translate to triple-diget interest rates. Banks have essentially gone into the business of PAYDAY lending."*
>
> -Jean Ann Fox of the
> Consumer Federation of America

**Preventing Courtesy Overdraft Protection:**
**1.** Opt out. Call and request to have it removed. Follow it up in writing.
**2.** A more cost-effective way to combat against **COP** is to sign up for real overdraft protection, which will connect your checking account to a savings account, credit card or line of credit.
**3.** Start budgeting, keep your checkbook balanced and immediately enter any transactions into your checkbook ledger.
**4.** Get your bills under control with help from non-profit financial groups.

To learn more about **COP**, visit:
■ www.federalreserve.gov/pubs/bounce
■ www.bos.frb.org/consumer/spotlight/bounce.htm
■ www.bankrate.com/brm/news/chk/20071219
_overdraft_survey_results_a1.asp

## 3.) PAYDAY Loans:

■ Average **400%** or more
■ Can range between **17%** to **1955% APR**
■ **35** states allow payday loans
■ **11** states have **NO** restrictions or loopholes

**Why do people need PAYDAY loans?**
Groceries, car repair, medical bills, emergencies, etc.

**Example of how a PAYDAY loan works:**
**1.** You write a check for **$115** to borrow **$100**.
The payday lender agrees to hold the check until your next payday.
**2.** When loan comes due, lender deposits your check, or you **ROLL-OVER** the check by paying a fee to extend the loan for another two weeks
**3.** **$15** is the cost of the initial loan. However,
If you **ROLL-OVER** the loan 3-times, the finance charge would climb to **$60** to borrow **$100**

**Options before you take out a PAYDAY loan:**
**1.** Seek out a loan from family or friends
**2.** Consider a small loan from your bank
**3.** Try to get an advance pay from your employer
**4.** Get paid for your valuable fluids such as plasma, rare blood, etc.

**Preventive maintenance against PAYDAY loans:**
**1.** Start a savings account that can be used as collateral or secured loan in case of an emergency.
**2.** **$300-$500** in a savings account would eliminate the need for an emergency **PAYDAY** loan.

To learn more about **PAYDAY** loans, visit:
■ Better Business Bureau: **www.bbb.org/us/article/high -cost-payday-lenders-advertise-everywhere-527**
■ Bankrate.com: **www.bankrate.com/brm/news/loan/ 20040630a1can.asp**
■ FTC: **hwww.ftc.gov/bcp/edu/pubs/consumer/ alerts/alt060.shtm**

## 4.) ChexSystems (CS)

*"ChexSystems"* keeps a database of people who have a bad track record with one or more banks. **80%** to **90%** of the banking industry use *ChexSystems* to review potential clients banking history. If you have a negative listing in their database, it can be difficult to open a new checking, savings, or other accounts, for up to *5 years*.

**How do you get on *ChexSystems* list?**
**1.** Automatic debits & overdraft fees from closed account.
**2.** Bad checks (1or 2) written by mistake or intentional.
**3.** Closed account, too many *"Insufficient Funds"* notices.
**4.** A bank error. If you're a victim, *ChexSystems* will help you settle things with your bank and fix file.
**5.** Too many inquiries in their database.

**How do I get my *ChexSystems* report?**
If you've been denied an account after 60 days, contact You can also request a free copy of your report by writing to **ChexSystems** or by sending a fax:
**ChexSystems, 12005 Ford Road, Suite 600**
**Dallas, TX 75234-7253 / Fax: (972) 241-4772**

**For further instructions**, call *ChexSystems* toll-free customer service: **(800) 513-7125** or **(800) 428-9623** When contacting by mail or fax, include your name, address, and Social Security Number (SSN).
You can also request a copy of your *ChexSystems* report by visiting their Consumer Assistance site at:
**www.consumerdebit.com/consumerinfo/us/en/index. htm**
If you are on the **CS** database legitimately, you can send a note to explain your circumstances, but it won't delete factual listing unless instructed to do so by the closing bank.

**Staying out of *ChexSystems* Database:**
**1.** When closing a checking account, make sure all checks have cleared, and you have paid all fees.
**2.** Make sure to stop all automatic debits stopped.
**3.** Don't write checks without money in account.

**If you made the *ChexSystems* hit-list:**
**1.** Don't close checking or savings accounts, and keep balances in the black.
**2.** Pay all overdraft fees ASAP.
**3.** Make good on checks.
**4.** If you paid overdraft fees, and you have satisfied everyone who received a bounced check, get a short explanation inserted into your **CS** file.

**Can't get a checking account thanks to CS?**
You can join either **www.newchecking.com** or for a **$35** fee **www.passchecking.com**. Both have nationwide lists of banks that don't use *ChexSystems*.

To learn more about **"*ChexSystems*,"** or a way to fight or go around their system, visit:
■ **www.chexsystemsvictims.com**
■ **http://chexsys.tripod.com/contactchex.html**
■ **www.creditinfocenter.com/FeaturedArticles/Chex Systems.shtml**
■ **http://en.wikipedia.org/wiki/ChexSystems**
■ **www.bankrate.com/finance/checking/chexsystems. aspx**
■ **http://stopchex.com**

Are you having trouble paying your bills, are creditors' sending notices, are you losing your home, car, or both? You are not alone!

According to Defense Manpower Data Center 2005 Survey of Active Duty Service Members (junior enlisted 3 to 5 years of service):

- **21%** were pressured to paying bills
- **19%** failed to make minimum credit card payments
- **12%** had telephone, cable or internet cut off
- **12%** got a payday loan (average rollover **4.9%**)
- **11%** bounced checks
- **6%** failed to make a car payment
- **5%** fell behind paying mortgage and rent
- **2%** had car, appliance or furniture repossessed
- **1%** filed bankruptcy

Another report provided by DoD/Rand stated that:

- 55% of Army enlisted members have less than two weeks of emergency savings
- 24% of Air Force's financial assessment survey of E-3s through E-5s said they had no savings. In addition, 29% said they had less than $1,000 in savings
- 54% of Navy junior sailors reported having less than $1,000 in savings

A 1998 study by the Military Family Institute provided insight into the financial condition of many military members and their families. The study revealed:
- An estimated **$117 million** spent for the direct administrative costs of handling the consequences of service members' financial mismanagement.

Furthermore, the study found that, out of the Navy's **430,000** members at that time:

- **99,000** wrote bad checks on the Navy Exchange System
- **35,000** had their wages garnished
- **43%** reported problems paying monthly bills

<u>Fact:</u> Of all the **security clearances revoked**, an average of **60%** involved financial reasons.

I can get myself out of debt, if I hit this jackpot!

However, I guess it will have to wait until next week to play *"Paycheck Roulette,"* again.

## Quiz: 8 questions to ask if you are in debt?

1. Do you use credit today to buy many of the things you bought last year with cash?

2. Have you taken out loans to consolidate your debts, or asked for extensions on existing loans to reduce monthly payments?

3. Your standard of living has stayed pretty much the same, but does your checkbook balance get lower by the month?

4. You used to pay most bills in full each month but do you now pay only the minimum amount due on your charge accounts?

5. Have you begun to receive repeated late notices from your creditors?

6. Have you been drawing on savings to pay regular bills that you used to pay out of your monthly paycheck?

7. You've borrowed before on your life insurance, but this time, are the chances of paying it back more remote?

8. Do you depend on extra income, such as overtime and dividends, to get you through to the end of the month?

**Be honest—if you answered *"yes"* to two or more of the above 8 questions, it's time to take a close look at your budget.**

**Reasons why we get in debt:** Many people face financial crises at some point in life. Crises such as:

- Personal or family illness
- Divorce or separation
- Major home or auto repairs
- The loss of a job or separation from the service
- Over-reliance upon credit, over-extension of credit obligations or irresponsible use of credit

**Tools to help you get out of debt:** Financial problems can seem overwhelming, but can be overcome. The fact of the matter is that your financial situation does not have to go from bad to even worse.

If you or someone you know is in a financial mess, consider these options in this order:

- Track spending habits (**page 33**).
- Start a budget (**page 153**).
- Organize: Pay crucial bills first (**page 38**).
- Get rid of collection calls (if needed see **page 39**).
- Negotiate with creditors to lower debt (**page 40**).
- Reduce debt: Use the program PowerPay (**page 41**).
- Seek credit counseling from reputable organization (**page 42**).
- Debt consolidation (**page 42**. Second to last resort)
- Look into bankruptcy (**page 42**. Last resort).

C-4

# 8 Steps when dealing with credit problems

## 1. Try to stay current with your obligations:

■ Make an effort to get your payments mailed or delivered to your creditors by due dates.
■ Follow your creditors instructions concerning how, when, and where to make bill payments.
■ Try to make the minimum payments due every month.

## 2. Keep all lines of communication open with your creditors:
Whatever your reasons are, it is crucial to keep the lines of communication open with your creditors. By contacting your creditors early on, you will probably have more repayment options available to you. In addition, the earlier credit problems are resolved, the less potential damage to your credit files there will be. If your problems are in the early stage, you may simply need to explain the reasons for your current dilemma and give assurances of your intent to pay.

## 3. Determine where your money is going:
Keep precise records of your spending every month with a small notebook and jot down your purchases, such as cigarettes, sodas, parking, gas, etc. (see page 33 for more information)

## 4. Develop a budget:
A budget will help you to determine what resources you have left to set up a systematic spending plan to pay off your creditors, or save each month (see **page 153** for more information).

## 5. Develop a plan to pay off your creditors:
Try to pay off your obligations as quickly as possible. Pay off loans that have high interest rates, late payment charges, over-the-limit-fees, etc.

## 6. Develop a repayment plan:
If bills are overdue and creditors are harassing you, then contact them to negotiate repayment plans. Make sure you provide enough information to each creditor about your financial situation, so they feel confident that there is some basis as to why you should be granted special consideration.

## 7. Get help through a non-profit credit counseling service:
Professional help in dealing with credit problems is available through non-profit credit counseling services. These agencies will assist you to set up a budget, deal with your creditors, etc. and possibly, lower payments, reduce interest rates, or waive fees (see **page 42**).

## 8. Try to avoid declaring bankruptcy:
Some people with credit problems may be tempted to file for bankruptcy as an *"easy way out."* Bankruptcy protection, however, should be viewed as a last resort. It is appropriate for a very small percentage of people whose debts are so staggering there is no realistic way of repayment.

**What bills should you pay first?** If a bill collector bugs you to pay a bill, you will probably pay it to get rid of him. However, paying the wrong bill at the worst time could leave you in a bad fix (lose car, home, etc.). Therefore, two lists provided below, have been broken into two categories, critical (pay) and minor bills (pay below minimum). Make the right decision.

**Critical bills (that must be paid):**
■ **Car payment:** If you live in a warm climate, you can sleep in a car and still use to get to work.
■ **Rent / mortgage:** if you live, where it is cold, pay this first, and consider working from home.
■ **Utility bills:** Heating is important, if its 21º below.
■ **Child support:** Garnished wages, along with other punishments merited out, if you do not pay. Pay whatever you can, but do not stop paying.
■ **Secured Loan(s):** If loan(s) secured against item (home, car, etc,), pay loan(s) or lose item(s).
■ **Unpaid Taxes:** The IRS can and will garnish your wages if you do not pay. Do not stop paying. Send whatever you can afford (call and make arrangements).

**Minor bills (pay below minimum):**
■ **Unsecured loans, credit and charge cards:** Do not stop paying. Send $1 each month if that is all you can afford. **NOTE:** May lose credit and charge cards.
■ **Department store and gasoline charge cards:** Pay cash at the pump from this day forward.
■ **Education loans:** try to defer your loans.
■ **Legal, medical and accounting bills:** Do not stop paying. Send $1 each month if that is all you can afford.
■ **All subscriptions:** Cancel all, and use free library.

**Bargain or barter with creditor(s):**
**Example:** Landlord agrees to reduce rent payment, or allows back payments each month. Send certified letter to landowner to confirm agreement made together (see sample letter below).

## Sample letter:

Bill Bonehead
234 Dumpsite Rd.
Col. Springs, CO 80935

June 23, 2008

Dear Mr. Bonehead,

This letter is to confirm the conversation we had June 13, 2009. My lease requires that I pay rent of $795 per month. You agreed to reduce my rent to $395 per month, beginning June 26, 2009, and lasting until I can get up on crutches, but not to exceed six months.

This includes my services ($200 per month) as an accountant for you.

My rent will go back to $795 per month starting November 22, 2008. However, I will continue as your accountant, until I make up the difference in back rent.

Thank you so much!

Sincerely,

Linda Julie Kelly

**Dealing with your new pals, debt collectors:** The Fair Debt Collection Practices Act is the federal law that mandates how and when a debt collector may bother you. A debt collector cannot contact you before 8 a.m. or after 9 p.m., or at work, especially, if collector knows that your employer disapproves of such calls. Collectors may not make false statements, use unfair practices, or harass you when they try to obtain a debt. When you send a written request to **cease contact** with you, debt collectors must honor it.

**Turn debt tuff collectors into wimps:** The letter below, will stop collection agencies from calling you, and give you ammunition to parley a better deal with them, if they are not budging. After the agency receives your letter, they are allowed to contact you one more time and that's only to tell you what will happen (another chance to deal).

Your letter cuts off the hands of the collection agency. The collection agency more than likely will return your debt to the original creditor, who might be more inclined to negotiate with you. You can always call collection agencies to make a new offer and possibly profit from it.

## Sample *cease contact* letter to a collection agency:

Shyster Collection Service
453 Pirate Cove Ave.
Long Beach, CA 67456

August 25, 2007

Attention: Kutcher Calls

Re: Jane Plain
    Account No. 6745-9909

Dear Kutcher Calls,

For the past four months, I have received several phone calls and letters from you concerning my overdue plastic surgery enhancement account. As I have informed you, I cannot pay this bill at this time.

Accordingly, under 15 U.S.C § 1692c, this is my formal notice to you to cease all further communications with me except for the reasons specifically set forth in the federal law.

Yours truly,

Jane Plain

**Control your emotions and keep yakking:** Before sending **cease contact** letter to a collection agency, try to keep the lines of communication open, so you can make a better deal for yourself. Think twice before you send one to your mortgage or your car lender. Most mortgagers and car lenders will work with you and help you to get current with your mortgage or car payments.

For more information on collections and your rights, visit:
- www.law.cornell.edu/uscode/15/usc_sec_15_00001692---c000-.html
- www.fdic.gov/regulations/laws/rules/6500-1300.html
- www.15usc1692k.com

## Record letters sent to collection agencies to cease verbal contact

Agency: _____

Address: _____

Date Sent: _____ Phone: _____

Agency: _____

Address: _____

Date Sent: _____ Phone: _____

Agency: _____

Address: _____

Date Sent: _____ Phone: _____

## Record collection agencies phone calls after you send your *cease contact* letters

If you are unfortunate to run into an unethical collection agency, report it at once to your State Attorney General's Office, your local consumer affairs bureau and file a complaint with the Federal Trade Commission at the following address:

**Federal Trade Commission**
Consumer Response Center
600 Pennsylvania Avenue, NW
Washington, DC 20580

Call toll free at: **877-382-4357**
File a complaint: **www.ftccomplaintassistant.gov**
Keep a record of all phone calls from collection agencies for proof of their misdeeds and send a copy to the FTC.

| Agency | Date Called | Time Called |
|---|---|---|
|  |  |  |
|  |  |  |
|  |  |  |
|  |  |  |
|  |  |  |
|  |  |  |

"Pay us, Deadbeat!"

Creditors hate debtors who hide their head in the sand to escape their liability and hope everything will go away. When a debt collector takes your account, at that point, creditors have given up on you. However, creditors would rather keep customers, and avoid the collection process altogether. Creditors often extend time to pay, will reduce payments, drop late fees, etc., if they believe you are giving an honest effort to deal with your debt.

Call or write (see sample letter) to creditors at once if you are having trouble making ends meet. Tell them why it's difficult for you to pay your bill, such as, a divorce, loss of a job, etc. Be sure to mention any development that points to an encouraging financial situation.

## Sample letter to creditor:

Customer Service Department
Grabit and Hideit Bank
711 Steel Ave.
Las Vegas, NV 89102

February 12, 2009

Re: Greg and Wendy Whiner
    Account # 666-5674-Loan

To whom it may concern,

On March 22, 2006, you granted us a loan of $5,000. Our agreement requires us to pay $188 per month, on the 15th of each month, and we have made those payments on time. However, we're now faced with a big problem.

I am separating from the service on April 24, 2009, and have only a few job prospects lined up, when I get back home to Barstow, CA. I hope to have a job by June/July. The good news is my wife Wendy, recently got a job at the local Del Taco as a cook.

Therefore, what we are requesting is a modified payment plan from $188 to a more manageable $5 or $10 per month. However, as soon as I get a job, I should be able to increase my payment back to $188.

Thank you for your understanding. We expect a response within 20 days. Please call (702) 555-8765 in the evening and ask for Greg or Wendy.

Sincerely,

Greg and Wendy Whiner

Cc: Tracey Isfullofgas, President

## When writing these letters:
- Send a copy to the company president (helps).
- Keep a photocopy of all your letters for your records. You might need them.
- Send the letters through certified/return receipt mail. This is proof that you sent the letter.
- Send letter to the correct address, by addressing your envelope to the address on the back of the bill.

**Important:** If you cannot make a deal with your creditor for a lower payment plan, then send the lower payment anyway, attached with a letter that explains your situation. Your payment emphasizes to your creditor that you are very serious about paying your bills; however, you can't pay the full amount at this moment.

**Tactics in negotiating with creditors:** Here are some basic guidelines:
- Know your bottom line.

**Example:** If you owe a doctor $2,000 and are unwilling to pay more than $1,200 on the debt over 12 months, don't agree to pay more.

- Try to find the creditors bottom line.

**Example:** If a lender offers to waive three months interest as long as you pay the principal on your car loan, that may mean the lender will certainly waive four or five months of interest.

**Push your deal through:** One thing you need to know, bill collectors lie a lot. If they think you can pay $200, they will vow that $200 is the rock-bottom amount they can accept. Do not believe them.

A creditor may agree to settle at 60% of the total debt, that is if you pay a lump sum, however, if you pay monthly installments, they could insist on 100%. Best bet is to find the money to pay the 60% and settle the score. Maybe your parents or relatives will help and give you a loan. If you settle the debt, or are put on a new payment schedule, insist that they clear the negative information off your credit report and re-age the account as current so long as you keep payments current.

Do not agree to split the difference. If you offer a low amount to settle a debt and the creditor counters that you split the remainder between his higher demand and your offer, do not agree to it. Look upon this split-the-difference number as a new top and counter an amount between that and your original offer.

If you do not feel comfortable negotiating with creditors, ask a relative or friend to negotiate on your behalf. This tactic often works well, as long as your negotiator knows and keeps to your bottom line, it will be hard to shame or guilt you into agreeing to pay more.

**Crucial negotiation:** Make sure creditor does not list your negotiated deal as a *charge-off* that will affect your credit rating for years. To learn more on how to negotiate a deal, and still keep your credit clean, see **page 48 & 49**.

For more information on negotiating with creditors, visit:
- **www.militarymoney.com/credit/1148481943**
- **www.creditinfocenter.com/debt/settle_debts.shtml**
- **http://scaretactics101.com**

"I can only afford to pay you $1 per month, and that's my final offer, Dude."

"What the…?"

*PowerPay* is an effective and valuable financial tool that within minutes can compare several ways of trimming debt, cut payments and interest costs and shorten time required to repay debts. *PowerPay* does all of this and more, because you don't have to increase the amount that you typically budget toward monthly debt.

With *PowerPay* you can easily compare debt pay off sequences for maximum emotional boost from early debt repayment; see the impact of adding a little extra to the total monthly payments, calculate savings from making a one-time lump sum payment at a specified future date and explore possible savings from consolidating some or all debts.

*PowerPay* generally works like this, as soon as you pay a debt off, merely roll that monthly amount into another debt until all debts are paid. In order for *PowerPay* to work, you must make a commitment *NOT* to assume any new debts during the repayment period or *CHARGE* any new items on existing accounts.

Repayment Schedule: In the example below, there are two columns, one without *PowerPay* and with *PowerPay*, along with creditors and debt information. The program arranges creditors with the highest interest rates first. The amount of time and money saved by making PowerPayments is summarized at the bottom of the chart. In this example, the five creditors are paid 3.5 years ahead of schedule with a total saving of $1,417.21.

### Example: Repayment Schedule

| Creditor Name | % | Without PowerPayments | | | With PowerPayments – High Interest First | | |
| --- | --- | --- | --- | --- | --- | --- | --- |
| | | # of Payments | Total Paid | % Paid | # of Payments | Total Paid | % Paid |
| Department Store | 21% | 41 Months | $1,430.98 | $ 414.98 | 29 months | $1,365.99 | $ 349.99 |
| Credit Card 1 | 15% | 93 Months | $9,588.87 | $4,088.87 | 51 Months | $8,236.65 | $2,736.55 |
| Bank | 15% | 44 Months | $5,427.41 | $1,250.41 | 44 Months | $5,427.41 | $1,250.41 |
| Credit Card 2 | 16% | 48 Months | $5,998.29 | $1,498.29 | 48 Months | $5,998.29 | $1,498.29 |
| Gas Card | 13.9% | 22 Months | $1,079.21 | $ 129.21 | 22 Months | $1,079.21 | $ 129.21 |

| | |
| --- | --- |
| Total Monthly Payments: **Varies** | Total Monthly Payments: **$441** |
| Months To Repay: **93 Months** | Months To Repay: **51 months** |
| Loan Amount Repaid: **$16,143** | Loan Amount Repaid: **$16,143** |
| Interest Paid: **$7,381.76** | Interest Paid: **$5,964.55** |
| Total Amount Paid: **$23,524.76** | Total Amount Paid: **$22,107.55** |

**Benefits of PowerPayments:** Time reduced by **44 months** to pay-off all debts. Amount of money saved **$1,417.21**

To use PowerPay or for more information: https://powerpay.org or
www.extension.iastate.edu/Publications/PM1873A.pdf

# *Power Hardball: Yet, another way to rid yourself of DEBT*

### Problem: Lots of bills

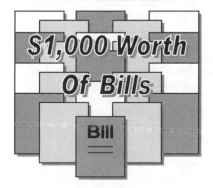

21 bills (unsecured)
with total payments
of $1,000 per month

### Solution: Pay only $200 per month toward bills

Pay $5 x 20-bills (left side) = $100 per month
toward bills. Pay $100 per month toward one
bill (right side), when paid off, take the next bill
and add $5 to $100 = $105, when paid off, take
the next bill and add another $5 to $105 = $110 etc.

### SAVE IT!!!

$800

Here are some interesting and helpful Internet resources and their tools on money management.

## CREDIT COUNSELING

To find an Accredited Financial Counselor (AFC) nearest you, contact the Association for financial counseling and Planning Education at: 614-485-9650 / Website: www.afcpe.org

■ **National Foundation for Credit Counseling:** www.nfcc.org
Topics: Non-profit organization provides education and counseling services on budgeting and credit. To learn more about information on the free Consumer Credit Counseling Service in your area call:
**1-800-777-PLAN** or visit www.afcpe.org

■ **American Consumer Credit Counseling:** www.consumercredit.com
Topics: Credit counseling, debt management, financial resources, etc.

## CREDIT COUNSELING AND CONSOLIDATION

■ **Military Debt Management Agency (MDMA):** 800-323-3343 / www.militarydebt.org
Topics: MDMA assists servicemembers with security clearances through debt management programs. It is an IRS qualified 501c (3) nonprofit charitable organization. Most MDMA programs have creditors PAID IN FULL at half the cost and time. Programs can be implemented overseas, combat zones and ships at sea. Throughout the years, MDMA has saved numerous military careers.

## BANKRUPTCY

■ **American Bankruptcy Institute:** www.abiworld.org
Topics: Offers daily news about bankruptcy and is a gateway to ABI On-Line, a private bankruptcy research library.

■ **Bankruptcy Law Center (LexisNexis):** http://law.lexisnexis.com/practiceareas/BankruptcyLawCenter
Topics: Bankruptcy news, blogs, downloads, etc.

■ **InterNet Bankruptcy Library:** http://bankrupt.com
Topics: News, articles, forums and other resources

■ **U.S. Bankruptcy Law (Cornell):** www.law.cornell.edu/topics/bankruptcy.html
Topics: Bankruptcy law primer

■ **The Law Guru:** www.lawguru.com/ilawlib/index.php?id=311
Topics: Forms, library, federal & state laws, etc.

WOW! You're really good at this. Do you tango?

No! However, I'm really good at dropping extremely heavy metal objects onto men's feet that don't know how to act in public with a woman, Fresh Guy!

■ **U.S. Courts:** www.uscourts.gov/bankruptcycourts.html
Topics: Provides answers to frequently asked questions about bankruptcy and other topics such as:
Bankruptcy basics: www.uscourts.gov/bankruptcycourts/bankruptcybasics.html
Filling bankruptcy without a lawyer: www.uscourts.gov/bankruptcycourts/prose.html
Link to Internet sites of courts around the U.S. www.uscourts.gov/links.html

■ **Lawyers.com:** http://bankruptcy.lawyers.com/consumer-bankruptcy/Bankruptcy-Law-In-Your-State.html
Topics: Lists state-by-state bankruptcy laws and other lawyer services.

■ **SPANISH LANGUAGE: Que Es La Quiebra** www.quiebras.com
Topics: Provides an explanation of both Chapter 7 and Chapter 13 bankruptcy.

## MONEY EDUCATION

■ **Bankrate:** www.bankrate.com
Topics: All aspects of financial price comparisons, financial planning calculators and tools.

■ **Institute of Consumer Financial Education:** www.financial-education-icfe.org/default.asp
Topics: Full spectrum of financial education

■ **MoneyInstructor.com:** www.moneyinstructor.com
Topics: Basic money skills, interactive lesions, saving, kids section, etc.

■ **Mymoney.com:** www.mymoney.gov/default.shtml
Topics: U.S. government's website that teaches the basics about financial education.

■ **FDIC:** www.fdic.gov/consumers/consumer/moneysmart/ mscbi/mscbi.html
Topics: Financial education program

## CREDIT, CREDIT CARDS AND MORE

■ **Credit Card Comparison:** www.cardweb.com/cardtrak
Topics: Comparison of costs and features of credit cards.

■ **Credit Infocenter:** www.creditinfocenter.com
Topics: Bankruptcy, credit card rates, credit reports, rebuilding credit, etc.

■ **Credit and Banking Laws and Regulations:** www.cardreport.com/laws/credit-laws.html
Topics: News, credit and banking laws, regulations, credit articles, etc.

■ **Federal Trade Commission:** www.ftc.gov
Topics: Credit and loans

■ **Federal Reserve:** www.federalreserve.gov
Topics: Your credit rights & how the law protects you.

## DEBT MANAGEMENT AND TOOLS

■ **Debt and Credit:** www.nolo.com
Topics: Nolo Press articles on using credit, strategies for repaying debts, student loans, debt collection, bankruptcy, and credit repair.

■ **Debt Management:** http://quicken.intuit.com/personal-finance-tips/index.jsp?lid=site_banner
Topics: Debt reduction planner

## FINANCIAL CALCULATORS

■ **Dinkytown.net:** www.dinkytown.net
Topic: Lists over 350 financial calculators.

■ **Financial Calculators:** www.financialcalculators.com
Topic: Lists over 125 financial calculators.

■ **Bankrate.com:** www.bankrate.com/brm/calc_home.asp
Topic: Lists several financial calculators.

"Okay, let's run Zebra Red on two! Make sure you block your…OOPS! Wrong meeting. YO, listen up! Don't even think about neglecting your credit reports! You need to be all over your credit history as if it's a ball in play, constantly keeping tabs on where it is and what it's doing, and like a football, make sure no one else gets their hands on it. Shield your credit from the thieves out to wreck your score. If it's already out of your hands, I'm here to tell you what you can do to get it back under control, so I can get you back in the game!"

**Fifth Commandment:
"THOU SHALL CHECK AND
PROTECT THY CREDIT"**

IGNORE CREDIT HISTORY

KEEP TABS ON CREDIT

C-5

# STAY AWAKE

Credit has become a significant part of many people's financial lives. When purchasing a car or house on credit, your credit rating will be the number one factor in qualifying for loans from lenders. Having good credit will allow you to borrow money, but more importantly, at lower interest rates. Having a low score typically triggers higher interest rates that can cost you lots of money. Therefore, it's in your best interest to have and maintain the best credit score possible. Because having a good score is important, it's crucial to understand how the credit reporting system works.

## HOW THE CREDIT SYSTEM WORKS

The largest and foremost Credit Reporting Agencies (CRA's) are Equifax, Experian, and TransUnion. They are the main companies that collect, compile, and store information on individual consumers that allows them to produce a credit score. It is estimated that these agencies have credit information on almost 200 million Americans.

The CRA's in constant contact with banks, credit unions, finance companies, and other lenders who continually update them on the status of an individual's account. This allows them to track the payment status and balances of your credit cards, auto loans, and mortgages. In addition, the CRA's hire teams of professionals to inspect court records to track down bankruptcy information, civil judgments, or tax liens.

Don't hate me because my FICO score is beautiful.

After collecting and compiling the data, the CRA then applies a formula to determine each individual's credit score. What can hurt and lower your credit score?

- Late payments
- Having a high amount of debt or credit
- All derogatory information in your file

Most negative information will stay on your credit report for seven years, but Bankruptcy is held in your file for ten years.

## VANTAGESCORE and FICO

### VANTAGESCORE – www.vantagescore.com
VantageScore is a new scoring technique, the first one that was developed collaboratively by the three credit reporting companies. This model provides a more predictive score for consumers, even for those with limited credit histories, which reduces the essential need for creditors to manually review credit information. VantageScore features a common score range of 501-990 (higher scores represent lower likelihood of potential risk). A key benefit of VantageScore is that as long as the three major credit bureaus have the same information regarding your credit history, you will receive the same score from each. A different score alerts you that there are discrepancies in your report.

### FICO – www.myfico.com
Historically, FICO has been the most well known credit scoring system. The information in your credit report is used to calculate your FICO credit score, a number generally between 300 and 850 that rates how risky a borrower you are. The higher your score, the less risk you pose to creditors. Your FICO score is available from **www.myfico.com** for a fee.

### FICO SCORING SYSTEM: FICO score is based on your financial history as collected in your credit report. Creditors can use this score to evaluate whether you are able to pay a loan back on time. The higher the score the more likely you are to pay off a loan on time and the less of a credit risk you pose. The FICO or credit score ranges are broken down as follows:

**720-850** - This represent the best score range
**700-719** - Able to obtain favorable financing terms
**675-699** - This is still considered a decent score range
**620-674** - May have trouble getting good credit terms
**560-619** - May have trouble securing credit
**500-559** - Time to work on improving your score

**FICO FORMULA:** Although the exact formulas for calculating credit scores are closely guarded secrets, Fair Isaac has disclosed the following five components and the approximate weighted contribution of each:

- Payment History – 35% (only includes payments later than 30 days past due)
- Amounts Owed – 30% (credit card balances, etc. & credit limits, debt ratio)
- Length of Credit History – 15%
- Types of Credit Used – 10% (installment, revolving, consumer finance)
- New Credit – 10% (amount of new credit recently obtained)

**HOW TO ORDER YOUR CREDIT REPORT & SCORE:**
The federal Fair Credit Reporting Act requires each of the major credit reporting bureaus to provide consumers with a free copy of their credit report, once every 12 months. To order your free report, go through **www.annual creditreport.com** or call **877-322-8228 (toll FREE)**. If you space your free reports correctly you can get one every 4 months. Example:
- March report from **EXPERIAN**
- July report from **TRANSUNION**
- November from **EQUIFAX**

Although your free credit report will allow you to check your credit report for errors, it will not tell you your credit score. To acquire your score, each CCR maintains a website on which they sell credit reports that contain your score.
- Equifax: **(800) 685-1111** -www.equifax.com
- Experian: **(888) 397-3742** -www.experian.com
- TransUnion: **(800) 888-4213** -www.transunion.com

**IMPROVE CREDIT SCORES:** Here are a few reasons why it's in your best interest to improve credit scores:

- Lower your interest rates, auto insurance
- Speed up credit approvals
- Reduce deposits required by utilities
- Get approved for apartments
- Get better credit offers, car loan, mortgage, etc.

## TIPS TO IMPROVE CREDIT SCORES

**Payment History:**
- Pay on time. If you can't, notify your lender ASAP and work something out
- Get current on past due accounts

**Amounts Owed:**
- Keep balances low (35%) on credit cards. High debt levels can hurt your score and other "revolving credit."
- Apply for and open new credit accounts only as needed.

**Length of Credit:**
- Keep old accounts open if you've been a good borrower.
- Start building credit ASAP.

**New Credit Category:**
- When shopping for new credit, keep it all within 14 days or less.
- If credit history is bad you can improve credit scores by opening a new account and managing it responsibly.

**Types of Credit:**
- Installment debt (fixed monthly payments to eliminate debt) is "better" than revolving debt (open-ended debt).
- Certain finance company debts (buying product with retailer financing) can lower your score.

**Bottom Line:** Have patience, because it takes time and discipline to improve credit scores.

## BIG CREDIT MISTAKES TO AVOID

**Canceling old credit cards:** If 15% of your credit score depends on length of credit history, it's deemed a big mistake to cancel old credit cards. In addition, canceling an old credit card can worsen your debt ratio (makes up 30% of your score), if you have balances on other cards. Finally, if you don't have credit cards older than seven years, do not cancel your oldest credit card.

**Late on payments:** Since 35% of your score depends on payment history and only payments over thirty days late affect your score, it is critical to pay on time. One late credit card payment can drop your credit score by 20 points, missing a car payment can down your credit score by nearly 100 points and if auto payment is late by 90 days or more it can plunge another 25 points. Therefore, if you're going to be late on any loan, contact your lender ASAP and work out a deal, most are very understanding. If that doesn't work, borrow from your savings, family or friends to keep current or juggle payments a bit, but make sure you're not too late on any one loan.

**Having too many open lines of credit:** 10% of your score comes from the types of credit used. If you have a lot of revolving credit, creditors see you as a risk, as you have the potential to rack up a lot of debt quickly. Make it a policy not to open any store credit cards, and if you have some already cancel them once they're paid off.

**Maxing out cards:** 30% of your credit score depends on the ratio of credit card debt and limits. Therefore, maxing out cards will cause your credit score to drop, even if you

keep up with the payments. Instead of charging more, focus on paying down cards.

**Avoiding credit cards:** If you are avoiding credit cards, you should still consider getting one to start or improve credit history. Purchase gas with the card and pay it off in full each month. Having a solid credit score will be useful later when you are ready to purchase a home, car, etc., at lower interest rates.

**Requesting credit limit reduction:** Never reduce your credit limit on cards, because it will affect your debt ratio and lower your credit score. Only set a limit reduction if it has a huge psychological value for you.

**Not researching a credit counseling service:** If you intend to use a credit counseling service, find legitimate credit counseling services listed in the Yellow pages, Google, etc. and follow up with the Better Business Bureau for any complaints. See **page 42** to assist you in finding the right counseling service for you. Remember, your credit score will affect many of your financial moves for years, so do not skimp on research.

**Declaring bankruptcy:** With new bankruptcy laws now in effect, people who would have gone forward with bankruptcy before the law now must go through credit counseling before filing bankruptcy. To find credit counseling service see **page 42**. Bankruptcy can decimate your credit score for 10 years. Quite often, there are better solutions, such as negotiating with creditors and so forth.

**Playing credit card roulette:** Rolling credit debt to other credit cards can seriously damage your credit score, if you are not an expert. If you make an error, your credit score could easily be blown up.

**Never checking credit report:** Since 25% of credit reports contain errors (that are serious enough to deny credit), and identity theft is common today, therefore, it would be wise to get your free credit report from **www.annualcreditreport.com** at least once a year, and correct any mistakes on the report.

**To learn more, visit:**
- www.bankrate.com/brm/news/cc/20010223a.asp
- http://library.hsh.com/?row_id=86
- www.pbs.org/wgbh/pages/frontline/shows/credit/more/scores.html
- www.federalreserve.gov/pubs/creditscore/default.htm
- www.bankrate.com/finance/credit-debt/tips-for-boosting-your-credit-score-1.aspx
- http://ezinearticles.com/?10-Tips-to-Improve-Credit-Score&id=838554

Jane, since I'm still having difficulty qualifying for credit cards, let's head out and do some serious damage to your cards!

Home Sweet Home!

Do you have a head injury? Keep reading and pay attention, Dick!

The Credit bureaus don't have time or capacity to substantiate the accuracy of information they report and that's the secret to credit repair, challenge them.

> A U.S. Public Interest Research Group study found that *25% of consumer credit reports contained errors serious enough to lead to a denial of credit*
> - Source: Freedman, J. (2004, September) Credit Check. Money, p. 30
>
> Over 82 million American's live with poor credit scores
> - Source: Government Accountability Office

Furthermore, with all those errors and mistakes credit bureaus make, they then manage to compound the problem by reselling the information to other companies.

If you demand that credit bureaus perform at the level implied by law, they'll often clear records more willingly than spend time and effort investigating individual cases.

The credit bureaus often can't confirm older items even when they're true (bad archival records).

The chart below will assist you with whether to dispute a negative mark through a creditor or with credit bureaus. A creditor's pledge to clear an item will clear the problem with all three of the major credit bureaus. The more erroneous credit items you can repair with creditors, the easier time you'll have with the credit bureaus.

## CREDIT REPAIR LEGEND:

| Age of credit items: | Late payments: |
| --- | --- |
| **"O"** Old (more than two years) | **"S"** Scattered late payments |
| **"N"** New (less than two years) | **"P"** Patterned late payments |

### Retail Store Credit / Department Stores

| Creditor Negotiation | O / S: Possible | O / P: **Excellent** |
| --- | --- | --- |
| | N / S: Possible | N / P: **Excellent** |
| **Tip** Customer service orientation favors negotiation. | | |
| Use Letters | **#1, 2, 3, 5** if you owe | **#6, 7** |
| Bureau Dispute | O / S: **Good** | O / P: **Excellent** |
| | N / S: Possible | N / P: **Good** |
| Use Letters | #8 - #14 | |

### MasterCard / Visa and Other Credit Cards

| Creditor Negotiation | O / S: Possible | O / P: **Good** |
| --- | --- | --- |
| | N / S: Poor | N / P: Possible |
| **Tip** Patterns, problems in correct billing address, amounts; most corrections done through Bureau's | | |
| Use Letters | **#1, 2, 3, 5** if you owe | **#6, 7** |
| Bureau Dispute | O / S: **Good** | O / P: **Excellent** |
| | N / S: Possible | N / P: **Good** |
| Use Letters | #8 - #14 | |

### Banks and Credit Unions

| Creditor Negotiation | O / S: Fair | O / P: **Good** |
| --- | --- | --- |
| | N / S: Poor | N / P: Possible |
| **Tip** Patterns are important; Go through Bureau's to fix | | |
| Use Letters | **#1, 2, 3, 5** if you owe | **#6, 7** |
| Bureau Dispute | O / S: **Good** | O / P: **Excellent** |
| | N / S: Poor | N / P: **Good** |
| Use Letters | #8 - #14 | |

### Mortgage Credit

| Creditor Negotiation | O / S: Possible | O / P: **Good** |
| --- | --- | --- |
| | N / S: Poor | N / P: Possible |
| **Tip** Older late payments, most likely to repair | | |
| Use Letters | #1, 5 | |
| Bureau Dispute | O / S: **Good** | O / P: **Excellent** |
| | N / S: Poor | N / P: **Good** |
| Use Letters | #8 - #14 | |

### Auto Loans

| Creditor Negotiation | O / S: Poor | O / P: Possible |
| --- | --- | --- |
| | N / S: Poor | N / P: Poor |
| **Tip** Older paid accounts most likely to repair. | | |
| Use Letter | #3 (repossession) | |
| Bureau Dispute | O / S: Possible | O / P: **Good** |
| | N / S: Poor | N / P: Possible |
| Use Letters | #8 - #14 | |

### Student Loan Agencies / Universities

| Creditors Negotiation | O / S: Possible | O / P: Possible |
| --- | --- | --- |
| | N / S: Possible | N / P: Possible |
| **Tip** Credit bureau disputes best. | | |
| Use Letters | #4 (still in school or No job) | |
| Bureau Dispute | O / S: **Good** | O / P: **Excellent** |
| | N / S: Poor | N / P: **Good** |
| Use Letters | #8 - #14 | |

### Medical: Dentists, Doctors, and Hospitals

| Creditors Negotiation | O / S: **Good** | O / P: **Excellent** |
| --- | --- | --- |
| | N / S: **Good** | N / P: **Excellent** |
| **Tip** Creditors: Haggle best when you owe money. Credit Bureaus: If your account is paid in full. | | |
| Use Letters | **#2, 3** if you owe | |
| Bureau Disputes | O / S: **Good** | O / P: **Good** |
| | N / S: **Good** | N / P: **Good** |
| Use Letters | #8 - #14 | |

### Collection Agencies

| Creditor Negotiation | O / S: **Excellent** | O / P: **Excellent** |
| --- | --- | --- |
| | N / S: **Good** | N / P: **Good** |
| **Tip** Creditors: Haggle best when you owe money. | | |
| Use Letters | **#2, 3** (if you owe money) | |
| Bureau Disputes | O / S: **Good** | O / P: **Excellent** |
| | N / S: Possible | N / P: Possible |
| Use Letters | #8 - #14 | |

### Public Records (Bankruptcies, Judgments, Etc.)

| Creditor Negotiation | O / S: Impossible | O / P: Impossible |
| --- | --- | --- |
| | N / S: Impossible | N / P: Impossible |
| **Tip** Negotiations impossible; work through bureaus. | | |
| Use Letters | NA | |
| Bureau Disputes | O / S: **Good** | O / P: **Good** |
| | N / S: Possible | N / P: Possible |
| Use Letters | #8 - #14 | |

**First, order your credit report**: It's important to get your credit report from each of the three major credit bureaus, because bureaus often report different things, and you won't know which bureau the lender is using to check your credit. This means that you have to contest similar items on different credit reports, from each credit bureau. Cleaning an item off one bureau's report won't clear it off another, but if you clear an item off one report, you should succeed with the other credit bureaus. See **page 44** to order your free credit report.

**Your credit reports have arrived:** At this point, If you have received and deciphered your credit reports from the three major credit bureaus, and after analyzing the reports, you have found no damaging information that they are reporting about you, skip over to "*Protect Your Identity From Thieves,*" on **page 53**.

> Wahoo! I have great credit! I'm the king of the world!

However, after reading your credit report and if you're not ecstatic like the picture above, more than likely, you found damaging data that the credit bureaus are reporting about you. Now, you are ready to change and fix your credit.

The first thing you need to do is to negotiate with your creditors to repair your particular bad mix of credit items. The systematic strategies and letters will help you to repair your credit (cheer-up).

## Part 1: Time to contact your creditors

**How to negotiate with creditors:** The secret to dealing with creditors is that they want to be paid, and yet, keep you as a customer. They will often clear credit if you call to negotiate through their customer service departments. Their job in customer service is to clear customer credit. They do it daily. Follow the strategies below:

■ **Misunderstanding:** Even if you owe them money, call a customer service rep and speak plainly to have your *misunderstanding* (always call it a misunderstanding) cleared off your credit reports. You may want to tell them that their negative report is stopping you from buying a car, house, etc. Be adamant; always bring up the fact that you have been a loyal customer, and that you really don't want to take your business elsewhere, because of a little misunderstanding.

■ **Work it:** If you have to, work your way up to a supervisor and while keeping your temper in check, let them hear an inkling of the irritated customer who would be happy, if this little credit problem were to go away.

■ **Loyal customer:** Creditors with a customer service department usually cave in to the technique of, *"I'm a loyal customer, and I'm not going to quit."* Be firm, even when all seems impossible, because their system is not set up for people who won't take *"no"* for an answer.

■ **If you're current with payments:** If you're current, creditor may say, *"Since our records show that you've been paying on time, we'll be happy to clear your credit."* If very delinquent or matter preceded a lawsuit or judgment against you, some companies won't clear it at all.

■ **If you owe money:** Ask the creditor to clear your credit upon payment. Include **"Restrictively Endorsed"** letter **#1** (**page 48**) and follow the directions precisely. Alter letter to the particular terms you've negotiated with the creditor.

■ **If you owe more money than you are willing or able to pay:** Bargain to repay money you owe according to a firm payment schedule; possible repayment terms extended and to have debt reduced. Using **"Term and Debt Schedule"** settlement letter **#3** (**page 48**).

■ **One is the loneliest number:** If you have one late payment showing, make a plea of, *"it wasn't my fault that my payment was late"* or *"everybody deserves a second chance."* If it doesn't work, then use **"Restrictively Endorsed"** settlement letter **#1** (**page 48**).

■ **Clarify bill:** Can't be late paying a bill that is in doubt (even though you must continue to pay contested bills). See **"Billing Clarification"** letter **#6** (**page 49**).

■ **Address changed:** Can't be late for not paying a bill that you never received, even if the creditor argues differently. See change of **"Billing Address"** letter **#7** (**page 49**).

■ **State your own terms:** If your negotiations don't succeed with customer service, state your own terms using **"Restrictively Endorsed"** letter **#1** (**page 48**), assuming that they cash your check. Furthermore, you can use **"Terms and Debt schedule"** **#3** (**page 48**). Be sure to mail letter **#1** or **#3** along with letter **#5** (**page 49**) to credit bureaus to make sure that creditors unfavorable data that you have bargained off with creditors is removed.

■ **Follow up:** Be sure to report all successful and unsuccessful negotiations with letters to credit bureaus. Sometimes just stating your case and cause is enough to spur a credit bureau to clear an item, even if creditor disagrees. If the credit bureau doesn't want to choose sides, they'll delete the item from your report. See **"Documentation"** letter **#5** (**page 49**).

■ **Other strategic options:** If you have exhausted all your options with creditor, and they still won't agree to clear your credit, move on and skip to **Part 2** (see **page 50**).

> Hey, I just got credit card #20 in the mail today. Let's celebrate and go shopping. Lunch is on me!

> I'm so there!

## "Restrictively Endorsed" Settlement Letter #1

Your terms become an agreement when creditor cashes your check with this letter. Even if a creditor does not honor your call for clearing your credit, credit bureaus must and will (see **"Documentation"** letter **#5**). Shrewd people have sent restrictive endorsement agreements to credit bureaus claiming that they sent letters to creditors with payment.

---

*Creditor name*                              Date:
*Creditor address*
*Creditor phone*

Dear Customer Service,

Please find payment for my account attached to this letter. Your acceptance of this check signifies that my account is current (paid and up to date or paid in full) and that you will remove all negative remarks with all the credit bureaus that you report too.

Thank you. I want to give my thanks to the customer service department for being so helpful with this misunderstanding.

Yours truly,

---

## Collection Agencies Agreement Letter #2

This letter is for creditors who do not report to credit bureaus, but instead, hand-off past due accounts to collection agencies. It should not be a surprise to find that collection agencies are active credit bureau reporters.

The intent of this letter is to get the original creditor to call off the assigned collection agency. If you do not do this accurately, collection agency will report your overdue account as **PAID COLLECTION ACCOUNT**, which is a flawed mark on your credit report. If collection agency agrees to clear your bad credit, then you will not need this letter, but that is normally more difficult to accomplish than getting a creditor to agree to this letter. This letter states it in writing, so if the creditor doesn't follow through, you still have proof of the agreement for the credit bureaus (see **"Documentation"** letter **#5**).

The word *"misunderstanding"* is the best way to describe your collection situation without admitting or assigning any fault or blame. Tie this agreement together with **"Term & Debt Schedule"** letter **#3**.

---

*Creditors name*                              Date:
*Creditors address*
*Creditors phone*

Dear (use contact's name),

I'm pleased that we're able to settle our misunderstanding. Please find my payment attached to this letter (full, or if you're using a repayment schedule, the first installment). Your acceptance of check signifies that my account is up to date (or paid in full). You also agree to contact credit bureaus that you report too and direct your collection agencies to remove all collection accounts and all damaging credit remarks.

I appreciate your cooperation from the bottom of my heart. Thank you.

Yours truly,

---

## "Term and Debt Schedule" Settlement Letter #3

When you bargain to repay a debt through regular payments, repayment terms can deviate widely, but the major point is that you want your credit repaired as soon as you begin making payments to creditors.

Lump sums will more than likely motivate a creditor to accept your offer of a partial payment. Debt counselors normally use 40-month repayment plans, Chapter 13 bankruptcy often involves 60-month repayment plans, so an offer of payment in 12 to 24 months will appear relatively fast to them. The next best thing to a lump sum payment is to keep a payment schedule below a year.

---

*Creditor name*                              Date:
*Creditor address*
*Creditor phone*

Dear Customer Service:

Because of financial hardship and health problems within my family, it is imperative that I settle my debt with you the best I can.

With this letter, I offer to settle my owed debt to you for 30% of its total amount. In other words, I am offering you:
$ _____ to be paid in _____ monthly payments of
$ _____. As long as I adhere to these payment terms, you will agree to eliminate all negative credit remarks with all the credit bureaus that you report too and claim my account as current.
If these terms are acceptable to you, please sign and date below and return to me.

Thank you. I want to express my thanks to your customer service department for being so helpful with this misunderstanding.

_____
Creditor name &   Date                Your name
_____   Your address
Creditor signature                         Your phone

Yours truly,

---

## Student Loan "Forbearance Notification" Letter #4

Student loans that have after *graduation repayment plans* require borrower to inform all lenders about their school enrollment or other circumstances that would provide forbearance on repayment of loan. If lender forces your loan into default, you'll want to prove to bureaus that you served the lender with a forbearance letter (see **"Documentation"** letter **#5**).

---

*Student loan lender name*                  Date:
*Student loan lender address*
*Student loan lender phone*

Dear Customer Service:

Please consider this notification of my being in school, thereupon terms of forbearance of my student loan as it is still in effect today. I will inform you when I have graduated—and following my grace period expiration date, by mailing you a check for the first payment on my student loan.

Thank you,

## "Documentation" Letter #5

Use this letter as a follow-up to an unsettled dispute with a creditor. The plan is to push the credit bureau to remove damaging items that the creditor may not have repaired. You can send any documentation with this letter (the more the better), but settlement letters such as **"Restrictively Endorsed"** (letter **#1**) or **"Debt Schedule"** (letter **#3**) are especially effective, because they verify an agreement between you and the creditor. Therefore, include with all documentation's, photocopies of certified postal return receipts and canceled checks whenever possible. It's unscrupulous to send copies of letters to credit bureaus that you truthfully never sent to creditors, but evidence indicates that the credit bureaus don't usually investigate factual documentation sent from consumer.

Credit Bureau name        Date:
Credit Bureau address
Credit Bureau phone

Dear Customer Service:

The following mistake is still on my report, despite the fact that I have valid documentation (enclosed) showing evidence that this should no longer be reported as derogatory credit. I would not press such a small matter if the consequences weren't so grim. I stand to lose $30,000 if this is not corrected quickly.

Nevada Bank, account # 1289-7890

The enclosed documentation verifies that this mistake should be corrected immediately to mirror my good credit.

Yours truly,

## "Billing Clarification" Letter #6

The Fair Credit Billing Act requires all revolving credit lenders to bill you correctly to the address you declare on a monthly basis. This means that your payment is not delinquent if, within two billing cycles, you send in a formal request for clarification of amounts due. Under the Act, this request for clarification is categorized as a billing error and payment cannot be reported as late. With a certified return receipt proof of having mailed this clarification letter, you can demand that reported lateness on your credit report be deleted. Even without return receipt proof, sending a copy of the letter is often enough to get either the creditor or credit bureau to correct the delinquency (See **"Documentation"** letter **#5**).

Creditor name        Date:
Creditor address
Creditor phone

Dear Customer Service:

On my most recent bill (be specific about card number and billing date), I am at a complete loss of the amount I owe you. I am not certain if one of the charges is correct (list the charge).

Since I am writing you within two billing cycles of the actual charge, I ask that you not report this payment as late.

I want to give my thanks to the customer service department for being so helpful with this misunderstanding.

Yours truly,

## "Change of Billing Address" Letter #7

With revolving credit you can borrow and pay on a monthly basis, with credit ceiling and minimum payment. It differentiates from installment loans, which are typically mortgages, student loans, or car-loan payments that have a prearranged monthly payment. This means, 10-days before end of any billing cycle, you can change your billing address. If the creditor does not bill you at new address you stipulated, then you haven't been billed and your payment shouldn't be counted as late.

You can also use change of address form, if one came with bill. You can always send in a blank copy of the same form as proof that you already sent in a completed form.

With a certified return receipt, you have proof of having mailed this change of address letter; you can demand that your delinquent payment on your credit report be repaired. Even without a certified return receipt, sending a copy of such a letter is generally enough to get either the creditor or credit bureau to correct your delinquency (See **"Documentation"** letter **#5**). Customer service departments will generally neutralize your Fair Credit Billing Act rights with arguments like "We don't have to bill you, it's just a courtesy" or "If you charged it, you should have known about it"; "The bill wasn't returned, so it must have been received." Don't be intimidated by their arguments.

Creditor name        Date:
Creditor address
Creditor phone

Dear Customer Service:

This letter is to notify you of a change in my billing address for my account with you (be specific about account number).

Thank you. I am a satisfied and loyal customer.

Yours truly,

### IMPORTANT: Always remember to:

■ Make sure all of your letters are in your own words. You do not want to look as though you are being coached or copying (like letters in this chapter).
■ Photocopy and keep all of your letters for records of proof. Copies needed later in the repair process.
■ For proof that you sent letters, send with certified return receipt mail.
■ Creditor address: It's crucial to send letters to the correct address. The address on back of your bill is one to use.
■ Don't give up. By using wear-you-down tactics and their vast experience, credit bureaus count on you giving up.

## Part 2: Dealing with the credit bureaus:

**How to dispute your credit problems:** When you have three or fewer items to contest with each of the bureaus, you should dispute them all at the same time. If there are nine or more bad items on your three credit reports, divide them up into three groups of three and contest one group with each bureau. Example:

**1.** Send dispute letter **#8**. RULE; never contest more than three items at a time! You'll have a chance to add more items later, but only after the first disputes are resolved.

**2.** After 30 days, send dispute letter **#9**, credit bureaus by law have 30 to 45 days to respond to your objection, hold them to this.

**3.** If 10 days after letter **#9**, the credit bureaus still haven't written back to you, send the FTC dispute letter **#13** with a copy of letter **#9** to both the FTC and the credit bureaus.

**4.** When you finally get a response from the credit bureaus, there are three possibilities:
■ They have removed all of the damaging items that you contested, so you've won! The credit repair is complete or if there's more, start the process from the top again or send off letter **#12**.
■ They cleared some, but not all of the damaging items that you contested. This is a tactic to frustrate individuals from repairing one's credit. Do not settle. Finish what you started. Send dispute letter **#11**.
■ None of your items is repaired. Don't give up. This is a normal delaying tactic of there's.

**What to do next:** Send letter **#10**. If you're using strategy of disputing different items with different credit bureaus, then play to win. Contest an item that's been deleted by one bureau with others. Hold items that were not deleted to side for re-disputing at later date. By pursuing this strategy, you'll go right back to beginning of your dispute with letter **#8**.

The second possibility is that you have more items to contest, but they're so few (one or two) that you want to re-contest one or two of original discarded items ASAP. In this case, send dispute letter **#12,** in which you will add, one or two new disputes to original items that weren't deleted by your first dispute.

If however, you have no new items to contest, send dispute letter **#10** to re-contest the uncorrected items with stronger language. This works because your more specific objections make the credit bureau either choose an expensive investigation or delete your bad credit. The credit bureaus have a limited number of barriers they're inclined to enforce, and if you've made it to this particular point, you've already smashed through one of them.

If, by the end of sequence of letters, you still have not won and have worked on every possible way to contest your derogatory credit (it's unlikely in simple cases; more than likely in severe dismal situations), then send letter **#14**.

The credit bureaus are required to let you have your day in the sun, by allowing you to write a statement, with up to **100 words** clarifying every damaging credit item that was insufficiently settled in your dispute. This is an end-of the road technique, after you've given up (don't be a quitter) and it's not really a repair tactic, because it doesn't help your credit. However, in impossible cases such as car repossessions, it's still better than nothing. By making a positive effort to write reveals that, more than likely, you will be reliable in future credit transactions to creditors.

### Credit Bureau Dispute Flowchart

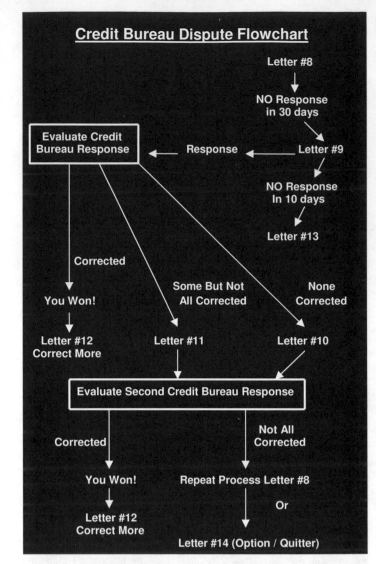

**50**

## *How To Write Letter's To Credit Bureaus*

1. Put your name, address and phone number and Social Security number (See dispute letters).
2. Put the credit bureau name and address on the same page (for addresses see *How to Order Your Credit Report*).
3. **Important:** Include a copy of a recent bill (phone, electric, etc.) to prove who you are and your address.
4. Write an opening paragraph and mention three points:
   A. "You have disregarded my complaints of mistakes in my credit report."
   B. Financially, the mistakes have hurt me personally and are continuing to do so."
   C. Express the ways in which you have been financially punished for their mistake. In one or two sentences, say what you individually stand to lose (can't refinance a mortgage; get a car loan, which means you cannot get to work).
5. Do not use sample dispute letters as form letters to be copied word-for-word. Why? The credit bureaus may be familiar with repair strategy you're using and give you a hard time.
6. Give the name of creditor that sent derogatory remarks against your credit and your account number with that creditor. List each creditor, account number, and contest individually if you are contesting more than one item.
7. Mention specific reasons why the credit item is incorrect, as letters are sent, you may want to go into more detail each time. Never admit any fault or blame for your problems.
8. After letter **#8** and letter **#9**, make clear in your own words that you are going to take stronger action if they don't correct their mistakes soon (i.e., call your lawyer, sue in small claims court, report credit bureau to the Federal Trade Commission or your attorney general).
9. Finish your letter by signing your name.
10. **Important:** Send letter through certified/ return receipt mail, or else credit bureau will know that you don't have legal proof that you sent letter and they may ignore it.

### Dispute Letter #8: To the Credit Bureau

This is the first dispute letter that you will send to credit bureaus to resolve credit problems.

Date:                                      Your name
                                           Your address
                                           Your phone #
                                           Your Soc. Security #

Customer Service
*Credit bureau name*
*Credit bureau address*

Dear Customer Service:

The following mistakes are ruining my chances of buying a home for my family and furthermore, if you don't fix these mistakes soon, I will lose a $20,000 deposit.

This account is incorrect: Nevada Bank, account # 1289-7890

My Nevada Bank account should be a good account. Your report says that I was late 30 days once and 60 days late twice. I have always paid this account on time.

I expect a quick response from you, in writing.

Yours truly,

### Dispute letter #9: To the Credit Bureau

Send letter **#9,** if you get no reply within 30 days with letter **#8**. Include copy of a certified receipt and letter **#8**.

Date:                                      Your name
                                           Your address
                                           Your phone #
                                           Your Soc. Security #

Customer Service
*Credit bureau name*
*Credit bureau address*

Dear Customer Service:

What is going on? It has been a month since I sent you my first letter (attached is a copy of my certified mail receipt and first letter). Legally, you must respond within a certain time limit (I am now marking the days off on my calendar).

Your mistakes are killing my chances of getting this house for my family. If you don't fix your mistakes soon, I will lose my $20,000 deposit. **PLEASE, HELP ME!**

This account is incorrect: Nevada Bank, account # 1289-7890

The Nevada Bank account is a good account. Your report says that was late 30 days once and 60 days twice. I have always paid this account on time.

I expect a quick reply from you, in writing.

Yours truly,

### Dispute Letter #10: To the Credit Union

Use letter **#10** if the credit bureau writes back to either letter **#8** or letter **#9** with an unwillingness to fix any of the problems.

Date:                                      Your name
                                           Your address
                                           Your phone #
                                           Your Soc. Security #

Customer Service
*Credit bureau name*
*Credit bureau address*

Dear Customer Service:

Not long ago, I wrote and asked you to investigate a mistake on my credit report. You claimed the item is correct as stated on report, but my account is still incorrect. You must be ignoring all my evidence, I sent you as proof that it's wrong.

Either you correct the mistake, or I will take serious measures to defend myself. This will include holding you at fault for any of my forthcoming financial losses.

This account is incorrect: Nevada Bank, account # 1289-7890

My Nevada Bank account is a good account. Your report says that I was late 30 days once and 60 days late twice. I paid this account on time. Please tell me how I can contact the person who is supplying you with all of this derogatory information.

Legally, you are liable for this mistake. If you don't correct this misunderstanding ASAP, then I will take stronger measures.

Yours truly,

## Dispute Letter #11: To the Credit Bureau

Use this letter #11 if the credit bureau writes back to either your letter #8 or letter #9 with an unwillingness to fix some of the problems on your credit report. If the credit bureau refuses to fix any of the problems, use dispute letter #10. If the credit bureau fix's all or only some of the problems, and you want to contest more problems, use letter #12.

Date:

Your name
Your address
Your phone
Your Soc. Security #

Customer Service
*Credit bureau name*
*Credit bureau address*

Dear Customer Service:

In my latest credit report from you, I see that you have repaired some of your mistakes, but not all of them. You must be ignoring some of the evidence, I've sent to you as proof.

You allege that you have validated the problems, but I don't know how that could be possible, since they're wrong. I feel like you're just blowing me off and could not care less about my problem.

This account is incorrect: Nevada Bank, account # 1289-7890 My Nevada Bank account is a good account. Your report says that I was late 30 days once and 60 days late twice. I paid this account on time. Please tell me how I can contact the person who is throwing out all of this derogatory information.

Legally you are liable for this mistake. If you don't correct this misunderstanding ASAP, then I will take stronger measures.

Yours truly,

## Dispute Letter #12: To the Credit Bureau

Use this letter if the credit bureau responds to either letter #8 or letter #9 by repairing some or all of the mistakes and you want to contest more mistakes.

Date:

Your name
Your address
Your phone #
Your Soc. Security #

Customer Service
*Credit bureau name*
*Credit bureau address*

Dear Customer Service:

Your credit reports are so mystifying to me that I've only now come across another mistake on my credit report.

The mistake is: Credit Zero, account # 555-1234

Your report says that I was 30 days late twice, but it's really not my mistake. That payment was delinquent because I did not receive a bill. The bill was sent to an old address, even though I had formally notified the company in writing that I moved.

Please correct this problem and misunderstanding ASAP.

Yours truly,

## Sample FTC Letter #13: To the FTC

Use this letter #13 if the credit bureaus don't answer letter's #8 and #9 within six weeks. When you send letter #13 to the FTC, also send a copy to each of the dawdling credit bureaus to indicate that you really mean business.

Date:

Your name
Your address
Your phone #
Your Soc. Security #

Federal Trade Commission
Pennsylvania Ave. and 6th St. N. W.
Washington, DC 20580
(202) 326-2000

Date:

Dear Consumer Complaints:

*Credit bureau name,* won't answer my objections about mistakes on my credit report. Attached, is a copy of my written complaint, and copy of certified return receipt card. Please help me.

Yours truly,

## Dispute Letter #14: To the Credit Bureau (100 words)

The Fair Credit Act obligates credit bureaus to let you write a statement from up to 100 words explaining, each and any damaging credit item from your point-of-view. When writing, do not assign any fault. Indicate how you have taken full responsibility for your actions and troubles you have faced.

*Credit bureau name*
*Credit bureau address*

Date:

Dear Sir or Madam:

Please attach the statement below to my credit report with regards to the following account.

Honda Accord, account # 6660666

At the end of 2006, I left the Armed Forces for a new career and job. When I got to my new job assignment, I was told that I was laid off because of the recession. Without a job, I could not continue making my car payments, so I voluntarily gave up my car. I took the layoff as another chance to be retrained for a new career that I now have with my current employer. Since I have a job once again, I am pleased to report that I am current with all my credit obligations. I consider credit vital to me and revere it as keeping my word.

Thank you. Please send me a copy of my revised credit report.

Yours truly,

## Credit Bureau Stalling Tactics:

■ They'll send you a form letter telling you that they are researching your objections, even though they are not.
**Solution:** Blow off letters and continue with next step.
■ They will send you a form letter telling you that your objections were not precise enough to research or repair.
**Solution:** See **page 51**, **"How to write Letter's to the Credit Bureaus."**

During a long day, you may write a check, charge dinner and a movie, rent a car or apply for credit. In each transaction, you reveal bits of personal information, like your bank and credit card account numbers; your income; your Social Security number (SSN); including, your name, addresses, and phone numbers. Once a thief has your information, it can be used (without your knowledge) to commit serious fraud or theft.

People who have had their identities stolen can spend months or years and thousands of dollars cleaning up the mess. In addition, identity victims may lose job opportunities, be refused loans or credit, and arrested for crimes they didn't commit. Shame, anger and frustration are among the feelings victims experience as they trudge through the process of rescuing their identity. The following information will give you strategies on how to protect your identity or wrestle it back from thieves.

## How identity thieves get your personal information:
They get information from businesses or other institutions by:

■ While they are on the job, they may steal records, datum, bribe an employee (who has access to these records), hack records, or even con information out of employees.

■ Stealing mail, bank and credit card statements, credit card offers, new checks, and tax information.

■ Rummaging through trash from businesses or public trash dumps.

■ Obtaining credit reports by abusing their employer's authorized access to them, or posing as property owner, employer, or someone else who may have legal right to access report.

■ Stealing credit or debit card numbers by capturing the information in a data storage device in a practice known as *"skimming."* They may swipe your card for an actual purchase, or attach the device to an ATM where you may enter or swipe your card.

■ Stealing wallets or purses.

■ Sending a "change of address form" to divert your mail to another location.

■ Stealing information they find in your home.

■ Stealing information from you through email or phone by posing as legitimate companies and claiming that you have a problem with your account. This practice is known as *"phishing"* online or *"pretexting"* by phone.

■ Glean information off your business card(s).

## How identity thieves use your personal information:
They may:

■ Call your credit card issuer to change the billing address on your credit card account. The imposter then runs up charges on your account. Since your bills are being sent to a different address, it may be awhile before you realize the problem.

■ Open new credit card accounts in your name. When they use the credit cards, and don't pay the bills, delinquent accounts are reported on your credit report.

■ Set up a phone or wireless service in your name.

■ Open a bank account in your name and write bad checks on that account.

■ Counterfeit checks, credit or debit cards, or authorize electronic transfers in your name, and drain accounts.

■ File bankruptcy under your name to avoid paying debts they've incurred under your name, or to avoid eviction.

■ Buy a car with a loan using your name.

■ Get identification such as a driver's license issued with their picture, in your name.

■ Get a job or file fraudulent tax returns in your name.

■ Give your name to the police during an arrest. When they don't show up for their court date, a warrant for arrest is issued in your name.

## What can you do to protect yourself from identity theft?
Here is a list of things you can do that can lower risk of information being stolen:

■ Check your credit report regularly. The major credit bureaus are required to provide you with a free copy of your credit report, at your request, once every 12 months. You can get these free reports by going to **www.annualcreditreport.com.** Consider spacing these out so that you get one every four months.

■ Instead of depositing your outgoing mail in your own mailbox, take it to the post office collection mailboxes where items are more secure. Identity thieves can easily steal your mail and use that information against you.

■ Never give personal information over the phone, unless call is initiated by you. Make sure household members know not to give out such information.

■ Never leave receipts at bank machines, bank windows, or gas pumps. These receipts contain information that Identity thieves can utilize.

■ Shred any financial trash, especially credit card offers or cash advance/check offers (If a thief gets one of these applications, they can apply in your name).

■ Notify credit card companies and financial agencies in advance of address and phone number changes. Don't let your mail continue to go to your old address.

■ If you applied for a credit card, and it doesn't arrive promptly, immediately contact the credit card company.

■ Report lost or stolen credit cards immediately.

■ Sign all new credit cards upon receipt.

■ Carefully review your credit card bills and bank account statements each month.

■ When making online purchases, consider using only one card that you check frequently.

■ Beware of any official looking requests to confirm information from businesses or federal entities that you receive via email. These are usually Identity thieves *"phishing"* for information.

■ Use "strong" passwords that aren't easy to guess. For example, do not use your anniversary, birth dates or other significant dates that a thief could easily discover.

■ **Option C:** If you want to receive calls, but keep your phone number private, use call forwarding service. The person calling will dial a number that will connect to your phone, without knowing your real number. There is several call forwarding services, just Google to find one.

■ **Opt out on the internet:** Stop sharing of online cookie data with advertisers by visiting: **www.networkadvertising.org**

■ **Use privacy search Engines:** The search engine *"Ixquick"* deletes search queries after 48-hours. Conversely, **Yahoo** retains search queries for 13-months and **Google** 18-months. To download, visit: **www.ixquick.com/eng/download_ixquick_plugin.html** Furthermore, the search engine **Ask.com** offers a privacy feature called *"AskEraser"*. Go to **www.ask.com**, click on *"AskEraser"* and your search activity is deleted from **Ask.com** servers.

■ **Freeze credit report:** You can deny *"access"* to your credit reports in all 50 states. This will reduce your risk of identity theft. To learn more, visit: **www.consumersunion.org/campaigns//learn_more/003484indiv.html**.

■ **To remove your name** from national companies that do direct mail marketing, telemarketing, rents or sells your name to other companies, send your letter / post card with your name address and phone number to:

**1. DMA Mail Preference Service**
P.O. Box 643, Carmel, NY 10512 or you can register by phone: **212-768-7277, ext. 1500**
**2. DMA Telephone Preference Service**
P.O. Box 1559, Carmel, NY 10512
**3, DMA E-Mail Preference Service at www.dmachoice.org:** Follow instructions to remove your e-mail address from many direct e-mail lists.

If you write to the DMA you'll be removed from the DMA-member lists for five years, but it may take several months before you see a decrease in amount of solicitations. Opting out will not end solicitations from all local merchants, religious and charitable associations, professional and alumni associations, politicians, and companies. To eliminate mail from these groups – as well as mail addressed to "occupant" or "resident" – write directly to each source.

■ **Opt out of pre-approved unsolicited credit card offers:** Get rid of credit offers for 5-years with a call, or permanently, by mailing the Opt-Out form, through their web site. Call **888.567.8688** or visit **www.optoutprescreen.com**.

■ **Opt Out of Acxiom:** Acxiom is one of the sources of addresses and phone numbers for telemarketers and mass mailers. To Opt-Out call **877.774.2094** or by e-mail **optoutUS@acxiom.com**. Should opting out with Acxiom become a problem, visit the website **www.private-citizen.com** to help get rid of them.

■ **Opt out of Abacus:** Abacus collects a cooperative database of catalog customers. When you order products from one catalog, that company is likely to sell your contact information to other catalog companies. To opt-out of the Abacus database, write to **Abacus, P.O. Box 1478, Broomfield, CO 80038** or by email at **abacusoptout@epsilon.com**. Include full name (add middle initial) and current address (and previous address if you have moved within the last 6 months). For more information, visit **www.abacusoptout.com**

■ **Protect Your Financial Privacy:** Read privacy notices from your bank, credit card, insurance, and investment companies. By law, as a requirement, financial institutions must mail privacy notices to you yearly. Take full advantage of any opt-out opportunities regarding the sharing of customer data.

**What to do if you fall victim to ID Theft:** If you are unfortunate enough to become a victim of ID theft, there are several crucial steps you must take in order to restore your credit and identity:

**STEP 1:** Close accounts that you know, or believe to have been tampered with or opened fraudulently. Call and speak with someone in security or fraud department of each company. Follow up in writing, and include copies (not originals) of supporting documents. It is important to notify credit card companies and banks in writing. Send your letters by certified mail, return receipt requested, so you can document what the company received and when. Sample letters are available at **www.FTC.gov.** Keep a file of your correspondence and enclosures.

**STEP 2:** Contact the Credit Bureaus Equifax, Experian, and TransUnion, and place a fraud report on your credit report. This fraud alert will make it difficult for Identity thieves to continue stealing by stopping them from opening new lines of credit.

■ **Equifax:** 1-800-525-6285; www.equifax.com P.O. Box 740241, Atlanta, GA 30374- 0241
■ **Experian:** 1-888-397-3742 www.experian.com/consumer/cac/InvalidateSession.do?code=SECURITYALERT P.O. Box 9532, Allen, TX 75013
■ **TransUnion:** 1-800-680-7289 www.transunion.com Fraud Victim Assistance Division, P.O. Box 6790, Fullerton, CA 92834-6790

**STEP 3:** Contact local police and file a police report. This will help you to validate the authenticity of your claim, so that later, if you need to challenge transactions or notations on your credit report you have some form of proof that you were the victim of theft. Sometimes, local police are unresponsive to reports, in which case, you can also contact your State Attorney General's Office.

**STEP 4:** Contact the FTC and file a complaint at: **www.FTC.gov**

Although, these steps can help mitigate the harm done when your identity is stolen, the most important thing you can do is follow the steps laid out in this article to decrease your risk of having your identity stolen. For more information visit:

■ **Department Of Justice:** www.usdoj.gov/criminal/fraud/websites/idtheft.html
■ **Social Security Administration:** www.ssa.gov/pubs/idtheft.htm
■ **Privacy Rights Clearing House:** www.privacyrights.org/identity.htmVictims

**You won our mystery grand prize!**

It's a mystery prize. Now, in order to get that prize out to you, I'll need several forms of ID, including...

**HUH? I WON? OH MY GOD, WHAT?**

I'll get my purse. If you need my spouse information, I have that too! I can't believe...

We're almost half way through our journey, but you still look a tad out of shape. I'll remedy that a little later, Peaches. In this chapter, I have tried to simplify the process of purchasing a car. You'll find information that will assist your research, including strategies that will save lots of money when striking the final deal. In addition, I'll teach you how to shop for the best financing and auto insurance and more. **Tip:** <u>**DO NOT RUSH INTO BUYING A CAR ON IMPULSE**</u>. Getting stuck with an expensive ($450 average) payment plus car insurance will burden you with an unnecessary large obligation and limit your ability to create wealth. You really can't afford to screw this one up. **Tip 2: Never step on a car lot unprepared to make a deal** (be sure to get all your ducks in a row). It's time I teach you a little secret that will save you serious transportation dollars. Have you ever wondered how man traveled long distances before horses, cars, etc.? Well, they ran and ran and ran, just as you're about to do. I'll have you in tip top shape in no time. So, get on your mark! Get set! Go! Run, Skippy! Ruuuuun!

**Sixth Commandment:**
**"THOU SHALL NOT PURCHASE BIG TICKET ITEMS ON IMPULSE"**

NEW CAR: $$$$$$

USED CAR: $$$

C-6

NEW CAR

USED CAR

USE EXTREME CAUTION

SPEED LIMIT 10

The first thing you should do when looking to purchase a used car (recommended) is to find one that is dependable. Nowadays, buying a used car is not as risky as it once was thanks to Consumer Reports (CR). They compile lists from their reader responses (Annual Questionnaire) from year to year. CR scores only the models in which they have sufficient data. However, problems with the engine, engine cooling, transmission, clutch and driveline are considered more heavily than other problems.

The following lists will assist you in choosing a used car. The first list is cars rated "Consumer Reports Good Bets." According to CR, these cars performed well over the years, and their overall reliability has been better than average for the model years 1999 to 2008. The second list is used models from 1999 to 2008 whose overall records have been much worse, and you should not consider these used cars at any price. For detailed information on specific auto makes, models and their troubles, you can obtain that information and more for a small fee ($5.95 for one-month access) at **www.consumerreports.org/cro/cars/index.htm.**

## GOOD BETS

### ACURA
Integra
MDX
RL
RSX
TL
TSX

### BMW
M3
Z3
Z4

### BUICK
Lucerne (V8)

### FORD
Fusion
Mustang (V6)

### HONDA
Accord
Civic
Civic Hybrid
CR-V
Odyssey
Pilot
Ridgeline
S2000

### HYUNDAI
Santa Fe

### INFINITI
FX35
G20
G35 (Sedan)
I30
I35
M35
QX4

### LEXUS
ES
GS (6-cyl., RWD)
GX
IS
LS
RX
SC

### LINCOLN
MKZ, Zephyr (FWD)

### MAZDA
MX-5 Miata
Protégé
Mazda3

### MERCURY
Milan

### MITSUBISHI
Outlander

### NISSAN
350Z
Altima
Maxima
Xttera (05-08)

### PONTIAC
Vibe

### PORSCHE
Boxster

### SCION
tC
xB

### SUBARU
Baja
Forester
Impreza WRX/STi
Outback (6-cyl)
Tribeca

### TOYOTA
4Runner
Avalon
Camry (except 2008 V6)
Camry Solara
Celica
Corolla
Echo
Frontier (05-08)
Highlander
Land Cruiser
Matrix
Prius
RAV4
Sequoia
Sienna
Tacoma (05-08)
Tundra

### VOLVO
S60

## BAD BETS

### Audi
A6 Allroad
A8

### BMW
X5 (V8)

### BUICK
Rendezvous (AWD)

### CADILLAC
SRX

### CHEVROLET
Blazer
Colorado (4WD)
S-10 Pickup (4WD)
Uplander
Venture

### CHRYSLER
Pacifica
Sebring convertible
Town & Country (AWD)

### DODGE
Grand Caravan (AWD)

### GMC
Canyon (4WD)
Jimmy
S-15 Sonoma (4WD)

### JEEP
Grand Cherokee

### KIA
Sedona

### LAND ROVER
Discovery
LR3

### MAZDA
RX-8

### OLDSMOBILE
Bravada
Silhouette

### PONTIAC
Aztec
G6 (V6)
Montana
Montana SV6
Cayenne

### SATURN
Relay

### VOLKSWAGEN
Cabrio
Jetta (V6)
New Beetle (turbo)
Passat (V6, FWD)
Touareg

### VOLVO
XC90 (6-cyl.)

Son of a day on the beach! I've got to get rid of this piece of Junk!

To run out and purchase a car first, without researching the cost of auto insurance is foolish, especially if later you find that the policy is too expensive and you cannot afford it. By law, you must have auto insurance coverage for your vehicle, which protects you from losses. The next four pages of tips and ideas will help you find affordable auto insurance at a reasonable price, or review your current policy to find a better one. If you are looking to buy a new car, do the proper research, and maybe it won't be stolen.

**Tip #1:** Compare auto insurance prices by contacting your **State Insurance Department** (**SID**) who may provide comparisons of prices charged by major insurers. See **SID** phone numbers and websites below:

**ALABAMA:** 334-269-3550
www.aldoi.gov/Consumers/AutoInsurance.aspx
**ALASKA:** 907-269-7900 / 907-465-2515 / www.commerce.
state.ak.us/insurance/pub/2008_Auto_Guide.pdf
**ARIZONA:** 602-364-2499 / 602-364-3100 / 800-325-2548
www.id.state.az.us/consumerautofaq.html
**ARKANSAS:** 501-371-2600 / 800-282-9134
www.insurance.arkansas.gov/PandC/SurveyPPAall/09PPA
Survey/SurveysPPA.htm
**CALIFORNIA:** 1-800-927-4357 (in CA) / 213-897-8921
www.insurance.ca.gov/0100-consumers/0060-information-
guides/0010-automobile
**COLORADO:** 303-894-7490 or 7499 / 800-930-3745
www.dora.state.co.us/insurance/consumer/AutoMain.htm
**CONNECTICUT:** 860-297-3800 / 800-203-3447
www.ct.gov/cid/cwp/view.asp?q=390260
**DELAWARE:** 302-674-7310 / 800-282-8611 (in DE)
http://delawareinsurance.gov/auto/auto_topics.shtml
**DISTRICT OF COLUMBIA:** 202-727-8000
http://disr.dc.gov/disr/cwp/view,a,1299,q,643793.asp
**FLORIDA:** 877-691-5236 / 850-413-3140
www.myfloridacfo.com/Consumers/Guides/Auto/index.htm
**GEORGIA:** 404-656-5875 / 800-656-2298
www.gainsurance.org/ConsumerService/Home.aspx
**HAWAII:** 808-586-2790 or 2799 / http://hawaii.gov/dcca/
areas/ins/consumer/consumer_information/mvl
**IDAHO:** 208-334-4250 / 800-721-3272 (in ID)
www.doi.idaho.gov/consumer/automobile.aspx
**ILLINOIS:** 312-814-2420 (Chicago) / 217-782-4515
http://insurance.illinois.gov/autoinsurance/shopping_auto_i
ns.asp
**INDIANA:** 317-232-1990 / 800-622-4461
www.in.gov/idoi/2333.htm
**IOWA:** 515-281-5705 / 877-955-1212
www.iid.state.ia.us/index.asp
**KANSAS:** 785-296-3071 / 800-432-2484
www.ksinsurance.org/consumers/auto.htm
**KENTUCKY:** 502-564-3630 / 800-595-6053
http://insurance.ky.gov/kentucky
**LOUISIANA:** 225-342-5900 / 800-259-5300 / www.ldi.la.
gov/consumers/misc_pubs/2008AutoRateGuide.pdf
**MAINE:** 207-624-8475 / 800-300-5000
www.maine.gov/pfr/insurance/consumer/auto.htm
**MARYLAND:** 410-468-2000 / 800-492-6116
www.mdinsurance.state.md.us/sa/jsp/Mia.jsp
**MASSACHUSETTS:** 617-521-7794 / www.mass.gov
?pageID=ocasubtopic&L=4&L0=Home&L1=Consumer&L2
=Insurance&L3=Automobile+Insurance&sid=Eoca
**MICHIGAN:** 517-373-0220 / 877-999-6442
www.michigan.gov/dleg/0,1607,7-154-
10555_13222_13224-66774--,00.html
**MINNESOTA:** 651-296-2488 / 800-657-3602
www.state.mn.us/portal/mn/jsp/content.do?subchannel=null
&programid=536914935&sc3=null&sc2=null&id=-
536893703&agency=Insurance
**MISSISSIPPI:** 601-359-3569 / 800-562-2957
www.mid.state.ms.us/consumer/auto_insurance.aspx

**MISSOURI:** 573-751-4126 / 800-726-7390
www.insurance.mo.gov/consumer/auto/index.htm
**MONTANA:** 406-444-2040 / 800-332-6148
www.sao.state.mt.us/consumers/Auto%20Guide%2009.pdf
**NEBRASKA:** 402-471-2201 / 877-564-7323
www.doi.ne.gov/brochure/autorateguide.pdf
**NEVADA:** 775-687-4270 (CC) / 702-486-4009 (LV)
www.doi.state.nv.us/G-AutoGuide-12-24-08.pdf
**NEW HAMPSHIRE:** 603-271-2261/ 800-852-3416
www.nh.gov/insurance/consumers/auto.htm
**NEW JERSEY:** 609-292-7272 / 800-446-7467 / www.state.
nj.us/dobi/division_consumers/insurance/auto.htm
**NEW MEXICO:** 505-827-4601 / 800-947-4722
www.nmprc.state.nm.us/final.htm
**NEW YORK:** 518-474-6600 / 800-342-3736
www.ins.state.ny.us/cauto.htm
**NORTH CAROLINA:** 919-733-2032 / 800-546-5664
www.ncdoi.com/Consumer/consumer_auto.asp
**NORTH DAKOTA:** 701-328-2440 / 800-247-0560
www.nd.gov/ndins/consumer/auto-insurance-information
**OHIO:** 614-644-2658 / 800-686-1526 / www.insurance.
ohio.gov/Consumer/Pages/AutoToolkit.aspx
**OKLAHOMA:** 405-521-2828 / 800-522-0071
www.ok.gov/oid/Consumers/Buying_Insurance/Automobile
_Insurance/index.html
**OREGON:** 503-947-7984 / 888-877-4894
www.cbs.state.or.us/external/ins/consumer/auto-
insurance/auto.html
**PENNSYLVANIA:** 717-787-2317 / 877-881-6388 / www.ins
.state.pa.us/ins/cwp/view.asp?a=1274&q=543098&PM=1
**PUERTO RICO:** 787-722-8686 / 888-722-8686
www.ocs.gobierno.pr/ocspr
**RHODE ISLAND:** 401-462-9500 / 401-462-9520
www.dbr.state.ri.us/documents/divisions/insurance/property
_casualty/com_guide-auto_insur.PDF
**SOUTH CAROLINA:** 803-737-6160 / 800-768-3467
www.doi.sc.gov/consumer/auto.htm
**SOUTH DAKOTA:** 605-773-3563 / www.state.sd.us/drr2/
reg/insurance/consumer/autoinsurance.htm
**TENNESSEE:** 615-741-2176 / 800-342-4029
www.state.tn.us/commerce/insurance/consumerRes.shtml
**TEXAS:** 512-463-6169 / 1-800-252-3439 / www.opic.state.
tx.us/guideline.php?p_guideline_id=6&p_section_id=2
**UTAH:** 801-538-3800 / 800-439-3805
www.insurance.utah.gov/auto/auto.html
**VERMONT:** 802-828-3301 / 800-964-1784
www.bishca.state.vt.us/InsurDiv/insur_index.htm
**VIRGIN ISLANDS:** 340-774-7166 / http://ltg.gov.vi
**VIRGINIA:** 804-371-9967 / 800-552-7945 / 877-310-6560
www.scc.virginia.gov/division/boi/webpages/boipublications
.htm#autoinsurance
**WASHINGTON:** 360-725-7103 / 800-562-6900 / www.insur
ance.wa.gov/consumers/insurance_types.shtml#auto
**WEST VIRGINIA:** 304-558-3354 / 888-879-9842
www.wvinsurance.gov/Default.aspx?alias=www.wvinsuranc
e.gov/consumerservices
**WISCONSIN:** 608-266-3585 / 800-236-8517
http://oci.wi.gov/faq/auto.htm
**WYOMING:** 307-777-7401 / 800-438-5768
http://insurance.state.wy.us/consumer.html

C-6

**TIP #2:** Get quotes from different insurers, but do not shop price alone. Ask friends and relatives for their recommendations. Consider picking an agent or company representative willing to take the time to answer your questions. Furthermore, compare quotes from insurers by using the checklist provided on **page 61**.

**TIP #3:** Before purchasing a car, compare insurance costs. Car insurance premiums are based in part on car's sticker price, cost to repair, overall safety record, and likelihood of theft. Many insurers offer discounts for features that reduce the risk of injuries or theft (see checklist **page 61**). To help you decide what car to buy, you can get information from the Insurance Institute for Highway Safety (**www.iihs.org**) or The National Insurance Crime Bureau (**www.nicb.org**).

## TOP 10 LEAST EXPENSIVE CARS TO INSURE:
1. Hyundai Santa Fe
2. Kia Sportage
3. Hyundai Entourage
4. Kia Sedona
5. Kia Rio5
6. Honda Odyssey
7. Smart Fortwo
8. Saturn Vue
9. Mazda Tribute
10. Chrysler Town & Country

## TOP 10 MOST EXPENSIVE CARS TO INSURE:
1. Nissan GT-R
2. Dodge Viper
3. BMW M6
4. Ford Shelby GT500
5. Mercedes-Benz G-Class
6. Audi S8
7. BMW M5
8. Hummer H2
9. Lexus IS-F
10. Porsche 911

- Insure.com 2009

## MOST STOLEN CARS 2008:
1. 1994 Honda Accord
2. 1995 Honda Civic
3. 1989 Toyota Camry
4. 1997 Ford F-150 Pickup
5. 2004 Dodge Ram Pickup
6. 2000 Dodge Caravan
7. 1996 Jeep Cherokee/Grand Cherokee
8. 1994 Acura Integra
9. 1999 Ford Taurus
10. 2002 Ford Explorer

- National Insurance Crime Bureau 2009

## TOP 10 STATES FOR AUTO THEFT 2008:
1. California
2. Texas
3. Florida
4. Arizona
5. Michigan
6. Washington
7. Georgia
8. Illinois
9. Ohio
10. New York

- National Insurance Crime Bureau 2008

## TOP IIHS SAFETY PICKS 2009:
The Insurance Institute for Highway Safety (IIHS) declared that seventy-two vehicles earned their Top Safety Pick award for 2009. Vehicles must pass several rigorous tests conducted by the IIHS in order to earn this award, which typically, is no easy thing.
To see the seventy-two 2009 Top Safety Pick winning vehicles and runner-ups, please visit:
**www.iihs.org/ratings**

**TIP #4:** Deductibles are what you pay before your insurance policy kicks in. By requesting higher deductibles, you can substantially lower costs.

**Example: Increasing deductible from $200 to $500 could reduce collision and comprehensive coverage cost by 15 to 30%. Going to a $1,000, deductible can save you 40% or more.**
**WARNING:** Before implementing higher deductible, set aside enough money to pay it if you have a claim.

**TIP #5:** Consider dropping collision and/or comprehensive coverage on older cars. If your car is worth less than 10 times the premium, purchasing coverage may not be cost effective. Auto dealers and banks can tell you the worth of cars. Furthermore, you can look up price online at Kelley's Blue Book (**www.kbb.com**). Review your coverage at renewal time to make sure your insurance needs have not changed.

**TIP #6:** Several insurers will give discounts if you buy two or more types of insurance (homeowners, auto, etc.). Also, if you have two or more vehicles, be sure to ask for a reduced rate. Some insurers lower rates for long-time customers. However, it still makes sense to shop around, because you may save money buying from different insurance companies, compared with a multi-policy discount.

**TIP #7:** Companies offer discounts to policyholders who have not had any accidents or moving violations for a number of years. You may also get a discount if you take a defensive driving course. If there is a young driver on the policy who is a good student, has taken a drivers education course or is at a college out of the area without a car, you could also qualify for a lower rate.

**TIP #9:** In the event you get a traffic ticket, more than likely you will passively go to court, pay the fine, and then watch helplessly as your auto insurance rates skyrocket. Alternatively, you could put the gloves on and fight your ticket; win your case in court and all without the expensive help of a lawyer.

There is a very informative, self-help book titled, *"Fight Your Ticket" by David W. Brown,* which gives advice and strategies on how to defend yourself in Traffic Court and keep your auto rates low. Your local library should carry the book or you can buy it from **www.amazon.com.**

**TIP #10:** Good credit can cut insurance costs. Insurers are aggressively using consumer's credit histories to price auto insurance policies. To protect your credit rating, pay bills on time, don't obtain more credit than you need and keep your credit balances as low as possible. Check your credit record on a regular basis and have any errors corrected ASAP so that your record remains solid.

**TIP #11:** Some insurers give discounts to motorists who drive lower than average number of miles each year. Discounts can also apply to drivers who carpool to work.

**TIP #12:** Some companies offer reduced rates to drivers who purchase insurance through group plans from their employers, professionals, business and alumni groups, or other associations. Ask employer and inquire with groups or clubs you are a member of to see if this is possible.

**TIP #13:** Young singles typically pay higher rates for insurance, but when singles marry, they usually get a price cut. Couples with different insurers should review their policies to see which company offers the best price and service. Once they start a family, young parents tend to become more careful behind the wheel and generally enjoy a mature driver insurance discount.

**TIP #14:** Young adult drivers can add from 50 to 100% to the family's auto insurance cost. It's typically cheaper to have a teenage driver on the family's policy rather than purchasing a separate policy. To help lower insurance rates, select a car with a high safety rating. Other discounts may be available for good students. If a college student doesn't have a car during the school year and attends a school at least 100 miles from home, tell insurer. Rates may be lowered for students away from home.

**TIP #15:** If you pay monthly, your insurer may charge anywhere from $3 to $5 per month for this type of billing. Pay every six months if possible. If you have to pay monthly, use automatic pay. Charges are less because they only send a bill if amount changes.

**TIP #16:** If you live in a *"high risk"* neighborhood, you could end up paying a higher premium. In addition, it is very important to know that if you are living in a city, expect to pay more for automobile insurance. Therefore, beware of your surroundings, because it can either save or cost you money.

**TIP #17:** Make sure that your vehicle information is correct. Auto insurance companies aren't perfect and may record the details about your car wrong, such as recording your four door vehicle as two-door, or as supercharged instead

of GT or SE version. Correcting errors will definitely help to cut your insurance costs tremendously.

**TIP #18:** Your driving record may be incorrect. Only a few consumers have examined their C.L.U.E. (Comprehensive Loss Underwriting Exchange) file to see what their driving record says. Thus, if there are some misleading claims and outdated entries it will cause you to pay higher auto-insurance rates and to make matters worse; the insurer not the consumer's spoken word decides what's on the report. If you think you have error(s) on your report, or just curious, under the federal Fair Credit Reporting Act you can request a copy of your C.L.U.E. report from ChoicePoint Consumer Disclosure, P.O. Box 105108, Atlanta, Georgia 30348-5108, or call toll free **866-527-2600 / (800) 456-6004** or visit **www.choicetrust.com**.

**TIP #19:** After filing a claim, many insurers will raise rates, so if you can afford it, pay the claim yourself to avoid a rate increase.

**TIP #20: NEVER DRIVE WITHOUT CAR INSURANCE.** There are just too many risks to driving without insurance protection for you and others. If you've been turned down for insurance, contact the office of the insurance regulator in your state (**http://consumer action.gov/insurance.shtml**) and ask if your state has an uninsured motorist fund.

**TIP #21:** Consider other modes of transportation other than owning a car that do not require auto insurance. For some, it may be feasible to get by without a car and this choice can save you a ton of money.

**TIP #22:** Keep in mind, the key to savings is not discounts, but the final price. A company that offers few discounts may still have a lower overall price.

**For more information, call the National Insurance Consumer Helpline (NICH) toll free at 800-942-4242**

# RECOMMENDATIONS FOR CAR COVERAGE

### BODILY-INJURY LIABILITY
**Coverage:** Pays medical treatments, in accidents where you're at fault, rehabilitation, or funeral costs incurred by another driver, other driver's passengers, passengers in your car, and pedestrians. For non-monetary losses (pain and suffering), it pays legal costs and settlements.
**Available:** Coverage limits can be as low as your state requires and as high as $500,000 per person and $1,000,000 per accident.
**Recommendation:** Buy $100,000 per person, $300,000 per accident, if you have a home, bank accounts, and a good-paying job. Buy less if you have very little assets or income to protect. If a court rules that you owe more, you might have to sell-off your other assets, so buying an umbrella policy might be smart to have additional coverage. A policy of $1,000,000 costs about $200 a year and pays for losses beyond what's protected by an auto or homeowners policy.

### PROPERTY-DAMAGE LIABILITY
**Coverage:** Repairs or replaces other people's property or vehicles that someone insured on your policy damages in an accident (like your teenager).
**Available:** States require drivers to have property-damage liability, typically $15,000 per accident. Maximum coverage you can purchase $100,000.
**Recommendation:** Purchase an umbrella policy for the extra margin of safety you might need. In several parts of the country, minimums won't cover possible losses.

### COLLISION & COMPREHENSIVE
**Coverage:** Regardless of who's at fault, collision pays for replacement of the car market value or repair. If the auto has been stolen or damaged because of events such as a flood, fire, etc. comprehensive pays for replacement or repairs after the fact.
**Available:** Most auto insurers sell this coverage in increments of $250, normally up to a $1,000 deductible.
**Recommendation:** Minimum collision deductible of $500. Only buy if the car is worth more than $4,000 or less than four years old. Keep in mind, bigger the deductible cheaper the coverage.

### MEDICAL-PAYMENTS COVERAGE
**Coverage:** It pays for hospital bills and physicians, rehabilitation costs, and covers some funeral expenses for you and your passengers. It also pays limited compensation for needed convalescence services. Coverage is sometimes called "med pay."
**Available:** You can buy it in increments of $1,000 or $5,000 and up to $25,000, but this coverage is optional. There is no deductible.
**Recommendation:** You may want to purchase more coverage if your health plan or homeowner's policy doesn't already cover you (see policies), or if you have high health-insurance deductibles and co-payments.

### PERSONAL-INJURY PROTECTION (PIP)
**Coverage:** Covers medical and funeral costs for you and members of household. It also pays a portion of costs of in-home assistance and lost wages. PIP is optional in many states, but mandatory in some states with no-fault auto insurance.
**Available:** Basic required coverage is usually with upper limits set at $50,000. In some states, there is a PIP deductible with coverage.
**Recommendation:** If your state doesn't require you to have PIP, and you already have good health, life, disability insurance, don't buy it. Otherwise, buy only required minimum.

### UNINSURED & UNDERINSURED-MOTORIST
**Coverage:** If you have an accident resulting from a hit-and-run driver, or by a driver who lacks sufficient insurance or who has no insurance at all, it pays you and members of your household for medical costs, rehabilitation, funeral costs, and losses from pain and suffering. Coverage is mandatory in several states.
**Available:** Limits are similar to bodily-injury liability, and most state laws will not allow you to buy more of this coverage than liability coverage you carry.
**Recommendation:** If you drive in a densely populated state, especially where many people drive uninsured, then this coverage is essential.
**Example:** More than one in four drivers has no insurance in California. Where such limits are offered, buy at least $100,000 per person and $300,000 per accident.

### UNINSURED-MOTORIST PROPERTY DAMAGE
**Coverage:** Pays for property damaged by someone without enough insurance to reimburse your costs or someone without insurance.
**Available:** Maximum coverage is $25,000.
**Recommendation:** Where offered, purchase this coverage only if you don't have collision.

### GLASS BREAKAGE
**Coverage:** Regardless of how it occurred to your car, this coverage will replace damaged glass.
**Available:** Usually adds to the cost of your comprehensive coverage 15% to 20%; there is no deductible.
**Recommendation:** If you do not live in an area that has dirt roads, wayward rocks or lots of car break-ins, this coverage is not worth purchasing if it costs more than a few dollars a year (recommended: Colorado and Texas).

### RENTAL REIMBURSEMENT & TOWING
**Coverage:** This is used after an accident, for towing your damaged car and payment for a rental while your auto is being worked on.
**Available:** Costs $15 to $25 a year for rental coverage, but generally pays about $15 per day for up to 30 days. Costs about $5 per car, per year for towing coverage and normally pays up to $50 per tow.
**Recommendation:** If you have only one car and no alternative transportation then purchase rental coverage. The only way you can collect on towing is when your car is not drivable after an accident, and you were at fault or damaged it, other than through a collision.

*Source: Consumer Reports, Federal Trade Commission, Insure.com, National Insurance Crime Bureau and Insurance Institute for Highway Safety.*

# REDUCE COST: AUTO-INSURANCE CHECKLIST

Use checklist to find best auto-insurer to cover your car(s). Remember: Companies with lowest price is not always the best company. Good luck with your search.

## DISCOUNTS TO ASK FOR:

__ **Multiple-Cars:** Save **10–25%** overall
__ **Auto / Homeowner Combo:** Save **5–15%** overall
__ **Long-Time Customer**
__ **Marriage Discount:** Save **5–15%** overall
__ **Good Driver (renewal):** Save **5–20%** overall
__ **Defensive Driver Course:** Save **5–15%** overall
__ **3-Years of Driving Experience:** Save **10–15%**
__ **No Moving Violations in 3 Years**
__ **No Accidents in 3 Years**
__ **Over Age 25 Discount:** Save **5–15%** overall
__ **Mature Driver Discount:** Save **5–15%**
__ **Low Annual Mileage:** Save **10%**
__ **Auto Club, Occupational, or Association Discount**

### EDUCATION DISCOUNTS:
__ **Student Driver Training:** Save **5–20%** overall
__ **Good Student (B average):** Save **5–25%**
__ **Resident Student:** Save **5–15%**
__ **Student Away at College:** Save **10–40%**

### CAR DISCOUNTS:
__ **Automatic Seat Belts:** Save **10–30%** medical
__ **Air Bags:** Save **10–30%** medical
__ **Anti-Theft:** Save **5–50%** comprehensive
__ **Anti-Lock Brakes:** Save **5–10%** overall
__ **Automatic Daytime Headlights:** Save **5%**

### PERSONAL DISCOUNTS:
__ **Non-Smoker:** Save **5%**
__ **Non-Drinker:** Save **5%**
__ **Alcohol or Drug Awareness Training:** Save **5%**

### MISCELLANEOUS DISCOUNTS:
__ **Carpooling:** Save **15–20%**
__ **Garage (Car parked inside at night):** Save **5%**
__ **Farm (Farm or rural usage):** Save…?
__ **Seasonal Usage of Vehicle:** Save…?

### Tips to keep your insurance rates low!

❑ Maintain a clean driving record.
❑ Buy a car with lower rates.
❑ Don't file small claims.
❑ Get a copy of your C.L.U.E. report.
❑ Eliminate all duplicate coverage's.
❑ Maintain good credit.
❑ Pay annually or Simi-annually.
❑ Assign high-risk drivers to low risk cars.
❑ Waive collision insurance on an older vehicle.
❑ Shop for the best rate annually.

❑ Other:_____

| | |
|---|---|
| **Insurance Co.:** _____ | |
| **Contact person:** _____ | |
| **Website:** _____ **PH #:** _____ | |

## HOW MUCH COVERAGE DO YOU NEED?  —  COST OF COVERAGE

**1. Bodily injury liability:**

$_____     $_____

**2. Property damage liability:**

$_____     $_____

**3. Medical payment:**

$_____     $_____

**4. Uninsured motorist:**

$_____     $_____

**5. Underinsured motorist:**

$_____     $_____

**6. Personal injury (PIP):**

$_____     $_____

**7. Collision:**

| | | |
|---|---|---|
| A. | $100 Deductible | $_____ |
| B. | $250 Deductible | $_____ |
| C. | $500 Deductible | $_____ |
| D. | $1,000 Deductible | $_____ |

**8. Comprehensive:**

| | | |
|---|---|---|
| A. | NO Deductible | $_____ |
| B. | $50 Deductible | $_____ |
| C. | $100 Deductible | $_____ |
| D. | $250 Deductible | $_____ |
| E. | $500 Deductible | $_____ |

**Other Charges:**

**Membership Fees:**      $_____

**Surcharges:**      $

**SUBTOTAL:**      $_____

**Discounts: Subtract from SUBTOTAL** $_____

**GRAND TOTAL: $_____**

To get a great deal on a new or used car, you have to do more than just twist the dealer into giving you a great price. You also must haggle and bargain for best terms and interest rate for your new car loan. Usually, car dealerships will give in to your tactics to lower the price of car, but will launch a full-scale assault when it comes to car financing. That is because a dealership makes most of their money on car financing.

To be fair, it is the goal of any good business to make money, and that is what a good dealership should do. Furthermore, a dealership has a full arsenal of schemes and tricks to get the job done. However, it is the right of any consumer to research and gain knowledge in order to get the best deal possible. With a little insight, you can fine-tune yourself into a consumer who knows his way around a dealership and guard against dealer traps.

According to **www.edmunds.com**, in the United States the average car deal consists of:
- Down payment of $2,400
- Amount financed $24,864
- Monthly payment of $479.

The most popular loan term is 6-years. Nowadays, you can finance up to 100% of the manufacturer's suggested retail price, plus taxes, tags and fees. Even if you are **"upside down"** on your old car loan (you still owe money after the trade-in), it's no longer a deal breaker.

However, car loans can vary from 0% to as high as 30%. Therefore, it is extremely important to know that dealers put their most gifted, brightest and toughest closers in the finance/insurance office. This is the place where you are shown offers for extended warranties and other add-ons, including tons of paperwork that can exhaust you to the point of giving in.

The following strategies will help prevent you from being **"taken for a ride"** in a dealer's finance office.

**Strategy #1:** To begin with, arrange financing first from an outside source. A good place to start looking for a car loan is through local credit unions, which mostly, have the lowest interest rates. If you don't belong to a credit union already, join one fast. Car loans are only one of many benefits of belonging to a credit union. All military personnel can belong to a credit union.

To find credit unions in your area, call the Credit Union National Association (CUNA) at **800-358-5710** or visit **www.cuna.org**.

Once you find a few credit unions, call them over the phone; compare their loan rates with other institutions offering car loans, such as local banks, thrifts, savings-and-loan, etc.

Once you have your financing in place, start your search for the car you want, but do not tell the salesperson that you already have your car loan secured, until you have the car's price in writing.
**Danger:** Not researching the best terms and financing before purchasing a car, and assuming that dealers offer the best deal when it comes to financing a car loan, to which, consumers later learn to their angst of longer and higher payments.

**Lesson:** Dealers are just **"middlemen"** when it comes to car financing between you and car lending institution. Dealers typically try to finance your car at a higher interest rate set by their source, so they can increase their profit margin.

**Example:** If you qualify for a 6% rate, but the dealer charges 8% on a 60-month, $20,000 car loan, you pay over $1,100 more in interest (extra profit for the dealer).

**Auto Loan Calculator:** Use calculator to check interest rates to see how much car you can afford at: **www.bankrate.com/calculators/auto/auto-loan-calculator.aspx**

**WARNING:** Do not forget to include auto insurance payments, especially, when considering how high a price you want to pay for a car.

## Dealing with car lenders

**Get ready. Set. Go!** Once you make the decision on what would be best car for you, about one week before going out to buy the car, have your car loan in place.

**Example:** Fill out a car loan application at a lending institution to qualify for a loan.

**Strategy #2:** Talk to a lender and tell them the amount you want to borrow.
**Important:** Only credit unions will commit to financing a used car, even if you are not sure of make and condition of the car you want to purchase.
**Danger:** Do not agree to a rate without trying to bargain for lower one. Once you have researched rates and terms offered by several lenders, call them back and ask them to beat your lowest bid.

## Consumers, dealers just love to look for

**Consumer A:** Dealers dream of consumers who go to a dealership thinking, I will not pay more than $9,000, including trade-in for the new car.

However, by thinking only about the new car's price, you might overlook your real trade-in value, and rip yourself off in the process.

**Consumer B:** Being the type of consumer dealers love to outwit, such as, just like any good salesperson, car dealers look for mannerisms in consumers that will give him or her chance to make some money.

**Consumer C:** Dealers love the type of consumer, who goes into a dealership demanding a certain price for the trade-in, which unfortunately, could lead to a bait-and-switch tactic by the dealer. In other words, you will not get the car model you came to buy, but you will get your price you want for the trade-in. **Example:** Dealer might say, "I can give you $6,000 on your old car, but only if you buy this other model."

**Consumer D:** Dealers adore consumers who bargain from the monthly car payment they prefer. Keep the car payment to yourself, because dealers will give you your desired monthly payment, but, in the process, you might be stuck with longer loan on the vehicle.

**Consumer E:** Dealers, lick their chops just thinking about the consumer who goes to dealership uninformed. If you go to a dealership with only limited knowledge about the process of financing a vehicle, you will probably fall prey to every dealer trick in the book. Do not step foot onto a car lot until you know how the games played, or suffer the financial consequences.

## How dealers throw the uninformed off guard

**"We have credit unions that lend money for cars":**
That is a true statement; however, if you finance your car through their credit union you will pay the commission that they give to the dealer for bringing in your business, which will cost you 1% to 2% or more.

**"Our loan rate is 6%, which is lower than your credit union's loan rate of 8.75%":** That may be true; however, the dealer might have conveniently forgotten to factor your rebate into that equation.

**Example:** $14,000 car financed by a dealer at 6% for 48-months, payment would be $328.72 a month. However, by applying a rebate of $1,500 toward down payment, and loan financed through credit union at 8.75%, monthly payment would be $309.50. That would be a nice tidy savings of $922.56 over a 48-month loan.
**Important:** Make sure car manufacturer sends rebate check directly to your residence.

**Buying credit disability insurance or credit life:**
These insurance polices pay car payment obligations off in case of death, or if one should become disabled. Typically, they are over-priced policies that you do not need. Consider the policies as optional coverage, no matter what the dealer insists. Besides, even if you decline the policy and die later, your estate is liable for all car payments.
**Other solution:** Purchase cheap term insurance policy.

**Before signing any contract:** Make sure that the dealer or lender has not added an insurance policy to the contract without your knowledge. Adding a policy will leave you with a higher payment than expected. Calculate monthly car payment by using loan table (on right); then make doubly sure this is the correct figure, before signing your name on the contract.
**Important:** Several credit unions do not charge anything extra for such insurance policies.
**Bonus:** Several credit unions believe that a death cancels loan obligations.

**Getting a loan for the loooooooongest period:**
Typically, consumers finance long-term loans, for lower monthly car payments, or when financing a costlier car than they can readily afford.
**Problem:** The longer the loan, the more interest you will pay, and on top of it, be charged a higher interest rate. However, when purchasing a used car, the interest rate is generally the same for two or four year loans.
**Danger:** By borrowing money too long, you may end up paying far more than the car is truly worth, which would be costly if you try selling it.

### Example: Financing $14,000 car

| Length of Loan | Interest Rate | Monthly Payments | Total Interest |
|---|---|---|---|
| 3 year | 6% | $425.88 | $1,331.68 |
| 4-year | 7% | $335.16 | $2,087.68 |
| 5-year | 8% | $283.92 | $3,035.20 |
| 6-year | 9% | $252.36 | $4,169.92 |
| 7-year | 10% | $232.42 | $5,523.28 |

**Strategy #3:** Lower payments will make it easier on your budget each month, but payments will seem like an eternity. Look for more "*reasonably priced*" cars that come with affordable payments and shorter pay-off plan.

**Note:** To lower and shorten payments take out a loan for no more than 80% of loan value of the car, and then pay difference with down payment.

**Calculate payments:** The table below will help you to figure monthly payments with a mixture of interest rates and for any dollar amount.

**Example:** Car costs $14,000, with 48-month loan at 10% interest rate. Divide amount of the loan $14,000 into $1,000: **$14,500 ÷ $1,000 = 14**. Locate 10% rate on table; then on right, under 48-months you will find the factor of 25.36. Multiply 14 by 25.36 and you will have an exact monthly payment of **$355.04**.

| Interest Rate | 36-months per $1,000 | 48-months per $1,000 | 60-months per $1,000 |
|---|---|---|---|
| 11.00 | 32.73 | 25.84 | 21.74 |
| 10.75 | 32.62 | 25.72 | 21.61 |
| 10.50 | 32.50 | 25.60 | 21.49 |
| 10.25 | 32.38 | 25.48 | 21.37 |
| 10.00 | 32.26 | 25.36 | 21.24 |
| 9.75 | 32.14 | 25.24 | 21.12 |
| 9.50 | 32.03 | 25.12 | 21.00 |
| 9.25 | 31.91 | 25.00 | 20.87 |
| 9.00 | 31.79 | 24.88 | 20.75 |
| 8.75 | 31.68 | 24.76 | 20.63 |
| 8.50 | 31.56 | 24.64 | 20.51 |
| 8.25 | 31.45 | 24.53 | 20.39 |
| 8.00 | 31.34 | 24.42 | 20.28 |
| 7.75 | 31.22 | 24.29 | 20.15 |
| 7.50 | 31.10 | 24.17 | 20.03 |
| 7.25 | 30.99 | 24.06 | 19.91 |
| 7.00 | 30.87 | 23.94 | 19.80 |
| 6.75 | 30.76 | 23.83 | 19.68 |
| 6.50 | 30.64 | 23.71 | 19.56 |
| 6.25 | 30.53 | 23.59 | 19.44 |
| 6.00 | 30.42 | 23.48 | 19.33 |

**Lease payments:** To familiarize yourself with the complexity of car leases, see: **www.LeaseGuide.com**.

For the most part, used cars are sold without warranties. This means that a thorough inspection of a vehicle inside and out is really the best warranty you can get. The most reliable way to check out a used car is to have a professional do it for you, either a trusted local mechanic, or AAA-recommended inspection service (contact your local AAA auto club—this service is available for both members and non-members).

In addition to mechanic's checkup, a careful inspection of the auto can give you a number of clues as to how the vehicle was treated, and will give you a chance to ensure that the car will be equipped with all the features you require.

**TIP:** Shop for a car during daylight hours. Sunlight can reveal more flaws than can usually be found under cover of darkness.

The following is a 48-point checklist to help insure that the used vehicle of your choice will indeed be a best buy.

**Year:    Make:         Model:**

| EXTERIOR | Yes | No |
|---|---|---|
| **Is paint color on inside the door or engine compartment different from paint on rest of the car?** | | |
| **Are there different paint colors on outside of the car?** | | |
| **Is there lots of chipping paint and rust?** Check for rust spots around body edges, behind bumpers and inside trunk. Probe with finger to see if rust is only on the surface or working through from beneath. Shun cars that are excessively rusty (Repairing rust is far more expensive than most mechanical repairs, and rust does more to depreciate value of a car than any other single item). | | |
| **Does exterior look as if it has just been repainted or repaired?** Be suspicious of new paint. Rippled areas and grainy patches suggest accident (Use a magnet to help detect any repair work in metal body of vehicle). | | |
| **Do doors, trunk, and hood all open and close easily & tightly?** | | |
| **When closed, do doors have a gap between bodies of the car?** An uneven space can be a sign that car has been in an accident or may have high mileage hidden by rolled-back odometer. | | |
| **If car is a convertible, is there a hole in the roof?** Inspect top by parking in bright sunlight, and examine roof from inside for any holes or cracks. | | |
| **Are there brand-new tires on car?** Brand-new tires may indicate a serious wheel-alignment problem exists. Older tires tell an important story about the car—inspect carefully for wear and scuffing. If car has 25,000 miles or less on odometer, it should have its original tires. | | |
| **Park car on level surface and inspect from squatting position about 20 feet behind vehicle. Are front wheels in visible alignment?** If not, car may have severe frame problem (Do not buy). Also, check to see that car is level. | | |
| **After pushing up and down on each corner of car, does car bounce more than once when you let go of fender?** Bad shock absorbers can lead to big problems. | | |
| **Do wheels wobble?** Few dealers leave tires untouched, but it's easy to spot recaps; the tread is new while the sidewalls are slightly grazed. Have the salesperson drive the car slowly away from you, or better yet have a friend follow behind you and check to see if car wobbles or crabs that means a bent frame. **DO NOT BUY.** | | |

| EXTERIOR | Yes | No |
|---|---|---|
| **Remove gas cap. Look for notices on fuel-filter door or dashboard that indicate unleaded fuel only should be used. Has gas-pipe opening been tampered with?** Opening should be small enough to prevent filling from larger, leaded fuel-pump nozzles (leaded fuel can damage an engine designed for lead-free gas). | | |
| **Examine tailpipe, after car has cooled down, check it by rubbing your finger along inside; it should reveal either a white or a powdery substance. If residue is black and sooty, car may simply need a tune-up. Is there black and gummy residue?** This means car probably has problem with its valves or piston rings, and is burning oil. | | |

| INTERIOR | Yes | No |
|---|---|---|
| **Does car smell musty or heavily deodorized?** If it does, it probably leaks; worse, it may have been under-water at one time. **DO NOT BUY.** | | |
| **Are all accessories and instruments (dashboard) operational?** Make sure each instrument and accessories are in working condition with key turned on, but without engine running. | | |
| **Are there any cracks or scratches on front, back or side windows?** | | |
| **Is it hard to roll windows up or down?** Try door handles, window cranks, electric door switches. Minor items can be costly to repair. | | |
| **Are seats, floor mats, and pedals badly worn?** Check for signs of wear on "rubbing points." Wear is a better clue to mileage than an odometer, an untrustworthy gauge. | | |
| **If floor mats are new, is there a hole in floor, or is floor badly worn?** | | |
| **Is brake or clutch pedal worn?** Press brake pedal down hard. If it continues to sink instead of stopping, there is a leak most likely in master cylinder, or possibly in wheel cylinders or lines. | | |

| UNDER THE HOOD | Yes | No |
| --- | --- | --- |
| **Start engine with hood up and listen. Are there unusual hissing, squealing, grinding or grating noises?** | | |
| **Are there wet spots on radiator?** | | |
| **Does water in radiator look rusty or dirty?** | | |
| **Are hoses cracked or flaking?** | | |
| **Is air filter dirty?** | | |
| **Is electrical wiring frayed or cracked?** | | |
| **Is oil on dipstick very heavy or dirty?** | | |
| **Has engine been freshly painted?** Don't be fooled by new looking engine. Most dealers steam clean engines, some even repaint it. | | |

| UNDER THE CAR | Yes | No |
| --- | --- | --- |
| **Are there leaks under the car?** If liquid is black and dark, it could be oil leaking from engine or manual transmission. **DO NOT BUY**. If it's oily, but has little odor, it's probably brake fluid; if it's gasoline, you'll recognize smell. However, if the seepage is clear water, it's usually condensation from air conditioning system and is not a sign of trouble. | | |
| **Are there any holes in muffler or exhaust pipes?** | | |
| **Does either of the front wheels make a clanking noise when turned or shaken?** Grab a front wheel at top and give it a good shake. If you hear clanking noises or discover unexpected looseness, wheel bearings and ball joints may need replacement. Make this check while car is off ground. | | |

| BEHIND WHEEL: ROAD TEST | Yes | No |
| --- | --- | --- |
| **Do you hear odd noises?** For comparison's sake, drive a well-tuned car and listen carefully. | | |
| **Does transmission work smoothly?** Go forward and backward several times from a full stop to make sure transmission works smoothly | | |
| **When you accelerate car does it sputter?** Accelerate rapidly from 20 to 60 mph. If car gains speed smoothly without sputtering, you can be confident that engine is in fair shape. | | |
| **Does car shift gears roughly?** | | |
| **Is there a lot of black smoke during acceleration?** Race the engine and have a friend check exhaust. Blue smoke means burning oil and this could mean that major engine repairs are needed. **DO NOT BUY!** | | |
| **Does car swerve when braking?** At 50 mph, brake hard. Brakes should hold equally on all four wheels, without grabbing or causing car to pull to one side or the other. | | |
| **Are there grinding noises when braking?** | | |
| **Does car vibrate when braking?** | | |
| **Does car vibrate during acceleration?** | | |
| **Does car overheat?** | | |
| **Does the car make a lot of noise on bumpy roads?** | | |

| BEHIND WHEEL: ROAD TEST | Yes | No |
| --- | --- | --- |
| **While turning steering wheel to the far left and right does wheel surge or bounce?** Conduct a do-it-yourself stress Test. If car is equipped with power steering, run engine at idle, air conditioning on full power, lights on high beam, radio on, and foot on brake pedal, put engine in gear and turn steering wheel all the way to the left and right. All accessories should continue to run smoothly. Listen for screeches in power steering, and feel for smoothness in steering wheel (there should be no surges or bouncing in your hand). | | |

| CHECK PAPERWORK | Yes | No |
| --- | --- | --- |
| **Are owner's manual, original warranty and maintenance papers in glove box?** These items are valuable and can be a wealth of information. | | |
| **VERY IMPORTANT: Make sure cars vehicle identification number corresponds with associated paperwork:** You can find **VIN** by looking through windshield on the driver's side dashboard. *If the plate looks tampered with, beware.* | | |
| **Make sure any mileage disclosures match the odometer reading on the car.** | | |
| **Check warranty. If a manufacturer's warranty is still in effect, contact manufacturer to make sure you can use coverage.** | | |
| **Examine dealer documents carefully.** Make sure you are buying—not leasing vehicle. Leases use terms such as "balloon payment" and "base mileage" disclosures. | | |

**BOTTOM LINE:** If you answered most of these questions **YES**, forget the car. If you answered **NO**, the car might be a good buy. Take the car to a diagnostic center or garage for an impartial appraisal. A professional check-up should include the engine (for compression), brake linings, frame, cooling system, exhaust system, and front end (for alignment). Try to persuade mechanic to test-drive the car for an analysis of its transmission and drive shaft; then you will have done best you can.

## OTHER THINGS YOU CAN CHECK:

**Check cars recall history:** You can usually check this with a new-car dealer, who can tell you if particular make and model has ever been involved in a recall, and whether a problem has been corrected on that specific car. You can also check specific makes and models by calling the U.S. Department of Transportation's toll-free recall and safety hotline at Toll free: **1-888-327-4236** or visit **www.nhtsa.dot.gov.**

If a vehicle has been recalled, ask the dealer for proof that the defect has been repaired.

Used vehicles should also have a current safety inspection sticker if your state requires one.

■ **The Insurance Institute for Highway Safety (www.hwysafety.org):** Uses offset-frontal car crashes to assess protection provided by a vehicle's structure.

■ **Consumers Union (www.consumersunion.org):** *Consumer Reports'* annual auto issue rates vehicles in terms of overall safety. Its safety score combines crash test results with a vehicle's accident avoidance factors—emergency handling, braking, acceleration, and even driver comfort.

C-6

■ Your state motor vehicle department can research the car's title history. Inspect the title for "salvage," "rebuilt or similar notations.
■ **www.carfax.com** and **www.autocheck.com** sell information on history of vehicles.
■ The National Highway Traffic Safety Administration (www.nhtsa.dot.gov) lists VINs of its crash-test vehicles and will let you search an online database of manufacturer service bulletins.
■ The Center for Auto Safety (www.autosafety.org) provides information on safety defects, recalls, and lemons, as well as service bulletins.
■ Visit www.safetyforum.com for a free online search of its database of lemons registered by previous owners.

## BEWARE: CURB STONING & TITLE WASHING:

Curb stoning occurs when a dealer has an inferior or damaged car that can't sell on a lot. Dealer gives the car to a salesperson to sell through the classifieds, as if it was a private party sale. A title history report will show that title recently changed hands and could reveal that it is a lemon or an otherwise branded car. Be suspicious if seller's name is different from the name on title. Title washing occurs when scam artists try to sell a salvage vehicle by concealing its history of damage from a buyer. Although vehicle's title should show if it has been damaged or salvaged, some states do not document titles in the same way as other states. By moving a vehicle and its title through several different states, con artists try to "wash" out the title branding of salvage or damage. The way to avoid this trick is to buy only from reputable dealers and/or to get a title guarantee in writing.

### BUYING FROM A PRIVATE OWNER CHECKLIST

When shopping for a used car, ask private owners these questions before running off to see the vehicle. You'll save yourself tons of frustration and needless trips.

**What condition is the car in?** _____
_____

**What's wrong with the car?** _____
_____

**Do you sell many cars?**                    Yes        No
If the answer is yes, hang up the phone.
*Private advertiser* may have a sideline selling problematic cars or is a dealer.

**Are you the original owner?**          Yes        No

**How long have you owned the car?** _____
_____

**Who drove the car?** _____
_____

Insurance companies charge single males under 25 higher premiums than males and females over 25, because they tend to do more cruising and partying than caring for their cars. Older drivers, particularly woman, are usually more careful, maintaining the car according to schedule and driving slower. Don't underrate this factor.

**Has the car been maintained according to the manufacturer's manual?**          Yes        No

**How often has the oil been changed?** _____
_____

**Do you have repair receipts?**          Yes        No

**When was the car last inspected?** _____
_____

*Super important* in states where the title cannot be transferred unless the car passes an inspection.

**Where did you buy the car?** _____
_____

**Where did you drive the car?** _____
_____

Freeway miles (hopefully), long trips, or the city.

**What is the mileage?** _____
_____

**Is the odometer correct?**          Yes        No

**Has the car ever been painted?**          Yes        No

**If so, why?** _____
_____

**Has the car ever been recalled?**          Yes        No

**If so, may I see verification of the correction?**          Yes        No

**Can I take the car to my mechanic?**          Yes        No

**Are there any liens on the car?**          Yes        No

**Special notes:** _____

**CAUTION: A car reaches the twilight of its life around:**     100,000 miles = 4-cylinder
125,000 miles = 6-cylinder
150.000 miles = 8-cylinder

By Jove, I think you've got it!

Make copies of this checklist for each vehicle you drive. Plan your own test route and not the scenic tour that the salesperson will have you go on. Your route should include:

**In town:**
- ❑ An area that has steep hills, rough and bumpy roads.
- ❑ A side street, so you can check out the cornering ability, braking power and turning circle.

**On the interstate:**
- ❑ Check acceleration and passing ability.

**Option:**
- ❑ You might include your travel route from home to work.

Your evaluation of the vehicles you test should give you a clear picture of which car is the best for you.

## YOUR FUTURE CAR?

**Make:** _____

**Model:** _____ **Year:** _____

**Body Type:** ☐ Coupe ☐ Convertible ☐ Hatchback

☐ Sedan ☐ Station Wagon ☐ Minivan ☐ Pickup

☐ Utility ☐ SUV Other: _____

**Type of Drive:**

☐ Front ☐ Rear ☐ 4-Wheel ☐ All-Wheel

**Size of Engine:** _____ Liters _____ Cylinders

☐ Turbocharged ☐ Supercharged

**Horsepower:** _____ **Torque:** _____

**Miles Per Gallon:** City _____ Highway _____

☐ Unleaded Gas ☐ Premium Gas ☐ Diesel

**Transmission:** ☐ Manual ☐ Automatic

**Resale Value:**

2 Years $_____ 4 Years $_____

**Suggested Price:** $_____

**Dealer Invoice:** $_____

**Target Price:** $_____

**Comments:**

## Time to test the CAR

Judge the vehicle in the 6 major categories below: For all but safety features, use the following scale:

| | |
|---|---|
| **0 – Bomb** | **3 – C** |
| **1 – F** | **4 – B** |
| **2 – D** | **5 – A** |

**1. Comfort and Convenience:**

Entry and exit: ____
All-around visibility: ____
Use of controls: ____
Seat comfort: ____
Front and rear legroom: ____
Headroom: ____
Trunk or cargo space: ____
Interior noise level: ____
**TOTAL** (40 points maximum): ____

**2. Ride and Handling:**

Engine and transmission smoothness: ____
Cornering stability: ____
Smoothness over bumps: ____
Steering response: ____
Turning circle: ____
**TOTAL** (25 Points maximum: ____

**3. Acceleration and Braking:**

Acceleration from stop: ____
Acceleration to pass: ____
Lane-change quickness: ____
Hill-climbing power: ____
Braking ability: ____
**TOTAL** (25 points maximum): ____

**4. Production Quality:**

Absence of squeaks and rattles: ____
Quality (fit, finish and paint job: ____
**TOTAL** (10 points maximum): ____

**5. Design Quality:**

Exterior: ____
Interior ambiance: ____
**TOTAL** (10 points maximum): ____

**6. Safety Equipment:**

10-Points standard    5-Points optional    0-Points none

Driver-side bag:       ☐ Standard....................: ____
Passenger air bag: ☐ Standard....................: ____
Anti-lock brakes:      ☐ Standard   ☐ Optional: ____
Traction control:      ☐ Standard   ☐ Optional: ____
TOTAL (40 points maximum): ____

### The Final Tabulation:

1. Comfort and Convenience: ____
2. Ride and Handling: ____
3. Acceleration and Braking: ____
4. Production Quality: ____
5. Design Quality: ____
6. Safety Equipment: ____

**TOTAL (150 points maximum)**

C-6

**Why should you buy a used car?** A new car loses value (depreciates) as soon as you drive it off the dealer's lot. That's why year old cars are worth significantly less than what you paid for them from the factory. If you want to beat the high cost of depreciation and save money, buy a used car that's two to three years old and with low mileage instead of a new one.

From yesteryear, the stigma that's always been associated with buying a used car is that "you're buying someone else's problem." Presently, car dealerships have many used cars that come off two or three year leases in great condition. Most dealerships are even offering extended warranties that are almost like those that you would get with buying a new car.

**Find a reliable model:** You can lower your risk of purchasing a used lemon if you buy a vehicle that has a good dependability record. ***Consumer Reports*** publishes an annual list of good and bad used cars. The report is based on an ***"Annual Survey"*** from its reader's miseries dealing with repair shops on their automobiles. This annual list depicts the dependability and history between the years 1995 to 2002. From those records, they put together a list of the best and worst used cars.

## Where can you buy a "good" used car?

**Superstores and new-car dealerships:** They generally carry the best quality in used cars, because many of them still have the original manufacturer's warranty in effect, on account of a short two or three year lease. Many of your dealers today offer their own warranties as well, but they are normally in effect just long enough to let you make sure the vehicle is not a lemon (it might be longer on some high-end models).
**Tip on warranties:** Try to negotiate an extension to the manufacturer's original warranty.
**Important features:** New-car dealers have onsite repair facilities. Some dealers lease used cars.
**Bottom line price:** Prices at superstores and new-car dealerships tend to be higher.

**Independent used-car dealers:** Their stock may be lower in quality. Independent dealers usually get their stock from superstore or new-car dealership rejects, wholesale auctions, police departments, taxi fleets, etc.
**Important features:** Most of your independent dealers, who sell only used cars, usually do not have a repair shop, which means their cars may have cosmetic repairs only before being ***"paraded"*** out on the sales lot.
**Bottom line price:** Prices are usually lower than a superstore / new-car dealership. Check with the Better Business Bureau for past consumer abuses.

**Auctions, banks, credit unions, etc.:** What is the condition of these cars? Cars may immediately break down, run in reverse, have unsafe conditions, odometers turned back, etc. Cars normally auctioned off have been abandoned, repossessed or seized.
**Auction tips:** For auctions, look in local papers; Internet for local Municipal, State and Government auctions (see **pages 80-84**).
**Bottom line price:** You can pick up some great deals at an auction, so bring cash and remember that all sales are usually final (buyers beware).

**Car rental companies:** Usually, the quality of most rental cars is very good, because they have been well maintained and have service records available. In addition, rental cars are often driven for under a year and for relatively short distances.
**Rental car tip:** To find out when is the next rental sale to the public, contact the rental companies.
**Bottom line price:** You can find some great deals, but you cannot trade in your car to buy a rental car and be prepared to arrange your own financing. It is possible to rent the car first and then have your rental payments applied to the car if you purchase it.

**Private owners:** Try to buy from someone you know, because they will be less likely to lie to you. This may allow you to double-check their version of the car's maintenance history.
**Caution:** Before you buy from a private owner, take the car to a reliable mechanic to get their expert opinion.
**Bottom line price:** Private owners tend to charge the lowest prices and be more willing to wheel and deal.

## Do homework before you buy

- Start here with these helpful websites:
   1. www.edmunds.com
   2. www.carbuyingtips.com
- Your best buy will be a car less than three years old, with warranty and low mileage.
- Avoid high performance cars, because your insurance will be sky-high.
- Call the auto safety hotline at **1-800-424-9393** to find out if the model you're looking at has a defect or **www-odi.nhtsa.dot.gov/cars/problems/recalls**
- **National Automobile Dealers Association:** The price of a used car is usually close to retail in a "blue book" (NADA), so look for the price range you can afford. You can buy a "blue book" for used car prices, for around $10.00 in any bookstore or contact: Retail Consumer's Guide at **1-800-544-6232** or **www.nada.com** or **www.nadaguides.com**
- If you are dealing with an independent dealership, check with the Better Business Bureau (BBB). The dealer must follow the Federal Trade Commission ***"used car rule,"*** which means the buyer guide must be in the window informing you of all warranties. The car must be safe, but the dealer is not required to tell you of known defects. If you buy from a private seller, you have little protection under the law. You can usually save money, because the seller has probably bought another car, but the car is sold in ***"as is"*** condition.

## Homework finished. Start shopping!
- Try not to fall in love with a certain car too quickly, even if you want one badly, do not show it.
- Look and be informed. Whether you're going to a dealer or an individual seller, show up with a pen, paper, and calculator. Let the seller see that you are in the know by having relevant information about the car(s) you're looking at, such as the price of the car when it was new, whether it has manufacturer problems (recalls), what it will be insured for, safety records, and fuel efficiency.
- Always inspect a vehicle in the daylight. Lights can play tricks and not allow you to see all the defects.
- When buying from a dealer, ask how long the car has been on the lot (longer dealer has had it around, the more eager he'll be to sell). Dealers often have larger margins on used cars than on new ones, so don't be afraid to offer your own estimate of the car's value, not theirs.

- Test-drive the car at different speeds. Be sure you are covered by insurance. Take the car to a reliable mechanic for a possible list and estimate of needed work (if repairs needed, use cost as a bargaining tool).
- Now that you have decided to buy and your offer is accepted, the following things will happen. If you went through a dealer, you will receive a "contract of sale." This includes:

1. Guarantees, if any
2. Full price
3. Description
4. Trade-in allowance
5. Repayment terms
6. Insurance premium, if applicable
7. Sales tax
8. Finance charge, if financed through the dealer.

Do not sign a contract with any blank spaces. Specify conditions. Example: If your state requires an emission test for registration, make a simple condition that the auto must pass emissions. You should also get a mileage disclosure.
- Make a final check of the automobile before signing (signals, radio, under the hood, etc.).
- If you pay cash, write on the check "full purchase price." If you have to arrange financing, be sure to have the contract state "based upon being able to finance," or something similar. To avoid this problem, have your financing in place before signing.
- Don't forget your sales tax and ownership tax. Some states have very high ownership (personal property tax). Call your Department of Motor Vehicles for more information.
- Get a bill of sale. You will receive the title and registration at the time of sale. If you finance the car, the bank, etc. will hold the title.

Do I have a deal for you, Kid! I've been waiting to show this dreamboat to someone like you that would really appreciate the value of this **"one in a million beauty."**

Gee, I don't know, Mr.

What's not to like? Go ahead; kick the tires…except this one. All this tire needs is just a little air and love.

Do you have something else I can look at?

Tell you what I'm going to do; I'll throw in some used floor mats. Do we have a deal?

But, umm, what's the price, Mr.?

I'm going to make an offer you can't refuse. How about 24% financing, with 7-year payments?

**WOW!** Sounds too good to be true. Where do I sign?

- Repossessed cars: Look for repossessed cars at a bank or credit union. When you find a car that you are interested in, test drive it and have it checked by a mechanic. Remember that banks and credit unions are not in the automobile business, so they want to dispose of repossessions and will normally finance the transaction. **Do not pay the asking price.**

## Examine a car's title for rip-offs:

Don't pay a penny for a used car until you have carefully examined the title of the car. The following title problems are potential signs of a rip-off in the making.
- If the title is not in the same name as the seller, ask why. Ask if the person is authorized to sell the vehicle. Contact the owner listed on the title before proceeding. If the dealer's name is on the title, the car may have been bought at an auction, a bad sign. The history of an auction car is difficult to trace.
- If the title lists an owner from a different state, has a post office box for an address, or is an auction company, be very suspicious. This could be a car with a history of problems.
- Make sure that there are no liens listed on the title. You do not want to be held responsible for someone else's debts.
- Be suspicious if the title is new for a car that is already several years old. Beware if it is stamped "duplicate," because it could be a fake. Look for staple marks purposely covering up alterations or any changes in the original printing on the document. Look out for any decimal points added to the odometer.
- If there are any rubber-stamped codes on the title, check with the DMV to determine what the code means. The stamp on the title (called branding) could mean the vehicle was damaged, salvaged, a lemon, or stolen and recovered. It could also mean that the odometer has already turned over 100,000 miles or that the odometer reading has been altered. For example, the mileage shown as 37,564.2 was actually 75,642 before the fraud.
- For a small fee, you can check out the history (problems) of a used car at: **www.carfax.com** or **www.autocheck.com**.

## Price the car through your Credit Union

| Wholesale | Retail | Dealers Price |
|-----------|--------|---------------|
| **$2,500** | **$3,500** | **$4,995** |

Normally, you have to get on your hands and knees, and then beg a dealer to drop $500 off the price of a used car, if you step foot onto a dealership unprepared to purchase a vehicle. Example:

| Dealers price: | $4,995 |
|----|----|
| After all day negotiations: | - 500 |
| Final price: | $4,495 |

**Solution:** A simple way to bypass the *"all day negotiations"* nightmare is to call your credit union and get the **HIGH** and **LOW** book information on a car you want. Add the two prices together, divide by two and this will be your offer that you can feel safe and confident to bargain with.

**Example:**  Add **HIGH** book price  $3,500
Add **LOW** book price  + 2,500
$6,000
÷ 2
$3,000

Dealers price:  $4,995
Your offer:  -$3,000
$1,995

**YOU SAVE**
**$1,995**

**69**

Nowadays, there is a wealth of information to use when purchasing new cars, however, most consumers rush out to a dealership, without any advice, unprepared to purchase a car. From this point forward, make a pact with yourself never to set foot on a car lot before putting in the necessary research to purchase a vehicle.

The following is an effective list of information on how to get the best deal when looking to buy a new car.

**Start your research with the Internet:** The Internet is a great place to begin your research to buy a new car. The web sites below will provide information such as:
1. Reviews and invoice price on new cars.
2. Advice on how to buy a new car.
3. Incentives, rebates and holdbacks in your area.
4. New dealer tricks (**www.carbuyingtips.com**).
5. Guide to discount buying sites.
6. Online car loan sites.
7. Extended warranty tips and more.
8. Help with purchasing vehicle at lowest price.

- www.ftc.gov/bcp/menues/consumer/autos.shtm
- http://consumerguideauto.howstuffworks.com/ consumer-guide.htm
- www.edmunds.com
- www.caranddriver.com
- www.costcoauto.com/enterzipcode.aspx? gotourl=%2fDefault.aspx
- www.cars.com
- www.autos.com
- www.autoweb.com
- www.invoicedealers.com
- www.car.com
- www.autousa.com

9. Look to sites that have knowledge of manufacturers who are offering rebates that will help lower the cost of cars that you are interested in. To learn more, visit:
- **www.carsdirect.com** and
- **www.autopedia.com/html/Rebate.html**

### CR Tips on how to buy a new car

A great place to learn and get good deals on new cars is *Consumer Reports (CR)*. According to *CR*:

**Begin by narrowing your choices:** Visit a few dealerships; decide what type of vehicle and size fits your needs. Do not fall in love with a particular vehicle. Absolutely, do not start negotiating with a dealership at this time. *GO HOME!*

**Find out the "invoice cost" of the car:**
*Consumer Reports,* for $14 on one car and $12 for each additional vehicle, will send online, mail or fax you a detailed report of the *"invoice"* cost of what a dealer paid for a car that you are interested in, and *"sticker"* price of what the dealer wants you to pay for the auto. This report also includes the invoice and sticker prices for all options and packages; current rebates, factory-to-dealer incentives and holdbacks.

Contact *CR*-New Car Price Service at **800-888-8275** or visit: **www.ConsumerReports.org/carprices/new6**

**Do the research:** Make a worksheet for each car. Write down the make, model and trim line. List each option, or

both columns (fixed charge and dealers take no markup on it). Total columns and subtract any factory-to-dealer rebate from the *"invoice"* column. The difference between the final *"invoice"* and *"sticker"* price represents how much bargaining room you have.

| Vehicle Worksheet | | | | |
|---|---|---|---|---|
| **Make:** | | **Model:** | | |
| **Year:** | | **Trim line:** | | |
| Invoice | $ | Sticker | | $ |
| Option 1 | $ | Option 1 | | $ |
| 2 | $ | 2 | | $ |
| 3 | $ | 3 | | $ |
| 4 | $ | 4 | | $ |
| | | | | |
| | | | | |
| | | | | |
| | | | | |
| Destination Charge | $ | Destination Charge | | $ |
| Sub-total | $ | | | |
| Rebates | - $ | | | |
| Factory to Rebates | - $ | | | |
| Holdbacks | - $ | | | |
| **Total** | $ | **Total** | | $ |

**When is the best time to buy a new car?**
**Aug**, **Sept** and *last two weeks in* **Dec** are the best time to bargain for a new vehicle. Other options are to arrive late to a car lot in the daytime, particularly on Saturday, when their salespeople are tired and worn down from other consumers low-ball tactics. Another idea is to go late in the month, when dealers are closing their books, and want good sales figures, or when the salespeople are under strong orders to meet sales quotas.

**Go to the dealership and start bargaining:**
- Bring your worksheet to the dealership.
- When you get to the dealership, find the receptionist and ask for the fleet manager. Also, do not ask a saleperson for the fleet manager, because they may claim to be fleet manager. A fleet manager will not have to run back and forth to the sales manager for pricing. If they do, more than likely, they are not the fleet manager, and just a salesperson impersonating one.
- Explain to the fleet manager precisely what you want and car that interests you.
- Investigate the window sticker and see if it differs from your figures. If it does, find out why.
- Examine the vehicle carefully for dents and scratches. Once you take delivery, they are all yours.
- Ask if there are any undisclosed incentives that they are sharing with the customers.
- Submit your figures to the fleet manager and ask for the *rock-bottom* markup over dealer cost that the dealership will agree to. If they dispute your figures, ask to see documents that prove why they are wrong.
- When negotiating, always bargain up from the invoice and not down from the dealer's sticker price. Do not discuss financing, leases, or your trade-in, until you reach a solid price for the new car.
- Most dealers don't own the cars they sell. They pay carrying costs until they are sold, so paying $200

below or $300 over invoice is fair for most models. Never pay more than $300 above dealer cost for a car valued at $30,000 or less. If the fleet manager says **NO**, leave. If you are dealing with a sales rep and he/she states that it has to be approved by the sales manager and returns with a note saying **NO**, stick around. This is a common trick. Tell them you want a fast answer and price in writing.

■ **Beware:** You might have to pay the *"full sticker"* price or close to it, for a hot-new model.

■ As for sales (and prizes), dealers just mark up prices, so they can mark them down.

■ A conveyance or documentation fee may be added into the final price to cover the cost of preparing the paperwork of $300 or more. You probably will not be able to bargain the fee away, so add it into the price of the car.

■ If you are dealing with a salesperson, you'll probably be made to wait for long periods of time while a salesperson submits your offer to the dealership's sales manager. Long waits is their designed strategy to wear you down. Stay focused, because you might not bargain well if you are upset or angry.

■ Don't tell the Fleet Manager/Salesperson what you're willing to pay each month, because this will give them the excuse to spread your payments over a longer time period. Longer loan terms will allow you lower payments, however, you will pay more for the car in the long run, including possible higher interest rate.

■ Do not rush into a decision. A deal that is good today should be good tomorrow or even a week later.

■ Let the dealership know that you're willing to shop for a better deal through their competitors. If you feel you are being jerked-around, get up and leave.

■ Before you talk about leasing or financing, be sure you have a rock solid price for your new car.

■ Do not give any money to show good faith. You can show good faith, when they reach your budgeted price, which will help you to get a *"better price"* that much quicker.

**Your trade in:** Do not tell the dealer that you have a trade-in until you have agreed on a price. Your trade-in has nothing to do with the price of the car. Walk out, if the dealership says the trade-in value on your old car depends on what you pay for your new car.

■ If you want to trade-in your car, you should know what it is worth first. Libraries and bank loan officers carry copies of the *NADA Official Used Car Guide* or the *Kelly Blue Book* (**www.kbb.com**)*,* which will give you the worth of your car. You can get a verbal quotation, faxed, mailed or downloaded online 24/7 on your used car with prices updated daily through Consumer Reports New Car Price Service for $12. Call **1- 800-888-8275** or visit: **www.consumerreports.org/cro/cars/used-cars.**

■ Eventually they will need to get your trade-in appraised. Before giving them your keys, tell them you want them back immediately after they finish their appraisal. Do not continue to negotiate until you get the keys back. When a dealership keeps your keys, it is a way to intimidate you, and keep you from leaving, so they can continue to negotiate and get the best price out of you.

**After agreeing on a price:** Before signing the contract, check the vehicle again for dents, scratches and parts not aligning correctly. Point out any problems and have them corrected. Once you sign, the car is yours.

■ It is customary to sign the transaction sheet and leave a deposit.

■ Taxes and other charges will be listed at the bottom of the sheet. Know your state laws and your tax rate for automobiles, sometimes the tax rate is different.

■ *Read the contract carefully*. If you believe an item should be included, or you see something you don't like, ask for changes. Make sure an officer at the dealership signs the contract.

**If you're considering a service contract:**
Although a factory warranty is included in the price of a new car, a dealership will definitely offer a service contract to you, which will provide for the repair of problems, or certain specified parts. Manufacturers, dealers, or independent companies offer service contracts. If you're contemplating a service contract, remember it does not go into effect until the factory warranty expires. Keep in mind, a 5-year service contract may only pay claims for 2-years, if the factory warranty is for three years. If mileage is a factor, then be your own judge. Before you decide to purchase a service contract, read it carefully and think about the following questions:

■ What is the difference between the coverage under the warranty and the service contract?

■ What types of repairs are covered?

■ Who pays for the labor and parts?

■ Can repairs be made anywhere or only at a specific place?

■ How long does the service contract last?

■ What is their cancellation and refund policy?

**Finally:** Keep your eyes peeled for:
■ Dealer finance managers that may try to "flip" your purchase into a lease. Look for balloon payment and *"base mileage"* disclosures that indicate a lease.
■ The number of payment months. Instead of 60 months (5 years), it may say 72 months (6 years).
■ Worthless or overpriced add-ons like undercoating, rust proofing, fabric protection, credit life, accident and health or window etching of vehicle identification number.

To learn more, visit:
■ FTC: **www.ftc.gov/bcp/edu/pubs/consumer/autos/ aut11.shtm**
■ FCIC: **www.pueblo.gsa.gov/cic_text/cars/newcar/ newcar.htm**
■ BBB: **www.bbb.org/us/article/buying-a-new-car-405**
■ DMV: **www.dmv.org/autos/buying-new-cars.php**
■ Bankrate.com: **www.bankrate.com/finance/auto/ buying-a-new-car-vs-buying-used.aspx**
■ Consumer Energy Center: www.consumerenergycenter .org/transportation/buying_a_car/index.html

71

Under the federal Consumer Leasing Act, as a consumer, you have rights to information about the costs and terms of a vehicle lease. These pages will help you compare lease offers and negotiate a lease that best fits your financial needs and driving patterns.

The information provided is for a closed-end lease, the most common type of vehicle lease. With closed-end leases, you may return the vehicle at the end of the lease term, pay any end-of-lease costs, and walk away.

## LEASING vs. BUYING A VEHICLE

| LEASING: | BUYING: |
|---|---|
| You use it, but must return it at the end of the lease, unless you choose to buy it. | You own the vehicle and get to keep it at the end of the financing term. |
| Up-front costs may include the first month's payment, a refundable security deposit, a capitalized cost reduction (like a down payment), taxes, registration and other fees. | Up-front costs include the cash price or a down payment, taxes, registration and other fees. |
| Monthly lease payments are usually lower than monthly loan payments because you are paying only for the vehicle's depreciation during the lease term, plus rent charges, taxes, and fees. | Monthly loan payments are usually higher than monthly lease payments because you are paying for the entire purchase price of the vehicle, plus interest and other finance charges, taxes, and fees. |
| You are responsible for any early termination charges if you end the lease early | You are responsible for any pay-off amount if you end the loan early. |
| You may return the vehicle at lease-end, pay any end-of-lease costs, and "walk away." | You may have to sell or trade the vehicle when you decide you want a different vehicle. |
| The lessor has the risk of the future market value of the vehicle. | You have the risk of the vehicle's market value when you trade or sell it. |
| Most leases limit the number of miles you may drive You can negotiate a higher mileage limit and pay a higher monthly payment. You will likely have to pay charges for exceeding those limits if you return the vehicle. | You may drive as many miles as you want, but higher mileage will lower the vehicle's trade-in or resale value. |
| Most leases limit wear to the vehicle during the lease term. You will likely have to pay extra charges for exceeding those limits if you return the vehicle. | There are no limits or charges for excessive wear to the vehicle, but excessive wear will lower the vehicle's trade-in or resale value. |
| At the end of the lease (typically 2-4 years), you may have a new payment either to finance the purchase of the existing vehicle or to lease another vehicle. | At the end of the loan term (typically 4-6 years), you have no further loan payments. |

**Lease calculators:** www.bankrate.com/calculators/auto/auto-lease-calculator.aspx or www.bankrate.com/calculators/auto/buy-or-lease-calculator.aspx

**Beginning, middle, and end-of-lease costs:**
■ **At the beginning of the lease,** you may have to pay your first monthly payment; a refundable security deposit or your last monthly payment; other fees for licenses, registration, and title; a capitalized cost reduction (like a down payment); an acquisition fee (also called a processing or assignment fee); freight or destination charges; and state or local taxes.
■ **During the lease,** you will have to pay your monthly payment; any additional taxes not included in the payment such as sales, use, and personal property taxes; insurance premiums; ongoing maintenance costs; and any fees for late payment. You'll also have to pay for safety and emissions inspections and any traffic tickets. If you end your lease early, you may have to pay substantial early termination charges.
■ **At the end of the lease,** if you don't buy the vehicle, you may have to pay a disposition fee and charges for excess miles and excessive wear.

**Compare different lease offers and negotiate some terms. Consider:**
■ The agreed-upon value of the vehicle--a lower value can reduce your monthly payment
■ Up-front payments, including the capitalized cost reduction
■ The length of the lease
■ The monthly lease payment
■ Any end-of-lease fees and charges
■ Mileage allowed and per-mile charges for excess miles
■ The option to purchase either at lease-end or earlier
■ Whether your lease includes "gap" coverage (protects you if vehicle is stolen or totaled in an accident).
■ Ask for alternatives to advertised specials and other lease offerings.

**Know your rights and responsibilities:** When you lease a vehicle, you have the right to:
■ Use it for an agreed-upon number of months and miles
■ Turn it in at lease-end, pay any end-of-lease fees and charges, and "walk away"
■ Buy the vehicle if you have a purchase option
■ Take advantage of any warranties, recalls, or other services that apply to the vehicle.

**You may be responsible for:**
■ Excess mileage charges when you return the vehicle. Your lease agreement will tell you how many miles you can drive before you must pay for extra miles and how much the per-mile charge will be.
■ Excessive wear charges when you return the vehicle. The standards for excessive wear, such as for body damage or worn tires, are in your lease agreement.
■ Substantial payments if you end the lease early. The earlier you end the lease, the greater these charges are likely to be.

**To learn more:**
■ www.federalreserve.gov/pubs/leasing/default.htm
■ www.leasecompare.com
■ www.carbuyingtips.com/lease.htm
■ www.leaseguide.com/lease03.htm
■ http://auto.howstuffworks.com/how-to-lease-a-car.htm
■ http://guides.wsj.com/personal-finance/buying-a-car/how-to-lease-a-car/
■ www.leaseguide.com/Articles/bad-credit.htm

This checklist will help collect information both before and while you shop for a vehicle lease. The questions feature vehicle leasing that you should consider before signing an agreement. Many terms and conditions in a car lease are negotiable. You can customize a car lease to fit your driving habits and financial needs. Nothing is final until you sign the lease agreement. It's important that you comprehend all the lease provisions before signing.

**1. Before shopping for a Lease:** How much can you afford to pay up front? $_____ Each month? $_____ At lease-end? $_____
Consider the beginning, middle, and end-of-lease costs, not just the monthly payment.

**2, Have you chosen a vehicle?**
_____Make/model/options
Length of time you expect to keep the vehicle? _____

**3. How long do you typically keep a vehicle?** _____
Don't lease for a term longer than you intend to keep the vehicle, because you may have to pay a large charge for early termination. The earlier you end the lease, the greater the charge is likely to be.

**4. How many miles do you drive yearly?** _____
Underestimating your mileage could cost you big at end of the lease. Check the odometer on your current vehicle to estimate the number of miles you normally drive.

**5. Want option in lease to buy the vehicle?** _____
You may want option to buy the vehicle at the end of the lease. However, the terms of the purchase option may affect other terms in the lease.

**6. What is your current insurance coverage:**
Bodily injury, property damage, and liability $_____
Collision and comprehensive $_____

**7. Cost of deductibles:**
Collision $ _____
Comprehensive $_____
**NOTE:** Your lease may require you to carry a higher level of insurance than you currently carry.

**While shopping for a Lease:** Record the following information while you're shopping for a lease to help you evaluate and compare leases. Also, make a copy of a leasing form that you can get from **www.federalreserve. gov/pubs/ leasing/form.htm** and bring with you when shopping. Ask the salesperson to fill out leasing form. If you responded to an advertisement, have the ad with you and compare the terms with other offers.

- **Vehicle year/make/model:** _____
**Lease term (number of months):** _____
**Mileage limit (per year):** _____
- **Amount due at lease signing (total up-front cost)?**
$_____
- **Capitalized cost reduction (down payment)?**
$_____
- **How much are the other costs that are included in the total?** $_____
- **How much credit will you receive for any trade-in or rebates?** $_____
- **What is agreed-upon value of vehicle?** $_____
- **Gross capitalized cost of the lease?** $_____
Ask for an itemization of the gross capitalized cost, and you can usually negotiate amount of some individual items.
- **What is the residual value?** $_____
- **Does lease include option to purchase the vehicle?**
_____
**Purchase-option price, including any purchase-option fee?** $_____ Fixed-price and fair-market-value purchase options may be available.

- **Rent charge?** $_____ This amount is like the interest or finance charge on a loan or credit agreement. You may be able to negotiate this figure, but a change in the amount may affect other amounts in the lease agreement.
- **What is total monthly payment, including taxes?**
$_____ Make sure the payment fits your budget.
- **What is the end-of-lease cost?** $_____
- **Disposition fee and other end-of-lease costs:**
$_____ **NOTE:** Your lease may impose a disposition fee if you do not purchase the vehicle.
- **Per mile charge for any excess miles you drive:**
$_____
- **Have you reviewed the standards for excessive wear?** _____ Your lease should specify these standards.
- **Are you responsible for the maintenance costs under the lease?** _____ You are generally responsible for seeing that the maintenance requirements are met.
**What are the insurance coverage requirements?**
Bodily injury to 1 person $_____
Bodily injury to 2 or more persons per accident $_____
Property damage $_____
- **Maximum deductibles allowed by the lessor?** _____
Check with your insurance company to see what the cost of insurance coverage will be.
Does the lease provide gap coverage if the vehicle is totaled or stolen? _____
If it does not, how much would gap coverage cost?
$_____ Gap coverage pays the difference between the early termination payoff and the insured value of the vehicle. It does not pay for such items as insurance deductibles and past-due payments.
- **How will an early termination payoff be calculated?**
_____ Different methods result in different payoff figures.
- **How much in additional fees, if any, are added to the payoff amount?** $_____
- **Have you asked about alternatives to the advertised lease?** _____ You can compare different lease offers.
- **Have you reviewed a copy of the lease?** _____
Read and understand the lease before you sign it. Make sure any oral promises are stated in the agreement. Federal law requires that you receive important disclosures in writing before you sign a lease agreement. You should receive and keep a copy of your signed lease and any disclosures. The disclosures may be in your lease agreement or on a separate form.
- **Options and Equipment:** Cars of the same make and model will have different prices if they have different options and equipment. Compare options and equipment packages on vehicles you are considering. Consider any differences in options and equipment along with the differences in lease payments to determine which the best choice is for you:

Engine size _____
Automatic transmission _____
Air conditioning _____
Stereo tape player _____
Compact disc player _____
DVD player or other video system _____
Cruise control _____
Power windows _____
Power locks _____
Power seats _____
ABS (anti-lock) brakes _____
Tilt wheel _____
Sun roof/moon roof _____
Premium wheels _____
Global positioning system (GPS) _____
Mechanical breakdown protection _____
Extended warranty _____
Roadside assistance _____
Other _____

**C-6**

Most soldiers have nothing or very little left over from their paycheck, after making a car payment ranging from $350 or higher; then add to the mix auto insurance, gas, maintenance, etc. When I am fortunate to come across soldiers without a car, I encourage them to focus and save at least $2,000 or more, and then once saved, have them take the cash and pay in full for a starter car. However, now that they have a car, but no payments, I want them to pretend that they do have a payment, and sock away the same money they saved to purchase the car. My hope is that they can drive the car and save for 5 years or longer. Likewise, for soldiers who have car payments, once paid off, I want them to deposit the ex-payment into savings or investment. Later, when these savers need a new vehicle, they can finance it themselves by using a secured or collateral loan at a low interest rate (for more information on loans, see **page 23** and **138**).

The chart below, illustrates deposits of 5-years saved monthly (without interest) in different denominations.

| $100 | $125 | $150 | $175 | $200 | $225 | $250 | $275 | $300 |
|---|---|---|---|---|---|---|---|---|
| $6,000 | $7,500 | $9,000 | $10,500 | $12,000 | $13,500 | $15,000 | $16,500 | $18,000 |

| $325 | $350 | $375 | $400 | $425 | $450 | $500 | $600 | $700 |
|---|---|---|---|---|---|---|---|---|
| $19,500 | $21,000 | $22,500 | $24,000 | $22,500 | $27,500 | $30,000 | $36,000 | $42,000 |

The example below shows two soldiers purchasing a new car. Soldier "A," having nothing in savings will finance his car through a typical bank loan. Soldier "B" having saved $325 monthly in savings account for 5 years, will finance the car himself, using savings as secured or collateral loan from his bank or lending institution that will give him a better loan.

| Soldier "A": $19,000 new car loan | | Soldier "B" = Finances $19,000 new car loan | |
|---|---|---|---|
| Savings in account: | 0 | Savings in account: | 19,500 |
| 5-Year bank loan @ 6%: | 377 | 5-Year collateral loan @ 6%: | 377 |
| Total cost of 60 payments: | 22,620 | Total cost of 60 payments: | 22,620 |
| Interest paid on car loan: | 3,120 | Interest paid on car loan: | 3,120 |
| Interest earned from savings: | 0 | Interest Earned from $19,500 @ 10%: | 11,941 |
| Interest made subtracting loan: | 0 | Interest made subtracting loan: | 8,821 |
| Savings in account after loan paid: | 0 | Savings in account after loan paid: | 31,441 |

**A tale of missed opportunity and fortune:** Whenever I hear the dreaded words, *"I have a car payment,"* I explain to that individual what the cost of the car will run him/her over time. Typically, their jaw drops when they learn the truth that they will be wasting hundreds of thousands of dollars and in some cases millions, because of their car payment.

**EXAMPLE:** 20 year-old with $300 a month 5 year car payments stands to lose $1,094,184 by age 65. However, same monthly payment of $300 put into savings for 5 years at 10%, amount would grow to $1,094,184 by age 65.

The projections below are based on the concept of when your car is paid-off, you continue payments and deposit them into a 10% account for the next 5 years (Plan: drive car for an additional 5 years) and allow sum to mature until age 65:

| Age | $100 | $150 | $200 | $250 | $300 | $350 | $400 | $450 | $500 |
|---|---|---|---|---|---|---|---|---|---|
| 18 | $441,324 | 661,986 | 882,648 | 1,103,310 | 1,323,972 | 1,544,634 | 1,765,296 | 1,985,958 | 2,206,620 |
| 19 | $401,196 | 601,794 | 802,392 | 1,002,990 | 1,203,588 | 1,404,186 | 1,604,784 | 1,805,382 | 2,005,980 |
| 20 | $364,728 | 547,092 | 729,456 | 911,820 | 1,094,184 | 1,276,548 | 1,462,912 | 1,641,276 | 1,823,640 |
| 21 | $331,572 | 497,358 | 663,144 | 828,930 | 994,716 | 1,160,502 | 1,326,288 | 1,492,074 | 1,657,860 |
| 22 | $301,428 | 452,142 | 602,856 | 753,570 | 904,284 | 1,054,998 | 1,205,712 | 1,356,426 | 1,507,140 |
| 23 | $274,020 | 411,030 | 548,040 | 685,050 | 822,060 | 959,070 | 1,096,080 | 1,233,090 | 1,370,100 |
| 24 | $249,108 | 373,662 | 498,216 | 622,770 | 747,324 | 871,878 | 996,432 | 1,120,986 | 1,245,540 |
| 25 | $226,452 | 339,678 | 452,904 | 566,130 | 679,356 | 792,582 | 905,808 | 1,019,034 | 1,132,260 |
| 26 | $205,860 | 308,790 | 411,720 | 514,650 | 617,580 | 720,510 | 823,440 | 926,370 | 1,029,300 |
| 27 | $187,152 | 280,728 | 374,304 | 467,880 | 561,456 | 655,032 | 748,608 | 842,184 | 935,760 |
| 28 | $170,148 | 255,222 | 340,296 | 425,370 | 510,444 | 595,518 | 680,592 | 765,666 | 850,740 |
| 29 | $154,680 | 232,020 | 309,360 | 386,700 | 464,040 | 541,380 | 618,720 | 696,060 | 773,400 |
| 30 | $140,616 | 210,924 | 281,232 | 351,540 | 421,848 | 492,156 | 562,464 | 632,772 | 703,080 |
| 31 | $127,836 | 191,754 | 255,672 | 319,590 | 383,508 | 447,426 | 511,344 | 575,262 | 639,180 |
| 32 | $116,208 | 174,312 | 232,416 | 290,520 | 348,624 | 406,728 | 466,032 | 522,936 | 581,040 |
| 33 | $105,636 | 158,454 | 211,272 | 264,090 | 316,908 | 369,726 | 422,544 | 475,362 | 528,180 |
| 34 | $ 96,036 | 144,054 | 192,072 | 240,090 | 288,108 | 336,126 | 384,144 | 432,162 | 480,180 |
| 35 | $ 87,312 | 130,968 | 174,624 | 218,280 | 261,936 | 305,592 | 349,248 | 392,904 | 436,560 |
| 36 | $ 79,368 | 119,052 | 158,736 | 198,420 | 238,104 | 277,788 | 317,472 | 357,156 | 396,840 |
| 37 | $ 72,156 | 108,234 | 144,312 | 180,390 | 216,468 | 252,546 | 288,624 | 324,702 | 360,780 |
| 38 | $ 65,592 | 98,388 | 131,184 | 163,980 | 196,776 | 229,572 | 262,368 | 295,164 | 327,960 |
| 39 | $ 59,628 | 89,442 | 119,256 | 149,070 | 178,884 | 208,698 | 238,512 | 268,326 | 298,140 |
| 40 | $ 54,204 | 81,306 | 108,408 | 135,510 | 162,612 | 189,714 | 216,816 | 243,918 | 271,020 |

This year I hit 271,000 miles on my vehicle and it's still running strong. To get extra miles out of your car, begin with your owner's manual. Read suggested maintenance schedule and stick to it (most warranties are void if prescribed maintenance schedule is not followed). Therefore, preventive care = money saved. Besides, it is easier to schedule your car for maintenance than repairs at the worst time. If you decide to sell your car with low mileage, you will reap benefits from careful maintenance. Once a week, open the hood of your car (while engine is cold), and follow the life saving maintenance directions.

■ **Check Engine Oil (and Drive train):** Add oil if level is low (engine oil is #1 of all liquids for your car). Do not mix brands of oil, which breaks down protective components of the oil, leaving engine vulnerable. If changing brands, drain oil and change filter. Check engine oil weekly before starting car. Drain and replace oil every 3,000 miles or three months. Use 10W-30 oil, unless temperature drops below freezing, then use 5W-30 oil. For synthetic oil, drain and replace oil and filter every 7,500 miles or every six months. If synthetic oil is too costly, use one quart along with your regular oil. This should give you added protection of synthetic oil without extra cost. If you get oil changed at a shop, make sure quality filter is used (such as Purolator, Hastings or Atlas), it's money well spent. If not, buy your own filter at an auto part store and take with you. To keep oil clean between changes, select the biggest oil filter that will fit. Most cars accept either a "tall" or "short" filter. Tall always provides better filtration.

■ **Drive Train Oil:** Checking drivetrain oil is better left to mechanics. Ask your mechanic to check drivetrain next time they change your motor oil.

■ **Antifreeze / Coolant Level:** Most cars have see-through reservoirs with level markings (check when engine is cool). Pour in 50/50 solution of permanent antifreeze and water (keep 1 inch below filler neck). If level drops, have mechanic check for leak (leaking coolant can be disastrous). Check monthly or every 1,000 miles if under heavy use. Aluminum engines of today require proper mixture of coolant and additives to prevent corrosion and acid buildup. Fail to make periodic changes, you increase chances of blown head gasket or ruined cylinder head. Coolant turns acidic from combustion gases leaking into cooling system. Change coolant every two years or 25,000 miles. Dealer or experienced mechanic should do service for you. If done wrong, an air bubble can cause a blown head gasket.

■ **Brake Fluid:** If low, add approved fluid for car and check for possible leaks. Keep the fluid ½ inch from top unless otherwise marked and check monthly. Having brake fluid changed may prevent expensive brake repairs or catastrophic brake failure. Change fluid and inspect brakes every 30,000 miles or two years. Some ABS parts are ruined by old brake fluid (very costly mistake).

■ **Air Filter:** Once a month, take air filter and tap it against ground to clean and then run water through it for thorough cleaning (extends life of filter); however, tapping and water won't help if filter is clogged with oil). Replace air filter every 30,000 miles (more, if you drive in sand and dust). Furthermore, consider installing a reusable, long-life air filter. These filters can be cleaned and reused and do a serviceable job of filtering air.

■ **Battery and Terminals:** Check for loose cable connection and corrosion (above all during cold weather). Check battery fluid levels, covers and battery plates once a month. Always buy and install biggest and best battery, with longest warranty, that will fit in battery tray. Longer life, bigger battery, helps alternator to keep charged, and car starts better during cold weather. Replace battery six months before warranty expires. A marginal battery will require charging system to work full-time, possibly burning out alternator (costly repair).

■ **Fan Belts / Drive Belts and Hoses (check monthly):** Check belts with flashlight and replace worn, glazed or frayed ones. Tighten them when they have more than ½ inch of slack when depressed between the pulleys. Check hoses connecting motor to rest of car. Replace damaged hoses and tighten clamps when leaking. Inferior quality drive belts, timing belts, and hoses can fail prematurely (in some cases, damage other parts of engine). Best to stick with brand name parts.

■ **Transmission fluid:** Engine should be warm and running (parking brake on). Add fluid if low. Do not mix fluid types or overfill. Check every 3,000 miles or three months. Cars with front wheel drive (mainly, automatics), have expensive transmissions. It's cheaper to have transmission serviced than to have it fixed. Most cars with front wheel drive need service every 25,000 miles (more for city driving). Cars with rear wheel drive can run 50,000 miles between services. Many automatic transmissions have replaceable filters, but some have filters that are cleaned and reused. Ask dealer which type of filter system your vehicle uses. Don't pay for filter replacement if it's supposed to be reused, or let them reuse old filter. For service, use transmission specialist or dealership. Manual transmissions and differentials require less care and can withstand more abuse, and no filters to replace. Manual transmissions with front wheel drive have transaxles (differential located in front axle). Rear wheel drives have separate differentials (in rear axle). Have differential or transaxle serviced every 50,000 miles.

■ **Power-Steering Fluid:** Check fluid when car is warm (in park), by removing, wiping and reinserting reservoir dipstick. Fluid should be maintained between "full" and add" markers. Check every 6,000 miles or six months. Most carmakers don't call for power steering fluid changes, but dirty fluid can cause power steering failure. Change power steering fluid every 30,000 "miles (plus filter), when applicable. Power steering repairs are very expensive, but power steering fluid changes are cheap insurance against major problems later on.

■ **Tune-ups:** Follow your owner's manual instructions for regular tune-ups, typically every 30,000 miles. However, some cars can run 60,000 and even 100,000 miles between tune-ups. Tuning a car regularly can be done yourself with the aid of owner's manual, or by a trained mechanic whom you know and trust.

■ **Exterior Tires:** For recommend pressure; check tire itself or sticker on the driver's-side doorjamb for level, probably between 26 and 36 pounds per square inch (psi). Check with a gauge when tires are cool (check spare tire). Inspect for cuts, bulges, nails, and excessive wear. Uneven wear indicates misalignment or out-of-balance tires. Rotate tires every 5,000 to 10,000 miles and align periodically, or whenever you notice the car veering to one side in order to extend their life. In most cases, when you buy tires, you can often get tires rotated free, simply by asking. When mechanics take your wheels off, they replace them with the use of an air-driven impact gun, which often over-torques the lug nuts. This can warp the brake rotors and permanently damage them. Therefore, whenever your wheels are remounted at a shop, retighten lug nuts yourself. A torque wrench is inexpensive and easy to use.

**C-6**

Feeling ripped off by the escalating price of gasoline these days. Utilize the great ideas below to help you save and go further on a tank of gas.

**Check the Internet for cheapest gas prices:** Find lowest gas prices in your local area by using.
- www.motortrend.com/gas_prices
- www.gasbuddy.com
- www.gaspricewatch.com

**Benefits of club memberships:** See what club memberships, wholesale clubs, automobile clubs, and number of other organizations offer as gas discounts to members. Some grocery stores even provide money saving coupons for gasoline with their grocery receipts.

**Pay with gas card:** If you prefer to use credit at the pump, think about getting a gasoline credit card that offers a 5% or10% rebate back on every purchase.

**Credit and debit cards:** Some credit and debit cards provide reward points, coupons or other benefits for your purchase, so you can offset the price of gas with savings somewhere else.

**Buy gas in the middle of the week:** Weekends and holidays often see slightly higher fuel prices, so if you can fill up mid-week, you may save a few cents per gallon.

**Buy gas in the morning:** Get up to **5%** more gas in the summer if you fill up your gas tank before sun gets hot and expands gas in the station's fuel tanks.

**Fill your car with regular gas:** Most cars do not need high-octane fuel to run efficiently. In truth, low-octane fuel is great for energy conservation, due to less crude oil per gallon. Using premium gas in a car intended to run on regular wastes gas, money, and causes car problems. However, using regular gas in a car intended to run on premium can quickly destroy an engine.

**Keep tires inflated:** The Department of Energy estimates that properly inflated tires can save the average car owner **3.3%** with each tank of gas. Under-inflated tires can lower gas mileage by 0.4% for every 1 psi drop in pressure of all four tires. Bias-ply tires are not as fuel-efficient as radial tires. Properly inflated tires are safer and last longer.

**Use correct oil:** You can improve your gas mileage by **1%-2%** by using the manufacturer's approved grade of motor oil. Look for motor oil that says *"Energy Conserving"* on the API performance symbol, to be sure it contains friction-reducing additives.

**Get tune-ups:** Two worn-out spark plugs can cost you **20%** or more of your fuel economy. If your car has a faulty oxygen sensor, your gas mileage may improve as much as **40%**. Tune-ups will improve performance as well as gas mileage (estimated annual savings is $53).

**Change dirty air filter:** When changing dirty air filter, you can improve car's gas mileage by as much as 10% and protect the engine too.

**Change your filthy fuel filter:** Clean fuel is crucial for long engine life. Change your fuel filter every 10,000 miles or check owner's manual for schedule.

**Warm your car up:** A cold engine will use about **20%** more gas than a warm one, so warm up your car briefly and at first drive slowly.

**Avoid excessive idling:** An Idling engine gets 0 miles per gallon and devours up to 1/2 gallon of gas per hour, You're better off turning car off. In addition, it takes less gas to turn car back on again than it does to leave it on.

**Drive within speed limit:** Gas mileage decreases rapidly at speeds above 60 mph. You can save an average of **7%** to **23%** by driving within speed limit. When driving, you'll pay $0.10 for every 5 mph over 60 mph.
**Take your time getting there:** Rapid acceleration, speeding and braking wastes gas. It can lower your gas mileage by **33%** on highway and by **5%** driving in town.

**Should I or shouldn't I use air conditioning?**
City driving uses up to *3 miles per gallon* when using AC, but if you drive at a constant speed while driving on a highway, AC use doesn't matter.

**Lighten your load:** Don't carry needless gear and luggage in a vehicle. Gasoline mileage decreases 1%-2% for every extra 100 lbs of weight. When going on a trip, fill up trunk and spare passenger areas before adding luggage racks or trailers. These add drag, greatly reducing fuel cost-effectiveness.

**If car has fuel injection,** keep the gas tank at least ¼ full. This supplies enough fuel for the electric pump, which depends on a steady supply of fuel to lubricate its inner parts. Running your car low on fuel causes the pump to wear out, especially when cornering.

**Over-filling the gas tank causes charcoal evaporation emissions canister to saturate.** This part can cost $100 to replace. Stop fueling at first click of pump nozzle.

**To stop fuel lines from freezing,** add isopropyl alcohol (commercial additive) to the gas tank when filling up before and during especially cold weather.

**The gas tank must be kept full** when storing a vehicle. This limits amount of water forming (condensation) in the gas tank. Add a gas preservative if car will be stored for more than a month.

**Alliance to Save Energy Helps Consumers Get Better Mileage:** With gasoline prices nearing or hitting record levels in many states and regions of the country, the Alliance to Save Energy offers consumers tips to cut gasoline use and protect their pocketbooks.
- www.ase.org/content/news/detail/862

**Fuel Economy for Cars:** Fuel economy information for 2009 cars, trucks, SUVs and vans is now available to assist consumers in making good environmental choices when buying new vehicles.
- www.fueleconomy.gov/feg/FEG2000.htm

**Gas Mileage Impact Calculator:** This calculator offers information correlating to gas consumption, fuel cost and emission of major pollutants.
- www.hybridcars.com/calculator

1. **STOP IMMEDIATELY and KEEP CALM.** Do not argue, accuse anyone, or make any admission of blame for the accident. **DO NOT LEAVE THE SCENE,** however, if the vehicles are operable, move them to the shoulder of the road and out of the way of oncoming traffic. **WARN ONCOMING TRAFFIC.**

2. **CALL MEDICAL ASSISTANCE** for anyone injured. Do what you can to provide first aid, but **DO NOT MOVE THEM UNLESS YOU KNOW WHAT YOU ARE DOING.**

3. Call appropriate law enforcement authorities.

4. Get information requested in this form.

5. Call your insurance company immediately

## Your Vehicle Information

Owner_____
Phone_____
Address_____
_____
Make/Model_____
Vehicle ID #_____
License Plate #_____State____
Driver's Name_____
Address_____
Phone_____
Driver's License #_____State____
Area of Damage_____
_____
_____

## Other Vehicle

Owner_____
Phone_____
Address_____
_____
Make/Model_____
Vehicle ID #_____
License Plate #_____State____
Driver's Name_____
Address_____
Phone_____
Driver's License #_____State____
Area of Damage_____
_____

## Injured Person

Name_____ Age____
Phone_____
Address_____
_____
Extent of Injury_____
_____

## Damage to Other Property

Owner_____
Phone_____
Address_____
_____
Nature of Damage_____
_____

## Accident Facts

Date_____ Time_____
Street_____
City_____ State____
Condition of road_____
Weather condition?_____
Which direction were you going?_____
How fast were you driving?_____
Estimated speed of the other car?____
Did police make a report?_____
Responding police department? _____
Case/Report Number?_____

**Please give brief description of how the accident occurred.**
_____
_____
_____
_____
_____
_____
_____

## Witnesses

Name_____
Phone_____
Address_____
_____
Name_____
Phone_____
Address_____

C-6

## HELP WITH LEMON CARS & OTHER TROUBLES:

**Autopedia:** Great source of information for state Lemon Laws.
www.autopedia.com/html/HotLinks_Lemon2.html

**CarFax:** Free Lemon Car check. www.carfax.com/cfm/general_check.cfm?partner=car_8

**Federal Trade Commission (FTC):** If you are having difficulty with a car dealer or questions about your new car warranty, contact the FTC.
www.ftc.gov/bcp/menus/consumer/autos/buy.shtm

**Consumer Protection Offices:** There are several cities, county and state consumer protection offices which provide a number of functions such as mediate complaints, conduct investigations, provide educational materials and more.
http://consumeraction.gov/state.shtml

**Better Business Bureaus (BBB):** The BBB promotes an ethical marketplace by encouraging truthful advertising and selling practices, and by providing alternative dispute resolution. Locate and contact your local BBB office if you need help with a consumer question or complaint.
www.consumeraction.gov/bbb.shtml

**AUTOLINE:** Offers third-party dispute resolution services, which is administered by the Council of Better Business Bureaus, Inc. http://welcome.bbb.org

**File a Complaint with the National Highway Traffic Safety Administration (NHTSA):** If you are having troubles with your automobile or its equipment and would like to file a formal complaint, please fill out a Vehicle Owner's Questionnaire and submit it to NHTSA's Office of Defects Investigation. www-odi.nhtsa.dot.gov/ivoq

**National Highway Traffic Safety Administration:** This site provides pertinent information of a wide variety of highway transportation issues including: air bags, child passenger safety, child seat inspections, crash tests, recalls, safety ratings, and more. www.nhtsa.dot.gov

**Vehicle & Equipment - NHTSA:** A wide-ranging resource that consist of recalls, test reports, news items, and more. www.nhtsa.dot.gov/portal/site/nhtsa/menuitem.bead436724af02e770f6df1020008a0c/

**Auto and Other Transportation Recalls:**
www.pueblo.gsa.gov/recallsdesc.htm

**ALLDATAdiy.com:** Offer information on technical service bulletins and recalls for your car or truck. Information is listed by year, make, models and engine option. www.alldatadiy.com/recalls

**Insurance Institute for Highway Safety (IIHS):** This Website provides datum on crashworthiness, and airbags to advice for buying a safer car. www.iihs.org

**Motorist Assurance Program:** The Motorist Assurance Program (MAP) was established to promote communication, education and cooperation among consumers, the automotive industry, and government. www.motorist.org/index.cfm

## OTHER AUTOMOVTIVE RESOURCES:

**NADAGuides.com:** National Automobile Dealers Association. N.A.D.A. Appraisal Guides is the world's largest publisher of value guides and has been the industry leader for over 69 years. N.A.D.A. provide informative Consumer Tips to the public. They help consumers to make informed, responsible decisions about the purchase, safe operation and proper maintenance of vehicles. http://nadaguides.com

**Leaseguide.com:** An e-Guide to consumer car leasing. It offers easy explanations of how leasing works, examples, advice, information, and tools that will assist you in getting the best possible deal on your lease. www.leaseguide.com/index2.htm

**AWARE (Americans Well-informed on Automobile Retailing Economics):** Tries to ensure that financing remains accessible and affordable to the broadest possible spectrum of consumers. www.autofinancing101.org/learning_suite/index.cfm

**DoItYourself.com - Cars, Trucks and Boats:** This site was created to inform consumers about different kinds of cars to buy, financing options, finding the right insurance, and how much to sell your car for. You will also find in this section safety and maintenance information you should know before you go out driving, boating, traveling, or playing on ATV's and go-carts. www.doityourself.com/scat/carstrucksandboats

**National Institute for Automotive Service Excellence:** ASE was founded in 1972 to improve the quality of automotive service and repair through the voluntary testing and certification of automotive technicians and provides useful tips for motorists. www.asecert.org

**Autosite:** Offers tips for maintenance (changing car fluids) to repair or replacement on things from your air - filter, brakes and headlights. www.autosite.com/content/own/maintain/index.cfm

**Allpar.com:** Repair and performance tips on a wide variety of Chrysler, Plymouth, Dodge, and DeSoto cars, and more. www.allpar.com

**Consumer's Checkbook:** A non-profit magazine dedicated to helping consumers find reasonably priced services. www.checkbook.org

That figures, lemon car = I'm a dead man! It's 120 degrees in the shade, no water, and I'm stuck in the middle of nowhere. *"Swing low, sweet chariot, coming for to carry me home. I looked over Jordan, and what did I...*

"Wake up and smell the coffee, Sleeping Beauty! Are you ready to spend *and* save? Brace yourself, you're about to learn the secrets of purchasing the things you want for less and save big time. Pay close attention to my advice, especially before purchasing any big-ticket items. It's go time! Prepare for battle and proceed to the checkout line, Muffin!"

**Seventh Commandment: "THOU SHALL THINK FRUGALLY & LOOK FOR THE BEST DEAL"**

C-7

GO AHEAD AND BUY IT! YOU DESERVE IT!

I DO DESERVE IT, RIGHT? RIGHT?

PURCHASE NOW - WHENEVER

RESEARCH - TIME PURCHASES

10%

## EXPLORE

When U.S. Customs confiscates a car, the DOD no longer needs a computer, or U.S. Marshals Service seizes land from a drug dealer; all these items may become available for purchase by the public. While some surplus and forfeited items are transferred to other Federal agencies or given to state and local governments, a variety of items from vehicles to real estate are made available to the public through Federal Government sales.

Before attending an auction, it's important to contact government agency and ask questions prior to the sale like:

- How and when the sale or auction will be held
- What bidding procedure will be used
- What special restrictions or unusual conditions apply
- What forms of payment such as money order, certified check, credit cards, cash, etc?
- Buyer's responsibility for property removal
- Inspection times prior to the sale
- Zoning rules if purchasing land in urban area

In most cases, the "*Invitation for Bid*," an informal piece released by the sponsoring federal agency containing a description of the property being offered for sale with the sale items and conditions will answer these types of questions. Most federal agencies maintain Internet web sites, which include detailed information about their particular sales program. It's wise to attend several sales to get-the-feel for the auction process. With a little research, you can obtain the information that you need to make a successful purchase.

**Most sales are final:** Because the sales items are mostly used, the condition of the goods will vary. For an example, some forfeited vehicles may be in excellent condition, while others may have high mileage or a striped interior. Even though information about the condition will be given, it is still necessary for you to inspect before you purchase. It's the buyer's job to verify that the description of the item fits its actual condition. Find out if the goods are sold "*as is*" or can be returned.

**Don't expect to buy a $1 car:** Goods sold in Federal Government sales are usually at fair market value. At many auctions, items are appraised prior to sale and will not be sold if the bid price is below what is reasonable; still, there are some great bargains to be had. For your convenience, most of the Federal agencies auctions and sales have been listed for your viewing pleasure. For more information visit: **http://usasearch.gov/search?v%3Aproject=firstgov-fcic&query=auction&x=25&y=9**

## GovSales.gov:
**www.govsales.gov/html/index.htm**
GovSales.gov is a single catalog to all surplus items and real estate for sale by federal government. From cars to commercial real estate to furniture, computers, and office equipment, you'll find everything you need in one place.
**Cars: www.usa.gov/shopping/cars/cars.shtml**

## General Services Administration Auctions:
**http://gsaauctions.gov/gsaauctions/gsaauctions**
Through the General Services Administration, you'll find things like aircraft, boats, cars, jewelry, computers, furniture, lab equipment and a lot more.
**Cars: www.autoauctions.gsa.gov**
**Real Estate: https://propertydisposal.gsa.gov**
**Furniture: http://gsaauctions.gov/gsaauctions/aucindx**
**Boats: http://gsaauctions.gov/gsaauctions/aucindx**

## Military Surplus:
**www.drms.dla.mil/sales**
The U.S. Defense Reutilization and Marketing Service is responsible for disposal of excess/surplus property received from the U.S. military services. You'll find furniture, appliances, camping gear, jeeps, computers, office supplies, radios and more.

## Department of Justice: U.S. Marshals Service - Seized Asset Information:
**www.usdoj.gov/marshals/assets/assets.html**
U.S. Marshals Service sells property to the public that has been seized by federal law enforcement agencies. Property for sale is residential and commercial real estate, business establishments, and personal property such as motor vehicles, boats, aircraft, jewelry, art, antiques, and collectibles.

## U.S. Treasury - Seized Vehicles Sales:
**www.treas.gov/auctions**
U.S. Treasury seized vehicles are usually offered for sale at the Miami/Ft. Lauderdale-Florida, Edison-New Jersey, Los Angeles-California, El Paso-Texas, Nogales-Arizona, and Chula Vista-California auction sales centers. Auctions take place in other states depending on availability.

## U.S. Treasury - IRS:
**www.treas.gov/auctions/irs**
When the U.S. government seizes property; you can benefit from others misfortune, through IRS auctions.

## Bid4Assets:
**www.bid4assets.com**
Bid4Assets is an online auction marketplace used by federal, state, and local governments to sell a wide variety of surplus.

## Customs and Border Protection, US Department of Homeland Security:
**www.robertsonauto.com**

## Federal Communication Commission Auctions:
**http://wireless.fcc.gov/auctions**
The Federal Communications Commission (FCC) conducts auctions of licenses for electromagnetic spectrums. These auctions are open to eligible company or individual that submits an application and an upfront payment, and is found to be a qualified bidder by the FCC.

DO I HEAR $375? 375? 375? GOING ONCE! GOING TWICE! SOLD TO THE GENTLEMEN IN BLUE AT $350! Now moving on to our next vehicle…

$375

$375

HELLO! I SAID $375! HELLO! HELLO!

## DEA Auctions:
**www.deaauctions.com**
The Official Premier National Headquarters for Police and Government Auctions information at all Local, States, and Federal Levels throughout the country with 24/7 instant online access 365 Days a year.

## Department of Energy (DOE) Surplus Auctions:
**http://management.energy.gov/?OpenDocument**
Office equipment, vehicles, furniture, trailers, generators, instruments and laboratory equipment, mechanical power transmission equipment, and heavy equipment are some of the items sold by the DOE. Personal property items for sale will vary with sale location. Most of DOE's real property is sold by the U.S. General Services Administration.

## Federal Deposit Insurance Corporation Auctions:
**http://www.fdic.gov**
The Federal Deposit Insurance Corporation (FDIC) sells a wide variety of assets from failed banks including loans; real estate such as undeveloped land, hotels, shopping malls, single-family homes, condominiums, and apartment complexes; personal property, including computers, phone systems, furniture, fixtures, and plants; and, specialty items such as crystal, china, and antiques.
**Real Estate: http://www2.fdic.gov/drrore**

## Government Printing Office (GPO) Auctions:
The Government Printing Office (GPO) prints, binds, and distributes publications for the Federal Government. As a result, you can purchase used printing and binding equipment by sealed bid. You may also find office furniture and business machines such as copiers, calculators, and typewriters. Sales are advertised through bidder's lists and the *Commerce Business Daily*. To be put on bidders list fax **(202) 512-1354** or write to Government Printing Office Specialized Procurement and Sales Section Mail Stop: MMPS 710 North Capitol St., NW Washington, DC 20401

## Government Surplus & Seized Marketplace USA:
**http://govassets4sale.com**
Buy planes, helicopters, vehicles, heavy equipment, office equipment, fire & rescue and law enforcement equipment, medical equipment, seized property and more directly from government agencies.

## USDA Properties for Sale:
**www.resales.usda.gov**
Looking for real estate? USDA sells government owned real estate and potential foreclosure sales for farms and ranch properties, houses, lots, and buildings. In addition, the USDA Housing and Community Facilities Programs provide a number of homeownership opportunities to rural Americans, as well as programs for home renovation and repair. HCFP also makes financing available to the elderly, disabled, or low-income rural residents of multi-unit housing buildings to ensure they are able to make rent payments.

## Small Business Administration Property for Sale:
**www.pueblo.gsa.gov/cic_text/fed_prog/ fedsales/sba.htm**
If borrower defaults on SBA loan or guaranty, SBA or a participating lender may sell property securing the loan. The assets for sale may range from commercial property, single-family homes, vacant land and personal property such as machinery, equipment, furniture, fixtures, and inventory that were used in business operations.

## TENNESSEE VALLEY AUTHORITY Surplus Auctions:
**www.tva.gov/surplus**

## Department of Housing and Urban Development (HUD) Homes for Sale:
**www.hud.gov/homes** and
**www.hud.gov/homes/homesforsale.cfm**
When a mortgage lender forecloses on a mortgage insured by the Federal Housing Administration (FHA), a division of HUD, the lender may convey the property to HUD in exchange for the mortgage insurance benefits. HUD sells homes to the public, nonprofit groups, and governmental entities at fair market value or at discounted price under special programs. Acquired properties are single-family homes (1-4 units), including town homes, condominiums, or other types of single-family dwellings.

## Veterans Affairs (VA) Sales:
**www.homesales.gov** or **www.ocwen.com**
VA acquires properties because of foreclosures on VA-guaranteed and VA-financed loans. Acquired properties are marketed for sale through a property management service. Properties are listed by local listing agents through local Multi Listing Systems (MLS). Properties for sale may also be viewed on websites above. If you are interested in buying a VA-acquired property when it is listed for sale by Ocwen Loan Servicing, LLC, please contact a local real estate broker of your choice to see the property.

## Department of the Interior: Bureau of Land Management (BML) Sales:
**www.blm.gov/wo/st/en.html** or
**www.blm.gov/nhp/what/lands/realty/tenure/sale.htmlln**
BML's undeveloped and unimproved lands, typically near growing communities, may be candidates for sale. These lands are largely located in 11 Western States and Alaska.

## Army Corps of Engineers Homes for Sale:
**www.sas.usace.army.mil/hapinv**
Homeowners Assistance Program (HAP) was enacted to assist eligible federal personnel, who were stationed at or near an installation scheduled for closure or realignment and who, through no fault of their own, are unable to sell their homes under reasonable terms and conditions.

## EBay Land Sale Auctions:
**http://realestate.listings.ebay.com/Land_W0QQfclZ3QQ sacatZ15841QQsocmdZListingItemList**
The government uses EBay to sell off many of its properties. If you're looking for land at almost lowest price, then bid through EBay.

## Sale of Surplus USPS Vehicles through EBay:
A variety of surplus vehicles may be available for sale via the Internet through **www.ebay.com** or local fleet managers will announce sales in local newspapers, notices posted on lobby bulletin boards at post offices. Seller, using following seller ID, can access online sales from the EBay home page, select search tool, and then search: **usps-al-pmsc.** You may also go directly to the EBay search by seller page.

Our next item for bid is an extremely rare vase from the 21st century S-Smart circa 2000 era. Let's start the bidding at, shall we say, $100,000?

State Surplus Auctions (SSA) has some of the lowest vehicle and equipment prices of all government agencies. Before bidding, know exactly what you're buying and take full advantage of the inspection period.

**ALABAMA Surplus:**
http://216.226.178.189/Surplus%20Property/default.aspx
**ALABAMA Surplus:**
www.justauctions.org/alabama_auctions.html
**ALABAMA (Tuscaloosa) Surplus:**
www.ci.tuscaloosa.al.us/FAQ.ASP?QID=25

**ALASKA Surplus:** www.state.ak.us/local/
akpages/ADMIN/dgs/property
**ALSAKA (Fairbanks) Surplus Auctions:**
www.fairbanksauction.com/past%20auctions.htm

**ARIZONA Land Auctions:**
www.land.state.az.us/programs/realestate/auctions.htm
**ARIZONA (Apache Junction) Sueplus:**
www.ajcity.net/index.aspx?NID=401
**ARIZONA (Flagstaff) Surplus:**
www.flagstaff.az.gov/index.asp?NID=507
**ARIZONA (Mesa) Surplus:** www.cityofmesa.org/auction
**ARIZONA (Peoria) Surplus:**
www.peoriaaz.gov/procurement/MaterialsAuctionsF.asp
**ARIZONA (Phoenix) Surplus & Police Auctions:**
http://phoenix.gov/invmgt or
**ARIZONA (Tucson) Surplus:**
www.publicsurplus.com/sms/tucsonaz.gov,az/browse/home

**ARKANSAS Surplus:** www.arstatesurplus.com

**CALIFORNIA Surplus:**
www.ofa.dgs.ca.gov/OSPR/default.htmor
**CALIFORNIA (Bakersfield) Surplus:**
www.bakersfieldcity.us/administration/financialservices/pur
chasing/city_surplus.html
**CALIFORNIA (Garden Grove) Police Auctions:**
www.auctionspluss.com/auctions.asp
**CALIFORNIA (La Mesa) Surplus:**
www.ci.la-mesa.ca.us/index.asp?NID=92
**CALIFORNIA (Los Angeles) Surplus:**
http://doingbusiness.lacounty.gov/surplus.htm
**CALIFORNIA (LA) Police Auctions:** www.lapdon
line.org/join_the_team/content_basic_view/9126
**CALIFORNIA (Santa Ana) Surplus:**
www.ci.santa-ana.ca.us/finance/FI-SurplusHome.asp
**CALIFORNIA (Sacramento) Surplus:**
www.cityofsacramento.org/pss/surplus.htm
**CALIFORNIA (San Diego) Police Dept. Surplus:**
www.sandiego.gov/police/auctions.shtml

**COLORADO Surplus:** www.coloradoci.com
**COLORADO (Colorado Springs) Surplus:**
www.springsgov.com/page.aspx?navid=1383
**COLORADO (Denver) Car Auctions:**
www.success-auctions.com/?Auction=5
**COLORADO (Denver) Surplus:**
www.success-auctions.com/?Auction=53
**COLORADO (Fort Collins) Surplus:**
http://fcgov.com/purchasing/surplus.php

**CONNENTICUT Surplus:** www.das.state.ct.us/
Surplus/No_Auctions.htm

**DELAWARE Surplus:** http://gss.omb.delaware.gov

**DISTRICT of COLUMBIA Surplus:** http://app.ocp.
dc.gov/RUI/information/ppd/ppd_main.asp
**DISTRICT of COLUMBIA Pol. Auc.:** http://mpdc.dc.gov/
mpdc/cwp/view,a,1242,q,558351,mpdcNav_GID,1541.asp

**FLORIDA Federal Surplus:** http://dms.myflorida.
com/business_operations/specialized_services/federal_pro
perty_assistance
**FLORIDA (Titusville) Surplus:**
www.titusville.com/Page.asp?NavID=945

**GEORGIA Surplus:** http://surplusproperty.doas.georgia
.gov/02/doas/surplus/home/0,2475,41113361,00.html

**IDAHO Surplus:** www.sco.idaho.gov/web/sbe/
surplusp.nsf/disclaimer.htm
**IDAHO State Police Surplus Auctions:**
www.isp.state.id.us/finance/surplus.html

**ILLINIOS Surplus:** www.cms.il.gov/cms/
1_buying/statesurp.htm
**ILLINIOS (Chicago) Surplus:**
http://notforprofitsales.com/sms/list/current?orgid=20549
**ILLINIOS (Naperville) Surplus:**
www.naperville.il.us/dynamic_content.aspx?id=976

**INDIANA Surplus:** www.in.gov/idoa/2286.htm

**IOWA Surplus:** www.iaprisonind.com/
html/surplus/state_geninfo.asp

**KANSAS Surplus:** www.da.ks.gov/surplus/default.htm
**KANSAS (Dodge City) Surplus:**
www.dodgecity.org/Bids.aspx?bidID=29
**KANSAS (Wichita) Surplus:** www.wichita.gov/
CityOffices/Finance/Purchasing/Auctions.htm

**KENTUCKY Surplus:** http://finance.ky.gov/internal/surplus

**LOUISANNA Surplus:** http://doa.louisiana.gov/lpaa
**LOUISANNA (New Orleans) Surplus:**
www.cityofno.com/pg-1-35-surplus-auctions.aspx

**MAINE Surplus:**
www.maine.gov/bgs/centralserv/surplus

**MARYLAND Surplus:** www.dgs.maryland.gov

**MASSACHUSETTS Surplus:** www.mass.gov/?page
ID=osdtopic&L=3&sid=Aosd&L0=Home&L1=Buy+from+a+
Contract&L2=Buying+Surplus+Property
**MASSACHUSETTS (Boston) Police Auctions:**
www.cityofboston.gov/transportation/auction.asp
**MASSACHUSETTS (Chelsea) Surplus:** http://register.
publicsurplus.com/sms/chelsea,ma/browse/home?tm=m

**MICHIGAN Federal Surplus Property Sales:**
www.michigan.gov/dmb/0,1607,7-150-9141_13135---
,00.html
**MICHIGAN Public Auction of Tax-Foreclosed Lands:**
www.michigan.gov/treasury/0,1607,7-121-1751_3437-
118951--,00.html
**MICHIGAN (Battle Creek) Surplus:** http://ci.battle-creek.
mi.us/Services/Purchasing/AuctionandSurplusSales.htm
**MICHIGAN (Birmingham) Surplus:**
www.ci.birmingham.mi.us/index.aspx?page=1143
**MICHIGAN (Rochester) Surplus:** www.rochesterhills.org/
city_services/purchasing/city_surplus_auctions.asp

**MINNESOTA Surplus:** www.fss.state.mn.us/mn03000.htm
**MINNESOTA (Minneapolis) Police Auctions:**
www.ci.minneapolis.mn.us/police/about/auctions.asp

**MISSISSIPPI State & Federal Surplus:**
www.dfa.state.ms.us/Offices/SurProp/SurProp.htm

**MISSOURI Surplus:** http://oa.mo.gov/purch/surplus.html
**MISSOURI (ST Charles) Surplus:** www.stcharlescitymo.
gov/Residents/SurplusAuction/tabid/342/Default.aspx

**NEBRASKA FEDERAL Surplus Property Sales:**
www.corrections.state.ne.us/federal_surplus/index.html
**NEBRASKA State Surplus:**
www.das.state.ne.us/materiel/surplus/surplus.htm

**NEVADA (NST) Surplus:** www.nstec.com/auction
**NEVADA Public Auction Announcements:**
http://purchasing.state.nv.us/property/auction.htm
**NEVADA Surplus Vehicle & Equipment Listing:**
http://purchasing.state.nv.us/property/vehicle.htm

**NEW JERSEY Surplus:** www.state.nj.us/treasury/dss
**NEW JERSEY Surplus Vehicles:**
www.state.nj.us/treasury/dss/csdssauc.shtm

**NEW MEXICO Surplus:**
www.generalservices.state.nm.us/tsd/SurplusProperty.html

**NEW YORK Federal Surplus Property Sales:**
www.ogs.state.ny.us/realEstate/sales/default.html
**NEW YORK State Surplus Public Sales:** www.ogs.state.
Us/supportService/fedSurplus/aboutfederal.html
**NEW YORK (New York City) Surplus:**
www.nyc.gov/html/dcas/html/auctions/auctions.shtml
**NEW YORK (NYC) Police Auctions:** http://home2.nyc.gov
/html/nypd/html/property_clerk/police_auctions.shtml
**NEW YORK (New York City) Sheriff Auctions:** www.nyc.
gov/html/dof/html/services/services_auctions.shtml

**NORTH CAROLINA Federal Surplus Property Sales:**
www.doa.state.nc.us/fsp/fsp.htm
**NORTH CAROLINA State Surplus:** www.ncstate
surplus.com/ssp/public/ssphomepage/ssp.htm
**NORTH CAROLINA (Greensboro) Surplus:**
www.greensboronc.gov/departments/finance1/AdminServic
es/surplusauction.htm
**NORTH CAROLINA (Lexington) Surplus:**
www.lexingtonnc.net/purchasing/auctions.asp

**NORTH DAKODA Surplus:** www.nd.gov/surplus/property

**OHIO Warehouse Surplus:** www.das.ohio.gov/GSD/
PropFac/Surplus/warehousenextauction.htm
**OHIO Auto Auctions:**
www.das.ohio.gov/gsd/PropFac/Surplus/nextauction.asp
**OHIO (Columbus) Police Auctions:**
www.columbuspolice.org/CommunityInteraction/AuctionsEv
ents/AuctionsEvents.html

**OKLAHOMA State Surplus:**
www.ok.gov/DCS/State_Surplus/index.html
**OALAHOMA (Tulsa) Surplus & Police Auctions:**
www.cityoftulsa.org/OurCity/Business/SurplusAuction.asp

**OREGON State & Federal Surplus:**
www.oregonsurplus.com
**OREGON (OSU) Surplus:** http://surplus.oregonstate.edu

**PENNSYLVANIA Surplus:** www.portal.state.pa.
us/portal/server.pt?open=512&objID=1393&&SortOrder=16
&level=2&parentid=1231&css=L2&mode=2

**SOUTH CAROLINA Surplus:**
www.ogs.state.sc.us/surplus/SP-index.phtm
**SOUTH CAROLINA (Georgetown) Surplus:**
www.cityofgeorgetownsc.com
**SOUTH CAROLINA (Myrtle Beach) Surplus:**
www.cityofmyrtlebeach.com/auction.html

**SOUTH DAKODA Surplus:**
www.state.sd.us/boa/Prop.%20Mgmt/propmgt.htm
**SOUTH DAKODA (Sioux Falls) Surplus:**
www.siouxfalls.org/Finance/surplus_auction.aspx

**TENNESSEE Surplus:** www.state.tn.us/generalserv/ba04s
**TENNESSEE (Knoxville) Surplus:**
www.cityofknoxville.org/purchasing/auctions.asp
**TENNESSEE (Oak Ridge) Surplus:**
www.cortn.org:8000/auction/auction/XcAuctionPro.asp

**TEXAS Surplus:** www.tfc.state.tx.us/communities/
supportserv/prog/statesurplus/index.html
**TEXAS (Austin) Surplus:** www.txauction.com
**TEXAS (College Station) Surplus:**
www.cstx.gov/index.aspx?page=918
**TEXAS (Dallas) Surplus & Police Auctions:** www.dallas
cityhall.com/business_development/auction_faqs.html
**TEXAS (Houston) Surplus:** www.publicsurplus.com/
sms/houston,tx/list/current?orgid=4154
**TEXAS (Midland) Surplus:** www.midlandtexas.gov/
departments/purchasing/auctions.html
**TEXAS (San Antonio) Police Auctions:**
www.sanantonio.gov/sapd/auction.asp?
**TEXAS (San Antonio) River Auth. Surplus:** www.sara-
tx.org/site/about/contracting/surplus_equipment.php
**TEXAS (Sugarland) Surplus:** www.sugarlandtx.gov/
administrative_services/services/online_auction/index.asp

**UTAH Surplus:** http://fleet.state.ut.us
**UTAH (Salt Lake City) Surplus:**
www.ci.slc.ut.us/purchasing/auction.htm

**VERMONT Federal Surplus Property Sales:**
http://bgs.vermont.gov/facilities/pms/propman/landsale
**VERMONT Surplus:** www.bgs.state.vt.us/gsc/surplus
**VERMONT State Police Auctions:**
www.dps.state.vt.us/vtsp/support/auction.htm

**VIRGINIA Surplus:**
http://159.169.222.200/dps/Surplus/surplus-bottom.htm
**VIRGINA (New Port News) Surplus & Police Auctions:**
www.nngov.com/purchasing/services/surplusregistration

**WASHINGTON State & Federal Surplus:**
www.ga.wa.gov/surplus/index.html
**WASHINGTON University of Washington Surplus:**
www.washington.edu/admin/surplus

**WEST VIRGINIA Surplus:**
www.state.wv.us/admin/purchase/surplus

**WISCONSIN Surplus:** www.doa.state.wi.us/section_
detail.asp?linkcatid=20&linkid=46&locid=2
**WISCONSIN (Milwaukee) Surplus:**
www.city.milwaukee.gov/Auction340.htm

**WYOMING Surplus:**
http://ai.state.wy.us/GeneralServices/Surplus/index.asp

**Other Auction Sources**
**National Association of State Agencies for Surplus:**
www.nasasp.org/site
**Government Deals:**
www.govdeals.com/eas/index.cfm

When it comes to getting airline tickets, nowadays you have plenty of outlets to buy them. However, how can you find the best possible deal? Fortunately for you, I have listed several ideas that will point you in the right direction when looking for bargain flights.

■ **Be Flexible with travel times:** One of the best ways to save on flights is to be flexible with travel times. The bigger your travel window, usually, the better deal.

■ **Book Early:** Book at least 14 days in advance to get lower rates.

■ **Find lower fares by using alternate airports.** I happen to live between Austin and San Antonio, Texas. When looking for best rates, I always check flights out of both airports and then arrivals to different airports. This strategy can save you a lot of money.

■ **Shop around:** Shopping around is a given when it comes to finding any type of bargain; travel is no different. Beware of sites that guarantee cheapest fares or offer other types of incentives; these offers tend to be loaded with conditions & aim more to mislead travelers into thinking they've found the best deal. Once you find the best rate through a search engine, go directly to airline's website to make sure you're getting lowest rate. Some search engines' include service fees (i.e. $10 per ticket).
**Recommended Website:**
**Kayak** searches 140+ travel sites at once and to find cheapest fares and compares results from all sites together - filter and sort instantly. You can also click to buy direct from airlines or agencies (Kayak is not a travel agent).**www.kayak.com**

■ **Package and save!** Package deals that offer flight + hotel can prove useful in saving money on entire cost of the trip. Try to package your trip when searching for lowest price, especially during holidays.
**Recommended Website: www.bing.com/travel** predicts the rise and fall of airfare ticket prices. Based on prediction, they provide a recommendation to buy now or buy later. Their service also includes whether or not a specific hotel is a deal. It compares an individual hotel's current rate to its observed historical rates.

■ **Watch out for taxes, surcharges, service fees & credit card fees:** Taxes and service fees can quickly make a cheap flight an expensive one. Taxes and surcharges can add significantly to a fare on some international routes up to 50% of ticket or more. Not all agents include these prices up front, so remember to include this in the final cost decision.

■ **Look for hidden extras:** Airport transfers, onboard meals, seat reservation fees etc. can add to the price of a ticket. Make sure you also tally up the cost of airport transport and any other extras when making a wise decision on airlines and prices.

■ **Consider frequent flyer programs:** If you travel a lot, find airlines that offers valuable frequent flyer programs that can save you money. Check to see if programs suit your needs and your travel patterns. **Use MileMaven:** This website lists frequent flyer promotions that could get you bonus miles per trip. **www.milemaven.com**
**Warning**: Do not focus on one particular airline just to earn airline miles, as airline miles are only worth about 1 cent each by the time you redeem them. Paying the premium on your airline tickets to earn miles doesn't make sense. Look for lowest fares and sign up for all airlines' mileage programs.
**NOTE:** Inventory frequent flier mileage balances in all of your accounts. Even if you do not have enough miles to earn a free ticket, you may be able to redeem unused miles for other benefits such as a discount coupon off a ticket you need to buy or a gift certificate.

■ **Subscribe to airlines' e-mail newsletters:** Find out about special promotions from e-mail newsletters because special promotional rates disappear fast.

■ **Sign up for** *"fare alerts"* **with travel search engines:** Fare alert systems allow you to name cities you'd like to visit with an estimated fare you'd be willing to pay. If airfares hit that price (or go below) you will get an email notice.

■ **Include a Saturday stopover:** Lower price of a round trip airfare as much as two-thirds by making certain your trip includes a Saturday evening stopover and by purchasing a ticket in advance.

■ **Take the "red-eye":** You can sometimes find especially good deals between midnight and 1 a.m.

■ **Last minute flights:** If planning a last minute, look at web deals on airline websites to take advantage of rock-bottom last minute prices.

■ **Travel on holidays:** If you and your family are flexible, traveling on the actual holiday (Thanksgiving, Christmas and New Year's Day) can get you incredible deals.

■ **Special fares:** Special fares such as a student, youth, companion and senior fare are also sometimes offered.

■ **Get best seating arrangement available:** Get the best seat on a plane, including view of in-flight movie screen, proximity to restrooms, and availability of power outlets with SeatGuru. You might even score an empty seat beside you. **www.seatguru.com**

Early in my marriage, my wife, occasionally, would come home with what seemed like a boatload of stuff from shopping all day. Our money was always tight back then, so being under pressure to stay financially afloat, in frustration, I'd bark out with something like, **"What bank did you rob to buy everything."** She'd immediately switch into **"KING COBRA"** mode with head bobbing antics from side to side, and try to glare me down with her deadly eyes; then lunge and strike for my jugular with this bite, **"I saved you money! Everything was on sale!"** With that, the fight would be on! The debate would last into the wee early morning hours, with the typical make-up, and the promise of *"It'll never happen again,"* until it happens again. Have I mentioned the joys of marriage, yet? Hey, you're getting me off the subject; we'll continue that story another time. Let's get back to our featured article.

Over the years, I found that she was right; you really can save 10% to 80%, **"if,"** you time your purchases. This page will assist you in scheduling the purchase of certain items of want or need, so you can save lots of money.
**Note:** Never bite the hand that feeds you.

| Items to Buy | Best Time to Purchase |
|---|---|
| Best Clothing Sales | After *Washington's Birthday, 4th of July, Easter, Christmas.* |
| Biggest Sales | *Jan, Aug* |
| | |
| Air Conditioners | *Feb, July, Aug* |
| Appliances | *Jan, April, Nov, Dec* |
| Appliances (Major) | *Jan, Mar, July* |
| Art Supplies | *Jan, Feb* |
| Auto Batteries | *Sept, Oct* |
| | |
| Bathing Suits | *After July 4th, Aug* |
| Bedding | *Feb, Aug* |
| Bicycles | *Jan, Feb, Sept, Oct, Nov* |
| Blankets | *Jan, May, Nov, Dec* |
| Blenders | *Jan* |
| Books | *Jan* |
| Builder Hardware | *June* |
| | |
| Camera Equipment | *Oct, Nov* |
| Camping Equipment | *Aug* |
| Car Seat Covers | *Feb, Nov* |
| Carpeting | *May, July, Aug, Sept* |
| Cars New | *Aug, Sept, Dec* |
| Cars Used | *Feb, Nov, Dec* |
| China | *Jan, Feb, Sept, Oct* |
| Christmas Gifts | *Anytime but December* |
| Christmas Supplies | *Jan and After Xmas Clothes* |
| Dryers | *Jan, Feb, March, April* |
| Clothing Children's | *April, July, Sept, Nov, Dec* |
| Clothing Men's | *Feb, April, Oct, Dec* |
| Clothing Women's | *Jan, Feb, April, Nov, Dec* |
| Clothing School | *Aug, Oct* |
| Clothing Summer | *June, July* |
| Coats Children's | *April, Aug, Nov, Dec* |
| Coats Men's | *Jan, Aug* |
| Coats Women's | *April, Aug, Nov, Dec* |
| Coffee Makers | *Jan* |
| Costume Jewelry | *Jan* |
| Curtains | *Feb* |
| | |
| Dishes | *Jan, Feb, Sept, Oct* |
| Drapes | *Feb, Aug* |
| Dresses | *Jan, April, June, Nov* |

| | |
|---|---|
| Electric Blankets | *Summer, Oct* |
| Fans | *May, Aug* |
| Fishing Equipment | *Oct* |
| Freezers | *Jan, March, July* |
| Fuel Oil | *July* |
| Furniture | *Jan, Feb, June, Aug, Sept* |
| Furs | *Jan, Aug* |
| | |
| Garden Equipment | *March, Aug, Sept* |
| Glassware | *Jan, Feb, Sept, Oct* |
| | |
| Handbags | *Jan, May, July* |
| Hardware | *Aug, Sept* |
| Home Decorating | *Nov* |
| Home Furnishings | *Jan, Feb, June, Aug, Oct* |
| Home Enter. System | *Jan, May to July, Nov, Dec* |
| Hosiery | *April, Oct* |
| Housecoats | *April, May, June, Oct, Nov* |
| House wares | *Jan, Feb, March, Aug to Oct* |
| | |
| Infant Wear | *Jan, March, April, July* |
| Irons | *Jan* |
| | |
| Lamps | *Feb, Aug, Sept* |
| Lawn Equipment | *March* |
| Lawnmowers | *Sept* |
| Lingerie | *Jan* |
| Luggage | *March, May, Nov* |
| Lumber (Wood) | *June* |
| | |
| Nursery Items | *Dec* |
| | |
| Paints | *April, Aug, Sept* |
| Porch Furniture | *April, May* |
| | |
| Radios | *Jan, Feb, July* |
| Refrigerators | *Jan, July* |
| Ranges | *April, Nov* |
| Rugs | *Jan, Feb, Mar, July, Aug, Sept* |
| | |
| School Supplies | *June, Aug, Oct* |
| Shoes Boy's & Girl's | *Jan, March, July* |
| Shoes Men's | *Jan, July, Nov, Dec* |
| Shoes Women's | *Jan, July, Nov, Dec* |
| Sheets & Spreads | *Jan, June, July, Dec* |
| Silverware | *Feb, Oct* |
| Ski Equipment | *March* |
| Sports Gear | *July, Sept, Oct* |
| Sporting Goods | *Feb, Aug* |
| Stereo Equipment | *Jan, Feb, July* |
| | |
| Television Sets | *May, June* |
| Tires | *May, June, end of Aug* |
| Toasters | *Jan* |
| Towels & Linens | *Jan, May, Aug* |
| Toys | *Jan, Feb, Nov* |
| | |
| Vacations | *Before Christmas* |
| | |
| Water Heaters | *Jan, Nov* |
| Winter Sports Gear | *March* |

**C-7**

I once counseled a young military couple (both in the service without children) about their finances. The couple wondered why they had no money left over at the end of each month. After doing a budget with them, to my surprise and theirs as well, we discovered that they had developed a habit of spending $800 monthly, dining out. They were then thrilled, when I gave them a plan where they had to prepare four meals a week at home, but by doing so, they could easily pocket and save $400 monthly. With our fast-paced lives, we don't seem to have time to plan meals, grocery shop and cook all day. However, if you're fed up with throwing money away to all of the food eateries you frequent, and want to reduce your food bill and eat healthier, just take the time and adhere to my following recipe.

## The ABCs of taking control of your food budget

**A. Get in the habit of eating real food again:** Why spread butter or sour cream on an ear of corn or whipped cream and chocolate on juicy strawberries when it covers-up their delicious natural flavor? Eating food in their natural state is inexpensive and usually healthier for you.

**B. Get organized:** Begin by getting your kitchen and pantry in order, so it's easier to cook. Devise a food-shopping strategy that gives you the most within budget. If organized, making meals from scratch instead from a pre-made mix makes sense. Besides, it is just as fast, cost is less, tastes better, and is free of additives and artificial flavor. In addition, preparing breakfast is not a hard task, and you'll save $500 or more a year, by frequenting fewer restaurants and fast food chains. When organized, leftovers are time and money savers. They allow you to brown bag lunch or heat up a quick meal after a long day, instead of wasting your food budget on outside eateries.

**C. Put fun into cooking:** Planning meals should be a creative undertaking, performed with fun and eagerness. Furthermore, you can recruit friends, spouse or even children to help with cooking. Remember the late sixties and seventies commercial, *"Its shake and bake, Daddy… and I helped."* Educating your kids on how to cook is a great way to spend quality time with them, while passing down family recipes that they'll enjoy and use later in life.

## 32 Tips: How to save money on food

**1. Use food list:** Before shopping, put everything you want on a food list (see **page 87**), but don't add to list once you get to the store. Statistics show that most consumers buy at least one item that was unplanned or unlisted in each aisle while shopping. Since the average market has 12 to 14 aisles that could add up to many unplanned purchases. Using a list will help to avoid impulse buying.

**2. Group your list:** By design, regularly purchased items such as milk, bread, etc., are found on opposite ends of the market. Grocers know bigger profits can be had by keeping consumers in their store longer, so they'll buy more. In addition, they know that most customers don't organize their shopping lists. One way to reduce your time in market and save is to *"group"* items on your list (see **page 87**).

**3. Pre-packaged foods are expensive:** Cereals, breads, desserts, beverages, etc., prepared at home are always a better value than prepackaged items.

**4. Plan meals in advance around sales:** Look for sales on the internet, store windows, newspapers and fliers sent by mail, etc., and scrutinize prices. Pay attention to days of the week sale prices are in effect, because some markets have no sales on Mondays. Buy a calendar and plan weekly or monthly meals. If chicken is on sale, purchase enough to make several meals. By using this system, you can trim 25% or more off your food bill. Pay attention to

meat and produce sales, which can account for 1/2 of the amount that you spend on food. Buy meat that you would normally use in large quantities and freeze some for later use. This method can save you up to 20%. Plan leftovers and freeze meals for future use.

**5. The Price is Right:** Use a book, software, etc., to keep a list of prices when looking for bargains in different stores. By keeping track of prices, you'll find the best places to shop each week. Your price list should also remind you when to redeem coupons, buy in bulk for further savings and will allow you to track deals for years. Dedicate one page to each distinctive food item and list its price in regular supermarkets, warehouse stores, etc; then list sales prices. Soon, you'll notice that certain items always go on sale, and *"bottom-line"* sale price for just about everything. While your savings may vary, you should be able to reduce your food bill 30%-40% within a few months, just by following this method. **Example:** Ice Cream

| Store | Brand | oz / gal | Cost | Cost lbs. | Coupons |
|-------|-------|----------|------|-----------|---------|
| Mega | Generic | 1 gal | 3.79 | $ .95 qt | 1 / .50 off |
| Safeway | Dryers | ½ gal | 3.99 | $2.00 qt | 1 / $2 off |
| HEB | Generic | ½ gal | 2.29 | $1.15 qt | 4 / $1 off |

**6. Eat a meal, dump spouse:** If you're food shopping while hungry, add spouse, kids, and you're shopping for more than one hungry mouth, which can inflate your bill. Before shopping, eat a meal and leave family home.

**7. Use cash:** Leave checkbook, credit and debit cards at home. Instead, get cash before heading to market. This way, if you should go over the top with limited cash on hand, and then find yourself holding up the line, while you pick and choose what items need be removed from shopping bags, so you come within budget (before dying a slow embarrassing death), you'll probably stick to your shopping list that much better. **NOTE:** Bring a calculator.

**8. Stay out of aisles:** Most stores position meats, dairy, produce and breads along walls. They place cookies, cereals, beverages, and canned goods in aisles. When shopping, stick with your list and plan all purchases to take advantage of sale products and 2 for 1 special's, if price is not inflated to compensate.
**FACT:** About 1/3 of all purchases are done on impulse.

**9. Don't spring traps:** Grocers, lay traps by promoting items displayed at end store aisles, because shoppers believe prices are reduced. Never assume that all items showcased at end aisles are on sale. More than likely, these *"end traps"* are just overstocked inventory sold at normal price and ready for you to spring their trap(s).

**10. Free food:** As a rule, when weighing pre-packaged produce such as 5 lb bag of potatoes that cost $2.99, it should weigh between 5½ to 6-lbs that means 15% free food.  Also, weigh non-pre-packaged produce like 2 cucumbers for a $1 or $3.99 for any size watermelon, etc. Weighing produce will yield more food and some free.

# Shopping List

**(Make copies)**

## Baking Products — Price
- __ Baking powder _____
- __ Cornmeal _____
- __ Flour _____
- __ Mixes _____
- __ Shortening _____
- __ Sugar / brown _____
- __ Vanilla extract _____
- __ _____

## Beverages
- __ Coffee / Tea _____
- __ Juice _____
- __ Soft drinks _____
- __ Water _____
- __ _____
- __ _____

## Bread, Cereal, Grains
- __ Bread _____
- __ Muffins / bagels _____
- __ Cereal _____
- __ Crackers _____
- __ Dried beans _____
- __ Oatmeal/grits _____
- __ Pasta _____
- __ Rice _____
- __ Rolls _____
- __ Taco Shells _____
- __ Tortillas _____
- __ _____
- __ _____
- __ _____

## Canned Goods
- __ Broth _____
- __ Chili / Raviolis _____
- __ Fish / tuna _____
- __ Fruit _____
- __ Soups _____
- __ Tomato sauce _____
- __ Tomato paste _____
- __ Vegetables _____
- __ _____
- __ _____
- __ _____

## Cleaning Supplies
- __ Bathroom cleaner _____
- __ Bleach _____
- __ Carpet cleaner _____
- __ Dish detergent _____
- __ Fabric softener _____
- __ Glass cleaner _____
- __ Laundry detergent _____
- __ Scouring pads _____
- __ Scouring powder _____
- __ _____

## Condiments — Price
- __ Catsup _____
- __ Gravy _____
- __ Jam / jelly _____
- __ Mayonnaise _____
- __ Mustard _____
- __ Oil _____ _____
- __ Peanut butter _____
- __ Pickles _____
- __ Relish _____
- __ Salad dressing _____
- __ Spaghetti sauce _____
- __ Spices / herbs _____
- __ Vinegar _____
- __ _____

## Dairy Products
- __ Butter / margarine _____
- __ Cheeses, hard _____
- __ Cheeses, soft _____
- __ Cream _____
- __ Eggs _____
- __ Milk _____
- __ Sour cream _____
- __ Yogurt _____
- __ _____

## Frozen Foods
- __ Breads / biscuits _____
- __ Frozen dinners _____
- __ Ice cream _____
- __ Juices _____
- __ Potatoes / fries _____
- __ Vegetables _____
- __ Waffles _____
- __ _____
- __ _____

## Meats, Poultry, Seafood
- __ Beef _____
- __ Chicken _____
- __ Fish _____
- __ Ground meat _____
- __ Ham / lamb _____
- __ Pork _____
- __ Sandwich meats _____
- __ Shellfish _____
- __ Turkey _____
- __ _____
- __ _____

## Paper, Storage Products
- __ Aluminum foil _____
- __ Food storage bags _____
- __ Facial tissue _____
- __ Napkins _____
- __ Paper Plates / cups _____
- __ Paper towels _____
- __ Plastic warp _____
- __ Sandwich bags _____
- __ Toilet paper _____
- __ Trash bags _____
- __ Waxed paper _____
- __ _____

## Produce — Price
- __ Apples _____
- __ Bananas _____
- __ Berries / Cherries _____
- __ Grapes _____
- __ Lemons / limes _____
- __ Melons / cantaloupe _____
- __ Nectarines _____
- __ Oranges/grapefruit _____
- __ Peaches _____
- __ Pears _____
- __ Plums _____
- __ Avocados _____
- __ Broccoli _____
- __ Cabbage _____
- __ Carrots _____
- __ Cauliflower _____
- __ Corn _____
- __ Cucumbers _____
- __ Garlic _____
- __ Green beans _____
- __ Greens _____
- __ Lettuce _____
- __ Mushrooms _____
- __ Onions _____
- __ Potatoes _____
- __ Spinach _____
- __ Tomatoes _____
- __ _____
- __ _____

## Snacks
- __ Candy _____
- __ Cake / cookies / pies _____
- __ Chips / Pretzels _____
- __ Dried fruit / raisins _____
- __ Nuts _____
- __ Popcorn _____
- __ Pudding _____
- __ _____

## Toiletries
- __ Bath powder _____
- __ Cotton swabs _____
- __ Deodorant _____
- __ Hand / body lotion _____
- __ Razor blades _____
- __ Sanitary nap./tampons _____
- __ Shampoo/conditioner _____
- __ Shaving cream _____
- __ Soap _____
- __ Toothpaste / floss _____
- __ _____

## Miscellaneous
- __ Baby-care items _____
- __ Baby diapers _____
- __ Baby food / formula _____
- __ Cold remedies _____
- __ First aid supplies _____
- __ Grill supplies _____
- __ Pet food _____
- __ _____

**11. Shop unit price:** The slogan, *"bigger the package, better the price,"* can't be said these days. A trick stores use is list price boldly, while hiding unit price (cost per ounce or other units of weight or volume). Unit price is found right below or beside the product price. If unit price isn't listed on display shelf, just divide price of food by its net weight or volume. Buying in bulk can save money, but it all depends on the product! Normally, you can save as high as 75% when purchasing non-perishable items in quantity such as rice, dried beans, dried peas, nuts, herbs, etc., because it's more expensive packaging small portions.

**12. We're going ballistic (generics)!** One of the easier ways to save money on food or products is to purchase house brands also known as generics. As a rule, these packaged products carry the store's name, but lack fancy labels or name recognition of nationwide brands. Overall, they cost 21% less than national name brands.

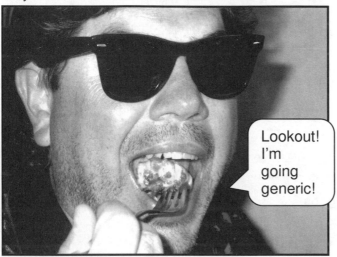

Lookout! I'm going generic!

**Why do most people select name brands?**
Researchers say it's a common buying tendency for shoppers to prefer well-known name brands and are more accustomed with them because they are highly promoted with ad campaigns. Most shoppers are certain they're getting "better quality" with name brands and are willing to pay more for them.
**FACT:** Most house brands are produced by the same name-brand competitors and sold to stores in modified packages. The only difference between products is the label.  Some items, by law, are mandatory to be precisely the same in content and composition. **Example:**

| Same in content and composition | | |
|---|---|---|
| Aspirin | Baking soda | Corn starch |
| Honey | Molasses | Peanuts |
| Pecans | Salt | Sugar |
| Flour | Vinegar | Vegetable oil |

**13. Use coupons during sales:** A big error is to redeem coupons too soon. If you really want to save money, put your coupons on hold until items you want are on sale. Manufacturers often encourage retailers to put products out on sale 1 to 4 times a year. Most product sales are not always timed to happen simultaneously with publication of coupons. Actually, you may have perceived that some retailers actually increase prices the week their coupons show up in fliers or newspapers. The best strategy is to wait for a sale, which occurs usually a month or two after coupons are put out. As a rule, if coupon is worth 25% of value of the item and product is on sale, you can cleverly save about one-half of its run-of-the-mill cost. Now and then, you can save more.

**Example:** A company offers a 75-cent coupon on one of its brands, and you clip out the coupon. A retailer marks the food item down from $3.69 to $1.49; use your coupon to purchase item for 74 cents. You save nearly $3 and percentage wise 80%.

**14. Become coupon King of the world:** If you know that you can save money buying an item on sale with a coupon, then why not save big by loading up on coupons and then buy items in bulk when they go on sale? To maximize your purchasing power, trade coupons you don't want for ones that are more valuable to you with family, friends, or neighbors. When trading, collect an abundance of coupons for items that are not on your shopping list, while contributing coupons that others need for their households. Once you get multiple coupons for the same item, you can buy in bulk and stock up. A great place to start collecting and saving coupons is through:

- www.coolsavings.com
- www.grocerycoupons.com
- http://discounts.shopathome.com
- www.couponmom.com
- www.thegrocerygame.com

**15. Use coupons with rebates and save big time:** A company issues a coupon for $1 off its product, which normally is priced at $1.89, instantly bringing cost down to 89 cents. Buy item and keep receipt. Week later, go back to store and find rebate slip for the product on store bulletin board for $1.89. Mail your rebate form along with saved receipt for product. Not only do you get the item free, but 89-cent profit, including cost of stamp to mail rebate. As a rule, save all receipts and check your supermarkets rebate board every time you go shopping. Whenever there's an ad campaign for a product, you'll probably see rebate slips.

**16. Non-food items:** Don't purchase non-food items in a grocery store. These items include pots, pans, film, paper and plastics, utensils, brooms, health and beauty aids, etc. These products have the *biggest margin* for most grocers, which is why they are highly displayed in stores.
*Solution #1:* Buy from discount drug stores, dollar stores and discount warehouses, etc.

**17. Don't buy unnecessary vitamins:** Essentially, all nutritionists concede that the vast majority of individuals can acquire all necessary vitamins and minerals from simply eating a balanced meal. What it boils down to is that unless you are diagnosed with a nutritional deficiency or are a nursing mother, you can safely skip buying vitamins.

**18. Make your own cleaning aids and clean-up:** Cleaning aids and cleansers are very expensive and prices vary notably with brands. The mightiest cleanser in kitchen, aside from powder is ammonia; therefore, there is NO need to buy a brand name. How to make your own cleanser: Start with 1/2 cup ammonia, 1/3 cup vinegar, 2 tablespoons of baking soda and 1 gallon of water.

**19. Brown-bag lunches:** The easiest way to reduce your food bill is to eat prepared lunches made from home. The typical adult eats out about 200 times a year. If working outside the home, nearly all your meals are for lunch. By making your own lunch at home, you'll cut costs by at least 40% or more. You can generally make your own lunch for well under $2, compared with buying out or ordering out which costs about $8. Sandwiches made from turkey, tuna, egg salad or peanut butter and jelly can be made for less than 45 cents a piece. A cup of soup in a thermos cost between 20 to 30 cents. Re-warmed chili or casseroles cost less than 40 cents per serving. Have some popcorn or vegetable sticks for about 15 cents per serving. How about hard-boiled eggs for 9 cents apiece with Tabasco sauce, and if you're not watching your weight try Jell-O, cookies or even fresh fruit for 20 cents a serving. Take along some juice in a thermos and you're just over the $1 mark. You'll save even more if you prepare a lunch-bag for school-age children. Most school lunches cost at least $1.50 and most kid-size brown-bag lunches are under $1.00. You can easily save $100 a year per child in cafeteria costs.

**20. Buy food in BULK:** In the USA, we buy groceries on a weekly basis, which is expensive on the pocket book and time consuming. Buying in bulk saves the average family $50 monthly. Even if you shop at more than one store, it still saves time. You'll probably still shop weekly for sales, milk and produce, but spend less time between aisles.

### Rules for buying in bulk:
■ **Rule A:** Never take for granted that one store has lower prices on every item regardless of type of store. To verify, track prices and frequency of sales using price list system. This information will tell you which market to purchase each item and how much to buy. A few hours spent doing this survey can save you hundreds of dollars over the year.
■ **Rule B:** Scrutinize all food sources in your area. Other than grocery stores, check out: food co-ops, bakery thrift shops, warehouse stores, salvage stores, and farmers.
■ **Rule C:** Sale items, on cover and back of sale fliers, will beat prices of any wholesale source of food. The grocer takes a loss on these items and counts on you buying other items at regular or higher price. Some foods never go on sale. Look for other ways to save on these items.
■ **Rule D:** Buy enough to get you to next sale or enough until it's advantageous for you to shop there again.
■ **Rule E:** Note date of any rare, unbeatable sales. In some cases, you might find a pattern on certain items that go on sale. If you can determine that olive oil goes on sale once every three months, you should buy a three-month supply.
■ **Rule F:** Find room for bulk foods, check for spaces in your apartment or home. People tend to think that all foods must be stored in kitchen. However, closets, spare rooms, under beds, attic, basement, even garage space can be converted into a pantry to store bargain foods.

Angel, can you find some more space, so I can store more... **fooooooooooouch!**

Oh! I'm so sorry, honey! When you grocery shopped, you forget to buy my diet soda again, love-chops.

■ **Rule G:** If buying in bulk, you should have a freezer; the savings far outweigh cost of electricity. While some families and singles may not have room for a freezer, I've known military families to make creative use of room by putting their freezer in bedroom or dining area.

**21. Use Co-ops & SAVE:** Many bulk foods are packaged in large quantities. A 50-pound sack of granola will not be practical for a small family. Co-ops came into existence to address this need. Generally, in the form of a buying club, groups of families join together to buy big quantities, then split it into smaller ones. As formal organizations, members are usually asked to donate a few hours of labor per month.

**Food Co-ops:** Co-ops vary greatly in character. Some deal only with organic foods while others carry a line of frozen and prepackaged foods. Finding one that suits your needs may prove difficult. An option is the informal Co-op. Small groups of friends, who buy similar foods, agree to split up large quantities or pick up large quantities of sale items for others in the group. This saves time, gasoline and money. This option addresses needs of smaller family units and those people with storage and time limitations. Buying in bulk can save the family $50 per month.

**Get started:** Most people do not buy food in bulk because they live from paycheck to paycheck. If money is tight, use previous steps on how to save money grocery shopping and live by them. Use savings surplus to begin buying in bulk. The additional savings will provide more cash to reinvest. Within months, you shouldn't have to worry about cost to buy in bulk. As you begin to buy in bulk, your food bill will be high the first month, but in time, the average will drop to a new low as you progressively eat a larger percentage of foods acquired at lowest possible price. Always keep eyes and ears open for sources of low-priced foods. Use the Food Co-op Directory below to find a local wholesale outlet. A wholesale outlet may or may not sell to individuals, or they may have minimum order requirements. However, they can give you names of storefront Co-op or buying club that they sell too.

### FOOD CO-OP DIRECTORY:
■ **Co-op Directory:**
www.coopdirectory.org/directory.htm
■ **CDS Consulting:**
www.cdsconsulting.coop/faq
■ **Local Harvest:**
www.localharvest.org
■ **Jim William's Food Co-op:**
http://niany.com/food.coop.html
■ **The Dollar Stretcher:**
www.strctcher.com/stories/971229a.cfm
■ **East End Food Co-op:**
www.eastendfoodcoop.com/co-oplinks.html
■ **National Co-op Business Association:**
www.ncba.org
■ **CG: Food Co-op 500:**
www.cooperativegrocer.coop/articles/index.php?id=654
■ **Green America:**
www.greenamericatoday.org/pubs/greenpages
■ **Organic Consumers Association:**
www.organicconsumers.org/purelink.html

**22. Buy vegetables by the case:** If you want fresh vegetables, purchasing a case isn't practical, since much will rot before you have a chance to use it. However, if you plan to make jellies, preserves, and sauces, you can save up to 50% purchasing produce by the case at farmers' markets. Farmers' markets render some great deals in bulk, as long as you wait for a huge quantity. All you need to do is call about one month before season's peak and plan to make purchases with the farmers themselves. To find the best purchasing seasons in your local area, get in touch with your local Co-op Extension Service officer (see Co-ops directory above) or refer to **TIP 23** seasonal charts on **page 90**.

**23. Seasonal bargains:** When it comes to perishable goods, you should be on guard for those items that are likely to be seasonal, abundant, and priced to sell, by taking a good look at the table below for ideas.

### WINTER: *December / January / February*

- **FRUIT: Apples, Cranberries, Grapefruit, Oranges, Grapes** and **Pears** (Dec).
- **VEGETABLES: Avocados, Bean Sprouts, Broccoli, Eggplant, Oriental Vegetables, Snow Peas, Sweet Potatoes** and **Winter Squash** (Dec).
- **MEATS: Poultry, Beef** (summer grilling steaks)
- **OTHER: Soup, Tea.**

### SPRING: *March / April / May*

- **FRUIT: Apples** (Mar), **Grapefruit** (Mar), **Oranges** (Mar), **Pears** (Mar), **Pineapple, Rhubarb,** and **Strawberries** (May).
- **VEGETABLES: Artichokes, Asparagus, Beans, Carrot, Cucumbers, Florida Bell Peppers, Onions, Tomatoes** and **Turnips** (May).
- **MEATS: Pork, Beef** (summer grilling steaks / Mar, April)

### SUMMER: *June / July / August*

- **FRUITS: Apples** (Aug), **Apricots, Berries** (July), **Cantaloupes, Cherries** (June, July), **Grapes** (July, Aug), **Lemons** (July), **Melons, Nectarines** (July, Aug), **Peaches** (July, Aug), **Pears** (Aug), **Plums** (Aug), **Strawberries** and **Watermelon** (June, July).
- **VEGETABLES: Beets, Carrots, Corn, Peas, Radishes, Snap Beans** and **Tomatoes.**
- **MEATS: Salmon, Beef** (winter cuts, roasts / July, Aug) **Pork** (Aug)

### FALL: *September / October / November*

- **FRUIT: Apples, Bananas, Cranberries** (Oct, Nov) **Grapefruit** (Nov), **Grapes, Oranges** (Oct, Nov), **Pears, Pomegranates** and **Pumpkin** (Oct, Nov).
- **VEGETABLES: Avocados, Broccoli, Brussels Sprouts, Cauliflower, Chestnuts, Green Peppers** (Sept), **Parsnips, Sweet Potatoes** (Oct, Nov), **Tomatoes, Turnips, Washington Potatoes, Winter Squash** (Sept).
- **MEATS: Beef** (summer grilling steaks / Nov)

**24. Blanch vegetables:** When buying fresh produce in bulk, you'll get more food than you could eat in a week, so what do you do before your produce spoils? Blanching is a method where you place produce in boiling water for a brief time and then instantly "submerge" in cold water before freezing. It's done so that vegetables store better and stay fresher longer. Just blanch for time indicated below, let cool, and then stash in freezer bags.

| | |
|---|---|
| **Asparagus / 3 min** | **Peppers / 2 min** |
| **Beets (small) / until tender** | **Spinach / 2 ½ min** |
| **Broccoli / 3 to 4 ½ m** | **Turnip greens / 2 ½ min** |
| **Brussels sprouts / 3 to 4 ½ m** | |
| **Corn (cut from ear) / 3 to 7 m** | |
| **Green peas / 1 ½ - 2½ m** | |
| **Green or Wax beans / 2 ½ m** | |
| **Lima beans / 1 ½ min** | |
| **Okra (medium) / 3 to 4 m** | |

To learn more, visit:
www.extension.umn.edu/distribution/nutrition/DJ0555.html

**25. Save money on poultry and meat:** If you have a freezer, you can save on your meat bill by buying it in abundance during seasons. If you buy summer meats in winter, fall or spring, you'll save about 15% over buying the same cuts in summer. You can save as much as 20%, by purchasing and hoarding winter meats in late summer. August is a good time to stock freezer with winter meats such as roasts and pork. If you don't have a freezer, you can save by buying out-of-season cuts when they're at lowest price.

**26. Chop and slice your own meat:** Butchers sell individual steaks at $6.98 per pound and whole strip loins at $4.59 per pound. If you buy whole strips and slice them into individual loins, you get meat at two-thirds of the cost (save 35%). Additional cuts recommended for the *"cut-it-yourself butcher"* include sirloin tip, brisket and peeled rib eye. You can also save money buying whole chickens and chopping them up yourself. All you have to do is educate yourself on how to cut it. Many supermarkets offer meat-cutting classes to shoppers. Just call your local supermarket and ask for information. You should buy two knives, which cost $15-20 each; a good long slicing knife and a stiff-bladed boning knife.

**27. Buy family packs of meat:** Supermarket meat departments and butcher shops offer price reductions on meat because big orders give them a steadier cash flow. The biggest savings are from purchasing whole sides of beef, which yields 240 lbs (+/-) of beef and can provide a household of four for six to eight months (if they eat meat three times per week). A side of beef can cost 20%-30% less than purchasing same quantity of meat over time. In contrast, buying family packs containing five or more pounds can result in discounts ranging 10 to 50 cents per pound, with savings of up to 20%. Before buying, research and know how you plan to use the meat, week by week. This will assist you in deciding how much and what variety of meat to purchase. In addition, make good use of freezer space and stock only what your family can use within recommended storage time (see storage chart **page 91**).
**Tip:** When looking for bargains on meat, bear in mind how many servings you'll get from each cut of meat. The guides below will you to help calculate cost per serving.

**Little Bone or Fat** (three to four servings per pound):

| | |
|---|---|
| Bone-in round steak | Flank steak |
| Boneless-beef chuck roast | Ground meat |
| Boneless ham | Stew meat |
| Boneless round roast or steak | |

**Some Bone or Fat** (two to three servings per pound):

| | |
|---|---|
| Bone-in chuck roast | Bone-in pork steak |
| Bone-in chuck steak | Whole chicken |
| Bone-in ham | Whole turkey |
| Bone-in pork chops | |

**Much Bone or Fat** (one to two servings per pound):

| | |
|---|---|
| Beef short ribs | Spareribs |
| Lamb rib chops | T-bone steak |
| Picnic shoulder roast | Veal rib chops |
| Porterhouse steak | |

**Tip:** Marinating for 20 minutes or as long as 24 hours, will make inexpensive and usually tougher cuts of meat more tender and better tasting. These involve stew meats, cubes, boneless roasts and flank steaks. You'll save close to 10 to 30% compared with purchasing more "tender" cuts and get a healthier chunk of meat, because tougher cuts of meat have less in fat.

# FOOD STORAGE CHART & MEASUREMENTS

| | Refrigerate | Freeze |
|---|---|---|
| **Meat (raw)** | | |
| Beef steaks | 1 to 2 days | 6 to 12 months |
| Beef roasts | 1 to 2 days | 6 to 12 months |
| Ground beef | 1 to 2 days | 3 to 4 months |
| Ground veal | 1 to 2 days | 3 to 4 months |
| Ground lamb | 1 to 2 days | 3 to 4 months |
| Beef stew meat | 1 to 2 days | 3 to 4 months |
| Ground pork | 1 to 2 days | 1 to 3 months |
| Lamb chops | 1 to 2 days | 6 to 9 months |
| Lamb steaks | 1 to 2 days | 6 to 9 months |
| Lamb roasts | 1 to 2 days | 6 to 9 months |
| Organ meats | 1 to 2 days | 3 to 4 months |
| Pork chops | 1 to 2 days | 3 to 4 months |
| Pork sausages | 1 to 2 days | 1 to 2 months |
| Veal Cutlets | 1 to 2 days | 6 to 9 months |
| Veal Steaks | 1 to 2 days | 6 to 12 months |

| **Poultry (raw)** | | |
|---|---|---|
| Chicken, cut-up | 1 to 2 days | 9 months |
| Chicken, whole | 1 to 2 days | 12 months |
| Chicken giblets | 1 to 2 days | 3 months |
| Duck, whole | 1 to 2 days | 6 months |
| Goose, whole | 1 to 2 days | 6 months |
| Turkey, whole | 1 to 2 days | 6 months |
| Turkey, cut-up | 1 to 2 days | 6 months |

| **Fish (raw)** | | |
|---|---|---|
| Fresh fish | 1 to 2 days | 6 to 9 months |
| Shrimp | 1 to 2 days | 2 months |
| Lobster | 1 to 2 days | 1 to 2 months |
| Crabs | 1 to 2 days | 1 to 2 months |
| Oysters | 1 to 2 days | 3 to 6 months |
| Clams | 1 to 2 days | 3 to 6 months |
| Scallops | 1 to 2 days | 3 to 6 months |

| **Cooked meat** | | |
|---|---|---|
| Beef roast | 3 to 4 days | 2 to 3 months |
| Beef stew | 3 to 4 days | 2 to 3 months |
| Chicken, fried | 1 to 2 days | 4 months |
| Chicken pieces In broth gravy | 1 to 2 days | 6 months |
| Chicken pieces Not in broth gravy | 1 to 2 days | 1 month |
| Chicken salad | 1 to 2 days | do not freeze |
| Tuna salad | 1 to 2 days | do not freeze |
| Fish | 2 to 3 days | 1 month |
| Fresh ham | 3 to 4 days | 2 to 3 months |
| Fresh pork | 3 to 4 days | 2 to 3 months |
| Meat broth | 1 to 2 days | 2 to 3 months |
| Meat gravy | 1 to 2 days | 2 to 3 months |

| **Cooked meat** | | |
|---|---|---|
| Meat loaf | 2 to 3 days | 3 months |
| Meat spaghetti Sauce | 3 to 4 days | 6 to 8 months |
| Pork or Lamb | 3 to 4 days | 2 to 3 months |

| **Cured meats** | | |
|---|---|---|
| Bacon | 1 week | 2 to 4 months |
| Corned beef | 1 week | 2 weeks |
| Frankfurters | 1 week | 1 month |
| Ham, canned (unopened) | 1 year | do not freeze |
| Ham, whole | 1 week | 1 to 2 months |

| Luncheon meat | 3 to 5 days | do not freeze |
|---|---|---|
| Sausage, smoked | 7 days | do not freeze |

| **Dairy products** | | |
|---|---|---|
| Butter, salted | 2 weeks | 3 months |
| Butter, unsalted | 2 weeks | 6 months |
| Cheese, hard | 2 to 3 months | 6 months |
| Cheese, soft | 2 weeks | 2 months |
| Cottage cheese | 5 to 7 days | 1 to 2 weeks |
| Cream cheese | 2 weeks | 2 weeks |
| Egg, whole | 2 to 3 weeks | do not freeze |
| Egg whites | 1 week | 6 to 8 months |
| Milk / cream | 1 week | 1 month |

| **Fruits** | | |
|---|---|---|
| Apples | 1 month | 1 year |
| Apricots, avocados | | |
| Bananas, grapes | | |
| Melons, nectarines | | |
| Peaches, pears | | |
| Pineapples, plums | 3 to 5 days | 1 year |
| Berries, cherries | 2 to 3 days | 1 year |
| Citrus fruits | 2 weeks | 1 year |
| Cranberries | 1 week | 1 year |

| **Vegetables** | | |
|---|---|---|
| Asparagus | 2 to 3 days | 6 months |
| Broccoli, spinach | | |
| Brussel sprouts | | |
| Lima beans, peas | | |
| Rhubarb, scallions | | |
| Summer squash | 3 to 5 days | 6 months |
| Cabbage | 1 to 2 weeks | 6 months |
| Carrots, parsnips | | |
| Beets, turnips | 2 weeks | 6 months |
| Cauliflower, celery | | |
| Green beans, peppers | | |
| Cucumbers, | | |
| Tomatoes | 1 week | 6 months |
| Lettuce, salad greens | 1 week | do not freeze |

## Measurement Equivalents

1 tablespoon (tbsp) = 3 teaspoons (tsp)
1/16 cup (c) = 1 tablespoon
1/8 cup = 2 tablespoons
1/6 cup = 2 tablespoons + 2 teaspoons
1/4 cup = 4 tablespoons
1/3 cup = 5 tablespoons + 1 teaspoon
3/8 cup = 6 tablespoons
1/2 cup = 8 tablespoons
2/3 cup = 10 tablespoons + 2 teaspoons
3/4 cup = 12 tablespoons
1 cup = 48 teaspoons
1 cup = 16 tablespoons
8 fluid ounces (fl oz) = 1 cup
1 pint (pt) = 2 cups
1 quart (qt) = 2 pints
4 cups = 1 quart
1 gallon (gal) = 4 quarts
16 ounces (oz) = 1 pound (lb)
1 milliliter (ml) = 1 cubic centimeter (cc)
1 inch (in) = 2.54 centimeters (cm)

C-7

**28. Stock up anytime and save:** The following products have a long shelf life. Buy when at best price.

| | | |
|---|---|---|
| Baking powder | Cornstarch | Rice |
| Baking soda | Cumin, ground | Rosemary |
| Balsamic Vinegar | Dark brown sugar | Salt |
| Bay leaves | Dijon mustard | Sesame oil |
| Beef bouillon | Flour | Soy sauce |
| Bread crumbs, unseasoned | Granulated sugar | Tabasco sauce |
| Cayenne pepper, ground | Honey | Tomato paste |
| Chicken bouillon | Italian Seasoning | Turmeric |
| Chili powder | Ketchup | Vanilla extract |
| Chili sauce | Nutmeg | Vegetable oil |
| Cinnamon | Paprika | Worcestershire |
| Cocoa, unsweetened | Pepper | White vinegar |

**29. Other tips and tricks (kitchen sink):**

■ Check out day-old bread stores (save 30% to 50%). They offer big savings on bread, pastry and some non-bread items that are still acceptable to eat.

■ Find supermarkets, food warehouses, etc, that sell *"day old"* goods such as meat, produce and bakery goods. The quality should still be acceptable.

■ Plan a few meatless meals during week. Meat's costly, so check the library for Mexican, Italian and oriental cookbooks, which feature vegetables rather than meat.

■ Make a pound of hamburger go further by adding bread-crumbs, oatmeal, tomato sauce or corn flakes. This will help stretch a high-cost food item with lower cost products.

■ Mix one part of reconstituted instant milk with one part of 1% or 2% milk. You are stretching a higher-cost product with a lower cost product that your family will never notice (hide the box). When buying milk, the lower the fat content, usually the less expensive the milk.

■ Plan the use of more leftovers.

■ Take snacks to work with you like oatmeal cookies, boiled eggs, pickles, carrot and celery sticks. Vending machines are expensive.

■ List food items that you discard when cleaning out your refrigerator. If after several cleanings, you see a pattern of underused items that spoil, change buying habits.

■ Eating at home saves money. Make a menu at home (laminate it) with everyone's favorite meal and discuss with family what to eat weekly. Twice a week, before setting meal on table, turn television off, play some light music (no singing to interfere with conversation) dim lights, and light a candle; include cloth napkins, your finest chinaware and a breadbasket for that restaurant atmosphere. *Bon appetite!*

**When you get to checkout counter:** Pay particular attention at the checkout counter. Sometimes a sale price is listed in a store, but not reflected at checkout. Group special sale items together when unloading the grocery cart, along with anything missing a price tag or tag that may be incorrect. Stay doubly alert when these items are rung up, they are the items most likely to be rung up wrong, even in stores using scanners. Look over sales receipt in the parking lot and compare prices with your food-shopping list. If there is a price discrepancy, go instantly and see the manager for a full return of your money.

**No money for food?** What would you do if you had no money for food? If an unfortunate situation like that should happen, first check with your installation "Family Support or Advocacy Center." See if they know of, or support, programs that can ably assist you in your time of need. Secondly, check your local church, or church groups for a free food pantry nearest you. Free pantries offer food and help to people who are struggling in tough times. If you'd like to get more information, willingly help donate food or volunteer time to a food pantry; just call your local church.

**30. Angel Food** is a non-denominational, organization (non-profit), devoted to food relief and financial support to communities throughout the USA. Started in 1994 (in Georgia) the program has now grown to serve more than 500,000 families monthly, with 5,200 (+) sites in 35 states.

■ **Blessings in a box:** Each month's menu is different and consists of fresh, frozen and packaged food. Food is purchased from the nation's top food suppliers, which provide quality and nutritious food at big discounts. One box of "**Angel Food**" cost $30 (value $65 (+/-), and feeds a family of four for about one week or single senior citizen for almost a month. In addition, the program offers "**Specialty Boxes**" of steak, chicken, pork or other foods. To view this month's menu, visit: **www.angelfoodministries.com/menu_0910en2.asp**

■ **FOOD STAMPS:** The program partakes in the **Food Stamp Program,** which is designed to help low-income families buy food they need for good nutrition. For more, visit: **www.angelfoodministries.com/food_stamps**

■ **Purchasing Angel Food:** There are no restrictions, conditions or forms to fill out to purchase Angel Food. The program is open to all and can purchase an unlimited number of boxes of food by placing an order with a local Angel Food host site. To find a host site and order food, visit: **www.angelfoodministries.com/hosts.asp**

**SIGNATURE BOX: $30.00** *(feeds family of four: 1- week)*
- 1.5 lb.  New York Strips Steaks (3 x 8 oz.)
- 1 lb.  Steak Fajita Strips
- 2 lb.  Chicken Stir Fry Skillet Meal
- 1 lb.  Lean Ground Beef
- 1.5 lb.  Breaded White Meat Chicken Tenders
- 1 lb.  Avg. Center Cut Ham Steaks (Hickory Smoked)
- 1 lb.  Bake or Fry Fish Sticks (32 sticks)
- 1 lb.  Pasta
- 25 oz.  Marinara Sauce
- 1 lb.  Frozen Baby Lima Beans
- 1 lb.  Frozen Mixed Vegetables
- 2 lb.  Bag Fresh Apples (8-10 ct.)
- 10 ct.  Flour Tortilla Wraps
- 32 oz.  2% Shelf Stable Milk
- Dozen Eggs
- Dessert

**SPECIAL 1: $23.00 (7 lb. Assorted Meat Grill Box)**
- 1.5 lb.  Ribeye Steaks (3 x 8 oz.)
- 2 lb.  Pork Chops (4 x 8 oz.)
- 2 lb.  Lean Hamburger Steaks (4 x 8 oz.)
- 1.5 lb.  Bratwurst Sausage with Cheese

**SPECIAL 2: $22.00 (4.5 lb. Assorted Steak)**
- 1.5 lb.  Bone-In Ribeye Steaks (2 x 12 oz.)
- 1.5 lb.  Kansas City Strip Steaks (2 x 12 oz.)
- 1.5 lb.  T-Bone Steaks (2 x 12 oz.)

**SPECIAL 3: $20.00 (10 lb. Breaded Chicken Box)**
- 4 lb.  Breaded Frying Chicken Pieces
- 2 lb.  Breaded Chicken Tenders
- 2 lb.  Breaded Chicken Breast Fillet
- 2 lb.  Breaded White Meat Chicken Nuggets

**SPECIAL 4: $22.00 (Fresh Fruit and Veggie box)**
- 1  Premium Sweet Golden Ripe Pineapple
- 3 lb.  Bag New Crop Florida Tangerines
- 1  Premium Vine Ripened Cantaloupe
- 4  Premium Washington State Bosc Pears
- 4  Premium Juicy Limes
- 3 lb. bag  Premium New Crop Large Red Potatoes
- 2 lb. bag  Premium New Crop Yellow Onions
- 1 head  Premium Green Cabbage
- 2 bulbs  Premium Jumbo Garlic
- 2 ct.  Premium Large Green Bell Pepper
- 3 lb. bag  Premium Bagged Idaho Potatoes
- 1 lb. bag  Premium Calif. Whole Peeled Baby Carrots

**31. SHARE Program: SHARE** offers families and individuals the most help in slashing the cost of groceries today. It's easy to do and the quicker you get started, the more money you will save. The information below will explain the program, how to qualify and locations nearest you.

## What is SHARE (Self Help and Resource Exchange)?

**SHARE** is a nationwide, neighborhood-based, self-help food distribution program and is sponsored by a network of churches, community centers, military bases, etc.

## What is a SHARE?

■ A **SHARE** is volunteering for 2 hours to help someone or an organization. You then qualify to buy a package of groceries worth $40 to $45 retail for $21 in cash or food stamps.
■ No limit on how many **SHARES'** a person may purchase.

**Example:** If you or family members donated 26 hours (can combine hours) of community service during month, you'd qualify to purchase thirteen **$21 SHARE** packages (value $40 +), which would be worth **$520+** in food value.

■ A person can give away his or her performed **SHARE's** for someone else to use.

## How the program works:

■ You pay cash (or in food stamps), for food during first 10 days of each month
■ You volunteer anywhere you want during the next 15-20 days (baby sit, coach, mow neighbors lawn, etc.).
■ You receive food during last 10 days of each month by picking up at your host site.

## Benefits to family and community:

■ Strengthens individuals, families and communities; it also cultivates dignity, acceptance and belonging.
■ Encourages new ideas and helps others.
■ Increases the amount of quality food available to families and it ensures people will have food the last few days of the month.
■ Helps military members to increase their chances of a promotion by volunteering time (EPS).

## Requirements to join SHARE:

■ **SHARE** is open to everyone, regardless of income or age. No documentation is required.
■ All you need are your cash or food stamps and a willingness to volunteer and help others.

### Locations and contacts to start with:

**California:**     www.goldensharefoods.com
                Services:  Southern CA
**Colorado:**     www.sharecolorado.com
                Services: KS, LA, MO, NE, NM, OK, SD, TX, WY
**Florida:**     www.shareflorida.com
**Illinois:**     www.sharefood-peoria.org/page6.php
                Services: IN
**Iowa:**     www.shareiowa.com
                Services: IA, MO, NE, SD
**New York:**     www.caproc.org/share.php
**Oklahoma:**     www.greatertulsa.com/frc/share.html
**Pennsylvania:** www.sharefoodprogram.org
                Services: DE, NJ, NY, MD
**DC Metro:**     www.sharedc.org
                Services: MD, VA
**Wisconsin:**     www.sharewi.org
                Services: IL, MI, MN, WI

**Note:** Make sure you sign up for next SHARE month on D-Day (Distribution Day). New menu will be provided to you to choose from at pick-up site or visit their web-site.

## EXAMPLE MENU

### *REGULAR Package: $21 (value $40 + or -)

| | | |
|---|---|---|
| 4 lb. | Whole Chicken | Lettuce |
| 1 lb. | Ground Beef | Broccoli |
| 1 lb. | Bacon | Celery |
| 14 oz. | Cooked White Turkey | Radishes |
| 2-7 oz. | Sausage Pizzas | 2 Cucumbers |
| 1 lb. | Pinto Beans | 5 Apples |
| 6 | Russet Potatoes | 5 Bananas |
| 4 | Onions | 5 Oranges |
| 1 lb. | Carrots | |

### *JR. Package: $11 (value $20 + or -)

| | | |
|---|---|---|
| 1 lb. | Meatballs | Lettuce |
| 2 lb. | Split Chicken Breast | Broccoli |
| 26 oz. | Spaghetti Sauce | Celery |
| 1 lb. | Spaghetti | 6 Russet Potatoes |
| 16 oz. | Salad Dressing | |

### *Grill Package: $21

| | | | |
|---|---|---|---|
| 1 lb. | Pork Chops | 3-1/2 lb. | Chicken legs ¼ |
| 10 oz. | (2) T-Bone Steaks | 1 lb. | Bratwurst |
| 6 oz. | (3) Fillet of Beef | 2 lb. | Chicken Breast |
| 6 oz. | (2) N.Y. Strip Steaks | | |

### *CHOICE Items: Can buy food in bulk

| | | | |
|---|---|---|---|
| _____ | $15.00 | 9 lb. | Variety Meat Box |
| _____ | 11.00 | 3 lb. | USDA Fillet Of Beef |
| _____ | 6.00 | 2.6 lb. | Italian Style Chicken Steak |
| _____ | 2.50 | 1 lb. | Mahi Mahi |
| _____ | 1.75 | 1 lb. | Bacon |
| _____ | 2.50 | 15 oz. | IQF Chicken Breast Tenderloin |
| _____ | 2.25 | 4 pk. | Pepperoni Hot Pockets |
| _____ | 1.65 | 1 lb. | Ground Beef 85/15 |
| _____ | 1.00 | 8 ct. | Fruit Bars |
| _____ | .80 | 15 oz. | Peaches |
| _____ | .50 | 15 oz. | Tomato Soup |
| _____ | .55 | 15 oz. | Tomatoes |
| _____ | 1.50 | 18 oz. | Corn Flakes Cereal |
| _____ | .40 | 6 oz. | Macaroni and Cheese |
| _____ | 1.00 | 15 oz. | Chili with beans |

**\* Items subject to change**

**NOTE: In some states, SHARE consumers can now order their groceries online.**

**TIP: 1. Be on time to pick up your food.**
       **2. Bring your receipt and volunteer slip**
       **3. Bring a couple of boxes to put food**

**32. Stay ahead of the food saving curve, visit:**
■ **Simple Debt Free Living:**
www.simpledebtfreeliving.com/grocerysavings.html
■ **Blogher:** www.blogher.com/how-you-can-save-money-food-and-still-eat-healthy
■ **Cook for good:** www.cookforgood.com
■ **Tree Hugging Family:** www.treehuggingfamily.com/organic-food-costs-rise-11-ways-to-save-money-on-organic-food
■ **SMOG:** www.save-money-on-groceries.com

As the father of five, I know there are many steps you can take to save money when having a new baby. Listed below are ways to cut corners in order to assist you in bringing up your baby and yet, still save.

## Before your bundle of joy arrives:

■ **Women, Infants, & Children (WIC):** The day you find you're pregnant, see if you qualify for WIC (a nutritional, supplemental food assistance program (see **page 95**).

■ **Buy used furniture:** Find baby furniture through thrift stores, garage, yard, divorce sales, etc. When no longer needed, resell at yard sale for same price you paid.

■ **Borrow and beg (furniture & clothing):** Contact family, friends, etc.; see what they can turn up. Our baby's room was furnished with all borrowed items; relatives and friends gave us tons of clothing.

■ **Throw baby shower:** What can't be found used may be given new through baby showers. Leave clues and hints to what you need or lack, especially with family.

■ **Put off items needed until found cheap:** Although you have to acquire key items for your baby, other items can be used instead. Here are some *"temporary"* ideas:

**Baby Tub:** Wash your baby in a sink, or hold carefully in a bathtub filled with 2 inches of warm water.

**Bottles:** Breastfeed your baby for a year or longer and then teach to drink from a cup.

**Car seat:** No substitute for this. Some hospitals rent them for a small fee per month, but It's a bargain to buy one new. Rental can be used until you find good used one.

**Changing table:** Use a towel on a bureau top or bed, with changing items in a nearby small box.

**Clothes:** If you don't receive free clothes from relatives and friends, get used clothes at garage and yard sale(s).

**Crib:** Use a drawer from a dresser bureau and put bedding in it for infant. Use a playpen and place bedding in it for an older child.

**Crib Bumpers:** Roll up a towel if worried about baby bumping his/her head.

**Diaper Bag:** Use any strong bag, backpack, etc.

**High Chair:** Use baby swing, stroller, walker or place baby in your lap and hold while feeding.

**Mobiles:** Babies tire of entertainment devices. Instead, hold and play with baby yourself (housework can wait).

**Playpen:** Baby proof room (doors, gates, etc.).

**Shoes:** Baby doesn't need them until he/she begins to walk. Use socks and booties when weather cools.

**Stroller:** Use baby backpack, until you get a stroller.

**Toys:** Babies love boxes, cups, lids, etc., and they usually end up getting more toys than they need.

**Walker:** Walkers aren't that important, but they can be used for many other things.

**Wind-up Swing:** My children enjoyed this device, but buy it used.

**Warning:** Think safety for your children always. Look over used equipment, homemade toys, etc. with a fine toothed comb. Educate yourself with current safety guidelines and use your brain.

## The stork arrives at your door step

■ **Formula:** Breastfeed if possible, it's better for your baby. Formula can cost up to $1,200 a year.

■ **Store-bought Baby Food:** Babies get adequate nutrition, as long as they are on breast milk or formula. When ready (six months more or less) to feed your baby foods, you can buy a hand-cranked device that grinds all sorts of foods to baby-food standards, but it's not really needed. Feed them applesauce, cooked cereals, or mashed potatoes. Foods like bananas, spaghetti, and salt-free canned green beans, mash with fork.

■ **Baby Diapers:** Generic diapers cost around $9 a box. Infant size box has 64. Most infants need changing 12 to 14 times a day, so you may end up using more than one box a week. You can buy a dozen pre-folded diapers for as little as $8. Mother with one baby would spend less than $40 for one-time purchase. By using cloth diapers, one can save $1,000 by the time infant learns how to potty train. **To wash:** Rinse out diapers in toilet. Wash diapers: Add ¼ cup of vinegar to neutralize; add detergent soap, and bleach with cold water.

■ **Saving for baby:** When is the best time to save for your baby? Save before the baby is born, Procrastinator. If you can save, consider a few options with the table below, which reflects what would happen if one were to deposit **$1,200** yearly in an account averaging **10%** for a child, then stop deposits after a period of 2 or 15-years; then allow sum to accumulate to age 65.

| 2-Year Deposits | | | 15-Year Deposits | | |
|---|---|---|---|---|---|
| Year | Deposit | Growth | Year | Deposit | Growth |
| 1 | 1,200 | 1,310 | 1 | 1,200 | 1,310 |
| 2 | 1,200 | 2,751 | 2 | 1,200 | 2,751 |
| 3 | 0 | 3.026 | 3 | 1,200 | 4,336 |
| 4 | 0 | 3,329 | 4 | 1,200 | 6,080 |
| 5 | 0 | 3,662 | 5 | 1,200 | 7,998 |
| 6 | 0 | 4,028 | 6 | 1,200 | 10,107 |
| 7 | 0 | 4,431 | 7 | 1,200 | 12,428 |
| 8 | 0 | 4,874 | 8 | 1,200 | 14,981 |
| 9 | 0 | 5.361 | 9 | 1,200 | 17,789 |
| 10 | 0 | 5,897 | 10 | 1,200 | 20,878 |
| 15 | 0 | 9.497 | 15 | 1,200 | 41,622 |
| 20 | 0 | 15,295 | 20 | 0 | 67,033 |
| 25 | 0 | 24.633 | 25 | 0 | 107,957 |
| 30 | 0 | 39.672 | 30 | 0 | 173,865 |
| 35 | 0 | 63,892 | 35 | 0 | 280,012 |
| 40 | 0 | 102.899 | 40 | 0 | 450,962 |
| 45 | 0 | 165,720 | 45 | 0 | 726,278 |
| 50 | 0 | 266,894 | 50 | 0 | 1,169,678 |
| 55 | 0 | 429,836 | 55 | 0 | 1,883,778 |
| 60 | 0 | 692,255 | 60 | 0 | 3,003,844 |
| 65 | 0 | 1, 114,884 | 65 | 0 | 4,886,036 |

Jane, we're so gosh darn lucky we don't have kids in our lives. Maybe we can plan to have one later, when I'm making more dough in the military. By the way, have you been putting on a little weight lately, Jane?

**OH NO!** If Dick only knew that I'm 6-months pregnant with his quintuplets!

Oh Dick, you and your silly goals and planning for the future! Don't you think it'd be fun to have a kid or four around here? Wait a second! **WHAT WEIGHT, DICK?**

**94**

## WHAT IS WIC?

WIC is a temporary assistance program for women; infants and young children who have a nutritional need for the program.

## WHAT DOES WIC PROVIDE?

■ **Nutrition Education**-information provided to help improve eating habits.
■ **Supplemental Foods**-vouchers to buy specific foods important for good health.

## WHAT ARE REQUIREMENTS FOR WIC?

Women must be pregnant, breast-feeding, or have recently delivered a baby. Children must be under five years of age.

### Participants must also:

■ Be determined as a nutritional risk by a health professional.
■ Receive regular medical check-ups.
■ Meet income guidelines.
■ Reside in a local agency's service area.

### WIC Vouchers are:

■ Used like checks.
■ Used to buy specific foods.
■ Used at the store selected by the participant.

### You may no longer be eligible (all participants) for WIC if:

■ You deliberately misuse or attempt to misuse your WIC vouchers.
■ Someone with a greater nutritional problem needs WIC.
■ You do not provide the WIC staff with adequate information to assess your eligibility.
■ You do not keep appointments to pick-up vouchers.
■ Your household income increases above the maximum allowed.
■ You provide the WIC staff with false information.

### For Women:

■ Six weeks after your baby is born if you are not breast-feeding.
■ One year after your baby is born if you are breast-feeding.

### For infants and children:

■ When child's nutritional problem has improved.
■ If it is determined that WIC is not improving your child's nutritional problem.
■ No child will be continued after the 5th birthday.

## While you are participating in WIC:

■ You will receive monthly vouchers for supplemental foods.
■ You will be provided with nutrition education.
■ You will be encouraged to receive regular health care.
■ Keep all medical appointments.
■ Keep your WIC appointment. Contact your WIC agency, if you cannot do so.
■ You will be expected to cooperate with the WIC staff, follow agency rules and use your vouchers correctly.

## WIC is a temporary assistance program:

■ Participation is for a limited period of time.
■ For infants and children, eligibility to participate will be re-evaluated approximately every 6 months.
■ For women, eligibility will be re-evaluated after the baby is born. For breast-feeding women, eligibility will be evaluated again when the baby is six-months old.
■ Eligibility determinations are called certifications.

## At each certification you will be required to provide:

■ Medical information.
■ Proof of address.
■ Proof of income.

**Note:** Your WIC agency may ask you to bring additional information and a form of personal identification.

Contact your **Family Support Counselor** for more information about WIC or go to WIC website at: **www.fns.usda.gov/wic**

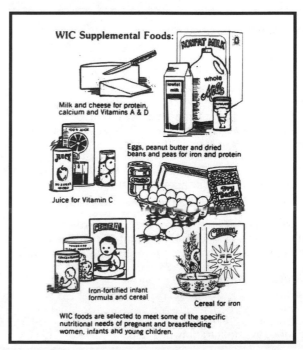

WIC Supplemental Foods:

Milk and cheese for protein, calcium and Vitamins A & D

Juice for Vitamin C

Eggs, peanut butter and dried beans and peas for iron and protein

Iron-fortified infant formula and cereal

Cereal for iron

WIC foods are selected to meet some of the specific nutritional needs of pregnant and breastfeeding women, infants and young children.

C-7

## U.S. Department of Agriculture (USDA)
### Food and Nutrition Service
3101 Park Center Drive
Alexandria, VA 22302
Administration: 1-800-221-5689
www.fns.usda.gov/fsp

Food and Nutrition Program is locally administered by district food stamp office. Check yellow pages for the nearest food stamp office in your area.

### Food Stamp Definition:
The Food Stamp Program helps low-income people to buy food that they need for good health. You may be able to get food stamps if you:
- Work for low wages.
- Is unemployed or work part-time.
- Receive welfare or other assistance payments.
- Are elderly or disabled and live on a small income.
- Are homeless.

The amount of food stamps you can get is based on U.S. Department of Agriculture Thrifty Food Plan, which is an estimate of how much it costs to give your household nutritious, low cost meals. This estimate is changed every year to keep pace with food prices.

### 2009 FINANCIAL ELIGIBILITY CRITERIA

| People in household | Gross monthly income limits | Net monthly income limits |
|---|---|---|
| 1 | $1,174 | $ 903 |
| 2 | 1,579 | 1,215 |
| 3 | 1,984 | 1,526 |
| 4 | 2,389 | 1,838 |
| 5 | 2,794 | 2,150 |
| 6 | 3,200 | 2,461 |
| 7 | 3,605 | 2,773 |
| 8 | 4,010 | 3,085 |
| Each additional person | +406 | +312 |

**Resources:** Under food stamp rules, resources such as bank accounts, cash, real estate, personal property, a vehicle and so forth are considered in determining whether a household is eligible to get food stamps. Some resources are counted and some are not. The agency representative will explain which are not. All households may have up to $2,000 worth of countable resources to be eligible. Households may have up to $3,000 and be eligible if at least one member is age 60 or older.

**Automobiles:** If the fair market value of your car exceeds $4,650, then any dollar above this amount counts against the $2,000 limit listed above.

**All Reported Income:** Under food stamp rules, almost all types of income are counted. For military personnel, add the following from left side of your LES:

1. Gross income
2. Base pay
3. BAS
4. BAH
5. Flight pay, Hazard duty pay, etc.

6. Cash and money in checking and savings accounts
7. Stocks, mutual funds, bonds, etc
8. Land, buildings, other than your home and lot that do not produce income
9. Licensed vehicle

**Note 1:** Military clothing allowance should not be included.

**Note 2:** It is best to obtain a written appraisal on your vehicle from a car dealer for a true estimate. This may be more accurate than blue book value.

### APPLYING FOR FOOD STAMPS

Obtain an application form and fill it out as correctly and honestly as possible. Give or send the form to the closest office in your area as soon as possible.

**Meeting with an Agency Representative:** After you have turned in your application, an agency representative will hold a private interview with you or another member of your household.

At the interview, agency representative will explain program rules and help you complete any parts of the application that you have not filled out. The representative will also ask you for proof of certain information you have given. Ask agency representative to explain anything you don't understand.

### Food Stamp Documentation:
**Proof of income:** You must provide proof of all incomes on all household members. **Example:** LES, pay stubs, other income.
- **Proof of bills:** In order to expedite your application you should have the following records.
**Example:** Child care costs, rents or mortgage, telephone, utility bills, account numbers for checking and savings.
- **Social Security cards:** You must have Social Security cards for all members of your household, including children and infants.

**Note:** To obtain Social Security cards contact your local social security office. If you are applying for an initial Social Security card, two forms of identification are required; birth certificate, immunization record, ID card, etc.

EAT ME!
I'm delicious.

## FINDING CHILD CARE & EARLY EDUCATION PROGRAMS

The **child care resource and referral agency (CCR&R)** can help you find available and affordable child care services and early education in your local area. Contact **Child Care Aware (CCA)**, a free, federally funded service, at **www.childcareaware.org** or call **1-800-424-2246** to find a local **CCR&R**. You can also use the **CCA** childcare connector online to find the nearest **CCR&R** center. Once you're in contact with **CCR&R**, they can give you the facts about child care, and a list of child care options in your area that may meet your needs.
Make sure to ask your **CCR&R** center these things:
■ What are the child care licensing requirements in my area?
■ How can I get information about child care complaints and licensing violations?
■ Are there any child care financial assistance programs that my family qualifies for?
**Visit and Ask Question:** Make sure you visit the child care center or home you are considering. Furthermore, investigate these key indicators of quality:

### FINDING MONEY FOR CHILD CARE
Your CCR&R may have information about child care programs that have special funding options or sliding fee scales.
**Child Care Aware's** brochures on help with funding child care are available on their Website. "Finding Help Paying for Child Care" (English):
**www.childcareaware.org/docs/pubs/110e.pdf**

"Cómo encontrar ayuda para cubrir el costo del servicio de cuidado de niños" (Spanish):
**www.childcareaware.org/docs/pubs/110s.pdf**

**Early Head Start** serves infants, toddlers, and children ages 3-5. Overall, **Head Start** serves children whose family income is at or below Federal Poverty Level. To find a **Head Start** program in your area, use the online Head Start Program Search Tool by visiting:
**http://eclkc.ohs.acf.hhs.gov/hslc/HeadStartOffices**

### CHILD & DEPENDENT CARE CREDIT
You can find more help with funding childcare through the IRS: Claiming the Child and Dependent Care Credit at:
**www.irs.gov/newsroom/article/0,,id=106189,00.html**

### CHILD TAX CREDIT
This credit is for people who have a qualifying child. It can be claimed in addition to the Credit for Child and Dependent Care expenses. To learn more, visit:
**www.irs.gov/newsroom/article/0,,id=106182,00.html**

### OTHER SOURCES: CHILD CARE HELP
The Department of Health and Human Services Administration for Children & Families (ACF) has a wealth of information about childcare, adoption & foster care, energy assistance, etc. Visit their website at:
**www.acf.hhs.gov/index.html**

The **ACF** has a **National Child care Information Center (NCCIC)** that is a national clearinghouse and technical assistance center linking parents, providers, policy-makers, researchers, and the public to early care and education information. **NCCIC** responds to requests from parents, childcare providers and other early education professionals, researchers, policy-makers, national organizations, businesses, and the public. **NCCIC** provides technical assistance and training to States, Territories, and Tribes. For more information visit:
**www.acf.hhs.gov/acf_working_with.html**

### QUESTIONS FOR CHILD CARE CENTER
■ **Adult to Child Ratio:** Ask how many children there are for each adult. The fewer children for each adult, the better for your child. You want your child to get plenty of attention. The younger your child, the more important this is. Babies need an adult to child ratio of no more than 1:4 (one adult for four infants); while four-year-olds can do well with a ratio of 1:10 (one adult for ten children).
■ **Group Size:** Find out how many children are in a group, because, the smaller the group, the better. Imagine a group of 25 two-year olds with five adults, in comparison to a group of 10 with two adults. Even though both groups have the same adult to children ratio, which group would be calmer and safer? Which would be more like a family?
■ **Caregiver Qualifications:** Ask about caregivers' training and education. Caregivers with degrees and/or special training with children will be better able to assist your child to learn. Are caregivers involved in activities to improve their skills? Do they attend classes and workshops?
■ **Turnover:** Check how long caregivers have been at center or providing care in their homes. It's best if children stay with the same caregiver at least a year. Caregivers who *"come and go,"* make it hard on your child. Getting used to new caregivers takes time and energy that could be spent on learning new things.
■ **Accreditation:** Find out if child care provider has been accredited by a national organization. Providers that are accredited have met voluntary standards for child care that is higher than most state licensing requirements. The National Association for the Education of Young Children (NAEYC) and The National Association for Family Child Care (NAFCC) are the two largest organizations that accredit child care programs.
■ **Make a Choice:**
Think about what you saw at each visit, and make the best choice for your child and family.
■ **Stay Involved:**
The work isn't over when you find good care for your child. You and your child's caregiver are partners now.

C-7

Today's lesson is to paint with a long stroke. Wrist up. Wrist down. Up. Down. In addition, do not forget to wax on. Wax off. Sand the...

When looking for ways to lower and save energy in your home, consider improving your existing heating and cooling system, but also consider energy efficiency of supporting equipment, making improvements by repairing, replacing with the latest system or installing new technologies to home and the possibility of either adding supplementary sources of heating or cooling.

## MAKE HOME ENERGY EFFICIENT

### PURCHASING AIR CONDITIONER & FURNACE:
■ **ENERGY STAR®** labeled products can cut your energy bills by up to **30%**. Find retailers near you at **www.energystar.gov** when you're ready to replace your heating and cooling systems.
■ For air conditioners, look for a high Seasonal Energy Efficiency Ratio (SEER). The current minimum is 13 SEER for central air conditioners.
■ If your air conditioner is old, consider purchasing a new, energy-efficient model. You could save up to 50% on your utility bill for cooling. Look for ENERGY STAR® and EnergyGuide labels.
■ When replacing furnace, look for high Annual Fuel Utilization Efficiency (AFUE) ratings. The national minimum is **78%** AFUE, but there are **ENERGY STAR®** models on the market that exceed **90%** AFUE.

### GET HELP FROM UTILITY COMPANIES & LIHEAP:
■ A home energy audit can identify ways to save up to hundreds of dollars a year on home heating and air conditioning. Ask electric or gas utility company if they can do this audit for free, or for a reasonable charge. If they cannot, ask them to refer you to a qualified professional.
■ An *"energy audit"* of home will identify air leaks and check for the proper level of insulation. Common sources of air leaks include cracks around windows and doors, gaps along baseboard, mail chutes, cracks in brick, siding, stucco or foundation, or where any external lines (phone, cable, electric, and gas) enter the home.
■ To test for air leaks on your own: On a windy day, light a candle and hold beside windows, doors, electrical outlets, or light fixtures to test for leaks. Also, tape clear plastic sheeting to the inside of your window frames if drafts, water condensation, or frost are present.
■ Enrolling in load management programs and off-hour rate programs offered by your electric company may save you up to $100 a year in electricity costs. Call your electric utility for information about these cost-saving programs.
■ Enrolling in **LIHEAP** can help subsidize your heating bill. For more information, see **page 100**.

### WEATHER STRIP, INSULATE, & SEAL EVERYTHING:
■ Adequate insulation in your attic, ceilings, exterior and basement walls, floors, and crawlspaces, as recommended for your geographical area, can save you up to 30% on home energy bills.
■ Insulate heating ducts in unheated areas such as attics, garage (rooms above) and crawlspaces and keeping areas in good repair will prevent heat loss up to 60%.
■ Insulating the attic and sealing air leaks will save on air conditioning and heating costs.
■ Cut heat and cooling loss in half by weather-stripping exterior doors, windows and attic.
■ Repair holes in the roof, walls, doors and windows to prevent heat loss.
■ Check to see if all windows have full putty around glass and caulk all cracks to keep in heat.
■ Seal gaps around pipes, wires and vents. This will improve energy performance in summertime and winter.
■ Plug all air leaks with caulking and sealing to save 10% or more on energy bill.

## FIX, REPLACE OR INSTALL LASTEST NEW STUFF:
■ Install a programmable thermostat that can adjust the temperature according to your schedule and make sure thermostat is not located in a cold or hot area.
■ When shopping for new windows, look for the National Fenestration Rating Council label; it means the window's performance is certified
■ Installing new, high-performance windows will improve home's energy performance. While it may take several years for new windows to pay off in energy savings, benefits of added comfort and improved aesthetics and functionality will make investment worthwhile.
■ In warm climates, where summertime heat gain is a main concern, look for windows with double glazing and with specially designed coatings that reduce heat gain.
■ In temperate climates with both heating and cooling seasons, select windows with both low U-values and low solar heat gain co-efficiency (SHGC) to maximize energy benefits. Remember when it comes to windows, the lower the U-value, better the insulation. In colder climates, a U-value of 0.35 or below is recommended.
■ In cold climates, **ENERGY STAR®** windows can reduce your heating bills by 30 to 40 percent compared to uncoated, single-pane windows, according to the Efficient Windows Collaborative.
■ Install exterior or interior storm windows; storm windows can reduce heat loss through windows by 25% to 50%. Storm windows should have weather stripping at all moveable joints; be made of strong, durable materials, with interlocking or overlapping joints. Low-e storm windows save even more energy.
■ Select windows with air leakage ratings of 0.3 cubic feet per minute or less.
■ When installing new windows, they must be installed correctly to avoid air leaks around the frame. Look for a reputable, qualified installer.
■ Apply sun-control or other reflective films on south-facing windows to reduce solar gain.
■ Install awnings on south and west-facing windows.
■ Install white window shades, drapes, or blinds to reflect heat away from the home.
■ Install tight-fitting, insulating window shades on windows that feel drafty after weatherizing.
■ Install a heavy-duty clear plastic sheet on a frame or tape clear plastic film to the inside of your window frames during the cold winter months. Remember, the plastic must be sealed tightly to the frame to help reduce infiltration.
■ Installing storm windows over single-pane windows or replacing them with **ENERGY STAR®** windows can reduce heat loss from air leakage, and reflect heat back into room during winter months to save even more energy.
■ In cold areas, use storm or thermal windows and install storm doors before cold weather arrives.
■ Fix and weatherize current storm windows, if necessary
■ Plant trees or shrubs to shade air conditioning units but not to block airflow. Place air conditioner on north side of house. A unit operating in the shade uses as much as 10% less electricity than same one operating in sun.
■ Install heat-resistant radiator reflectors between exterior walls and radiators.
■ Convert your home to solar heat. It costs the least.
■ Heat home with cheapest energy in your area. If wood is inexpensive in your area, install a wood burning stove.
■ A glass screen cover will reduce fireplace heat loss.

- Heat home with cheapest energy in your area. If wood is inexpensive in your area, install a wood burning stove.
- A glass screen cover will reduce fireplace heat loss.

## TRACK BILLS & TEACH YOUR CHILDREN WELL:
- Check all energy bills closely. Errors can be costly, and they do make mistakes occasionally.
- Teach your children to keep doors and windows shut, along with other energy-saving tips.

## SIMPLE TRICKS TO LOWER COOLING BILL: 56% (+/-)
of energy is used to cool and heat a typical U.S. home, making it the main energy expense for most homes.
- When using air conditioner, set thermostat at 78 degrees or higher.
- Don't set thermostat at colder setting than normal when you turn on air conditioner. It will not cool home any faster and could result in excessive cooling and extra expense.
- Don't place lamps or TV sets near air-conditioning thermostat. Thermostats sense heat from these appliances, and can cause air conditioner to run longer than necessary.
- Whole-house fans help cool home by pulling cool air through house and exhausting warm air through attic. They are effective when operated at night and when outside air is cooler than inside.
- Consider using an interior fan in conjunction with window air conditioner to spread cooled air more efficiently throughout home without greatly increasing power use.
- When using air conditioning in conjunction with ceiling fans, this will allow you to raise the thermostat setting about 4°F with no reduction in comfort.
- In summer months try not to use oven to cook meals. Cook outdoors or eat foods that do not need to be heated.
- When using air conditioning close windows, doors and air vents in unused rooms.
- Close curtains or shades on south and west-facing windows during the day to prevent solar gain.
- Make sure your front and back door are shut.
- Turn off air conditioning at night, open windows to let cool air in and turn ceiling fans on if needed.
- Turn off air conditioning when no one is home.
- When going away for extended periods set your refrigerator at lowest setting.

**A & E: NOT THE BRIGHTEST BULBS ON THE PLANET**

## SIMPLE TRICKS TO LOWER HEATING BILL:
- Heating can account for almost **50%** of the average family's winter energy bill. Make sure your furnace or heat pump receives professional maintenance yearly.
- Bleed trapped air from hot-water radiators once or twice a season, if in doubt about how to perform this task, call a professional.
- Remove your awnings from sun-exposed windows during winter.
- Clean warm-air registers, baseboard heaters, and radiators as needed; make sure they're not blocked by furniture, carpeting, or drapes.
- Keep windows on the south side of your house clean to let in winter sun.
- Inspect your furnace. Keep parts clean and replace air filters once a month.
- Set your thermostat at 68 degrees and 55 degrees at night. **Note:** Install an automatic timer.
- Turn heat off in the spring and fall.
- When going away for extended periods, turn off heat.
- Open shades and drapes in winter to let sun in, but close at night.
- Move furniture away from outside walls during winter.
- Make sure your front and back doors are shut and keep windows closed during cold weather.
- Close heating vents in rooms not in use such as attic, garage, basement, spare bedrooms, etc.

- Wear warm clothes indoors during the winter.
- Turn off heat when using fireplace and close fireplace damper when not using it.
- Avoid using your kitchen and bathroom fans in winter, they waste heating.
- Use of electric blankets is cheaper than heating home. Furthermore, insulate mattress and bed frame with wrapping or plastic sheets.

**SAVE ON HEATING WATER:** Water heating can account for 14%–25% of energy consumed in home. You can reduce monthly water heating bills by selecting appropriate water heater for home or pool and by using these energy-efficient water heating strategies below.
- You might qualify for tax credits or rebates for buying a solar water heater. Visit **Database of State Incentives for Renewable Energy** Website and see: **www.dsireusa.org.**
- Buy new energy-efficient water heater. While it may cost more initially than a standard water heater, the energy savings will continue during the lifetime of appliance. Look for the **Energy Guide label. NOTE:** Heat pump water heaters are very economical in some areas.
- Consider natural-gas on-demand or tankless water heaters. Researchers have found savings can be up to 30% compared with standard natural-gas storage tank water heater.
- Consider installing a drain water waste heat recovery system. A recent DOE study showed energy savings of 25% to about 30% for water heating using such a system.
- Install heat traps on the hot and cold pipes at the water heater to prevent heat loss. Some new water heaters have built-in heat traps.
- 85% to 90% of energy wasted is from hot water going down the drain. Install a drain-water heat recovery system to pre-heat new water using heat from drained water.
- Insulating hot water pipes will reduce heat loss and raise water temperature 2°F to 4°F hotter than non-insulated pipes. This allows for lower water temperature setting.
- Insulate first 6 feet of hot and cold water pipes connected to water heater.
- Insulate natural gas or oil hot water storage tank, but be careful not to cover water heater's top, bottom, thermostat, or burner compartment. Follow manufacturer's recommendations; when in doubt, get professional help.
- Insulate an electric hot water storage tank, but be careful not to cover thermostat. Follow manufacturer's advice.
- Install an **"automatic timer"** so water is heated only during hours needed.
- Install a **"low-flow showerhead"** with a flow rate of less than 2.5 gallons per minute for maximum water efficiency.
- Install a **"Sud saver"** on washer, so you can reuse hot water for several loads.
- Install an **"aerator"** on your kitchen sink faucet to save on hot water.
- Drain quart of water from the water tank every 3 months to remove sediment that impedes heat transfer and lowers efficiency of heater. To be on the safe side though, be sure to follow manufacturer's advice or instructions.
- Keep water heater thermostat set at 110-120 degrees. Lowering the thermostat on your water heater by 10°F can save you between 3%–5% in energy costs.
- Repair dripping faucets, because they can waste 15 gallons of hot water per day.
- When leaving for extended periods, turn off water heater.
- Take more short showers than baths (why not take a shower with spouse and save more?), because bathing uses the most hot water in average household.
- Wash only full loads of dishes and clothes.
- Although most water heaters last 10-15 years, it's best to start shopping for a new one if yours is more than 7 years old. Doing some research before your heater fails will

enable you to select one that meets your needs.

- If heating a swimming pool, consider a pool cover. Evaporation is by far the largest source of energy loss in swimming pools.

**SAVE MORE ON LIGHTING & DAYLIGHT:** The quantity and quality of light around us determine how well we see. Light affects our health, safety, morale, comfort, and productivity. In your home, you can save energy while still maintaining good light quantity and quality.

- Installing a skylight can provide home with daylight and warmth. When properly selected and installed, an energy-efficient skylight can help minimize your heating, cooling, and lighting costs.
- Install fluorescent light fixtures for all ceilings and walls that will be on for more than 2 hours each day.
- Use task lighting; instead of brightly lighting an entire room, focus light where you need it. For example, use fluorescent under-cabinet lighting for kitchen sinks and countertops under cabinets.
- Install dimmers, motion sensors, or occupancy sensors to automatically turn on or off lighting as needed and prevent energy waste.
- Use fluorescent fixtures with reflective backing and electronic ballasts for workroom, laundry room and garage.
- Use compact fluorescent light bulbs (CFLs) in place of comparable incandescent bulbs to save about 50% on your lighting costs. CFLs use only one-fourth the energy and last up to 10 times longer.
- Consider the use of high-intensity discharge (also called HID) or low-pressure sodium lights.
- Exterior lighting is one of the best places to use CFLs due to their long life. If you live in a cold climate, be sure to buy a lamp with cold weather ballast since standard CFLs may not work well below 40°F.
- Turn off decorative outdoor natural gas lamps; just eight such lamps burning year-round use as much natural gas as it takes to heat an average-size home during an entire winter.
- Use outdoor lights with a photocell unit or a motion sensor so they turn on only at night or when someone is present. A combined photocell and motion sensor will increase your energy savings even more.
- Consider using 4-watt mini-fluorescent or electro-luminescent night lights. Both lights are much more efficient than their incandescent counterparts. Luminescent lights are cool to the touch.
- If you have torchiere fixtures with halogen lamps, consider replacing them with compact fluorescent torchieres. Compact fluorescent torches use 60% to 80% less energy, can produce more light (lumens), and do not get as hot as halogen torches (fire risk hazard).
- Recessed down lights (also called recessed cans) are now available that are rated for contact with insulation (IC rated), are designed specifically for pin-based CFLs, and can be used in retrofits or new construction.
- Use CFLs in all portable tables and floor lamps in your home. Consider carefully the size and fit of these systems when you select them. Some home fixtures may not accommodate some of the larger CFLs.
- Consider three-way lamps; they make it easier to keep lighting levels low when brighter light is not necessary.
- Use **ENERGY STAR®** labeled lighting fixtures.
- Take advantage of daylight by using light-colored, loose-weave curtains on windows to allow daylight to penetrate room while preserving privacy. Also, decorate with lighter colors that reflect daylight.
- Consider light wall colors to minimize need for artificial lighting.
- During winter, open curtains on south-facing windows during day to allow sunlight to naturally heat your home, and close them at night to reduce the chill you may feel from cold windows.
- Turn off lights in any room you're not using, or consider installing timers, photo cells, or occupancy sensors to reduce the amount of time your lights are on.
- Turn lights off when leaving a room. Standard, incandescent light bulbs should be turned off whenever they are not needed. Fluorescent lights should be turned off whenever you'll be away for 15 minutes or more.

**Low Income Home Energy Assistance Program (LIHEAP):** By design, **LIHEAP** assists low-income households with winter home heating costs, but does not pay entire home heating bill. The program provides help with heating expenses during the period of *Nov 1* through *April 30* each year. Renters and homeowners are eligible for the program based upon family size and income.

**ELIGIBILITY REQUIREMENTS:**

- To determine whether a household is eligible for **LIHEAP**, assets such as bank accounts, cash, personal property, vehicles, etc., are considered. Some resources are counted and some are not. **Example:** Home and primary care are not counted as resources. Agency representative will explain which are not. All households may have up to $5,000 worth of countable assets and be eligible.
- Must be a permanent legal resident of the USA, and state that you reside in. **Note:** Servicemembers' stationed at their current duty station are considered residents of that state. **Example:** If your home of record is Texas, but stationed in Colorado, **LIHEAP** considers you a Colorado resident. **Income:** Your household income for the month before you submit your application must be within the guidelines listed on this page. "Household" means an individual who lives with you and for whom you are financially responsible.
**FINANCIAL CRITERIA:** For income guidelines, visit: **http://aspe.os.dhhs.gov/poverty/09poverty.shtml**

**Report Income:** The following is the financial eligibility requirements for **LIHEAP**. For military personnel, add the following from the left side of your LES.
Gross income, base pay, BAS, BAH, flight pay, hazard duty pay, etc. **Note:** Military clothing allowance is not calculated when determining financial eligibility requirements.

**Proof of income documentation:** You must show proof of income from all household members. **Example:** LES, pay stubs, grants, loans, etc. from the previous month. In order to expedite your application you should have the following:
1. Recent heating bill, company name and account number, copy of most recent rent receipt or rental agreement, if heating costs are included.
2. Proof of childcare expenses receipt.
3. Names and age of each child in child care.
4. Name, address, and phone number of the person who cares for them.
5. Bring account numbers of checking and savings.
6. Two forms of Identification.
7. All household members Social Security numbers.

**To learn more, and where to apply for LIHEAP, visit:**
- Start with **LIHEAP** Clearinghouse: **http://liheap.ncat.org**
- To apply: **www.acf.hhs.gov/programs/ocs/liheap/grantees/states.html**
- **For more help:** Call the National Energy Assistance Referral (**NEAR**) project on where you can apply for **LIHEAP**. You can speak to someone at **NEAR** Monday through Friday, from 6 a.m. - 6 p.m. (Mountain Time). Call toll-free: **866-674-6327** or send e-mail to: **energyassistance@ncat.org**.

Your home appliances and electronics are responsible for about **20%** of your energy bills. These appliances and electronics include washers, dryers, computers, water heaters, etc. When shopping for appliances, electronics and other products always look for **ENERGY STAR®** label. **NOTE:** You can achieve real savings in your monthly energy bill by just turning off appliances when not in use.

■ **ENERGY STAR®** label is government's seal of energy efficiency. The Energy Guide label estimates an appliance's energy consumption and meets strict efficiency guidelines set by U.S. Environmental Protection Agency and U.S. Department of Energy.

■ Saving energy starts with being an informed consumer. Estimate your appliance's annual energy cost by wattage used:

**Aquarium** = 50–1210 Watts
**Clock radio** = 10
**Coffee maker** = 900–1200
**Clothes washer** = 350–500
**Clothes dryer** = 1800–5000
**Dishwasher** = 1200–2400 (using the drying feature greatly increases energy consumption)
**Dehumidifier** = 785
**Electric blanket**- *Single/Double* = 60 / 100
**Fans:**   **Ceiling** = 65–175
      **Window** = 55–250
      **Furnace** = 750
      **Whole house** = 240–750
**Hair dryer** = 1200–1875
**Heater** *(portable)* = 750–1500
**Clothes iron** = 1000–1800
**Microwave oven** = 750–1100
**Personal computer:**
    **CPU** - awake / asleep = 120 / 30 or less
    **Monitor** - awake / asleep = 150 / 30 or less
    **Laptop** = 50
**Radio** *(stereo)* = 70–400
**Refrigerator** *(frost-free, 16 cubic feet)* = 725
**Televisions** (color):
    19" = 65–110
    27" = 113
    36" = 133
    53"-61" Projection = 170
    Flat screen = 120
**Toaster** = 800–1400
**Toaster oven** = 1225
**VCR/DVD** = 17–21 / 20–25
**Vacuum cleaner** = 1000–1440
**Water heater** *(40 gallon)* = 4500–5500
**Water pump** *(deep well)* = 250–1100
**Water bed** *(with heater, no cover)* = 120–380

■ "Phantom" loads occur in most appliances that use electricity, such as DVD players, televisions, stereos, computers, and kitchen appliances. The average U.S. home consumes **25%** of its electricity by home electronics, while products are turned off. This can be avoided by plugging electronics into power strips; turn power strips off when equipment is not in use.
■ For older appliances, use a ***power controlling device*** to reduce energy consumption of appliance's electric motor.

## DRYER:
■ Consider air-drying clothes on clothes lines or drying racks. Air-drying is recommended by clothing manufacturers for some fabrics.
■ When shopping for a new clothes dryer, look for one with moisture sensor that automatically shuts off machine when clothes are dry. Not only will this save energy, it will save wear and tear on clothes caused by over-drying.
■ Clean lint filter in dryer after every load to improve air circulation.
■ Now and then inspect your dryer vent to ensure it's not blocked. Not only will this save energy, it may prevent a fire. Manufacturers recommend using rigid venting material, not plastic vents that may collapse and cause blockages.
■ Don't over-dry clothes. If the machine has moisture sensor, use it.
■ Dry your towels and heavier cottons in separate load from lighter-weight clothes.
■ Wash and dry full loads. If you are washing a small load, use appropriate water-level setting.

## COMPUTERS:
■ **ENERGY STAR®** computers and monitors save energy only when power management features are activated, so make sure power management is activated on computer.
■ Consider purchasing laptop for next computer upgrade; they use much less energy than desktop computers.
■ A common fallacy is that screen savers reduce energy use by monitors; they do not. Using the automatic sleep mode or manually turning monitor off is always the better energy-saving strategy.
■ To maximize savings with a laptop, put AC adapter on a power strip that can be turned off (or will turn off automatically); transformer in AC adapter draws power continuously, even when laptop is not plugged into adapter.
■ Turn personal computer off when you're away from PC for 20 minutes or more, and both the CPU and the monitor if you'll be away for two hours or more.

## DISHWASHER:
■ Air dry your dishes instead of using dishwasher's drying cycle.

## BATTERIES:
■ Studies show that using rechargeable batteries for products like cordless phones and PDAs is more cost effective than throwaway batteries.
■ Unplug battery chargers when the batteries are fully charged or the chargers are not in use. Use the cool-down cycle to allow the clothes to finish drying with the residual heat in the dryer.

**C-7**

Today, almost everyone has a cell phone. We use them while driving, walking, at work, home and play. As a nation, we have become dependent upon their convenience and growing versatility. Cell phone technology changes rapidly and can become outdated quickly. Therefore, when you decide to purchase a new cell phone or service, do the research necessary to ensure that you will have the latest technology. The following information will help you to find the right cell phone and service.

## HOW MUCH DO YOU KNOW ABOUT CELL PHONE TECHNOLOGY?

Since there seems to be a never-ending plethora of new cell phone models, makes, features and technology that can make the latest cell phone outdated within months, nowadays you have to be a very knowledgeable consumer in order to purchase a cell phone that will stay ahead of the curve. Your best bet is to get informed and keep abreast of the latest news and trends through independent wireless sites.

## WHERE TO BEGIN:

■ **Federal Communication Commission:** www.fcc.gov/cgb/cellular.html
■ **Cellular Telecommunications Industry Association (CTIA):** www.ctia.org
■ **Telecommunications Research & Action Center (TRAC):** www.trac.org
■ **Mobile Phone Sales:** www.mobilephonesales.info/site-map.cfm/600/1
■ **Hearusnow.org:** www.hearusnow.org/homepage/7/consumertipswireless

## HOW WILL YOU USE YOUR CELL PHONE?

**1. What functions do you want and need?** Choose a phone with features that you can really use and don't waste money on functions that you'll seldom use or duplicate with your other electronic gadgets.

**2. Sound quality, display and color check out?** Check volume on phone; hear if it's loud and adequate enough for your needs. Make sure display features are easily readable, especially in difficult lighting conditions. If you want to watch videos or photos taken with a phone camera, then you'll need at least 65,000 colors (higher the number, better the picture quality). It would be wise to examine all these features physically at a store.

**3. Check the Quality of the Ring Tones**: Polyphonic ring tones are featured in all new cell phones and make it possible for a ring tone to sound like several instruments playing together. If a phone is a 16 polyphonic, it means that 16 instruments can be heard in a ring tone, and if you want a good sound then you'll need at least a 16.

**4. What accessories are Included with phone?** Check to see if phone comes with spare battery, earphone, leather casing, neck strap or antenna. If any of these accessories are optional, then your phone will cost more. Also, if you don't need an accessory now, but would like one in future, check to see if accessories for your model are easily available.

**5. How long will battery last?** It's common to find phones whose batteries have a three to seven-hour talk time, but you should also find out whether battery has enough stand-by time, so that you can make it through entire day without recharging.

**6. Consider look and feel of the phone:** Do not purchase a phone from catalog or Internet before handling, weighing, seeing layout of keyboard, buttons and if menus are easy to understand from a store. On some smaller phones, buttons are so small that it's difficult and tiresome to dial numbers or compose messages.

**7. Can your budget afford price?** Be smart, purchase a phone that lets you stay within budget and not force you to cut back on usual expenditures.

**8. What's sales service after purchase?** Make sure you find out where the phone can be serviced, and whether you will be given a replacement if phone develops problems. Be clear about service before choosing place where you will finally make your purchase.

## WHICH CARRIER SHOULD YOU CONSIDER?

Major carriers use one of two digital networks: CDMA (Alltel, Sprint, and Verizon) or GSM (AT&T and T-Mobile). Most GSM phones, offer more talk time on battery charge, typically five hours or more, compared with three or four hours for a CDMA phone. Another GSM plus is that phones have SIM card that stores your account information and phone book. When you switch to a new phone, you can remove card from inside the old phone and insert into new one. However, you can't use a T-Mobile SIM card in an AT&T phone, or vice versa. Also, GSM phones work more widely across the world than do CDMA models. CDMA phones typically have better voice quality than GSM models, and a few simpler models still offer analog backup, handy for rural areas where digital service is unavailable. CDMA data networks are usually faster than GSM, which enables them to deliver a wider variety of services and entertainment, but there is a trade-off, CDMA phones that support those advanced services lack analog backup.

## HELP WITH MAKING CHOICE:

■ **Consumer Reports:** www.consumerreports.org
■ **Ucan:** www.ucan.org
■ **Mobile-Broadband-Reviews.com:** www.mobile-broadband-reviews.com/wireless-broadband-reviews.html

## WHERE TO GET BEST DEAL, WHEN PURCHASING A CELL PHONE?

Cell phone prices differ by where you buy; carrier's rate plans do not. You'll frequently find superior phone deals online, from independent retailers. On the other hand, carriers often charge the highest prices for phones. Independent retailers set prices for their cell phones individually, and that makes a big difference. In addition, you'll find that online retailers that lack overhead of physical stores, have best prices of all. By investigating online retailers, you can find the best price.

**EXAMPLE:** At one time AT&T, Verizon, and T-Mobile websites showed the then popular Motorola RAZR V3 selling for $129.99 to $149.99 with new service, while the independent retailer MyRatePlan.com site had it for free.

## FIND CELL PHONE:

■ **MyRatePlan.com:** www.myrateplan.com/wireless
■ **LetsTalk.com:** www.letstalk.com/condor/home.htm
■ **Wirefly.com:** www.wirefly.com
■ **CellStores.com:** www.cellstores.com
■ **The-Cell-Phone-Advisor:** www.the-cell-phone-advisor.com/cell-phone-tips.html

## HOW TO FIND THE BEST WIRELESS SERVICE?

Finding the best wireless service is done by optimizing three things:

■ **Coverage:** Does phone work where and when I need it? Carrier coverage maps are great, but use only as a starting point; check with friends or neighbors who use same carrier you are considering to find out their experiences. Take full advantage of the trial period offered by most carriers.

■ **Expense:** Are rates within my budget?

■ **Rate Plan:** Am I spending as little as possible each month to get what I need from my service?

**NOTE:** FCC (2007) complaints, according to information obtained by PC World through Freedom of Information Act. Here's how carriers ranked concerning:

| Billing Complaints | Early Termination Complaints |
|---|---|
| T-Mobile | T-Mobile |
| Cingular/AT&T | Sprint/Nextel |
| Sprint/Nextel | Verizon |
| Verizon | Cingular |

| Carrier Marketing Complaints | Overall Complaints |
|---|---|
| | T-Mobile |
| T-Mobile | Sprint/Nextel |
| Cingular | Cingular |
| Sprint/Nextel | Verizon |
| Verizon | |

### FIND WIRELESS SERVICE:

■ **Consumer Reports:** www.consumerreports.org
■ **www.amazon.com** (good selection of different plans)
■ **www.phonedog.com** (good comparison site)
■ **www.jdpower.com** (provides satisfaction ratings for each carrier): www.jdpower.com/telecom
■ **LowerMyBills:** www.lowermybills.com
■ **LetsTalk.com:** www.letstalk.com/condor/home.htm
■ **MyRatePlan.com:** www.myrateplan.com
■ **The-Cell-Phone-Advisor:** www.the-cell-phone-advisor.com/cell-phone-tips.html
■ **SaveOnPhone.com:** www.saveonphone.com

### CONSIDER A REFURBISHED PHONE:

Refurbished phones are cell phones that were returned to manufacturer due to defects. These phones then go through tests, where any problems detected are fixed. These defective phones are brought back to "like-new" condition, but are deemed "used" because of former ownership. Prices on reconditioned or refurbished phones are cheaper and as a rule offer a 90 day warranty against future defects. You can find reconditioned phone models at EBay or Amazon.com. On Cingulars official website, you can also find refurbished phones.

### VOICE OVER INTERNET PROTOCOL (VOIP):

Voice over Internet Protocol (VoIP), is a technology that allows consumers to make telephone calls using a broadband Internet connection instead of regular (or analog) phone line service. It is a useful telecommunications alternative in many rural areas. Some VoIP services only work using special VoIP phones, while other services allow you to use a traditional phone with an adaptor. Today, many VoIP services are marketed to consumers as a substitute for traditional telephone service. For more information on whether VoIP is right for you, visit:

■ **Federal Trade Commission:** www.ftc.gov
■ **VoIP Now all things about VoIP:**
www.voipnow.org/2007/04/before_you_migr.html
■ **HelloDirect for latest equipment:**
www.hellodirect.com/hellodirect/Shop?PCR=1:1:5:15
■ **SaveOnVoip.com:** www.saveonvoip.com

## SKYPE, THE LATEST AND GROWING WONDER:

With Skype, you can make free calls from your computer all over the world. Other features: Sound quality is great, free high quality video calls, call phones and mobiles at cheap rates per minute or instant message when it's not a good time to talk. Forward calls and receive text messages when you're not online. Search web with Google Toolbar (optional to install).
**Skype:** www.skype.com/download/skype/windows

## EARN MONEY ON THAT OLD CELL PHONE:

Don't throw your old cell phone away; it may be worth something! Matter-of-fact, some current models may ring up to $200 dollars or more! There are several web sites online that can assist you to find out what your cell phone is worth or sell it yourself on EBay.
**CellForCash:** www.cellforcash.com

## USE UCAN CHECKLIST THAT STRIKES FEAR IN WIRELESS SALESPEOPLE:

Most complaints that UCAN (non-profit consumer protection agency out of San Diego, CA) get are from people who signed a contract that was misrepresented to them by a salesperson. That's why checklist on the next page is so useful. Its sole purpose is to confirm in writing that what salesperson told you about the contract was true. There are three reasons why a salesperson will refuse to sign form on the next page:

**1. They are hiding something.**
**2. They've been prohibited by their bosses to put anything they tell you in writing.**
**3. They don't want to provide written proof of lies they've told you.**

If they won't sign it, just walk away and then call UCAN at **619-696-6966**.

**Before visiting the store:** Write down any questions and bring checklist along (see **page 104**). If you are answering to an ad, be sure to keep a copy with your documents.

**Make sure salesperson answers** all of your questions: No answer; no sale. Remember, salespeople are trying to make a living. The more phones, minutes and extras they sell you, the bigger their commission.

**Ask salesperson to sign checklist:** Make sure sales rep completes and signs checklist. This is your proof that you are actually getting what's been promised. If salesperson will not sign it, walk away.

**After you get the contract signed:** Open box with care. Keep all packaging and literature together: You will need it if you return the phone within trial period. Use the phone extensively during the trial period. If you're not satisfied with coverage (i.e. it doesn't work from your home or office) take the phone back and cancel the contract. Don't accept excuses. If you are told that you must visit the store later, call carrier's Customer Service Department from your cell phone in the store. This will help document your cancellation. **Note:** Bring notepad.

**103**

***WARNING: DO NOT SIGN ANYTHING UNTIL SALESPERSON COMPLETES AND SIGNS THIS CHECKLIST!***

**Name of Calling Plan:** _____

_____

Plan cost per month:                    $_____

Estimated taxes/fees/
surcharges per month:                   $_____

**Contract Termination Fees:**
Carrier early termination/per phone:  $_____

Dealer/Agent early
termination/per phone:                  $_____

**Cancellation Period(s):**
(Maximum number of days
you have to cancel plan)

          Dealer/Agent:  _____ days

          Carrier:       _____ days

**Contract Length:**        _____ One Year

                            _____ Two Years

**Costs per Minute:**

#. Anytime Minutes per month:        _____

#. Night/Weekend minutes per month:_____

_____ Hrs: ___:___ PM TO ___:___ AM

Cost of additional minutes per minute: _____¢

Roaming charges per minute:          _____¢

**Free Mobile-to-Mobile:**

In-network only _____ Yes _____No

Number of minutes: _____

Unlimited minutes: _____

**Internet Use** (downloads,
ringtones, data, music, etc.):

Subscription per month:        $_____

_____ Opt-In _____ Opt-out _____ Internet blocked

**Text Messaging:**

Sending/receiving per message: _____¢

_____ Blocked _____ Not blocked

**International Calling** (verify rates with carrier before calling):

Country: _____

Per month:                        $_____

              @ _____¢ per min.

International roaming rate per minute: _____¢

Block international calls? _____ Yes _____ No

**Monthly Insurance:**      _____ Yes _____ No

Cost per month:                   $_____

With a deductible of:             $_____
(Replacement phones may be
refurbished comparable models.)

**Carrier Rebate:***        _____ Yes _____No

Amount:                           $_____

Deadline to apply for rebate expires on: ___/ ___/ ___

**Dealer Rebate:*** _____ Yes _____No

Amount:                           $_____

Deadline to apply for rebate expires on: ___/ ___/ ___

Rebate will be paid by company before: ___/ ___/ ___

**Manufacturer Rebate:*** _____ Yes _____No

Amount:                           $_____

Deadline to apply for rebate expires on: ___/ ___/ ___

Rebate will be paid by company before: ___/ ___/ ___

* Make copies of all rebates and documents before mailing.
Rebates more than $50 should be sent certified mail.

_____

**Salesperson Signature:**

                    **Date:** ___ /___/___

_____

**Customer Signature:**

                    **Date:** ___ /___/___

**Note: Save this document as proof of your negotiated contents of plan. Be sure you understand each item and that document is signed and dated before leaving.**

**Comments:**

Source: Ucan.com

The following savings tips (kitchen sink) will definitely help stretch your paycheck each month, if you use them.

## BENEFITS:
**1.** An overall resource for consumers on a variety of topics can be found at **USA.gov**.
**2.** To find what government benefits you and your family are eligible to receive, visit this free confidential tool at **GovBenefits.gov**.

## CAR RENTALS:
**1. Book early:** Cheapest rental cars sell out fast. Save yourself from expensive forced upgrade by booking car as soon as you have concrete travel plans.
**2. Comparison shop:** Prices offered through a rental company's website, 1-800 number and local office aren't always the same. To ensure getting best price possible, check all three sources; then compare those rates through travel sites like Orbitz, Travelocity, Expedia, etc.
**3. Reserve smallest car** that meets your needs, but later, ask for a free upgrade to a larger vehicle once you arrive to designation. Rental companies usually overbook their smaller fleets, resulting in upgrade for customers.
**4. Compare Daily & Weekly Rates:** Daily and weekly rental rates can fluctuate widely. Before booking a daily rental, check to see if renting the vehicle longer could get you a better rate.
**5. Rent car from non-airport facility:** Typically, you can save money-renting cars just outside the airport. Usually, they have company shuttle buses to take you to and from their off-site facilities. So shop and compare.
**6. Don't duplicate Insurance:** Rental car companies offer various insurances and waiver options. Check with your auto insurer and credit card Company (some cover rentals) in advance to avoid duplicating coverage you may already have.
**7. Ask for a discount:** Want a lower rate than quoted? Just ask. Rental companies have several special offers and discounts, such as AAA, AARP, military, etc. Some will lower their rates to beat their competition. Look for a better rate, and you'll likely find one.
**8. Fill tank yourself:** Make sure you deliver the rental with a full tank of gas or incur a hefty surcharge. Today's gas prices are bad enough! Check rental contract to see if this is part of the agreement, and if necessary, fill up the car before taking it back.

## CLOTHING:
**1.** Consider shopping at **discount stores**.
**2. Clearance** and **closeout sales** will net you new clothing for about same price or little more than thrift stores, yard and garage sales, and consignment shops.
**3. Department store clearance sales** are a great source for inexpensive clothes, if you buy only from clearance and closeout racks.
**4.** When **off season clothes shopping** you can get some real clothing bargains.
**5. Retail stores** discount clothing long before season ends. Stores begin stocking for the upcoming season more than a month ahead of schedule. This gives you the chance to buy great clothes at cheap prices for remainder of the current season or for the next season.
**6.** Planning ahead and buying for the next season is another great way to save on your clothing budget. Just be careful to consider growth patterns for children when using this strategy.
**7.** For **online clothing**, **clearance** and **closeout sales** always go to clearance link first! Not only can you

purchase new clothing at cheap prices, but get high quality in return. Recommended sites:
■ Blair.com Clearance Center: **www.blair.com/home.jsp**
■ Alloy: **http://store.alloy.com**
■ Classic Closeouts: **www.classiccloseouts.com**
**8. Buy wholesale by the case**, if you have a friend or group to share costs. Purchasing wholesale can make terrific clothes resource and amount to great savings for your clothing budget. Google "wholesale" and let the fun begin. Recommended Website: Dollar Days **www.dollardays.com**
**9.** Shop for clothing at rummage, garage sales, flea markets, thrift stores and used clothing at "like new" shops.
**10.** Watch newspaper ads for store sales, clearances, close-outs, etc.
**11.** Consider saving by ordering clothing items from mail order houses.
**12.** During sales, stock up on the basics: Sleep wear, underwear, socks, etc.
**13.** Buy only clothing items that are well made and will wear well.
**14.** Take care of leather clothing items for lifetime wear.
**15.** Consider buying or renting a sewing machine and making it yourself.
**16.** Alter adult's clothing for your children.
**17.** Change into older clothes for dirty at-home tasks.
**18.** Use worn-out clothing for cleaning and household wipes.
**19. Find clothing free from Freecycle organization**: Freecycle is a national organization that provides people with an on-line outlet to offer items they no longer want or give to someone who has a need for item. There are numerous offerings for adult and children's clothing on freecycle network. Website: **www.freecycle.org**
**20.** Teach children to care for their clothing.
**21.** Make children change into old clothes for rough play.
**22.** Save older children's clothing for hand-me-downs for younger ones.
**23.** Trade clothing items with friends and neighbors, especially children's.
**24.** Buy children's clothing items a size or two larger for longer wear.
**25.** Keep clothes clean and in good repair. They'll last longer.
**26.** Hang clothes on a clothesline instead of using dryer.
**27.** Buy clothing that does not need ironing.
**28.** Do not buy clothes that require dry cleaning.
**29.** Avoid dry cleaning bills. Many spots can be removed with cleaning fluids.

## EDUCATION:
**1.** Use the public library for reading materials.
**2.** Study to improve your qualifications for the job you hold or one that you covet.

## ENTERTAINMENT:

**1.** Eliminate cable or satellite TV and buy an antenna so you can watch free TV.

**2.** Go to a library and checkout books and movies. Read newspapers, magazines, or play on Internet.

**3.** Download *free* movies from Websites:

- **Movies Found Online.com** (very good): www.moviesfoundonline.com/movies.php
- **Entertainment Magazine:** http://emol.org/movies/freemoviesnew.html
- **Public Domain Flicks:** www.publicdomainflicks.com
- **Internet Archive:** www.archive.org/details/movies
- **Public Domain Movies:** http://movies.magnify.net
- **Public Domain Torrents:** www.publicdomaintorrents.com

**4.** Attend high school and sandlot sports events instead of more expensive college and pro events.

**5.** Use public parks and picnic areas.

**6.** Play board games or card games.

**7.** Start an inexpensive hobby.

**8.** Have potluck get-togethers with family and friends.

**9.** Do church functions as a family.

**10.** Vacation at home.

## FREE STUFF:

**1. Freecycle** is a national non-profit organization that provides people with an on-line outlet to offer items they no longer want or to give to someone who has a need for item. Freecycle has 4 million members with many local branches throughout the nation. Items are free if you are willing to pick them up. If you're lucky, some will offer to bring the item(s) to you or arrange meeting to pick up, generally though, rule is that you are responsible for pick up. Please follow guidelines of membership to keep program operating smoothly and as intended. It is not a free for all! If there is not a branch within reasonable distance to you, feel free to start one. You won't regret it! To find nearest branch visit: **http://www.freecycle.org**. For other inquiries, please contact: **info@freecycle.org**. The Freecycle Network, P.O. Box 294, Tucson, AZ 85702

**2. Free Antivirus Protection: avast! Home Edition** (**www.avast.com**) is free **antivirus** software that offers complete virus protection. Currently, 80,000,000 users receive daily automatic updates ensuring continuous data protection against all types of malware and spyware. avast! **Home Edition** is free, but must be registered yearly.

- **Tip:** When **downloading,** be sure you have top of the line security software running at **high protection levels** when you download files from anywhere, they are a notorious delivery mechanism for malware. In fact, I recommend you only download files from sources that you know are trustworthy as downloading files from unknown sources particularly from peer to peer networks or unfamiliar web sites is a highly risky activity.

- **Surfing the Web:** You can catch a malware download just from visiting a hacked web page – these drive-by downloads exploit vulnerabilities in browser, plug-in or other software on your PC to download malware onto your system. Virus software vendors are constantly delivering patches to plug these holes so make sure you are keeping your software up to date.

**3. Refdesk.com** is an amazing website to find free stuff, such as food, beauty items, coupons, samples and tons more. However, and more importantly, its real function is referencing. If you are looking for a subject, **www.refdesk.com** is the place to find anything and everything under the sun.

## HOUSING:

**1.** Learn to do simple repairs.

**2.** Do your own decorating.

**3.** Paint everything yourself.

**4.** Improvise furniture; shop at garage sales.

**5.** Buy unclaimed and repossessed furniture at warehouse sales.

**6.** Buy unpainted furniture and finish it yourself.

**7.** Try to buy wholesale. Some manufacturers have wholesale outlets.

**8.** When ordering carpeting, ask for remnants and save about half the cost.

**9.** Make some items yourself, such as curtains, draperies, bedspreads, etc.

**10.** Make your own cleaning supplies.

**11.** Add extra rooms instead of looking for a larger house.

## MAJOR APPLIANCES:

**1.** Consult Consumer Reports Magazine, available in most public libraries for information about specific brands and evaluates them, including energy use. There are often great price and quality differences among brands.

**2.** Once you've selected a brand, shop through Internet or call to learn what stores carry this particular brand; then check with at least four stores for prices of specific models. After each store has given you a quote, then ask if that's the lowest price they can offer. Comparison shopping can save you as much as $100 or more.

## PERSONAL:

**1.** Select cosmetics that are reasonably priced.

**2.** Do your own shampoos, sets and blow dries.

**3.** Cut children's hair yourself.

**4.** Set reasonable amounts for children's allowances and have a definite understanding of what the amount is to cover.

**5.** Carry only pocket change needed for bus fare and small items.

**6.** Spend only cash. Nothing affects the mind more than spending cash.

## PRESCRIPTION DRUGS:

**1.** Since brand name drugs are usually much more expensive than their generic equivalents, ask your physician and pharmacist for generic drugs whenever appropriate.

**2.** Since pharmacies may charge different prices for the same medicine, check with several. When taking a drug for a long time, also consider calling mail-order pharmacies which often charge lower prices.

**3.** Ask your doctor for samples.

**Example:** When diagnosed with high blood pressure, my doctor gave me three months worth of samples to lower pressure (savings: $180).

## TRANSPORTATION:

**1.** Use public transportation.

**2.** Get rid of one car.

**3.** Consider moving closer to work.

**4.** Drive small cars that cost less to operate.

**5.** Try to carpool with others.

**6.** Walk or ride bikes for small errands.

Hmmm?

Hmmm?

Let's roll! Find some! Get some!

We've finally found what we have been looking for.

For consumer information, guides, protection and services from U.S. government, visit:
**www.usa.gov/Citizen/Topics/Consumer_Safety.shtmland** and **www.usa.gov/Site_Index/index.shtml** .

**Air Travel Problems & Complaints:**
http://airconsumer.ost.dot.gov
http://airconsumer.ost.dot.gov
**Animal Cloning:**
www.fda.gov/AnimalVeterinary/SafetyHealth/AnimalCloning
/default.htm
**Attorneys General by State:**
www.naag.org/attorneys_general.php
**Automobile Safety & Recalls:**
www.nhtsa.dot.gov/cars/problems

**Bank Complaints:**
www.federalreserveconsumerhelp.gov
**Banking Authorities, by State:**
http://consumeraction.gov/banking.shtml
**Banking Questions – National Banks:**
www.helpwithmybank.gov
**Bankruptcy – How to File:** http://answers.usa.gov/cgi-
bin/gsa_ict.cfg/php/enduser/std_adp.php?p_faqid=452&p_c
reated=&p_sid=&p_lva=&p_sp=&p_li=&p_topview=1
**Better Business Bureaus:**
http://consumeraction.gov/bbb.shtml

**Cable TV Complaints:**
www.fcc.gov/cgb/broadcast.html
**Car Manufacturers' Customer Relations:**
http://consumeraction.gov/carman.shtml
**Car Safety:** www.safercar.gov
**Car Title Loans (Beware):** www.iowa.gov/
government/ag/consumer_advisories/auto/car_title.html
**Cars – Efficient Driving & Maintenance:**
www.energy.gov/yourcar.htm
**Cell Phones & Do Not Call Registry:**
www.ftc.gov/opa/2005/04/dnc.shtm
**Charities and Tips on Giving:** www.ftc.
gov/bcp/edu/pubs/consumer/telemarketing/tel01.shtm
**Complain About a Credit Union:** www.ncua.gov/Resour
ces/ConsumerInformation/Complaints/fcucomplaints.aspx
**Complain About a Product or Service:**
www.extension.iastate.edu/Publications/PM716.pdf
**Complain About Telemarketing & Junk Faxes:**
www.fcc.gov/cgb/complaints_tcpa.html
**Complaints – File with a Federal Agency:**
www.ftccomplaintassistant.gov
**Complaints – Top 10:**
www.ftc.gov/opa/2006/01/topten.shtm
**Computer Safety – OnGuardOnline.gov:**
http://onguardonline.gov/index.html
**Consumer Action Handbook:**
www.consumeraction.gov
**Consumer Information & Services:**
www.usa.gov
**Consumer Product & Safety Commission (CPSC):**
www.cpsc.gov
**Consumer Protection Offices, by State, City and
County**: http://consumeraction.gov/state.shtml
**Consumer Tips for teens:**
www.atg.wa.gov/teenconsumer
**Consumer Tips From the Federal Trade Commission:**
www.ftc.gov/bcp/consumer.shtm
**Corporate Consumer Contacts:**
http://consumeraction.gov/corpormain.shtml
**Credit:** www.ftc.gov/credit

**Credit Card Receipt Rules:**
www.ftc.gov/opa/2007/05/slipshowing.shtm
**Credit Reports – Free:**
www.ftc.gov/bcp/menus/consumer/credit/rights.shtm

**Digital TV – What you need to know:** www.dtv.gov
**Disasters & Emergencies:** www.usa.gov/Citizen/
Topics/PublicSafety/Disasters.shtml
**Do Not Call Registry:**
www.donotcall.gov/default.aspx
**Drinking Water Safety:**
www.epa.gov/safewater/dwh/index.html

**E-Commerce Complaints:**
www.econsumer.gov/english
**E-News Letters from the Government:**
http://apps.gsa.gov/CommonSubscriptionService.php
**Elected Officials – How to Contact:**
www.usa.gov/Contact/Elected.shtml
**EnergyGuide Labels for Appliances:**
www.ftc.gov/opa/2007/08/energy.shtm

**Family Health Information:**
www.fda.gov/consumer/default.htm
**Federal Citizen Information Center:**
www.info.gov
**Federal Communication Commission Consumer &
Government Affairs Bureau:** www.fcc.gov/cgb
**Federal Trade Commission – Complain About a
Specific Company or Organization:**
www.ftccomplaintassistant.gov
**Filing a Complaint:** http://esupport.fcc.gov/complaints.htm
**Food Safety Automated Questions & Answers:**
www.fsis.usda.gov/Food_Safety_Education/Ask_Karen/ind
ex.asp#Question
**Food, Drugs & Cosmetics Safety:** www.fda.gov
**Food – Borne Illness & Food Product Complaints:**
www.foodsafety.gov/poisoning/reportaproblem/index.html
**Foreclosure Resources for Consumers:**
www.federalreserve.gov/pubs/foreclosure/default.htm
**Fuel Economy Cars:** www.fueleconomy.gov

Back off,
Creeps!
There's a new
sheriff in town!

**Government Sales & Auctions:**
www.usa.gov/shopping/shopping.shtml

**Halloween Safety:**
www.cpsc.gov/cpscpub/pubs/100.html
**Highway Safety:** www.nhtsa.dot.gov
**Home Safety:** www.homesafetycouncil.org/Safety
Guide/sg_safetyguide_w001.asp
**Homeowners Resources:**
www.usa.gov/Citizen/Topics/Family/Homeowners.shtml
**Household Moves – Consumer Protection:**
www.protectyourmove.gov
**Household Product Safety Publications:**
www.cpsc.gov/cpscpub/pubs/house.html
**Household Product s Health & Safety Information
Database:** http://householdproducts.nlm.nih.gov

**Identity Theft:** www.ftc.gov/bcp/edu/microsites/idtheft
**Identity Theft: Trends and Issues**
www.fas.org/sgp/crs/misc/R40599.pdf
**Insurance Regulators by State:**
http://consumeraction.gov/insurance.shtml
**Internet Fraud:**
www.usa.gov/Citizen/Topics/Internet_Fraud.shtml
**Internet Fraud Complaints:** www.ic3.gov
**Investors Complaints to the Securities & Exchange
Commission:** www.sec.gov/complaint.shtml
**IRS E-mail & Phishing Scams:**
www.irs.gov/newsroom/article/0,,id=155682,00.html

**Kids Safety Sites:** www.kids.gov

**Long Term Care Ombudsman by State:**
www.ltcombudsman.org/ombudsman

**Mail Safety & Security:** www.usps.com/communications/
news/security/welcome.htm
**Meat & Poultry Hotline:** http://www.fsis.usda.gov/Food_
Safety_Education/usda_meat_&_poultry_hotline/index.asp
**Medical Products Complaints:**
www.fda.gov/medwatch/how.htm
**Mortgage Comparison Calculator:**
www.federalreserve.gov/apps/mortcalc
**Moving Tips to Protect your Move:**
www.protectyourmove.gov

**National Do Not Call Registry:**
www.donotcall.gov/default.aspx
**National Flood Insurance Program:**
www.floodsmart.gov/floodsmart/pages/index.jsp
**Nigerian Advance Fee Fraud:**
www.ftc.gov/bcp/edu/pubs/consumer/alerts/alt117.shtm

**Phishing Scams:** www.onguardonline.gov/phishing.html
**Postal Service Contacts:** http://faq.usps.com/eCustomer/
iq/usps/request.do?create=kb:USPSFAQ
**Privacy Resources:** www.hhs.gov/ocio/securityprivacy/
privacyresources/pias.html
**Publications – Order Free & Low-Cost Publications:**
http://permanent.access.gpo.gov/lps23/faqanswers.htm#ba
ckgrnd **or**
http://blog.usa.gov/roller/govgab/entry/free_publications_for
_you?comment=view

**Recall Resources from the Federal Citizen Information
Center:** http://www.recalls.gov/cpsc.html
**Recalls:** http://www.recalls.gov
**Report Product – Related Injury or Death:**
www.cpsc.gov/cgibin/incident.aspx
**RSS Feeds – Consumer Topics:** www.usa.gov/Topics/
Reference_Shelf/Libraries/RSS_Library/Consumer.shtml

**Scams & Frauds:**
www.fbi.gov/majcases/fraud/fraudschemes.htm
**Securities Administrators by State:**
http://consumeraction.gov/security.shtml
**Sex Offender Registry National Search:** www.nsopr.gov
**Spam E-mail: Help from the Federal Trade
Commission:**
www.ftc.gov/bcp/menus/consumer/tech/spam.shtm
**Spyware:**
www.ftc.gov/bcp/edu/microsites/spyware/index.html
**Stopping Unsolicited Mail, Telemarketing and E-mail:**
www.ftc.gov/bcp/edu/pubs/consumer/alerts/alt063.shtm
**Student Scholarship Scams:**
www.ftc.gov/bcp/edu/microsites/scholarship/psa.htm

**Tax Scams & Fraud Alerts:** www.irs.gov/compliance/
enforcement/article/0,,id=121259,00.html
**Telecommunications Issues:** www.fcc.gov/cgb
**Telephone Assistance Programs for Low-Income
Households:** www.lifeline.gov/lifeline_Consumers.html
**Telephone Service Complaints:**
www.fcc.gov/cgb/telephone.html
**Top Tax Scams for 2009:**
www.irs.gov/newsroom/article/0,,id=206370,00.html
**Topics & Information:**
www.usa.gov/Citizen/Topics/All_Topics.shtml

**Unclaimed Money:**
www.usa.gov/Citizen/Topics/All_Topics.shtml

**Workplace Health & Safety Education (CDC):**
www.cdc.gov/niosh
**Workplace Safety Complaints:**
www.osha.gov/pls/osha7/eComplaintForm.html
**Workplace Safety Policies & Regulations (OSHA):**
www.osha.gov

"At ease! One of the biggest benefits given to Servicemembers is the opportunity to purchase homes inexpensively through the Veterans Administration. This chapter covers VA home loans, mortgages, homeowners insurance and rental property. Your home is your castle, so let's get you one, Princess.

**Eighth Commandment:**
**"THOU SHALL BUILD EQUITY"**

C-8

FOR RENT

FOR SALE

RENT

OWN

For Rent

OPEN HOUSE

WHICH WAY?

Should I rent, or buy? In pondering that decision, many people ask themselves these questions: Can I afford to buy? Am I ready to be a homeowner? Do I really want to own a home? If the answer is yes, they assume buying is their best choice. However, you need to consider more than just finances. Honest answers can save you time and unpleasant ordeals later on. The chart below will aid you in deciding if buying or renting is better for you.

## RENTING vs. OWNERSHIP

### Payments: 5% inflation

| | |
|---|---|
| Payments may be temporarily lower, but can escalate, especially if rental property is scarce. | Payments may be higher at first, but will continue to stay fixed with a 15 or 30 year mortgage. |

**Renters payments:**
- Year 1 = $ 650
- Year 5 = $ 830
- Year 10 = $1,059
- Year 15 = $1,351
- Year 20 = $1,726
- Year 25 = $2,201
- Year 30 = $2,809
- Year 50 = $7,453

Rent never goes away.

**Owners payments:**
$100,000 mortgage
- Year 1 = $750
- Year 15 = $750
- Year 20 = $750
- Year 30 = $750

Your payments pay down mortgage and in time, possibly mortgage free.

### Appreciation: 5%

| | |
|---|---|
| Every payment you make gradually helps build equity in the rental property for landlord. | You'll build your own equity if your home goes up in value. History is on homeowner's side. |

**Renters equity:**
- Year 1 = $0
- Year 10 = $0
- Year 20 = $0
- Year 30 = $0

See landlord equity.

**Owners equity:**
- Year 1 = $100,000
- Year 5 = $127,628
- Year 10 = $162,889
- Year 15 = $207,893
- Year 20 = $265,330
- Year 25 = $338,635
- Year 30 = $432,194

### Tax Benefits

| | |
|---|---|
| Landlord gets all tax write-offs and benefits. | Not only can you write-off interest you pay on mortgage loan, but taxes as well. |

**Renters tax benefits:**
- Year 1 = $0
- Year 10 = $0
- Year 20 = $0
- Year 30 = $0
- Year 40 = $0
- Year 50 = $0

**Owners tax benefit:**
- Year 1 = $ 7,900
- Year 5 = $ 39,500
- Year 10 = $ 79,000
- Year 15 = $118,500
- Year 20 = $198,000
- Year 30 = $237,000

## INCOME PROPERTY (OPM): MULTIPLY THE MONEY

Here's a 6-step plan in becoming a landlord and earning lots of money, while in or out of the service:

**STEP #1:** VA offers Veterans' the opportunity to purchase multiplex properties such as 2-unit (duplex), 4-unit (4-plex), etc, using VA eligibility. State programs such as **California Cal-Vet** and **Texas Vet Home Loan programs** also allow purchase of multiplexes. Check with your state to see if there are any valuable real estate programs for veterans by visiting:
- ■ **www.va.gov/statedva.htm** or
- ■ **www.military.com/benefits/veteran-benefits/state-veterans-benefits-directory**

**STEP #1:** Purchase 4-plex property through VA.
**Cost of 4-plex:** $200,000
**Mortgage Loan:** Finance 15 years
**Payments per month:** $2,002

**STEP #2:** Renter's pay your mortgage, while you live in one unit free. **BONUS:** You get to save all your BHA.
**EXAMPLE:** BHA $800 x 12 months = $9,600 in savings.

| UNIT #1: YOU LIVE HERE "FREE" MONTHLY | UNIT #2: RENTER PAYS $667.33 MONTHLY | UNIT #3: RENTER PAYS $667.33 MONTHLY | UNIT #4: RENTER PAYS $667.33 MONTHLY |
|---|---|---|---|

**STEP #3:** After one year, purchase **"New"** home using Veterans' state real estate program (Cal Vet, Texas Home Loan, etc.). Rent out (your) Unit #1 and use income to supplement your new house payment.

**EXAMPLE:** Purchase new home through Texas Home Loan Program.
| | |
|---|---|
| **Cost of home:** | **$100,000** |
| **Mortgage Loan:** | **Finance 15 years (5.34%)** |
| **Payments per month:** | $808.62 |
| **Renter's payment:** | -$667.33 Monthly |
| **Adjusted payment:** | $141.29 Monthly payment |

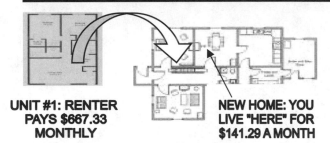

| UNIT #1: RENTER PAYS $667.33 MONTHLY | NEW HOME: YOU LIVE "HERE" FOR $141.29 A MONTH |
|---|---|

**STEP #4:** Raise renter's payments, in accordance with Government yearly inflation index.

**EXAMPLE:** Monthly payments based on 5% inflation.

| Renter's payments | Veterans house payments |
|---|---|
| Year 1: $2,002 | Year 1: $808.62 |
| Year 5: $2,555 | Year 5: $808.62 |
| Year 10: $3,261 | Year 10: $808.62 |
| Year 15: $4,162 | Year 15: $808.62 |

**Step #5:** In 15 years, mortgage on 4-plex is paid off, but payments continue:
**EXAMPLE:** After 15 years, renter's payments are **$4,162 x 12 months = $49,944** additional income.

**STEP #6:** In 16th year home mortgage is paid-off.
**REPEAT PROCESS** and purchase more rental property.

The **VA HOME LOAN PROGRAMS** are designed to assist you, the **VETERAN**, in obtaining the goal of home ownership.

■ VA offers **NO DOWN PAYMENT** home loans.

■ VA interest rates are competitive with other types of loans.

■ VA allows you to purchase **MORE HOUSE WITH LESS INCOME** than other types of loans.

■ VA allows the assumption of your loan by another party that assists you in selling your home.

■ VA allows you to refinance your VA loan to a lower rate with **NO APPRAISAL, NO CREDIT CHECK,** and **NO INCOME QUALIFYING.**

■ VA allows you to take **CASH OUT UP TO 100% OF THE CURRENT VALUE OF YOUR HOME.**

With the assistance of the information in this section, you can begin to enjoy:

■ **APPRECIATION in VALUE**

■ **GREAT** tax advantages

■ **FREEDOM** from **WASTED RENT**, landlords, base housing

■ **PRIDE** of **OWNERSHIP** in your **HOME**

## THERE ARE THREE TYPES OF VA HOME LOANS

**1. PURCHASE A VA HOME WITH NO MONEY DOWN.** You will be required to put down **"EARNEST MONEY"** when you write a purchase contract. This money will be returned to you at closing, and is usually used to pay closing costs. Closing costs will estimate around 3%-4% of your loan amount, or $5,250 on a $150,000 home. In addition to this, VA charges a **VA FUNDING FEE** that can be added to the loan and sales price. **VETERANS WITH 10% DISABILITY or MORE DO NOT HAVE TO PAY THIS FEE.** There are several ways to handle these costs!

■ You may pay them with your own funds

■ You may have the **SELLER** or **BUILDER** pay part or all of these costs for you.

■ You may get a rebate from the **REALTOR** to pay a portion of the costs.

**2. VA LOAN LIMITS:** Legislation now allows the VA to use a locality-based approach in determining ceilings on its no-down payment home loans. To see limits, visit: **www.homeloans.va.gov/docs/2009_county_loan_limits.pdf**. VA no-down payment loans are available for as high as $1,000,000 or more. If a large VA loan is needed, it may be obtained with a relatively small down payment.

**3. EASY INCOME QUALFYING:** The VA uses two methods of income qualifying. The first is that your new house payment and other monthly obligations cannot exceed 42% of your **GROSS INCOME** (not take home pay). A veteran making $3,400 per month, including allowances could afford a house payment of $1,428. If the veteran has a $220 car payment and a $50 credit card payment, these must be deducted.

| | |
|---|---|
| **Debt Free Payment** | **$1,428** |
| **Less Car Payment** | **- 220** |
| **Less Credit Card Payment** | **- 50** |
| **House Payment you can afford** | **$1,158** |

VA also uses a generous residual income approach that is more complicated. If you do not qualify by the 42% **method, see a** VA LOAN SPECIALIST **to get the** MAXIMUM AMOUNT YOU CAN BORROW. **Veterans**

can borrow **MORE** with less income than non-veterans can.

The benefits of Veteran vs. Non-Veteran purchasing a $150,000 home.

| VETERAN | NON-VETERAN |
|---|---|
| A debt free Veteran must make $2,753 per month. | A debt free Non-Veteran must make $4,128. |
| A Veteran buyer must put down $ 0. | FHA buyer must put down approximately $4,500. Home Conventional buyer must put down $7,500. |
| Veterans' have to add $250 in income, to make up $250 car payment. | Non-Veterans' have to add $750 in income, to make up a $250 car payment! |
| Typical closing costs $2,077. | Typical closing costs $2,822. |

## VA STREAMLINE REFINANCE

VA doesn't abandon you after closing like other loan types. Once you have your **VA LOAN**, you can refinance to a lower rate as long as you are current on your mortgage payments. Unlike other loans, the VA **STREAMLINE LOAN** can often be closed in a week! You do not need:

■ another appraisal

■ to have your credit checked

■ income to qualify

■ to come up with any money at closing

■ to live in the home anymore

VA wants you to have the lowest rate possible and will make it **SUPER EASY** for you.

## VA REFINANCE: CASH BACK, CONSOLIDATION

VA allows you to borrow up to 100% of the current appraised value of your house. The interest rates are the same as regular VA rates. Other types of loans charge higher rates and points for this loan. You will need to qualify to VA standards for this type of loan.

WOW! This VA home closed super fast. But, but, where's the lawn, Honey?

You have to install the grass yourself, Love-chops. You forgot to negotiate a lawn into our offer for the house. I'll supply the lemonade, while you install the lawn.

A Veteran can:

- Refinance another type of loan into a VA.
- Refinance VA loan to VA loan re-using the same eligibility.
- Consolidate a first mortgage and a high second mortgage.
- Pay off high interest credit cards and other obligations.
- Get cash out to make home improvements.
- Get cash out to invest in other real estate or for any other reason.
- Go on a trip, but don't forget to send in your house payment.

## STEPS TO PURCHASING A HOME

**1. PRE-QUALIFY FOR A LOAN:** Many lenders will accept your loan application and begin processing the loan for only the cost of a credit report, usually under $25. Pre-qualifying will:

- Tell you how much house you can afford to buy.
- Get your *CERTIFICATE OF ELIGIBILITY* ordered or updated.
- Check your credit, and begin repairs if necessary.
- Keep you from looking at a home you cannot afford.
- Home sellers and their realtors will look favorably on your offer because they can be confident that your loan will go through.
- If your credit report is in and your *ELIGIBILITY CERTIFICATE* is ordered, your loan will close much faster.

**2. LOCATE A REALTOR IN THE AREA YOU WANT TO LIVE IN:** As a purchaser, the Realtor works for you FREE (since the seller pays the commission). Certain Realtors will also help you with your closing costs. If a Realtor wants money from you to find you a home, *RUN*, don't walk, to another Realtor!

**3. WRITE A CONTRACT ON THE HOME YOU WANT:** Your Realtor will prepare this for you. VA contracts contain a clause called the *"VA ESCAPE CLAUSE"* which protects your *EARNEST MONEY* if the house does not appraise for the purchase price.

**4. APPRAISE THE HOUSE:** A VA approved appraiser will now determine the value of the home. He will note any obvious repairs that need to be done to bring the house up to *VA STANDARDS*. The VA then reviews his work to further safeguard your interest and issues a VA Certificate of Reasonable Value.

**5. LOAN APPROVAL & CLOSING:** VA or a lender's underwriter approved by VA now issues the final approval and the loan closing is scheduled. You will sign many papers, all approved by the VA. The lender and Title Company are limited in the closing costs; they can charge you. The VA will not let them charge UN-allowable closing costs. This does *NOT* prevent them from charging you too high an interest rate.

**6. MOVE IN:** Congratulations! You have taken a major step toward financial freedom and wealth building.

## OPM—THE SECRET TO WEALTH BUILDING

*OPM* stands for *OTHER PEOPLES MONEY*. If you borrowed $150,000 to purchase a home, you have $150,000 of someone else's money working for you. If your home goes up 5% in value each year, you are

getting richer by $7,500 per year or $625 per month! **PLUS**, now your gains compound!

**EXAMPLE:** 5% yearly appreciation on a $150,000 home over a 30-year period.

| | |
|---|---|
| 5th year: $191,442 | 20th year: $397,995 |
| 10th year: $244,334 | 25th year: $507,953 |
| 15th year: $311,839 | 30th year: $648,291 |

## MORE INFORMATION ON VA HOME LOANS

- **VA home loans (start here and explore):** www.homeloans.va.gov
- **State Veterans Affairs Offices (state home loan programs):** www.va.gov/statedva.htm
- **CalVet Home Loans:** Buy a 4-plex with OPM. **www.cdva.ca.gov/CalVetloans/Default.aspx**
- Texas Housing Assistance Program: **www.glo.state.tx.us/vlb/vhap/index.html**
- **Texas Veterans Land Board:** Because of a unique program, Texas veterans' can purchase land at great rates through the assistance of the Texas Land Board. **www.glo.state.tx.us/vlb**
- **How much can you borrow; payments calculator:** www.valoans.com/calculator_borrow.cfm
- **VA foreclosed homes (opportunity knocks):** va.reotrans.com
- **2009 VA County Loan Limits:** www.homeloans.va.gov /docs/2009_county_loan_limits.pdf
- **Home buying guide:** www.newbuyer.com/homes/ homeguide/buying/index.html
- **Bankrate.com:** www.bankrate.com/finance/mortgages/ va-loans-offer-good-deals-1.aspx
- **VALOANS.com:** www.valoans.com/geninfo-01a.cfm
- **Fannie Mae:** www.homepath.com

**REAL ESTATE AGENTS:**
- **How to Choose a Good Real Estate Agent:** www.housebuyingtips.com/realtor.htm
- **How to Negotiate Real Estate Commission Rates:** www.bloomkey.com/negotiate_real_estate_commission_r ates.php

**OTHER REAL ESTATE HELP:**
- **35 REAL ESTATE CHECKLISTS FOR BUYERS:** www.realestatechecklists.com/checklist.html

112

## STEP 1: PERSONAL INFORMATION CHECKLIST:

Before you start the loan process, you'll need to have information at hand before filing out loan applications:

- _____ Proof of income (Veterans: 1 month of pay stubs)
- _____ W2's for the past two years
- _____ If self-employed: Last 2 years tax returns with all schedules (if you are using commission, dividend or rental income to qualify then you will also need to provide your tax returns)
- _____ Copies of social security, pension, and/or retirement award letters
- _____ Names, addresses, account numbers and balances on all checking and savings accounts
- _____ Names, addresses, account numbers, balances and monthly payments on all open loans
- _____ Residence addresses for the past two years
- _____ Names and addresses of your employers over past two years
- _____ Addresses and loan information of other real estate owned
- _____ Estimated value of furniture and personal property
- _____ Certificate of Eligibility (veterans only)
- _____ Copy of DD214 (veterans only)
- _____ Documentation to support your funds to close
- _____ Explanation for any derogatory credit
- _____ Bankruptcy paperwork
- _____ Discharge paperwork
- _____ Divorce decree and settlement paperwork

## STEP 2: START MORTGAGE SHOPPING

**Company Name:** _____

**Phone Number:** _____

**Mortgage Type:** _____
(Fixed, adjustable)

**Mortgage Terms:**   15 years      20 years

_____ 30 years      _____ Other

**Interest Rate Quoted is:** _____ % Date: _____

**Number of Points:** _____

**Points Included in Loan Amount:**   Yes   No

**Interest Rate Lock-in:** Upon application? _____

At approval? _____

Lock in costs: $ _____

Effective how long: _____

Lower lock in rates drop? _____

**Minimum Down Payment Required:**

Without private mortgage insurance (PMI)? _____

With private mortgage insurance (PMI)? _____

Is mortgage insurance required?   Yes   No

Can it be financed?   Yes   No

Up-front costs? _____

Monthly premiums? _____

**Loan Processing Time:**
Days from application to approval? _____

Approval to closing? _____

**Closing Costs / Fees:**

Application fee: $_____      Credit report fee: $_____

Loan origination fee: $_____      Appraisal fee: $_____

Title search/insurance: $_____      Survey fee: $_____

Attorney fee: $_____      Transfer taxes: $_____

Other closing costs: _____

Will lender waive any closing costs or fees? _____

## STEP 3: FOR ADJUSTABLE RATE MORTGAGES

**Financial Index and Margin:** Treasury _____

LIBOR _____      Cost of Funds _____

Certificate of Deposit _____      Other: _____

What is the margin over the index used by the lender to calculate the fully indexed rate (e.g., prime interest rate plus 1%)? _____

**Initial Interest Rate:** _____ %

**Adjustment Interval:**
How often can the interest rate be adjusted ? _____

**Rate Caps:**
How much can the rate rise at each adjustment? _____

What is the lifetime interest rate cap? _____

**Conversion to fixed-rate loan:**
When can the loan convert? _____

How is the converted loan rate determined? _____

Conditions under which a conversion will not be offered?
_____

Is there a conversion fee? _____

## STEP 4: RESEARCH & RESEARCH SOME MORE

- **Mortgage buying guide:**
www.newbuyer.com/homes/mortgage/index.html
- **How get the best VA loan rate.**
www.mortgageresearchcenter.com/mortgagerates
- **VA MortgageCenter.com:** www.vamortgagecenter.com
- **Mortgage Market Info. Services:** www.interest.com
- **MBAA:** www.mbaa.org
- **Bankrate.com:** www.bankrate.com/finance/financial-literacy/conventional-va-fha-mortgage-1.aspx
- **FDIC:** www.fdic.gov/consumers/looking/index.html
- **U.S. Dept. of HUD:** www.hud.gov
- **HSH Association:** www.hsh.com

**C-8**

113

# THE ULTIMATE HOME BUYING CHECKLIST

The following checklist will help remind you of principal items that should be carefully thought about when buying a home. It does not cancel the need for dependable sound advice. The checklist does not cover everything, but it will make it handy to refer to as you look from one house to the next. Eventually, you'll fall in love with a home that will provide all the perks you want and need. Before starting your search, make several copies of this **"checklist."**

| The Neighborhood: Check the crime rate in the area ||
| Conveniences | Remarks |
| --- | --- |
| Work | |
| Supermarkets | |
| Shopping | |
| Restaurants | |
| Entertainment | |
| Child care | |
| Hospitals | |
| Doctor / Dentist | |
| Parks and Recreation | |
| Church / Synagogue | |
| Public transportation | |
| Airport | |
| Highways | |
| Absence of excessive traffic | |
| Absence of noise | |
| Absence of smoke and unpleasant odors | |
| Fire protection | |
| Police protection | |
| Snow removal | |
| Garbage service | |
| Age mix of residents | |
| Are there lots of children in the area | |
| Pet restrictions | |
| Zoning regulations | |
| Restrictions | |
| Covenants | |
| Other | |
| Your final thoughts | |

| Schools: Ask about after school activities in the area ||
| Description | Remarks |
| --- | --- |
| Age / Condition | |
| Reputation | |
| Quality of teachers | |
| Achievement test scores | |
| Play areas | |
| Curriculum | |
| Class size | |
| Distance of pre-school from home | |
| Distance of grade school from home | |
| Distance of middle school from home | |
| Distance of high school from home | |
| Distance of college / Univ. from home | |
| Busing distance | |
| Other | |
| Your final thoughts | |

| The Lot: Do you like the landscaping scheme? ||
| Description | Remarks |
| --- | --- |
| Size of front yard satisfactory | |
| Size of back yard satisfactory | |
| Size of side yards satisfactory | |
| Walks provide access to entrances | |
| Driveway provides easy access to garage | |
| Lot appears to drain satisfactory | |
| Lawn and planting satisfactory | |
| Septic tank in good operating order | |
| Well supplying adequate water | |
| Other | |
| Your final thoughts | |

## Exterior Detail: Observe the exterior detail of neighboring houses and determine whether the house being considered is as good or better in respect to each of the following features.

| Description | Remarks |
|---|---|
| Porches | |
| Terraces / Decks | |
| Garages | |
| Gutters | |
| Storm sashes | |
| Weather stripping | |
| Screens | |
| Other | |
| Your final thoughts | |

## Interior Detail: Consider each of the following to determine whether the house will afford living accommodations, which are sufficient to the needs and comfort of your family.

| Description | Remarks |
|---|---|
| Square footage | |
| Number of bedrooms | |
| Number of baths | |
| Practicality of floor plan | |
| Interior wall conditions | |
| Number of: Fireplaces, ceiling fans, etc. | |
| Cable or satellite connection | |
| Furniture will fit in all rooms | |
| Basement / Attic room | |
| Dining space large enough | |
| At least one closet in each bedroom | |
| At least one coat closet and one linen closet | |
| Sufficient storage areas and space | |
| Kitchen well arranged and equipped | |
| Laundry space ample and well located | |
| Windows provide sufficient light and air | |
| Sufficient number of electrical outlets | |
| Other | |
| Your final thoughts | |

## Exterior Construction: The following appear to be in acceptable condition.
**Warning:** Cracking, peeling, scaling and loose paint on stairs, decks, porches, railings, windows and doors may contain amounts of lead, which are harmful if eaten by children. Examine these areas carefully

| Description | Remarks |
|---|---|
| Wood porch and steps | |
| Windows, doors and screens | |
| Gutters and wood cornice | |
| Wood siding | |
| Mortar joints | |
| Roofing | |
| Chimneys | |
| Paint on exterior woodwork | |
| Other | |
| Your final thoughts | |

## Interior Construction: The following appear to be in acceptable condition. Keep on the lookout for water stains, cracks and leaks (could be expensive repairs).

| Description | Remarks |
|---|---|
| Plaster is free of excessive cracks | |
| Ceilings are free of water stains | |
| Walls are free of water stains | |
| Under kitchen sink no water leaks and stains | |
| Under bathroom sinks: No water leaks / stains | |
| Door locks work and move freely | |
| Windows move freely | |
| Fireplace(s) works properly | |
| Ceiling fan(s) work properly | |
| Basement is dry / will resist moisture | |
| Mechanical equipment works | |
| Electrical wiring and switches work | |
| heating and air conditioning suitable | |
| Adequate insulation in walls, floors | |
| Adequate insulation in roof and ceilings | |
| Other | |
| Your final thoughts | |

## Interior Finish Work: The following appear to be in acceptable condition.

| Description | Remarks |
|---|---|
| Wood floor finish | |
| Carpets | |
| Linoleum floors | |
| Tile floors | |
| Kitchen sink and tops | |
| Kitchen appliances | |
| Kitchen fixtures | |
| Bathroom sinks | |
| Bathroom fixtures | |
| Painting and wall paper | |
| Exposed joists and beams | |
| Other | |
| Your final thoughts | |

## Amenities: Usually this is a bonus, because it's been paid for already.

| Description | Remarks |
|---|---|
| Size of lot / acreage | |
| Single level, two-story, split level, other | |
| Garden(s), fire-pit, pathways, etc. | |
| Swimming pool, jacuzzi, lake, dock | |
| Fruit trees, orchard, crops, etc. | |
| Additional buildings, corrals, etc. | |
| Tennis court / basketball court | |
| Ceiling height | |
| Basement, garage, attic finished | |
| Den, workout room, sewing room, sauna | |
| Stained glass | |
| Slate, tile roof, etc. | |
| Sprinkler, drip system | |
| Views | |
| Exposure: north, south, east or west | |
| Easements | |
| Other | |
| Your final thoughts | |

## Financing Checklist: Add these figures and then compare them to your assets and monthly income

**Realtor listing #:**

**Address:**

**City:**

**County:**

**State:**                     **Zip code:**

| Description | Cost |
|---|---|
| Down payment | $ |
| *Closing costs | $ |
| VA funding fee | $ |
| Loan origination fee (1% of the loan) | $ |
| Discount points: Each Point equals 1% of the loan | $ |
| Title search and examination | $ |
| Various legal fees | $ |
| Credit report fee | $ |
| Appraisal fee | $ |
| Title insurance | $ |
| Recording fees | $ |
| Survey fees | $ |
| Other fees | $ |
| **Total down payment** | $ |

## Monthly Mortgage Payments

| Description | Payments |
|---|---|
| Monthly payment on mortgage | $ |
| Monthly payments on taxes and assessments | $ |
| Monthly payments for association fees | $ |
| Monthly payments for homeowners insurance | $ |
| Probable fuel cost (average per month) | $ |
| Probable monthly utility cost (electricity, gas, water, etc.) | $ |
| Monthly maintenance and repair expenses (estimated) | $ |
| Other | $ |
| **\*\*Total monthly payment** | $ |

\* If you don't know these amounts, you can use an average of about 3-1/2% of the loan amount, plus discount points.
\*\* The total monthly payment is the figure you should compare with your weekly or monthly income.

WARNING: Make sure that you will be able to comfortably pay the total monthly cost out of your income(s) and still have enough left over to meet all other items in your budget.

**HOMEOWNERS INSURANCE:** Homeowners' insurance is a big part of owning a home. Therefore, choose a homeowners' policy carefully to get the most insurance value for your money. The websites below will help you to find great deals:
■ **Homeowners insurance:** How to get the best coverage and value
http://fso.cpasitesolutions.com/Premium/LE/08_le_bi/fg/fg-Homeowner.html
■ **Insure.com: Homeowners insurance checklist**
www.insure.com/articles/homeinsurance/checklist.html

116

"Hey, you're starting to look fit as a fiddle! When it comes to deciding on what to do with their income tax refunds, Americans have the best intentions. In a survey by Principal Financial Group, 84% said they use this money to pay bills. HUH? Why is everyone waiting around for year or so to get a refund check to pay bills? **Tip:** Claim the tax deductions you're entitled to, then take the extra cash you'll receive on your paycheck, and *earn interest!* Furthermore, I have other great ideas on how to add extra income to your paycheck. By the way, if I find out you're receiving any tax refund checks, from here on out, then *"I must break you!"* Don't fumble my tip, instead, take it to the end zone and score six. Are you with me on that, Puke? Go long and get that pay raise!"

**NINTH COMMANDMENT:**
**THOU SHALL TAKE ADVANTAGE OF LAWS TO PAY LESS IN TAXES AND SAVE THE DIFFERENCE**

C-9

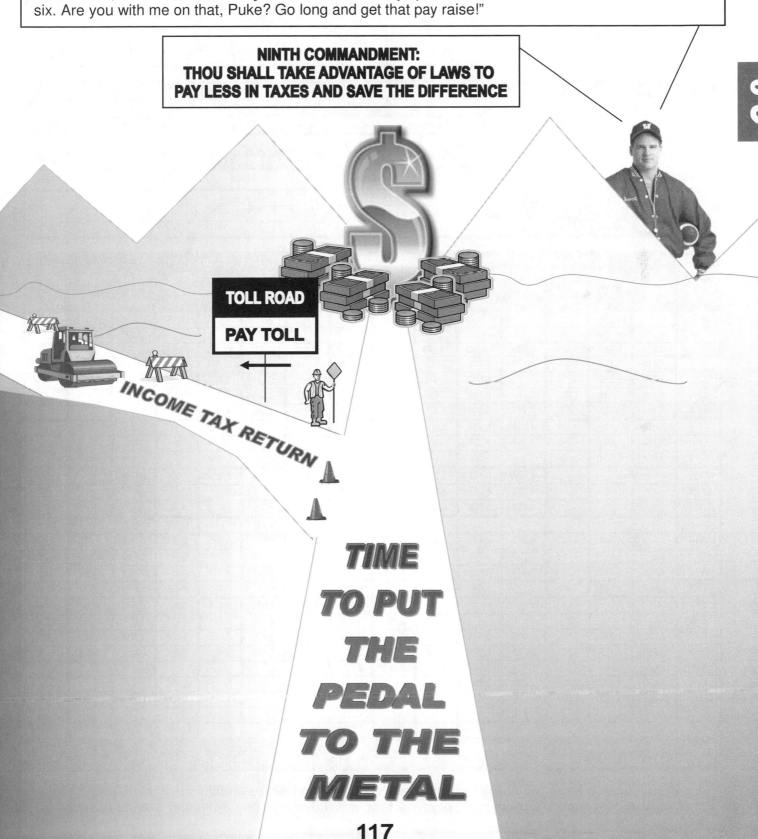

TOLL ROAD

PAY TOLL

INCOME TAX RETURN

**TIME TO PUT THE PEDAL TO THE METAL**

Track promotions, allowances, incentives, etc.; then save a portion or all of it for emergencies or your future. Two examples and open chart (below) have been provided to help keep track of your future raises.

## Save Future Promotions, Allowances & Incentives (Monthly)

| Date | 09 Basic Rate | New Rate | Differential | Other New Pay | Total | Saved Monthly | Add to Income |
|---|---|---|---|---|---|---|---|
| 09/09/15 | $2,128 (E-4) | $2,335 (E-5) | $207 | 0 | $207 | $100 | $107 |
| 09/11/15 | $2,335 (E-5) | 0 | 0 | $250 (FSA) | $250 | $150 | $100 |
| | | | | | | | |
| | | | | | | | |
| | | | | | | | |
| | | | | | | | |

| Jan 01, 2009 Allowances | | 2010 Standard Initial Clothing Allowance (Enlisted Members Only) | | | | | | | |
|---|---|---|---|---|---|---|---|---|---|
| | | ARMY | | NAVY | | AIR FORCE | | MARINE CORPS | |
| BAH: 6.9% increase | | Male | Female | Male | Female | Male | Female | Male | Female |
| BAH Differential: 3.9% Increase | | 1,426 | 1,702 | 1,594 | 1,823 | 1,314 | 1,597 | 1,691 | 1,768 |
| BAS Enlisted: $323.87 | | Cash Clothing Replacement Allowance (Enlisted Members Only) | | | | | | | |
| BAS Officer: $223.04 | | Male | Female | Male | Female | Male | Female | Male | Female |
| FSA (all pay grades): $250 | | | | | | | | | |
| Cash Clothing Replacement Allowance | Basic | 371 | 432 | 317 | 454 | 266 | 299 | 425 | 439 |
| | Standard | 530 | 619 | 317 | 454 | 382 | 428 | 608 | 626 |
| | Special | 0 | 0 | 662 | 518 | 0 | 0 | 0 | N.A. |

## Basic Pay Table for the UNITED STATES ARMED FORCES Effective January 1, 2010

| Rank | Under 2 Years | Over 2 Years | Over 3 Years | Over 4 Years | Over 6 Years | Over 8 Years | Over 10 Years | Over 12 Years | Over 14 Years | Over 16 Years | Over 18 Years | Over 20 Years | Over 22 Years | Over 24 Years | Over 26 Years |
|---|---|---|---|---|---|---|---|---|---|---|---|---|---|---|---|
| O-10 | | | | | | | | | | | | 15,188 | 15,262 | 15,579 | 16,132 |
| O-9 | | | | | | | | | | | | 13,284 | 13,475 | 13,751 | 14,234 |
| O-8 | 9,399 | 9,707 | 9,911 | 9,969 | 10,223 | 10,649 | 10,748 | 11,152 | 11,269 | 11,617 | 12,122 | 12,586 | | | |
| O-7 | 7,810 | 8,172 | 8,340 | 8,474 | 8,716 | 8,953 | 9,231 | 9,506 | 9,782 | 10,649 | 11,381 | 11,381 | 11,381 | 11,381 | 11,439 |
| O-6 | 5,788 | 6,359 | 6,777 | 6,777 | 6,803 | 7,094 | 7,134 | 7,134 | 7,537 | 8,254 | 8,675 | 9,096 | 9,335 | 9,577 | 10,047 |
| O-5 | 4,826 | 5,436 | 5,812 | 5,883 | 6,118 | 6,258 | 6,567 | 6,794 | 7,086 | 7,533 | 7,748 | 7,959 | 8,199 | | |
| O-4 | 4,164 | 4,819 | 5,141 | 5,213 | 5,511 | 5,831 | 6,229 | 6,540 | 6,755 | 6,880 | 6,952 | | | | |
| O-3 | 3,660 | 4,149 | 4,479 | 4,884 | 5,117 | 5,374 | 5,539 | 5,813 | 5,955 | | | | | | |
| O-2 | 3,163 | 3,602 | 4,149 | 4,289 | 4,377 | | | | | | | | | | |
| O-1 | 2,745 | 2,858 | 3,455 | | | | | | | | | | | | |
| O-3E | | | | 4,883 | 5,117 | 5,374 | 5,540 | 5,813 | 6,044 | 6,176 | 6,356 | | | | |
| O-2E | | | | 4,289 | 4,377 | 4,516 | 4,752 | 4,934 | 5,069 | | | | | | |
| O-1E | | | | 3,453 | 3,688 | 3,825 | 3,964 | 4,102 | 4,289 | | | | | | |
| W-5 | | | | | | | | | | | | 6,727 | 7,068 | 7,322 | 7,604 |
| W-4 | 3,783 | 4,068 | 4,187 | 4,301 | 4,499 | 4,695 | 4,892 | 5,192 | 5,453 | 5,703 | 5,905 | 6,104 | 6,396 | 6,635 | 6,909 |
| W-3 | 3,454 | 3,598 | 3,746 | 3,793 | 3,949 | 4,254 | 4,571 | 4,720 | 4,893 | 5,071 | 5,390 | 5,606 | 5,736 | 5,873 | 6,060 |
| W-2 | 3,038 | 3,212 | 3,364 | 3,473 | 3,569 | 4,003 | 4,156 | 4,306 | 4,490 | 4,633 | 4,764 | 4,919 | 5,021 | 5,103 | |
| W-1 | 2,682 | 2,903 | 3,050 | 3,145 | 3,397 | 3,694 | 3,828 | 4,014 | 4,198 | 4,342 | 4,475 | 4,636 | | | |
| E-9 | | | | | | | 4,571 | 4,675 | 4,805 | 4,959 | 5,113 | 5,361 | 5,571 | 5,792 | 6,130 |
| E-8 | | | | | | 3,742 | 3,907 | 4,010 | 4,133 | 4,265 | 4,505 | 4,627 | 4,834 | 4,948 | 5,232 |
| E-7 | 2,602 | 2,839 | 2,948 | 3,092 | 3,204 | 3,397 | 3,505 | 3,700 | 3,860 | 3,970 | 4,085 | 4,131 | 4,283 | 4,365 | 4,674 |
| E-6 | 2,250 | 2,475 | 2,585 | 2,690 | 2,801 | 3,051 | 3,149 | 3,336 | 3,394 | 3,436 | 3,485 | 3,485 | 3,485 | 3,485 | 3,485 |
| E-5 | 2,062 | 2,199 | 2,306 | 2,414 | 2,584 | 2,762 | 2,907 | 2,924 | | | | | | | |
| E-4 | 1,889 | 1,986 | 2,094 | 2,200 | 2,294 | | | | | | | | | | |
| E-3 | 1,706 | 1,813 | 1,923 | | | | | | | | | | | | |
| E-2 | 1,622 | | | | | | | | | | | | | | |
| E-1 | 1,447 | | | | | | | | | | | | | | |

**NOTE 1:** E-1 with less than 4 months of service receives $1,339 per month.
**NOTE 2:** Basic pay rate for Academy Cadets / Midshipmen and ROTC members / applicants is $961 per month.

For more information about pay tables', visit: **http://www.dfas.mil/militarypay/militarypaytables.html**
For other pays or specific requirements for pay, visit: **http://www.dtic.mil/comptroller/fmr/07a/index.html**

The pay chart below depicts monthly drill pay for members of the National Guard and Reserves for the calendar year of 2010. On top of one weekend of drill per month, members of the Reserves must perform a minimum of 14 days of active duty training per year. On the other hand, members of the National Guard are required to perform 15 days of training per year. Furthermore, Guard/Reserve members as a rule, are credited with 4 days active duty pay for a weekend duty.

In addition, when performing active duty other than weekend drills, Guard/Reserve members receive 1/30th of monthly active duty pay for each day served on active duty.

The chart below includes a 3.4 percent pay raise, effective on January 1, 2010. Guard/Reserve drill pay is based upon grade (rank) and years of service.

### Reserve Pay Table for Four Drills Effective January 1, 2010

| Rank | Under 2 Years | Over 2 Years | Over 3 Years | Over 4 Years | Over 6 Years | Over 8 Years | Over 10 Years | Over 12 Years | Over 14 Years | Over 16 Years | Over 18 Years | Over 20 Years | Over 22 Years | Over 24 Years | Over 26 Years |
|---|---|---|---|---|---|---|---|---|---|---|---|---|---|---|---|
| O-10 | | | | | | | | | | | | 2,025 | 2,035 | 2,077 | 2,151 |
| O-9 | | | | | | | | | | | | 1,771 | 1,797 | 1,833 | 1,897 |
| O-8 | 1,253 | 1,295 | 1,321 | 1,329 | 1,363 | 1,420 | 1,433 | 1,487 | 1,502 | 1,549 | 1,616 | 1,678 | 1,720 | | |
| O-7 | 1,041 | 1,089 | 1,113 | 1,130 | 1,162 | 1,195 | 1,230 | 1,268 | 1,304 | 1,419 | 1,518 | 1,518 | 1,518 | 1,518 | 1,525 |
| O-6 | 771 | 848 | 904 | 904 | 907 | 946 | 951 | 951 | 1,005 | 1,100 | 1,157 | 1,213 | 1,245 | 1,277 | 1,340 |
| O-5 | 643 | 725 | 776 | 785 | 815 | 834 | 876 | 906 | 945 | 1,005 | 1,033 | 1,061 | 1,093 | | |
| O-4 | 555 | 643 | 685 | 695 | 735 | 778 | 830 | 872 | 900 | 918 | 926 | | | | |
| O-3 | 488 | 553 | 597 | 651 | 682 | 717 | 738 | 776 | 794 | | | | | | |
| O-2 | 422 | 481 | 553 | 572 | 583 | | | | | | | | | | |
| O-1 | 366 | 380 | 460 | | | | | | | | | | | | |
| O-3E | | | | 651 | 682 | 717 | 738 | 776 | 805 | 823 | 848 | | | | |
| O-2E | | | | 572 | 583 | 602 | 634 | 657 | 676 | | | | | | |
| O-1E | | | | 460 | 492 | 510 | 529 | 547 | 572 | | | | | | |
| W-5 | | | | | | | | | | | | 896 | 942 | 976 | 1,013 |
| W-4 | 505 | 543 | 558 | 574 | 599 | 626 | 652 | 692 | 727 | 760 | 788 | 813 | 853 | 885 | 921 |
| W-3 | 460 | 480 | 500 | 506 | 526 | 568 | 609 | 630 | 652 | 676 | 720 | 748 | 767 | 783 | 808 |
| W-2 | 407 | 446 | 458 | 466 | 492 | 534 | 554 | 574 | 599 | 617 | 635 | 656 | 670 | 680 | |
| W-1 | 358 | 396 | 406 | 428 | 454 | 492 | 511 | 536 | 559 | 579 | 597 | 618 | | | |
| E-9 | | | | | | | 609 | 623 | 641 | 661 | 681 | 714 | 742 | 772 | 816 |
| E-8 | | | | | | 498 | 521 | 535 | 551 | 568 | 601 | 617 | 644 | 660 | 698 |
| E-7 | 346 | 378 | 393 | 413 | 427 | 453 | 467 | 493 | 515 | 529 | 545 | 551 | 571 | 582 | 623 |
| E-6 | 300 | 330 | 344 | 359 | 373 | 406 | 420 | 445 | 453 | 458 | 464 | | | | |
| E-5 | 275 | 294 | 307 | 321 | 344 | 368 | 388 | | | | | | | | |
| E-4 | 252 | 264 | 279 | 294 | 306 | | | | | | | | | | |
| E-3 | 227 | 242 | 256 | | | | | | | | | | | | |
| E-2 | 216 | | | | | | | | | | | | | | |
| E-1 | 193 | | | | | | | | | | | | | | |

**E1: Less than 4 months $179**

Track promotions, allowances, incentives, etc.; then save a portion or all of it for emergencies or your future. Two examples and open chart (below) is provided to help keep track of your future raises.

### Save Future Promotions, Allowances & Incentives (Monthly)

| Date | 09 Basic Rate | New Rate | Differential | Other New Pay | Total | Saved Monthly | Add to Income |
|---|---|---|---|---|---|---|---|
| 09/09/15 | $2,128 (E-4) | $2,335 (E-5) | $207 | 0 | $207 | $100 | $107 |
| 09/11/15 | $2,335 (E-5) | 0 | 0 | $250 (FSA) | $250 | $150 | $100 |
| | | | | | | | |
| | | | | | | | |
| | | | | | | | |
| | | | | | | | |
| | | | | | | | |
| | | | | | | | |

National Guard Drill Pay Calculator: **www.military.com/benefits/military-pay/reserve-and-guard-pay/national-guard-drill-pay-calculator**

For more information on pay, visit: **www.defenselink.mil/militarypay/pay/bp/index.html**

The future income chart below will help you to list and keep track of all future pay increases on a monthly basis. Hopefully, the second chart below (long-term savings) will motivate you to save some of those increases.

| Future income | Jan | Feb | Mar | Apr | June | July | Aug | Sept | Oct | Nov | Dec |
|---|---|---|---|---|---|---|---|---|---|---|---|
| Promotion | | | | | | | | | | | |
| New year mark | | | | | | | | | | | |
| Cost of living increase | | | | | | | | | | | |
| BAH | | | | | | | | | | | |
| BAS increase | | | | | | | | | | | |
| GI Bill paid-off | | | | | | | | | | | |
| Other | | | | | | | | | | | |
| Total | | | | | | | | | | | |

**Chart reflects varied pay raises saved monthly into a 10% account; stop after 20-years and let accumulate to age 65**

| Yr/Age | $50 = 600 a year | | $100 = 1,200 a year | | $150 = 1,800 a year | | $200 = 2,400 a year | | $250 = 3,000 a year | |
|---|---|---|---|---|---|---|---|---|---|---|
| 1 / 64 | 600 $ | 655 | 1,200 $ | 1,310 | 1,800 $ | 1,965 | 2,400 $ | 2,620 | 3,000 $ | 3,275 |
| 2 / 63 | 1,200 | 1,376 | 2,400 | 2,751 | 3,600 | 4,127 | 4,800 | 5,502 | 6,000 | 6,878 |
| 3 / 62 | 1,800 | 2,168 | 3,600 | 4,336 | 5,400 | 6,504 | 7,200 | 8,672 | 9,000 | 10,840 |
| 4 / 61 | 2,400 | 3.040 | 4,800 | 6,080 | 7,200 | 9,120 | 9,600 | 12,159 | 12,000 | 15,199 |
| 5 / 60 | 3,000 | 3,999 | 6,000 | 7,998 | 9,000 | 11,997 | 12,000 | 15,995 | 15,000 | 19,994 |
| 6 / 59 | 3,600 | 5,054 | 7,200 | 10,107 | 10,800 | 15,161 | 14,400 | 20,215 | 18,000 | 25,269 |
| 7 / 58 | 4,200 | 6,214 | 8,400 | 12,428 | 12,600 | 18,642 | 16,800 | 24,856 | 21,000 | 31,070 |
| 8 / 57 | 4,800 | 7,491 | 9,600 | 14,981 | 14,400 | 22,472 | 19,200 | 29,962 | 24,000 | 37,453 |
| 9 / 56 | 5,400 | 8,895 | 10,800 | 17,789 | 16,200 | 26,684 | 21,600 | 35,578 | 27,000 | 44,473 |
| 10 / 55 | 6,000 | 10,439 | 12,000 | 20,878 | 18,000 | 31,317 | 24,000 | 41,756 | 30,000 | 52,195 |
| 11 / 54 | 6,600 | 12,138 | 13,200 | 24,276 | 19,800 | 36,414 | 26,400 | 48,552 | 33,000 | 60,690 |
| 12 / 53 | 7,200 | 14,007 | 14,400 | 28,013 | 21,600 | 42,020 | 28,800 | 56,027 | 36,000 | 70,034 |
| 13 / 52 | 7,800 | 16,062 | 15,600 | 32,125 | 23,400 | 48,187 | 31,200 | 64,250 | 39,000 | 80,312 |
| 14 / 51 | 8,400 | 18,324 | 16,800 | 36,647 | 25,200 | 54,971 | 33,600 | 73,294 | 42,000 | 91,618 |
| 15 / 50 | 9,000 | 20,811 | 18,000 | 41,622 | 27,000 | 62,433 | 36,000 | 83,244 | 45,000 | 104,055 |
| 16 / 49 | 9,600 | 23,547 | 19,200 | 47,094 | 28,800 | 70,641 | 38,400 | 94,188 | 48,000 | 117,735 |
| 17 / 48 | 10,200 | 26,557 | 20,400 | 53,114 | 30,600 | 79,670 | 40,800 | 106,227 | 51,000 | 132,784 |
| 18 / 47 | 10,800 | 29,867 | 21,600 | 59,735 | 32,400 | 89,602 | 43,200 | 119,470 | 54,000 | 149,337 |
| 19 / 46 | 11,400 | 33,509 | 22,800 | 67,018 | 34,200 | 100,528 | 45,600 | 134,037 | 57,000 | 167,546 |
| 20 / 45 | 12,000 | 37,515 | 24,000 | 75,030 | 36,000 | 112,545 | 48,000 | 150,061 | 60,000 | 187,576 |
| 21 / 44 | | 41,267 | | 82,533 | | 123,800 | | 165,067 | | 206,334 |
| 22 / 43 | | 45,393 | | 90,786 | | 136,179 | | 181,574 | | 226,967 |
| 23 / 42 | | 49,932 | | 99,865 | | 149,797 | | 199,731 | | 249,664 |
| 24 / 41 | | 54,926 | | 109,851 | | 164,777 | | 219,704 | | 274,630 |
| 25 / 40 | | 60,418 | | 120,837 | | 181,255 | | 241,675 | | 302,093 |
| 26 / 39 | | 66,460 | | 132,920 | | 199,380 | | 265,842 | | 332,302 |
| 27 / 38 | | 73,106 | | 146,212 | | 219,318 | | 292,426 | | 365,533 |
| 28 / 37 | | 80,417 | | 160,833 | | 241,250 | | 321,669 | | 402,086 |
| 29 / 36 | | 88,458 | | 176,917 | | 265,375 | | 353,836 | | 442,294 |
| 30 / 35 | | 97,304 | | 194,609 | | 291,913 | | 389,220 | | 486,524 |
| 31 / 34 | | 107,035 | | 214,069 | | 321,104 | | 428,142 | | 535,176 |
| 32 / 33 | | 117,738 | | 235,476 | | 353,214 | | 470,956 | | 588,694 |
| 33 / 32 | | 129,512 | | 259,024 | | 388,536 | | 518,051 | | 647,563 |
| 34 / 31 | | 142,463 | | 284,926 | | 427,389 | | 569,856 | | 712,320 |
| 35 / 30 | | 156,709 | | 313,419 | | 470,128 | | 626,842 | | 783,552 |
| 36 / 29 | | 172,380 | | 344,761 | | 517,141 | | 689,526 | | 861,907 |
| 37 / 28 | | 189,618 | | 379,237 | | 568,855 | | 758,479 | | 948,097 |
| 38 / 27 | | 208,580 | | 417,161 | | 625,741 | | 834,327 | | 1,042,908 |
| 39 / 26 | | 229,438 | | 458,877 | | 688,315 | | 917,759 | | 1,147,198 |
| 40 / 25 | | 252,382 | | 504,764 | | 757,146 | | 1,009,535 | | 1,261,918 |
| 41 / 24 | | 277,620 | | 555,241 | | 832,861 | | 1,110,489 | | 1,388,109 |
| 42 / 23 | | 305,382 | | 610,765 | | 916,147 | | 1,221,538 | | 1,526,920 |
| 43 / 22 | | 335,921 | | 671,841 | | 1,007,762 | | 1,343,592 | | 1,679,612 |
| 44 / 21 | | 369,513 | | 739,025 | | 1,108,538 | | 1,478,061 | | 1,847,573 |
| 45 / 20 | | 406,464 | | 812,928 | | 1,219,392 | | 1,625,867 | | 2,032,331 |
| 46 / 19 | | 447,110 | | 894,221 | | 1,341,331 | | 1,788,453 | | 2,235,564 |
| 47 / 18 | | 491,821 | | 983,643 | | 1,475,464 | | 1,967,299 | | 2,459,120 |

How's this for a deal? You lend someone $2,500 without receiving payments or interest for 18 months. When you try to collect, borrower gives you a bunch of complex forms to fill out. Confused, you hire an expert to fill out forms, whose fee is $150. Once mailed, borrower then pays you back at their leisure, and that's if the forms were filled out correctly. Does this sound like a bad deal?

In 2009, **$2,675** was the average tax refund check, which means taxpayer's overpaid by **$222.92** monthly. Alas, most taxpayers don't realize what a mistake this is. The chart below illustrates what could happen by not claiming or claiming one allowance.

| YEAR & AGE | $547 yearly tax refund (no interest) | $547 saved once at 10% (up to age 65) | $547 saved yearly at 10% (up to age 65) |
|---|---|---|---|
| One allowance = $45.61 monthly x 12 months = $547 |||| 
| 1 / 64 | 547 | 602 | 602 |
| 2 / 63 | 1,094 | 662 | 1,209 |
| 3 / 62 | 1,641 | 728 | 1,877 |
| 4 / 61 | 2,188 | 801 | 2,612 |
| 5 / 60 | 2,735 | 881 | 3,421 |
| 6 / 59 | 3,282 | 969 | 4,310 |
| 7 / 58 | 3,829 | 1,066 | 5,289 |
| 8 / 57 | 4,376 | 1,173 | 6,365 |
| 9 / 56 | 4,923 | 1,290 | 7,549 |
| 10 / 55 | 5,470 | 1,419 | 8,851 |
| 11 / 54 | 6,017 | 1,561 | 10,284 |
| 12 / 53 | 6,564 | 1,717 | 11,859 |
| 13 / 52 | 7,111 | 1,888 | 13,592 |
| 14 / 51 | 7,658 | 2,077 | 15,499 |
| 15 / 50 | 8,205 | 2,285 | 17,596 |
| 16 / 49 | 8,752 | 2,513 | 19,903 |
| 17 / 48 | 9,299 | 2,765 | 22,441 |
| 18 / 47 | 9,846 | 3,041 | 25,232 |
| 19 / 46 | 10,393 | 3,345 | 28,303 |
| 20 / 45 | 10,940 | 3,680 | 31,680 |
| 21 / 44 | 11,487 | 4,048 | 35,396 |
| 22 / 43 | 12,034 | 4,453 | 39,483 |
| 23 / 42 | 12,581 | 4,898 | 43,978 |
| 24 / 41 | 13,128 | 5,388 | 48,923 |
| 25 / 40 | 13,675 | 5,927 | 54,363 |
| 26 / 39 | 14,222 | 6,519 | 60,347 |
| 27 / 38 | 14,769 | 7,171 | 66,929 |
| 28 / 37 | 15,316 | 7,888 | 74,169 |
| 29 / 36 | 15,863 | 8,677 | 82,133 |
| 30 / 35 | 16,410 | 9,545 | 90,894 |
| 31 / 34 | 16,957 | 10,499 | 100,530 |
| 32 / 33 | 17,504 | 11,549 | 111,131 |
| 33 / 32 | 18,051 | 12,704 | 122,791 |
| 34 / 31 | 18,598 | 13,975 | 135,617 |
| 35 / 30 | 19,145 | 15,372 | 149,726 |
| 36 / 29 | 19,692 | 16,909 | 165,246 |
| 37 / 28 | 20,239 | 18,600 | 182,318 |
| 38 / 27 | 20,786 | 20,460 | 201,097 |
| 39 / 26 | 21,333 | 22,506 | 221,754 |
| 40 / 25 | 21,880 | 24,757 | 244,477 |
| 41 / 24 | 22,427 | 27,232 | 269,472 |
| 42 / 23 | 22,974 | 29,956 | 296,967 |
| 43 / 22 | 23,521 | 32,951 | 327,211 |
| 44 / 21 | 24,068 | 36,246 | 360,479 |
| 45 / 20 | 24,615 | 39,871 | 397,074 |
| 46 / 19 | 25,162 | 43,858 | 437,329 |
| 47 / 18 | 25,709 | 48,244 | 481,609 |

**CLAIM THE CORRECT ALLOWANCES:** Time to stop giving cash free loans to the government and learn how to claim the correct allowances. Here's how to do it:

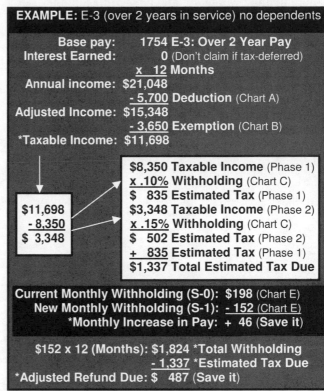

**EXAMPLE:** E-3 (over 2 years in service) no dependents

| | |
|---|---|
| Base pay: | 1754 E-3: Over 2 Year Pay |
| Interest Earned: | 0 (Don't claim if tax-deferred) |
| | x 12 Months |
| Annual income: | $21,048 |
| | - 5,700 Deduction (Chart A) |
| Adjusted Income: | $15,348 |
| | - 3,650 Exemption (Chart B) |
| *Taxable Income: | $11,698 |

$11,698
- 8,350
$ 3,348

$8,350 Taxable Income (Phase 1)
x .10% Withholding (Chart C)
$ 835 Estimated Tax (Phase 1)
$3,348 Taxable Income (Phase 2)
x .15% Withholding (Chart C)
$ 502 Estimated Tax (Phase 2)
+ 835 Estimated Tax (Phase 1)
$1,337 Total Estimated Tax Due

Current Monthly Withholding (S-0): **$198** (Chart E)
New Monthly Withholding (S-1): **- 152** (Chart E)
*Monthly Increase in Pay: **+ 46** (Save it)

$152 x 12 (Months): $1,824 *Total Withholding
 - 1,337 *Estimated Tax Due
*Adjusted Refund Due: $ 487 (Save it)

| CHART: A | 2009 Standard Deductions |
|---|---|
| SINGLE | $ 5,700 |
| HEAD OF HOUSEHOLD | $ 8,350 |
| MARRIED FILING SEPARATE | $ 5,700 |
| MARRIED FILING JOINTLY | $11,400 |

| CHART: B | 2009 Exemptions |
|---|---|
| PER PERSON | $ 3,650 |

**CHART: C  2009 Withholding Table: SINGLE**

| TAXABLE INCOME IS BETWEEN | TAX BRACKET IS |
|---|---|
| PHASE I: $ 0 and 8,350 | 10% |
| PHASE 2: 8,350 and 33,950 | 15%; plus $ 836 |
| PHASE 3: 33,950 and 82,250 | 25%; plus 4,675 |
| PHASE 4: 82,250 and 171,550 | 28%; plus 16,750 |
| PHASE 5: 171,550 and 372,950 | 33%; plus 41,754 |
| PHASE 6: over 372,950 | 35%; plus 109,216 |

**CHART: D  2009 Withholding Table: MARRIED**

| TAXABLE INCOME IS BETWEEN | TAX BRACKET IS |
|---|---|
| PHASE 1: $ 0 and 16,700 | 10% |
| PHASE 2: 16,700 and 67,900 | 15%; plus $ 1,670 |
| PHASE 3: 67,900 and 137,050 | 25%; plus $ 9,350 |
| PHASE 4: 137,050 and 208,850 | 28%; plus $ 26,638 |
| PHASE 5: 208,850 and 372,950 | 33%; plus $ 46,742 |
| PHASE 6: over 372,950 | 35%; plus $100,895 |

**CHART: E  2009 Monthly Withholding Table**

| BASE PAY | SINGLE | | | MARRIED | | |
|---|---|---|---|---|---|---|
| | 0 | 1 | 2 | 0 | 1 | 2 |
| $1,400 | $144 | $ 07 | $ 57 | $ 73 | $ 43 | $ 12 |
| 1,569 | 170 | 124 | 79 | 90 | 60 | 29 |
| 1,650 | 182 | 136 | 91 | 98 | 68 | 37 |
| 1,754 | 198 | 152 | 106 | 109 | 78 | 48 |
| 1,828 | 209 | 163 | 117 | 116 | 86 | 55 |
| 1,860 | 214 | 168 | 122 | 119 | 89 | 58 |
| 1,921 | 223 | 177 | 131 | 125 | 95 | 65 |
| 1,994 | 234 | 188 | 142 | 133 | 102 | 72 |

For more: //apps.opm.gov/tax_calc/withhold_calc/index.cfm
*NOTE: See a tax advisor to get the best possible results

# ADVANCED EITC: GET PAID MONTHLY

**2010 EARNED INCOME TAX CREDIT (EITC):** Earned income Tax credit (EITC) is designed to reduce tax liability for low- income families. The amount of credit varies with "earned income" of taxpayer.

That being said, hundreds of thousands of enlisted members—some in pay grades as high as E-6—may be eligible. The amount of earned income credit has increased substantially.  For example:

■ If you were raising one qualifying child in your home and you earned less than $35,463, or if you are married, filing jointly (income must be less than $40,463), you can receive an earned income tax credit up to $3,043.

■ If you were raising two qualifying children in your home and you earned less than $40,295, or if you are married, filing jointly (income must be less than $45,295), you can receive an earned income tax credit up to $5,028.

■ If you were raising three or more qualifying children in your home and you earned less than $43,279, or if you are married, filing jointly (income must be less than $48,279), you can receive an earned income tax credit up to $5,657.

■ If you are not raising children, and earning less than $13,440, or If you are married, filing jointly, your income must be less than $18,440: Earned income tax credit: Up to $458.

**EITC ESTIMATOR:** You can figure what EITC you'll receive for the year by using an earned income calculator at: www.cbpp.org/eic2009/calculator.

**WHAT IS ADVANCE EITC PAYMENT?** Most servicemembers' receive an EITC in one large check from the IRS, after filing a tax return. However, there is another choice:

■ Qualifying servicemembers' can add up to $1,826 ($152 monthly) to their EITC to their regular paychecks, and receive rest of credit after filing a tax return.

**SOME SERVICEMEMBERS' SHOULD NOT CHOOSE ADVANCE EITC IF:**
■ They hold more than one job.
■ Spouse works, unless *both* spouses take Advance EIC.
■ They get married during year and *both* spouses work.
■ Their earned income increases a lot.

**HOW DO I GET ADVANCE EITC PAYMENT?** Ask your finance office for a W-5 form. The W-5 form for 2009 is also available by calling 1-800-TAX-FORM or can be downloaded from IRS website at www.irs.gov/pub/irs-pdf/fw5.pdf.

Fill out W-5 form called *"Earned Income Credit Advance Payment Certificate"* and give bottom part to your finance office. You can file any time during the year, but you must file a new W-5 at the beginning of each year to continue getting the EITC in your paycheck. Married workers can choose advance payment, but if they do, both spouses should give a W-5 to their employers. The box on W-5 indicating worker's spouse also has a W-5 in effect should be checked "yes". This signals employers to figure the correct amount of advance payment and avoids an overpayment of EITC.

**WAIT! EITC IS NEWS TO ME. WHAT IF I WAS ELIGIBLE FOR EITC IN PAST YEARS?** If you fall under this category, Servicemembers' can file for EITC for the past three years. Fill out a FORM 1040X and attach to copy of the regular tax form you filed that year. Furthermore, fill out and attach a Schedule EITC for that tax year. For copies of prior-year forms, call 1-800-TAX-FORM.

**WHAT ARE RULES FOR MILITARY PERSONNEL?** Under the rules, allowances for housing and subsistence – including the value of meals and lodging furnished to personnel residing on military bases – are no longer considered earned income for EITC purposes. Veteran's Benefits and military retirement pay is not considered earned income. U.S. military personnel now can get EITC whether they live in the United States or overseas. Military personnel stationed overseas whose qualifying children remain in the United States can still claim EITC. Married couples living apart due to military assignment must file a joint return to receive EITC.

**WHO IS A 'QUALIFYING CHILD?** A son, daughter, stepchild, grandchild, foster child* or an adopted child who, at the end of tax year, was under age 19 (or a full-time student under the age of 24) and lived with you for more than six months of the year; a child of any age who is totally or permanently disabled and lived with you for more than six months of the year. In addition, a brother, sister, stepbrother, stepsister or any of their descendents may also qualify.
* A qualifying foster child must have been placed with you by an authorized placement agency.
NOTE: A child can only be a "qualifying child" for EITC on one income tax return.

**IF YOU WANT MORE INFORMATION OR HAVE ADDITIONAL QUESTIONS ABOUT EITC:** Call IRS toll free at (800) 829-1040 or visit their Website at
■ www.irs.gov/individuals/article/0,,id=96406,00.html
■ www.irs.gov/pub/irs-pdf/p596.pdf.
Also, you can call or see your finance or JAG office. Other options visit a local IRS office in person, locate one of the Voluntary Income Tax Assistance (VITA) sites that are set up around the state or visit www.irs.gov/individuals/article/0,,id=107626,00.html

If you qualify, tax credits can help pay the cost of raising a family, going to college, save for retirement; get daycare for dependents or lower tax liability to zero. However, each year, many taxpayers overlook these credits, even though they often qualify for one or more.

While tax deductions and tax credits can both save money, they are fundamentally different. A deduction lowers the income on which the tax is figured, while a credit lowers the tax itself.

The popular credits listed below can help either lower your tax bill or increase refund.

**First-Time Homebuyer Credit:** Those who bought a main home recently or are considering buying one may qualify for the first-time homebuyer credit. Normally, a taxpayer qualifies if she didn't own a main home during the prior three years. This unique credit of up to $7,500 works much like a 15-year interest-free loan. It is available for a limited time only — on homes bought from April 9, 2008, to June 30, 2009. It can be claimed on new Form 5405 and is repaid each year as an additional tax. Income limits and other special rules apply. To learn more, visit:
**www.irs.gov/newsroom/article/0,,id=187935,00.html**

**Child Tax Credit:** A taxpayer who has a dependent child under age 17 probably qualifies for the child tax credit. This credit, which can be as much as $1,000 per eligible child, is in addition to the regular $3,500 exemption claimed for each dependent. A change in the way the credit is figured means that more low-and moderate-income families will qualify for the full credit on their returns. The child tax credit is not the same as the child care credit. Details on figuring and claiming the child tax credit can be found at **www.irs.gov/pub/irs-pdf/p972.pdf**. To learn more, visit:
**www.irs.gov/newsroom/article/0,,id=106182,00.html**

**Credit for Child and Dependent Care Expenses:** An individual who pays someone to care for a child so he or she can work or look for work probably qualifies for the child and dependent care credit. Normally, the child must be the taxpayer's dependent and under age 13. Though often referred to as the child care credit, this credit is also available to those who pay someone to care for a spouse or dependent, regardless of age, which is unable to care for him-or herself. In most cases, the care provider's Social Security Number or taxpayer identification number must be obtained and entered on the return. Form 1040 filers claim the credit for child and dependent care expenses on Form 2441. Form 1040A filers claim it on Schedule 2. IRS Publication 503 (PDF version) **www.irs.gov/pub/irs-pdf/p503.pdf.** To learn more, visit:
**www.irs.gov/newsroom/article/0,,id=106189,00.html**

**Education Credits:** The Hope credit and the lifetime learning credit help parents and students pay for post-secondary education. Normally, a taxpayer can claim his or her own tuition and required enrollment fees, as well as those for a dependent's college education. The Hope credit targets the first two years of post-secondary education, and an eligible student must be enrolled at least half time. A taxpayer can also choose the lifetime learning credit, even if she is only taking one course. In some cases, however, she may do better by claiming the tuition and fees deduction, instead. The education credit and the tuition and fees deduction cannot both be claimed for the same student in the same year. Special rules, including income limits, apply to each of these tax breaks. Education credits are claimed on Form 8863. Details on these and other education-related tax breaks are contained in Publication 970 (PDF version) **www.irs.gov/pub/irs-pdf/p970.pdf.** To learn more, visit: **www.irs.gov/individuals/article/0,,id=121452,00.html**

**Saver's Credit:** The saver's credit is designed to help low-and moderate-income workers save for retirement. A taxpayer probably qualifies if his income is below certain limits and contributes to an IRA or workplace retirement plan, such as a 401(k). Income limits for 2009 are:
■ $27,751 for singles and married taxpayers filing separately
■ $41,626 for heads of household
■ $55,501 for joint filers
Known as the retirement savings contributions credit, the saver's credit is available in addition to any other tax savings that apply. There is still time to put money into an IRA and get the saver's credit on a 2009 return. 2009 IRA contributions can be made until April 15, 2010. Form 8880 is used to claim the saver's credit. To see or retrieve form, visit: **www.irs.gov/pub/irs-pdf/f8880.pdf.** To learn more, visit:
**www.irs.gov/publications/p590/ch05.html**

**Other Credits Available:** IRS.gov has information on these additional credits:
■ **Recovery Rebate Credit**, claimed on Form 1040 Line 70, Form 1040A Line 42 and Form 1040EZ Line 9. FS-2009-3 has further details. To learn more, visit:
**www.irs.gov/newsroom/article/0,,id=186065,00.html**
■ **District of Columbia first-time homebuyer credit**, claimed on Form 8859. To see or retrieve form, visit:
**www.irs.gov/pub/irs-pdf/f8859.pdf**
■ **Foreign tax credit**, claimed on Form 1040 Line 47 Credit for the elderly or the disabled, claimed on Form 1040 Schedule R. To learn more, visit:
**www.irs.gov/businesses/article/0,,id=183263,00.html**
■ **Adoption credit**, claimed on Form 8839. To see or retrieve form, visit: **www.irs.gov/pub/irs-pdf/f8839.pdf.** To learn more, visit: **www.irs.gov/taxtopics/tc607.html**
■ **Residential energy efficient property credit**, claimed on Form 5695. To see or retrieve form, visit:
**www.irs.gov/pub/irs-pdf/f5695.pdf.** To learn more, visit:
**www.irs.gov/newsroom/article/0,,id=206871,00.html**
■ **Alternative motor vehicle (including hybrids) credit**, claimed on Form 8910. To see or retrieve form, visit:
**www.irs.gov/pub/irs-pdf/f8910.pdf.** To learn more, visit:
**www.irs.gov/businesses/corporations/article/0,,id=20 2341,00.html**
■ **Credit for prior year minimum tax**, claimed on Form 8801. To see or retrieve form, visit:
**www.irs.gov/pub/irs-pdf/f8801.pdf**

Department of the Treasury
**Internal Revenue Service**

C-9

As you know, your *"home of record"* never changes, but what you might not know is your *domicile* can. Domicile is a legal residence that you consider home. During a military career, a servicemember will have been stationed in a number of different states and any one of them could have become the member's domicile. So, where is your domicile? In order to change your domicile; you must be physically present in that state with the intent to make it your permanent home Once you've met all the criteria to change your domicile, pick up and fill out form **DD-2058** from your finance office. That's it, but changing your domicile is sometimes complicated and varies according to circumstances. Don't be your own lawyer. If you have questions regarding domicile, consult with a military legal assistance office.

**WARNING:** Research the state tax structure before changing your domicile, so you won't get yourself into a financial mess by having to pay higher state taxes. The states below either have **NO** state tax or conditions that will allow you to skip paying them:

1. **NO** state tax - **Alaska, Florida, Nevada, South Dakota, Texas, Washington, Wyoming**
2. **NO** state tax while in service - **Connecticut, Illinois, Michigan, New Hampshire, Tennessee, Vermont, West Virginia**
3. **NO** state tax while out of state - **California, Idaho, New Jersey, New York and Pennsylvania**

**If paying less taxes after changing domicile, save difference. The projections below reflect ex-state tax dollars deposited monthly into a 10% account; stopped after 20-years, and funds continue to accumulate until age 65.**

| Years | $25 = 300 | | $50 = 600 | | $75 = 900 | | $100 = 1,200 | | $125 = 1,500 | |
|---|---|---|---|---|---|---|---|---|---|---|
| 1 | 300 $ | 328 | 600 $ | 655 | 900 $ | 983 | 1,200 $ | 1,310 | 1,800 $ | 1,638 |
| 2 | 600 | 688 | 1,200 | 1,376 | 1,800 | 2,063 | 2,400 | 2,751 | 3,600 | 3,439 |
| 3 | 900 | 1,084 | 1,800 | 2,168 | 2,700 | 3,252 | 3,600 | 4,336 | 5,400 | 5,420 |
| 4 | 1,200 | 1,520 | 2,400 | 3,040 | 3,600 | 4,560 | 4,800 | 6,080 | 7,200 | 7,600 |
| 5 | 1,500 | 1,999 | 3,000 | 3,999 | 4,500 | 5,998 | 6,000 | 7,998 | 9,000 | 9,997 |
| 6 | 1,800 | 2,527 | 3,600 | 5,054 | 5,400 | 7,581 | 7,200 | 10,107 | 10,800 | 12,634 |
| 7 | 2,100 | 3,107 | 4,200 | 6,214 | 6,300 | 9,321 | 8,400 | 12,428 | 12,600 | 15,535 |
| 8 | 2,400 | 3,745 | 4,800 | 7,491 | 7,200 | 11,236 | 9,600 | 14,981 | 14,400 | 18,726 |
| 9 | 2,700 | 4,447 | 5,400 | 8,895 | 8,100 | 13,342 | 10,800 | 17,789 | 16,200 | 22,236 |
| 10 | 3,000 | 5,220 | 6,000 | 10,439 | 9,000 | 15,659 | 12,000 | 20,878 | 18,000 | 26,098 |
| 11 | 3,300 | 6,069 | 6,600 | 12,138 | 9,900 | 18,207 | 13,200 | 24,276 | 19,800 | 30,345 |
| 12 | 3,600 | 7,003 | 7.200 | 14,007 | 10,800 | 21,010 | 14,400 | 28,013 | 21,600 | 35,017 |
| 13 | 3,900 | 8,031 | 7,800 | 16,062 | 11,700 | 24,094 | 15,600 | 32,125 | 23,400 | 40,156 |
| 14 | 4,200 | 9,162 | 8,400 | 18,324 | 12,600 | 27,485 | 16,800 | 36,647 | 25,200 | 45,809 |
| 15 | 4,500 | 10,405 | 9,000 | 20,811 | 13,500 | 31,216 | 18,000 | 41,622 | 27,000 | 52,027 |
| 20 | 6,000 | 18,758 | 12,000 | 37,515 | 18,000 | 56,273 | 24,000 | 75,030 | 36,000 | 93,789 |
| 21 / 44 | | 20,633 | | 41,267 | | 61,900 | | 82,533 | | 103,167 |
| 22 / 43 | | 22,697 | | 45,393 | | 68,090 | | 90,786 | | 113,483 |
| 23 / 42 | | 24,966 | | 49,932 | | 74,899 | | 99,865 | | 124,832 |
| 24 / 41 | | 27,463 | | 54,926 | | 82,389 | | 109,851 | | 137,315 |
| 25 / 40 | | 30,209 | | 60,418 | | 90,628 | | 120,837 | | 151,046 |
| 26 / 39 | | 33,230 | | 66,460 | | 99,691 | | 132,920 | | 166,151 |
| 27 / 38 | | 36,553 | | 73,106 | | 109,660 | | 146,212 | | 182,766 |
| 28 / 37 | | 40,209 | | 80,417 | | 120,626 | | 160,833 | | 201,043 |
| 29 / 36 | | 44,229 | | 88,458 | | 132,688 | | 176,917 | | 221,147 |
| 30 / 35 | | 48,652 | | 97,304 | | 145,957 | | 194,609 | | 243,261 |
| 31 / 34 | | 53,518 | | 107,035 | | 160,553 | | 214,069 | | 267,588 |
| 32 / 33 | | 58,869 | | 117,738 | | 176,608 | | 235,476 | | 294,346 |
| 33 / 32 | | 64,756 | | 129,512 | | 194,269 | | 259,024 | | 323,781 |
| 34 / 31 | | 71,232 | | 142,463 | | 213,695 | | 284,926 | | 356,159 |
| 35 / 30 | | 78,355 | | 156,709 | | 235,065 | | 313,419 | | 391,775 |
| 36 / 29 | | 86,190 | | 172,380 | | 258,571 | | 344,761 | | 430,952 |
| 37 / 28 | | 94,810 | | 189,618 | | 284,429 | | 379,237 | | 474,048 |
| 38 / 27 | | 104,290 | | 208,580 | | 312,872 | | 417,161 | | 521,452 |
| 39 / 26 | | 114,720 | | 229,438 | | 344,159 | | 458,877 | | 573,598 |
| 40 / 25 | | 126,191 | | 252,382 | | 378,575 | | 504,764 | | 630,957 |
| 41 / 24 | | 138,811 | | 277,620 | | 416,432 | | 555,241 | | 694,053 |
| 42 / 23 | | 152,692 | | 305,382 | | 458,075 | | 610,765 | | 763,459 |
| 43 / 22 | | 167,961 | | 335,921 | | 503,883 | | 671,841 | | 839,804 |
| 44 / 21 | | 184,757 | | 369,513 | | 554,271 | | 739,025 | | 923,785 |
| 45 / 20 | | 203,233 | | 406,464 | | 609,698 | | 812,928 | | 1,016,163 |
| 46 / 19 | | 223,556 | | 447,110 | | 670,668 | | 894,221 | | 1,117,780 |
| 47 / 18 | | 245,912 | | 491,821 | | 737,735 | | 983,643 | | 1,229,558 |

There is a staggering amount of $16 billion of unclaimed money sitting around in state coffers awaiting claims of rightful owners. However, 44 states (including the Province of Alberta) and MissingMoney.com, the only free, state endorsed national database have teamed together to help the public search, identify and file claims for lost assets.

With the help of **www.missingmoney.com**, you can search for unclaimed funds such as paychecks that have not been cashed, uncollected security deposits and undeliverable refunds. You can also search on the behalf of relatives and friends who misplaced financial assets. Thus, if you have mislaid money, there is now a free and easy way to look for it.

MissingMoney.com, established in November 1999, is the only database endorsed by the National Association of Unclaimed Property Administrators (NAUPA).

MissingMoney.com has had several successes in reuniting money to rightful owners as a few stories attest:

*"About 2 months ago I was watching the news on TV when I saw a story that featured your site. The story told of a local man who had used your site to locate a little over $400. The news story intrigued me and led to my going online and searching for myself.*

*I was astounded to find that I had not one, but two accounts I did not even know about being held in my home state of Virginia. In just over a month after filling out the claim forms, I received a check for over $1400! The monies were from two annuities my parents had purchased when I was young and had never told me. As my parents are now both deceased this money really had even more special meaning to me. One last gift from two loving parents.*

*I cannot thank MissingMoney.com enough for the services you provide. What truly left me amazed was the fact that there was no finder's fee at all involved in my receiving this money. What you do is certainly special. How you do it is even more so."*
**-- Jim, Florida**

*"Our family was referred to your web site by a cousin. She had seen something on the evening news about unclaimed properties. Since checking into it (with the aid of missingmoney.com) we found unclaimed money for my grandfather, grandmother, mother, father, sister, and myself. The amounts ranged from a couple dollars to a couple thousand, but the best part was the fun and excitement it brought to the family. I have encouraged everyone I know to log onto your web site, because it costs nothing and if you don't look you'll never find out."*
**-- Christopher, Oklahoma**

## Search Tips

**Search you, family members or businesses:** Start individual search by using your last name (current or prior name) and your full or partial first name. Family search only requires last name. Business search requires entering your business name in the last name field.

**Whom can you search?** Anyone, however, you may only file a claim for property that belongs to you or for which you are the legal heir. If you are a business owner, you may also file on behalf of your business.

**Common name:** You can narrow down your search results by specifying the City and/or State where you have lived (see **"Advanced Search"** & **"Exact Match."**).

**Advanced search:** You can restrict the records you are interested in searching by selecting a single State from the list. You can also filter the results to only show records where the city begins with some value. These are all very useful to filter results for common names.

**Exact match:** Click the *"Exact"* check box on the Search Results page. This option is only available after a performed search; it is not available from their Home Page. When checked, it will now return records of the entire first and last name match that you enter. With the option turned off (blank check box), records with a similar first name will also appear in the list.

**Save time and set up profiles:** Set up profiles for you, family and friends (include maiden or previous names). To set up search profiles click on the *"Create / Maintain Profiles"* menu option under *"My Profiles"* to add additional profiles. You must be a member to set up profiles. You can join under *"My Profiles."*

**Deceased family members:** Join membership; then set up profiles for each family member you would like to search. However, only rightful heirs can claim property.

**State search:** To search states directly, click *"State Contact Information"* on left side of home page. On next page, you will see a US Map. To search a state, click on that state's *"Unclaimed Property Page."* You should also search federal agency websites using their links page. In addition, search as often as you like, and check back frequently (database is constantly updated).

**Length of time it takes to receive money:** Processing claims vary from state to state and by property type. However, processing usually takes between 4 -16 weeks.

**Find status of claim:** The state in which you filed your claim is accountable for all claims and paper work. Ask questions directly to the state.

**Match:** You have a match! However, have you ever lived in that state? Do you recognize company name listed? Bear in mind, you need to submit proof of eligibility to collect claim.

For more information or begin your search to find money, visit **www.missingmoney.com**

I feel like a million bucks. Gosh, I love sunbathing on a beach, while sipping cool drinks, after partying all night in Jamaica in February. Glad I found all that misplaced money before my family did.

C-9

Need money? Welcome to Amazon and eBay, where you can set up a business, and within an hour, start-making money worldwide. Below, you'll find tips to speed your learning curve and help master Amazon and Ebay that much faster. Furthermore, I've thrown in how to make money by getting rid of your junk through a successful yard or garage sale(s). Making money is now at your fingertips, so go and get it!

## AMAZON.COM

**ITEMS NEEDED TO START YOUR NEW BUSINESS:**
■ Desktop or laptop computer and printer, digital camera (highly recommended, but not required)
■ Get DSL connection, especially if you intend to bid on things, and an e-mail account.

**Amazon.com** is by far the easiest business to start up and sell. How to set up your account and sell:

1. Go to **www.amazon.com** and set up a seller account (simple process). Once your account is set up you're now open for business. Start selling.
**EXAMPLE:** Sell new **"Capricorn One"** Soundtrack CD

2. Go to search engine at top left.

Click on **"Music,"** then type in **Capricorn One** soundtrack and click **"Search"** on right.

3. Scroll down until you come to picture that matches item.

4. When you find item that matches, click on Capricorn One INTRADA LTD. ED. by Jerry Goldsmith.

5. On this page look to the right and you will see **"Sell yours here"** and click on.

> 4 used and new from $129.95
> **See all buying options**
> Have one to sell?   Sell yours here

6. On new page look for **"Condition"** and click on new:

**Condition:** | New

7. Then find **"Condition note:"** (below) and describe something about the CD (see how other sellers describe their product).

> New & Out of Print. Limited Edition. Fast shipping

8. Once your item is described, click **"Continue"** button.

9. Next, find **"Pricing Details"** on right and click on **"new"** to see what the item is selling for (new page will pop up):

> **Pricing Details for Your Product**
> Title
> Capricorn One INTRADA LTD. ED.
> **Competing Marketplace Offers**
> **2 New** from $165.00 ◄
> **2 Used** from $129.95

Click on **"New"**

10. After seeing what the going rate is for the item, go back to page with **"Your price"** and put your price in the box.

> $163.11

11. Just below, list **"quantity: 1** (unless you have more).

12. Next, see shipping; click expedited shipping box, but not **"International."** There is a learning curve on how to package and ship items correctly. Until you have shipping down pat, pass on international shipping.

13. After shipping, click **"Continue"** (just below).

14. Review your order. If things look correct, then click **"Submit your listing"** and you're done. Sell more by repeating sequences #2 through #14, **good luck!**

15. Transfer money daily to yourself, in case there is a dispute that freezes your funds until problem is solved.

## EBAY.COM

**A FEW THINGS NEEDED TO GET STARTED:**
■ Get checking account with debit or credit card (separate from regular household account).
■ Open **PayPal** account at **www.paypal.com**. PayPal will streamline business and keep track of transactions, collect money from clients, transfer money to you, etc.
**TIP:** Transfer money daily to yourself, in case there is a dispute that freezes your funds until problem is solved.
■ Find Items to sell: EBay estimates that the average household has $1,200 or more in unused items lying around the house. Take inventory of things you're not using, old hobbies, collections, etc. or find a product with a cheap source to sell.

**SIGN UP & DO REQUIRED RESEARCH ON EBAY:**
■ Start by visiting eBay at **www.ebay.com**, register and then sign in. **TIP:** An important task at this point is to create a user ID that lets everyone know who you are. Therefore, you may want to tie your user name to your market or product. Don't offend others by using vulgar ID.
■ Once you're signed in, the first page you'll see will be a **"Favorite Categories"** on left hand side, just above it, a search tool with advance feature. On the top right side, you'll see Buy, Sell, My eBay, Community, etc.
■ Pick a category (something you have to sell); then explore and familiarize yourself with how sellers list their items to sell such as how do they word their item for bidding? On the other hand, how they present their item? Do they use their own or eBay stock pictures?

**TIP:** When starting out, use your own pictures; because it shows bidders that you actually have the product in hand (trust issue in the beginning), however, once you are established, you can list with or without pictures.

Buy from me and get a killer deal!

- **TIP:** I've found that by listing items at $0.99 that starts the bidding process that much faster. Furthermore, it builds an attachment with customers once they bid on your item. In addition, by listing at .99, fees are less.
- **TIP:** Do not **overcharge** on shipping. Make sure you purchase **"Delivery Confirmation"** on all of your packages through the Post Office, just in case you get that rare customer who never received their package.

## SECRET SELLER TECHNIQUES:
- **Don't list items late at night or early in the morning:** Most bidders are asleep during those hours.
- **End auctions in prime time:** You'll catch the most bidders between the hours of 6:00 PM and 8:00 PM PST.
- List your items to end on Sunday evening or end on Tuesday or Wednesday evening around 7:00 PM PST.
- **Don't end listing on Friday or Saturday nights:** That's when most bidders are not at home. **TIP:** If you're looking to buy, Monday, Friday and Saturday nights are great for getting deals.
- Avoid ending your auctions on holidays, less bidders. **Tip:** On Holidays, buy and score some terrific deals.
- **Avoid listing first week of the month:** Rent and bills are usually due on the first.
- By the end of March, it's the season for income tax, and it's definitely slow on eBay.
- Between June and middle of August things slow down. Hey, it's vacation time.
- **Set your price high enough to cover your cost, in most cases:** But, if you know your item will sell at a higher price, then list lower to attract more bidders looking for deals. **EXAMPLE:** I list a movie at $0.99, even though my cost to this point is over $9. Why? Because I know that this particular movie will sell over $100.
- Price one item high to make your other auctions look like huge bargains.
- **Offer incentives:** when listing you might add free shipping. **EXAMPLE:** Some movies are listed at $0.99, but when you add shipping cost of $4.75, the total for the movie comes to $5.74. What I do is list the same movie at higher price of $6.99; then offer free shipping with the deal. It works great and usually drives prices higher.
- **List item for 7-days:** 7-days guarantee that your item(s) will be shown over the weekend.

**THERE'S MORE TO LEARN:** I've given you plenty of ideas to get you started in the right direction, but keep learning. I recommend that you read, **"Tricks of the eBay Masters"** by Michael Miller. You can find it in any used bookstore. When done reading, sell it on EBay or Amazon.

## YARD AND GARAGE SALES

As a nation, most of us have crammed junk in attic spaces, basements, storage units, garages, etc. Apparently, we love junk! However, if you're finally tired of all your junk, maybe It's time to pass yours on to other junkaholics, and while you're at it, make a few bucks. This means throwing a yard/garage sale, but not just any sale, a successful yard/ garage sale. The yard/garage successful sales formula is fairly simple:
1. Marketing strategy
2. Low prices
3. Great selection
4. How organized you are throughout sale process
5. And your willingness to wheel and deal

without them, you'll still have a pile of junk at the end of your sale, and less money and profit. By the way, trust me when I say that it's a lot easier hauling junk out to the

sale than dragging it back, then re-stuffing and lifting it back from which it came.

Follow the yard/garage sale step-by-step countdown and you'll be moving stuff that has cluttered your home for years for profit. However, the sale will more than likely help you to clear out room for more junk (sigh).

### 2-3 WEEKS BEFORE SALE: Get prepared
- Put a sale date on your calendar. Ask neighbors and relatives if they want in. Remember, larger the sale event, bigger the interest, including drive-by traffic and profits.
- Begin moving your items to the garage. Clean and dust and get rid of the junk on your junk and make them pretty (use polish for furniture, etc., so you'll get better prices). Furthermore, sort them by category.
- Bring home boxes from supermarkets, price clubs, etc. The boxes can be used as extra display surfaces (when closed and laid upside down) or can hold loose items.
- Collect lots of plastic bags and newsprint to bag and wrap fragile items when they sell.

### 1 WEEK BEFORE SALE: Advertise date & time of sale
- Time to let everyone know about your big sale event to friends, family (consider leaving out coworkers). To spread the news, make use of e-mail, Facebook, Twitter, social events, etc. In addition, use Craig's List and Kijiji and update them throughout week. List things you'll be selling (but not all, leave some mystery), like antiques, rare coins, collections, movies, furniture pieces, sizes of clothing, appliances, other interesting items.
- Ensure that you advertise sale in Thursday and Friday classified sections of the local print media. As a rule, advertising a Sunday sale on Saturday is good. However, advertising Saturday sale in Saturday media print is not good. Sale may conclude before people read about it!
- Go to your banking institution and get about $50 or more in small bills and plenty of change (mostly quarters).
- Make sure you have these items at hand during the sale: **Water, coffee, sunscreen, sunglasses, hat, markers, or price stickers, something to hold money (fanny pack),** and **lawn chairs.**

### NIGHT BEFORE SALE: Prep for success
- Post signs nearby road crossings & major intersections.
- Price your items, but be smart to price items cheap enough to get buyers to put cash in your hand, or room to bargain. Remember, it's junk.
- Have something to put money into after a sale. This is where a fanny-pack comes in handy.
- Need: Couple of heavy-duty electrical extension cords.

### D-DAY: Wake up early and start making money
- Set up tables and wares. Designate someone to get rid of Early Birds, if you're not ready to go.
- Group items together such as electrical power tools, kitchen devices, etc. on one table. Have extension cords plugged in nearby, so shoppers can try before they buy.

### START YOUR SALE: Smiles everyone, smiles!
- Once items and helpers are in place, start your sale.
- At 11:00 am, slash prices on remaining items 50%.
- At 12PM, offer "Buy Two, Get One Free," do a mini auction or other incentives to move the last of your stuff.

### THE END: 1 pm or 2 pm, pack it up & count money
- Time to end your sale.
- As for the remaining leftovers, haul them to Goodwill or other charity. Option: Put leftovers in one area and place a sign that reads, "FREE."

The checklist below will assist you to identify and keep track of future pay increases, lowering or paid-off bills, etc. The main objective is to help you plan and systematically set aside your newfound money into accounts that will pay you interest and build collateral, before temptation sets in to spend it or worse yet, create new bills.

**EXAMPLE: In May, $31.25 earned by claiming one dependent on W-4; then adds $102 promotion in June. In addition, LES increases $100 in July because GI Bill is paid. Total that can be put into savings: $233.25.**

| Categories | New Monthly Income | Month: | Month: | Month: | Month: | Total Accumulated |
|---|---|---|---|---|---|---|
| W-4 | | | | | | |
| W-5  (E.I.C) | | | | | | |
| Child Tax Credit(s) | | | | | | |
| State Taxes: | | | | | | |
| GI Bill | | | | | | |
| Promotion | | | | | | |
| Year Mark | | | | | | |
| Cost of Living | | | | | | |
| BAH | | | | | | |
| BAS | | | | | | |
| Signing Bonus | | | | | | |
| Hazard / Flight / Sea Pay | | | | | | |
| Clothing Allowance | | | | | | |
| Part Time Job | | | | | | |
| Spouse New Job | | | | | | |
| Spouse Raise / Promotion | | | | | | |
| Sell on EBAY | | | | | | |
| Other: | | | | | | |
| Soldiersmembers' C.R. Act | | | | | | |
| SHARE | | | | | | |
| WIC | | | | | | |
| Food Stamps | | | | | | |
| LIHEAP | | | | | | |
| Other | | | | | | |
| Mortgage / Rent Reduction | | | | | | |
| Groceries | | | | | | |
| Utilities (Elect, Gas, Water) | | | | | | |
| Cable / Satellite | | | | | | |
| Life Insurance | | | | | | |
| Auto Insurance | | | | | | |
| Home Own. / Renters Ins. | | | | | | |
| Long Distance / Cell Phone | | | | | | |
| Gasoline | | | | | | |
| Credit Cards | | | | | | |
| Loans | | | | | | |
| Car Loans | | | | | | |
| Child Support / Alimony | | | | | | |
| Social Security | | | | | | |
| Savings Bonds | | | | | | |
| Savings Accounts | | | | | | |
| Other: | | | | | | |
| Other: | | | | | | |
| **TOTALS:** | $ | $ | $ | $ | $ | $ |

| Put Money Into: | - | Starting The Month Of: | | - |
|---|---|---|---|---|
| Put Money Into: | - | Starting The Month Of: | | - |
| Put Money Into: | - | Starting The Month Of: | | - |
| TOTAL Left Over:      + / - $ | | TOTAL Left Over: | | + / - $ |

"I'm getting tired of seeing your mug around here, Egghead! Let's start by laying a rock-solid foundation that you can build upon financial brick by brick that will withstand the test of time. Do you remember the story of the three little Pigs? Well, one day there were these three…ah…err…scrap that. Just do yourself a favor, don't cut corners and build a flimsy house of cards that will crash when an unforeseen emergency arises. Be the ball, focus and finish what you've started, Pea-brain! We're almost there; it's time to suck it up! **LET'S DO THIS! GO! GO! GOOOOOOOOOOOOO!**"

**Tenth Final Commandment:**
**"THOU SHALL USE SAVINGS, INVESTMENTS AND SUPPLEMENTAL PLANS WITH LOW FEES THAT COMPOUND INTEREST TAX-DEFERRED"**

C-10

Hey Pal, over here! I have some hot stocks, interested?

FOUNDATION

PUT OFF UNTIL LATER

BUILD SOLID FOUNDATION

GO THE DISTANCE! FINISH WHAT YOU'VE STARTED!

**Create and build FOUNDATION:** Map out a financial plan, then implement plan by establishing goals (see **page 132**), a budget (see **page 153**), adequate insurance coverage (see **page 134-136, 154**), savings and investments (see **pages 139-148**). Furthermore, invest in accounts that can be used as security or collateral (see **pages 23** and **138**) in times of need that will allow you to keep your foundation intact.

# TAKE CAREFUL STEPS TO BUILD YOUR FOUNDATION

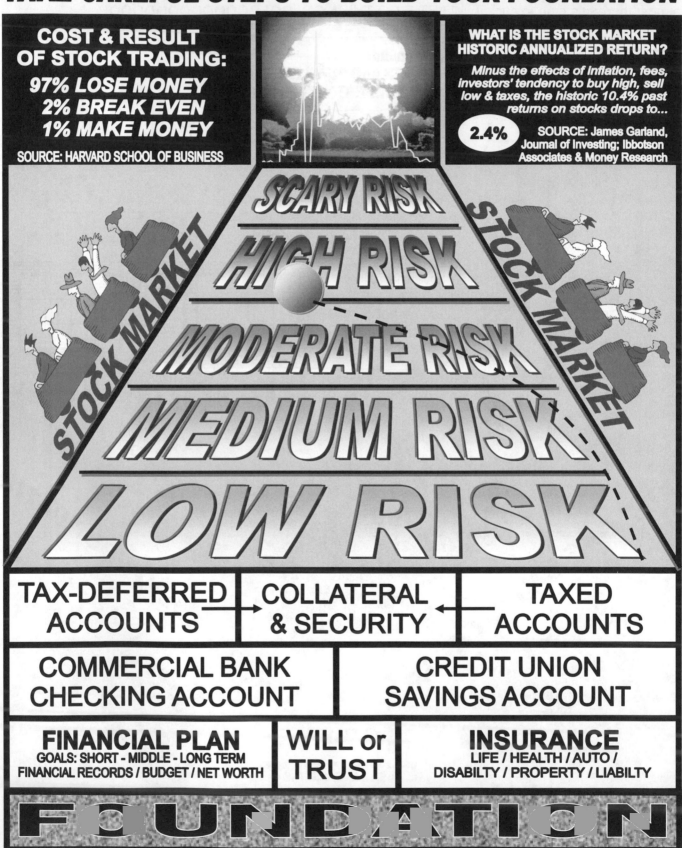

**COST & RESULT OF STOCK TRADING:**

**97% LOSE MONEY**
**2% BREAK EVEN**
**1% MAKE MONEY**

SOURCE: HARVARD SCHOOL OF BUSINESS

**WHAT IS THE STOCK MARKET HISTORIC ANNUALIZED RETURN?**

*Minus the effects of inflation, fees, investors' tendency to buy high, sell low & taxes, the historic 10.4% past returns on stocks drops to...*

**2.4%** SOURCE: James Garland, Journal of Investing; Ibbotson Associates & Money Research

SCARY RISK

HIGH RISK

MODERATE RISK

MEDIUM RISK

LOW RISK

STOCK MARKET

STOCK MARKET

| TAX-DEFERRED ACCOUNTS | COLLATERAL & SECURITY | TAXED ACCOUNTS |
|---|---|---|

| COMMERCIAL BANK CHECKING ACCOUNT | CREDIT UNION SAVINGS ACCOUNT |
|---|---|

| **FINANCIAL PLAN** GOALS: SHORT - MIDDLE - LONG TERM FINANCIAL RECORDS / BUDGET / NET WORTH | **WILL or TRUST** | **INSURANCE** LIFE / HEALTH / AUTO / DISABILTY / PROPERTY / LIABILTY |
|---|---|---|

## FOUNDATION

# ACTION: CREATE & IMPLEMENT FINANCIAL PLAN

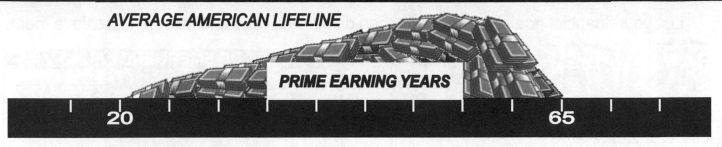

## AVERAGE AMERICAN LIFELINE

**PRIME EARNING YEARS**

20          65

C-10

As we learned on **page 12**, you can earn a fortune within your lifetime. Nevertheless, the age-old problem is how much of it will you keep? Most people live life without any written financial plan, goals or targets. The individuals that do have their financial game plan in order are standouts in business, government, education, etc. The process of creating a written financial plan identifies the direction you intend to take. However, to implement your plan, action and disposable income is the hammer needed to nail down targets, and turn goals from dreams into reality.

## ACTION: SAVE DISPOSABLE INCOME

List your monthly income and bills; then subtract income from bills. What you should have left over is *disposable income* (if negative, go back to Chapter 4 and start working toward getting out of debt).

### Monthly Bills:

| | |
|---|---|
| _____ | $_____ |
| _____ | _____ |
| _____ | _____ |
| _____ | _____ |
| _____ | _____ |
| _____ | _____ |
| _____ | _____ |

**Total Bills:**    $_____

**Monthly Income:**    $_____

**Disposable Income:**    $_____

If you have disposable Income, but no savings, then you are doing three out of four things (badly) with your money each month:

1. Spending it
2. Paying bills with it
3. Losing it

However, what I do know is that you cannot continue to put off saving, especially if you want to accomplish your financial goals and targets. Therefore, contemplate what amount of disposable income you can set aside (comfortably) each month and once that amount is determined, save and implement your goals. Take action today!

## ACTION: SAVE & IMPLEMENT GOALS

### PAY YOURSELF FIRST
- Save monthly to finance your goals (10% to 30%)

### TIME-LINE
- Begin with your next paycheck

### BENEFITS OF SAVING EACH MONTH
- Peace of mind
- Interest earned
- Emergency cash
- Increased worth
- Accomplishment

**SAVING STRATEGY**

Develop 3 or more different savings and investment plans

### METHODS
- Passbook Savings
- Savings Bonds
- CD
- Money Market Account
- Ins. policies: Universal or whole life, SIRP, etc.
- Traditional or ROTH IRA
- Stocks

## ACTION: TARGET FIRST $1,000,000

**Monthly savings financed for target: $_____**

**Example: $100** saved monthly at **8%** rate of return would accumulate to **$1,000,000** in 53 years

### TABLE: Monthly investment / Interest rate / Years

| % | $ 25 | $ 50 | $100 | $250 | $500 | $1000 |
|---|------|------|------|------|------|-------|
| 5 | 103 | 89 | 75 | 58 | 45 | 33 |
| 6 | 89 | 77 | 66 | 51 | 40 | 30 |
| 7 | 78 | 00 | 59 | 46 | 36 | 28 |
| 8 | 70 | 61 | 53 | 42 | 33 | 26 |
| 9 | 64 | 56 | 48 | 38 | 31 | 24 |
| 10 | 58 | 51 | 45 | 36 | 29 | 22 |
| 11 | 54 | 48 | 41 | 33 | 27 | 21 |
| 12 | 50 | 44 | 39 | 31 | 26 | 20 |

131

**List your financial goals; timeline and then disburse disposable income to achieve them.**

**LIST MINI GOALS: One year or less to accomplish.**

1. _____

2. _____

3. _____

**LIST SHORT TERM GOALS: Within two to four years to accomplish.**

1. _____

2. _____

3. _____

**LIST MEDIUM GOALS: Within five to seven years to accomplish.**

1. _____

2. _____

3. _____

**LIST LONG TERM GOALS: Within eight to ten years to accomplish.**

1. _____

2. _____

3. _____

## GOAL: SET UP EMERGENCY FUND

| | |
|---|---|
| Current emergency fund | $ |
| Goal: Create a fund of | $ |
| Goal date: | |
| Goal: Save each month | $ |
| Goal date: | |

## GOAL: HAVE ADEQUATE AMOUNT OF LIFE INSURANCE COVERAGE

| | |
|---|---|
| Current life coverage is | $ |
| Based on current expenses, I need extra coverage of | $ |
| Goal: Add extra coverage of | $ |
| Goal date: | |
| Goal: Insurance coverage on family members | $ |
| Goal date: | |

## GOAL: SET UP SAVINGS / INVESTMENT / RETIREMENT ACCOUNTS

| | |
|---|---|
| Current amount in savings | $ |
| Goal: Create a savings of | $ |
| Goal date: | |
| Goal: Save each month | $ |
| Current amount in investment(s) | $ |
| Goal: Create savings of | $ |
| Goal date: | |
| Goal: Save each month | $ |
| Current amount in retirement account(s) | $ |
| Goal: Create savings of | $ |
| Goal date: | |
| Goal: Save each month | $ |
| Current amount that can be used for secured loan(s) | $ |
| Goal: Create savings of | $ |
| Goal date: | |
| Goal: Save each month | $ |
| Current amount that can be used for collateral loan(s) | $ |
| Goal: Create savings of | $ |
| Goal date: | |
| Goal: Save each month | $ |

## GOAL: SET UP CHILDREN'S EDUCATION FUND

| | |
|---|---|
| Current amount saved for children's education | $ |
| Goal: Create savings of | $ |
| Goal date: | |
| Goal: Save each month | $ |

# YIKES! ESTATE TAX & PROBATE COSTS

Experts say that **$7 to $8 trillion** is sitting in potential estates simply waiting to be passed on to the next generation. The amount of wealth that will be transferred in the decades to come staggers the imagination. However, because of the **45%** maximum Federal estate tax rate **(55%** tax rate looming in 2011), plus any state death tax, estate taxes will erode much of this property. See what happened to the estates of the famous people below:

| This could happen to anyone, you included! | Gross Estate | Total Settlement costs | Net Estate | Percent Of Shrinkage |
|---|---|---|---|---|
| Dean Witter | $ 7,451,055 | $ 1,830,717 | $ 5,620,338 | 25% |
| Elvis Presley | $10,165,434 | $ 7,374,635 | $ 2,790,799 | 73% |
| Marilyn Monroe | $ 819,176 | $ 448,750 | $ 370,426 | 55% |
| Franklin D. Roosevelt | $ 1,940,999 | $ 574,867 | $ 1,366,132 | 30% |
| Frederick Vanderbilt | $76,838,530 | $42,846,112 | $33,992,418 | 56% |
| Gary Cooper | $ 4,984,985 | $ 1,530,484 | $ 3,454,531 | 31% |
| William Boeing | $22,386,158 | $10,589,748 | $11,796,410 | 47% |
| John D. Rockefeller Sr. | $26,905,182 | $17,124,988 | $ 9,780,194 | 64% |
| Walt Disney | $23,004,851 | $ 6,811,943 | $16,192,908 | 30% |
| J.P. Morgan | $17,121,482 | $11,893,691 | $5,227,791 | 69% |
| Alwin C. Ernst, CPA | $12,642,431 | $ 7,124,112 | $ 5,518,319 | 56% |
| Howard Gould | $67,535,386 | $52,549,682 | $14,985,704 | 78% |

-Source: www.finance.cch.com/text/c50s15d170.asp

| Estate Tax Brackets | | Estate Tax Schedule | |
|---|---|---|---|
| The percentage to the right is how much you'll pay if your estate is in the following ranges. These ranges are set for 2009. | | Estates valued at or more than the years will be subject to an estate tax. | |
| $2,000,001 | 0% | 2009 | $3,500,000 |
| $2,500,001 | 45% | 2010 | No estate tax |
| $3,000,001 | 55% | 2011 | $1,000,000 |

*-Source: Internal Revenue Service*

**State death taxes:** To find out if your state has death taxes, visit: www.mcguirewoods.com/news-resources/publications/taxation/state_death_tax_chart.pdf

**What is probate?** Probate is the court-supervised process of locating and determining the value of the assets owned in the individual name of a deceased person, referred to as a "decedent," paying the decedent's final bills and estate taxes and/or inheritance taxes (if any), and then distributing what's left of the decedent's assets to his or her heirs.

**How much does probate cost?** If you don't have an estate plan or have failed to completely fund your Revocable Living Trust, then your family will be faced with probating some or all of your assets. The overall cost of probate varies depending on the type and value of the property that's being probated. As a rule, the greater the value of the probate property, the more probate will cost. There are numerous fees and costs associated with probate.

#### Using life Insurance to avoid probate:
The importance of life insurance in every estate plan can't be overemphasized. In many estates, life insurance may be the largest single asset. The ability of life insurance to remove taxable property out of an estate is a very effective planning strategy. Life insurance, unlike any other asset, develops its optimum value at the time of death. Therefore, any technique that permits such

property to be transferred free of taxes and outside of probate has a high priority and importance.

Adequate life insurance coverage is one of the crucial components of a successful financial and estate plan. There are several reasons to acquire life insurance:
- To replace income lost by the death of a wage earner.
- To provide cash for an estate and thereby prevent the forced sale of assets to satisfy estate taxes.
- To shelter assets from estate taxes and thereby maximize the transfer of property.
- To create assets in an estate.

**Advantages of life insurance:** We often forget about favored income tax treatment life insurance generally receives such as:
- Probate free status
- Deferral of taxes on the internal growth that takes place with supplemental insurance polices (whole life, universal life and SIRP)
- Borrowing features are usually favorable and are tax-free. In addition, a loan does not have to be paid back, but is eventually deducted from the death benefit
- In most cases, supplemental insurance retirement policies (SIRP) can be used as collateral (see **page 136**).

**Bottom line:** Since you know that dying is inevitable, it would be smart to have a Will or living trust drawn up to contribute to your foundation. For more information on Wills, set a date with JAG or lawyer that specializes in estate planning; let them explain to you the several types of Wills and options that you can choose from.

**JOKE:** An elderly man had serious hearing problems for several years. One day, he went to see a doctor and the doctor fitted him with a set of hearing aids that now allowed the elderly man to hear 100%. Happy, the elderly man went home. However, within a month, the elderly man went back to see the doctor for a checkup. The doctor checked him out and said, "Your hearing is 100%. Your family must be thrilled you can hear again." To which the elderly man replied, "Oh, I haven't told my family a thing. I just sit around and listen to the conversations. I've changed my will five times."

133

**WHY LIFE INSURANCE?** We pay life insurance companies to provide protection from loss of income in case of death of the main family income provider. We also use it to pay bills, home mortgages and estate taxes that may exist after the insured passes away. Incredibly, I've seen service members (some with families) reduce their $400,000 Servicemans' Group Life Insurance (SGLI) to as low as $10,000 to save money.

I bring this up because, if we don't die before age 65; we will eventually, so why die cheaply or free.

**The Basics:** If you are the main family income provider, life insurance should be your top priority and your second priority should be your spouse. Thirdly, depending on how many children you have and their ages, decide how long they will need protection.

**TYPES OF INSURANCE POLICIES:** Finding the company and selecting the right type of insurance policy is an individual decision based upon one's needs and preferences. The three most popular insurance policies sold today are, **term, whole life** and **universal life.**

**Term Insurance:** This type of policy provides insurance protection for a specific length of time, such as 5, 10 or 20 years. The coverage ends when the term expires or when you stop paying the premiums. Payment is made to your beneficiary only when you die within the terms stated in the policy.

**Types of term coverage and important clauses:**
Term insurance may be:
■ **Level term:** The amount of level term insurance policy coverage remains the same over each renewal period, but at each renewal premiums for insurance increase.

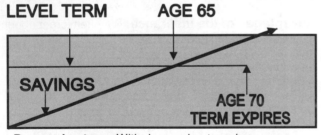

## LEVEL TERM        AGE 65

SAVINGS

AGE 70
TERM EXPIRES

■ **Decreasing term:** With decreasing term insurance, your premiums remain the same, but the amount of coverage decreases over time.

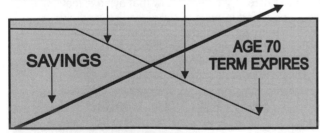

## DECREASING TERM  AGE 65

SAVINGS

AGE 70
TERM EXPIRES

■ **Renewability clause:** You can renew your policy to a specified period, usually until ages 65 or 70.
■ **Convertibility clause:** This feature will allow you to convert your term insurance to a whole life policy without a medical examination, but be prepared to pay higher premiums.
■ **Advantages:** Term insurance costs less than other types of life insurance for the same amount of coverage at a younger age.

■ **Disadvantages:** No cash value or loan value and in most cases, premiums increase with age.

**CASH VALUE INSURANCE POLICIES:**
■ **Whole Life Insurance** offers protection in case the insured dies and builds cash value. The policy stays in force for the lifetime of the insured, unless the policy lapses or is canceled. Policyholders usually pay a level premium for whole life, which does not increase, as the person grows older. The cash value portion of the plan accrues tax-deferred and can be borrowed against in the form of a policy loan. The death benefit is reduced by the amount of the loan, plus interest, if the loan is not repaid.
■ **Universal Life** combines the low-cost protection of term insurance with a savings portion, which is invested in a tax-deferred account earning money-market rates of interest. The policy is flexible; meaning, as age and income change, the policyholder can increase or decrease premium payments and coverage, or shift a certain portion of premiums into the savings account, without additional sales charges or complications.

**VGLI vs. NON-PROFIT MILITARY ASSOC. INSURERS:**
There are several non-profit military associations competing to replace your SGLI / *VGLI with their own insurance plans, especially when separating from service. Not only can these insurers save you serious money on life insurance premiums, they can also insure your spouse at low rates and children at no charge.

| Monthly insurance cost through the years | | |
|---|---|---|
| SGLI $250,000 | *VGLI $ 250,000 | Non-Profits $250,000 |
| Cost today **$17.25** **Problem:** Need to convert SGLI to VGLI, to continue coverage after separation | Age 18-29: **$ 20** | Age 18-30: **$16.25** |
| | Age 30-34: **$ 25** | **Note:** Can cover spouse / kids |
| | Age 35-39: **$ 32.50** | |
| | Age 40-44: **$ 42.50** | Age 40-49 **$18.75** |
| | Age 45-49: **$ 55** | |
| | Age 50-54: **$ 90** | Age 50-59: **$87.50** |
| | Age 55-59: **$167.50** | |
| | Age 60-64: **$270** | Age 60-89: **$160** |
| | Age 65-69: **$375** | |
| | Age 70-74: **$562.50** | |
| | Age 75 + : **$1,125** | |

| VGLI vs. Non-Profit Associations: $250,000 Coverage | | | |
|---|---|---|---|
| Age today | Insured to 80 | VGLI Cost | Non-Profit |
| 20 | **60 years** | $180,600 | $74,250 |
| 25 | **55 years** | $179,400 | $73,275 |
| 30 | **50 years** | $178,200 | $72,300 |
| 35 | **45 years** | $176,700 | $71,325 |
| 40 | **40 years** | $174,750 | $70,350 |

**SGLI REPLACEMENT AFTER SEPERATION:**
Servicemembers covered under SGLI have the option to convert their SGLI coverage to VGLI or an individual insurance policy within 120 days from the date of separation from the military. For more information or how to convert SGLI to VGLI with (62) participating commercial insurance companies, visit: **www.insurance. va.gov/sgliSite/VGLI/VGLI.htm** or call **1-800-419-1473**.

**To learn more about military insurance, visit the VA life insurance needs and calculator at:** www.in surance.va.gov/sgliSite/calcuator/LifeIns101.htm

**VETERANS GROUP LIFE INSURANCE (VGLI) vs. UNIVERSAL (UL):** If you're contemplating converting SGLI into either VGLI or UL (generic rates), check out the apples to apples comparisons of both (below). In addition, consider your income later in life, especially if it were to decline (due to job loss, health problems, etc.) and financial programs started at a younger age are no longer affordable; worse yet, no money to pay for it (see **pages 2-5**).

## AVERAGE AMERICAN LIFELINE

**PRIME EARNING YEARS**

20 | | | | | | | | 65

### AGE 20: VGLI (premium varies)

| Age | Yr Prem. | Paid Prem. | Cash Value | Coverage |
|---|---|---|---|---|
| 25 | 240 | 1,200 | 0 | 250,000 |
| 35 | 390 | 3,900 | 0 | 250,000 |
| 45 | 660 | 9,060 | 0 | 250,000 |
| 55 | 2,010 | 19,110 | 0 | 250,000 |
| 65 | 4,500 | 47,850 | 0 | 250,000 |
| 75 | 13,500 | 113,100 | 0 | 250,000 |
| 80 | 13,500 | 180,600 | 0 | 250,000 |
| **TOTAL:** | | $180,600 | 0 | $250,000 |

### AGE 20: UL (premium permanent)

| AGE | Yr Prem. | Paid Prem. | Cash Value | Coverage |
|---|---|---|---|---|
| 25 | 2,736 | 13,680 | 10,325 | 250,800 |
| 35 | 2,736 | 41,040 | 43,416 | 250,800 |
| 45 | 2,736 | 68,400 | 97,122 | 337,968 |
| 55 | 0 | 0 | 146,097 | 367,872 |
| 65 | 0 | 0 | 211,198 | 399,073 |
| 75 | 0 | 0 | 289,402 | 431,641 |
| 80 | 0 | 0 | 330,954 | 447,654 |
| **TOTAL:** | | $68,400 | $330,954 | $515,622 |

### AGE 25: VGLI (premium varies)

| Age | Yr Prem. | Paid Prem. | Cash Value | Coverage |
|---|---|---|---|---|
| 30 | 300 | 1,500 | 0 | 250,000 |
| 35 | 390 | 3,090 | 0 | 250,000 |
| 45 | 660 | 7,860 | 0 | 250,000 |
| 55 | 2,010 | 17,910 | 0 | 250,000 |
| 65 | 4,500 | 46,650 | 0 | 250,000 |
| 75 | 13,500 | 111,900 | 0 | 250,000 |
| 80 | 13,500 | 179,400 | 0 | 250,000 |
| **TOTAL:** | | $179,400 | 0 | 250,000 |

### AGE 25: UL (premium permanent)

| Age | Yr Prem. | Paid Prem. | Cash Value | Coverage |
|---|---|---|---|---|
| 30 | 3,216 | 16,080 | 12,448 | 250,133 |
| 35 | 3,216 | 32,160 | 29,622 | 250,133 |
| 45 | 3,216 | 64,320 | 80,530 | 280,230 |
| 55 | 0 | 80,400 | 140,782 | 354,489 |
| 65 | 0 | 0 | 203,489 | 384,505 |
| 75 | 0 | 0 | 278,812 | 415,846 |
| 80 | 0 | 0 | 318,832 | 431,257 |
| **TOTAL:** | | $80,400 | $318,832 | $431,257 |

### AGE 30: VGLI (premium varies)

| Age | Yr Prem. | Paid Prem. | Cash Value | Coverage |
|---|---|---|---|---|
| 35 | 390 | 1,890 | 0 | 250,000 |
| 45 | 660 | 6,660 | 0 | 250,000 |
| 55 | 2,010 | 16,710 | 0 | 250,000 |
| 65 | 4,500 | 45,450 | 0 | 250,000 |
| 75 | 13,500 | 110,700 | 0 | 250,000 |
| 80 | 13,500 | 178,200 | 0 | 250,000 |
| **TOTAL:** | | $178,200 | 0 | 250,000 |

### AGE 30: UL (premium permanent)

| Age | Yr Prem. | Paid Prem. | Cash Value | Coverage |
|---|---|---|---|---|
| 35 | 3,756 | 18,780 | 14,993 | 250,400 |
| 45 | 3,756 | 56,340 | 61,589 | 250,400 |
| 55 | 3,756 | 93,900 | 133,981 | 337,365 |
| 65 | 0 | 0 | 193,624 | 365,864 |
| 75 | 0 | 0 | 265,261 | 395,636 |
| 80 | 0 | 0 | 303,321 | 410,276 |
| **TOTAL:** | | $93,900 | $303,321 | $410,276 |

### AGE 35: VGLI (premium varies)

| Age | Yr Prem. | Paid Prem. | Cash Value | Coverage |
|---|---|---|---|---|
| 40 | 510 | 2,460 | 0 | 250,000 |
| 45 | 660 | 5,160 | 0 | 250,000 |
| 55 | 2,010 | 15,210 | 0 | 250,000 |
| 65 | 4,500 | 43,950 | 0 | 250,000 |
| 75 | 13,500 | 109,200 | 0 | 250,000 |
| 80 | 13,500 | 176,700 | 0 | 250,000 |
| **TOTAL:** | | $176,700 | 0 | 250,000 |

### AGE 35: UL (premium permanent)

| Age | Yr Prem. | Paid Prem. | Cash Value | Coverage |
|---|---|---|---|---|
| 40 | 4,500 | 22,500 | 18,196 | 250,000 |
| 45 | 4,500 | 45,000 | 42,445 | 250,000 |
| 55 | 4,500 | 90,000 | 111,828 | 281,584 |
| 65 | 0 | 112,500 | 188,231 | 355,674 |
| 75 | 0 | 0 | 257,854 | 384,587 |
| 80 | 0 | 0 | 294,841 | 398,807 |
| **TOTAL:** | | $112,500 | $294,841 | $398,807 |

### AGE 40: VGLI (premium varies)

| Age | Yr Prem. | Paid Prem. | Cash Value | Coverage |
|---|---|---|---|---|
| 45 | 660 | 3,210 | 0 | 250,000 |
| 55 | 2,010 | 13,260 | 0 | 250,000 |
| 65 | 4,500 | 42,000 | 0 | 250,000 |
| 75 | 13,500 | 107,250 | 0 | 250,000 |
| 80 | 13,500 | 174,750 | 0 | 250,000 |
| **TOTAL:** | | $174,750 | 0 | 250,000 |

### AGE 40: UL (premium permanent)

| Age | Yr Prem. | Paid Prem. | Cash Value | Coverage |
|---|---|---|---|---|
| 45 | 5,304 | 26,520 | 21,096 | 250,467 |
| 55 | 5,304 | 79,560 | 84,252 | 250,467 |
| 65 | 5,304 | 132,600 | 178,522 | 337,328 |
| 75 | 0 | 0 | 244,517 | 364,696 |
| 80 | 0 | 0 | 279,575 | 378,157 |
| **TOTAL:** | | $132,600 | $279,575 | $378,157 |

**Note:** If premiums are not paid, VGLI coverage lapses due to no cash value to maintain insurance coverage.

**Note:** If premiums are not paid, generally, UL coverage continues, unless there is no cash value available.

## Supplemental Insurance Retirement Policy

**(SIRP):** When I first came upon this product at Camp Pendleton, CA, I could not find anything about it in books or magazines, so I dubbed it an SIRP. An SIRP is unique, because it combines a small amount of (modified) whole life, with a high interest bearing accumulation account / fund. The (modified) whole life builds cash value (nice tidy sum), but unlike whole life, coverage amount at age 60 modifies to *"Face Value"* (reduced in half), and furthermore, coverage expires altogether at age 70-1/2. Therefore, what's the big deal? The big deal is life insurance in an SIRP, allows your contributions into the accumulation account / fund to be:

- **Probate free**
- **Guaranteed interest (set by Insurer)**
- **Tax-deferred**
- **Free from withdrawal penalties (in most cases)**
- **Used as collateral (whenever needed)**

### How an SIRP works

**Example:** 19-year old deposits $150 each month ($1,800 yearly), until age 65.

| Modified Whole Life | Tax-deferred Account |
|---|---|
| **First year:** $1,080 pays for life insurance | **First year:** $720 is deposited into tax-deferred fund |
| **Second year** and thereafter: $360 pays for life insurance | **Second year** and thereafter: $1,440 is deposited into tax-deferred fund |

### Upon Death

Life insurance + tax-deferred account  = Beneficiary

### Upon Retirement at age 65

Cash value: $8,725 + Tax-deferred account:
*$1,182,600
**Total: *$1,191,325**
*If tax-deferred account averages **10%**

**EXAMPLE SIRP (age 19): Tax-deferred account / fund**

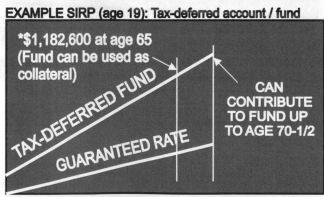

*$1,182,600 at age 65
(Fund can be used as collateral)

TAX-DEFERRED FUND
GUARANTEED RATE

CAN CONTRIBUTE TO FUND UP TO AGE 70-1/2

**EXAMPLE SIRP (age 19): (Modified) whole life policy**

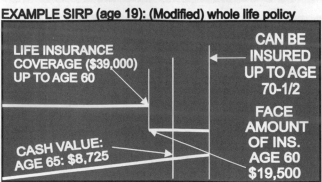

LIFE INSURANCE COVERAGE ($39,000) UP TO AGE 60

CASH VALUE: AGE 65: $8,725

CAN BE INSURED UP TO AGE 70-1/2

FACE AMOUNT OF INS. AGE 60 $19,500

## Purchasing Insurance Using Common Sense

### DEFINITION of common sense:
1. **Sound judgment not based on specialized knowledge.**
2. **The ability to make sensible decisions: judgment, sense, wisdom**
3. **Gumption, horse sense.**

Do you know if you possess common sense? Answer the three questions below to find out.

**1. *If you needed surgery for a medical condition, who would you want to perform your operation?***

A. Licensed physician / Doctor / surgeon
B. Friend
C. Co-worker / supervisor
D. Family member

**2. *If you needed legal advice on a crucial matter, who would you turn to for their expert advice?***

A. Licensed lawyer
B. Friends
C. Co-workers / supervisor
D. Family members

**3. *If an insurance program had all the benefits you could ask for, presented through a licensed and reputable agent, whose financial advice would you seek before implementing the policy?***

A. Rating Institution
B. Friends
C. Co-workers / supervisor
D. Family members

**Answers:** If you picked "A" to all three questions, then you have plenty of common sense.

As for question three, a consumer should research the financial strength rating of an insurance company, before purchasing insurance from them. Once purchased, follow up and check the strength ratings at least once a year.

Furthermore, five rating institutions analyze the insurance industry's financial strength. The chart below has phone numbers, websites of the rating Institutions, along with the total amount of insurers they rate.

| Rating Institutions | |
|---|---|
| **Company** | **Phone # / Web site** |
| **A.M. Best:** Rates 1,044 insurers | **908-439-2200** www.ambest.com |
| **Fitch Investors Services, Inc:** Rates 200+ insurers | **800-893-4824** www.fitchratings.com |
| **Moody's:** Rates 204 insurers | **212-553-0377** www.moodys.com |
| **Standard & Poor's:** Rates 710 insurers | **212-438-2400** www.standardandpoors.com |
| **Weiss Rating, Inc.:** Rates 1,242 insurers | **800-289-9222** www.weissratings.com |

**NOTE:** The opinions on the financial strength of an insurer are often alike between rating institutions; nevertheless, grades, or ratings sometimes differ. If you see an unusual difference in grading, then check all the available ratings of an insurer that appeals to you.

The services that banks and credit unions offer are often identical. **Bottom line:** You'll probably need the financial services of both through the years and as with any financial service, you'll want to shop around. The chart below reveals the key differences between banks and credit unions.

## Commercial Banks

Banks serve the public. However, the public has no voice in how the bank is run.

Banks are owned by investors who expect a good return on their investment

Only investors have privilege to vote. The public does not have the right to vote and cannot be elected to the board.

Only investors get an acquired share of the banks profits.

The government through the Federal Deposit Insurance Corporation (FDIC) insures banks. Taxpayers' dollars fund the FDIC. The FDIC does not operate as a pay-as-you-go system, which prevents the accumulation of annual losses. FDIC had to bail out several savings and loans in the late eighties and early nineties, costing taxpayers' billions of dollars. Some bank failures have tied up consumer funds for as long as a year.

Banks offer a full range of financial services, including 24-hour phone banking services. Large banks give you the convenience of several ATM's to access, which helps to save a few bucks by not having to use other banks ATM's which charge non-customer access fees.

**Business accounts:** Banks offer a full range of financial services to a business owner.

**National Banking Services Averages:**
Regular savings: 0.44%
Interest checking: 0.36%
Money market: 0.62%
One-Year CD: 2.26%
Credit card: 12.76%
48-month new car: 6.91%
48-month used car: 7.50%
36-month unsecured: 12.47%
HELOC: 4.90%
Five-year ARM: 5.71%
30-year fixed: 5.58%
Overdraft fees: $35-$39
-Source: Datatrac, Dec 2008/Liz P. Weston 4/09 MSN

Large banks can seem unfriendly with their many rules and new ideas to drum themselves up more money by creating fees, such as a $4 fee to deposit your paycheck into your account (BofA). However, banks are needed, especially if you require a full range of financial services.

**How to find a safe bank:** With 100 banks failing to date (Oct 2009), you would be smart to obtain the latest safety rating from **Veribanc** on any bank, thrift or credit union for a fee of **$10** for the first report, and **$5** for each additional report ordered at the same time by calling:
**(800) 837-4226** or **www.veribanc.com** or write to:
**Veribanc, PO Box 1610 Woonsocket, RI 02895**

## Credit Unions

Credit unions serve membership organizations. Each person that deposits money in a credit union is considered a member.

Credit unions are member owned and each member is an owner of the credit union.

Credit unions are run democratically. The volunteer board of directors is elected by the membership.

Credit unions are non-profit. After expenses are paid and reserves are set aside, surplus earnings are returned to members in forms of higher dividends, lower loan rates and free or low-cost services.

The full faith and credit of the U.S. Government back the National Credit Union Share Insurance Fund (NCUSIF). The NCUSIF is the only deposit insurance fund that operates on a pay-as-you-go system, which prevents the accumulation of annual losses. The NCUSIF has never had to use taxpayer' money. Most analysts agree there is better funding of the NCUSIF than the FDIC. This means you have a better chance of getting your money from a credit union than from a bank in the case of a failure.

Credit unions may be limited in their range of products and financial services. For example, they may offer personal loans and auto loans, but not mortgages. You won't have ease of 24 hour phone service or many ATM's to access, which means you could be hit with non-customer access fees when using other banks ATM.

**Business accounts:** You may have to shop for a credit union that accepts businesses and go through a forthcoming process that could include acceptance by the National Credit Union Association.

**National Credit Union Services Averages:**
Regular savings: 0.68%
Interest checking: 0.48%
Money market: 1.22%
One-Year CD: 2.93%
Credit card: 11.64%
48-month new car: 5.46%
48-month used car: 5.72%
36-month unsecured: 10.60%
HELOC: 4.70%
Five-year ARM: 5.54%
30-year fixed: 5.44%
Overdraft fee: $20-$25
-Source: Datatrac, Dec 2008/Liz P. Weston 4/09 MSN

Credit unions offer more personalized service, higher dividends, low-cost services (save up to $75-100 a year in bank fees alone) and loan rates. When you join a credit union, you're not only a member, but an owner too. Credit unions are needed competition, to keep banks in line from charging sky-high fees.

**Find safe credit union:** With 14 credit union failures to date (Oct 2009), it would be smart to obtain the Camel rating of your credit union or for one that you have interest in. Credit unions are rated from Code 1 (good) to Code 5 (bad). These codes are a reliable indicator of future success or failures. Contact the Camel rating system at: **703.518.6360 or www.ncua.gov**
■ Find a credit Union:
**www.creditunion.coop/cu_locator/quickfind.php**
■ Find a Federally insured credit union (USA):
**www.ncua.gov/DataServices/indexdata1.aspx**
■ Also try 2009 NCUA Credit Union Directory:
**www.ncua.gov/DataServices/Directory/cudir.aspx**
■ Start your own credit union: **703.518.6330**
**www.ncua.gov/Resources/CreditUnion Development/Start.aopx**
■ Federal Credit Union Complaints:
**www.ncua.gov/Resources/ConsumerInformation/Complaints/fcucomplaints.aspx**

■ **How to balance a checking account:**
**www.moneyinstructor.com/checkbalance.asp**

# NEED A LOAN? USE YOUR OWN MONEY!

**The problem:** A study by Hewitt Associates of 170,000 distributions (payouts) from defined contribution plans (retirement plans similar to the *Thrift Savings Plan*) indicated that **68% *of plan participants who changed jobs in 1999 took cash withdrawals from their tax-deferred retirement accounts.*** This means that **68%** of the plan participants, who had the option to avoid hefty tax penalties by leaving their money in the plan or roll their balances into new employers' plans or IRAs, instead, chose to pay the heavy tax penalties (Yikes!). *The highest percentage of cash payouts (78%) occurred among 20 to 29 year old investors.* There are numerous reasons why people take money out of accounts such as:

## LIFE'S LITTLE JOYS AND MISERIES

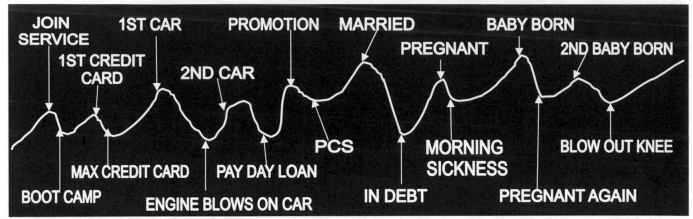

**Solution:** When an emergency arises, and you have depleted your emergency savings, your last line of defense may be your investments, retirement accounts or insurance policies. You cannot borrow from an IRA, and it's difficult to use mutual funds for collateral due to their volatility. That's why it's beneficial to have accounts that can be secured or collateralized. The examples below will help you to see the benefits of why it's in your best interest to use your own money to make loans to yourself. NOTE: Always search for the best available loan, and when found, negotiate the best terms possible from lender.

| Credit Union<br>**Passbook Savings** | Bank or Credit Union<br>**CD** | Insurance Company<br>**SIRP** | Insurance Company<br>**Universal Life (UL)** |
|---|---|---|---|
| 20-year-old deposits $100 monthly for 15 years into a passbook savings account, then **STOPS** deposits | 20-year-old deposits $100 monthly for 15 years into a CD, then **STOPS** deposits | 20-year-old deposits $100 monthly for 15 years into a SIRP, then **STOPS** deposits | 20-year-old deposits $100 monthly for 15 years into a universal life policy for 15 years, then **STOPS** deposits |
| 15 year savings average:<br>**2% (15% tax bracket)** | 15 year CD average:<br>**3% (15% tax bracket)** | 15 year SIRP fund average:<br>**10% (tax deferred)** | 16 year UL policy average:<br>**5% (tax deferred)** |
| Total saved by age 35:<br>**$20,971** | Total saved by age 35:<br>**$22,148** | Total accumulation fund by age 35: **$31,547**<br>Ins. coverage: **$26,000** | Total cash value by age 35:<br>**$18,288**<br>Ins. coverage: **$110,000** |
| **Situation:** Engine blows on car and needs another car ASAP. Cost of used car: $10,000 | **Situation:** Needs $10,000 for down payment on a lake vacation home | **Situation:** Wants to purchase a new car. Cost of vehicle: $25,000 | **Situation:** Wants to get out of $15,000 in credit card debt that totals $600 in monthly minimum payments |
| **Solution:** Use $10,000 secured loan against savings | **Solution:** Use $10,000 secured loan against CD | **Solution:** Use $25,000 collateral loan against SIRP | **Solution:** Take out $15,000 loan from insurer |
| 5 year loan rate:   - 4%<br>$20,971 earns:   + <u>2%</u><br>Loan average:   **- 2%** | 5 year loan rate:   - 6%<br>$22,148 earns:   + <u>3%</u><br>Loan average:   **- 3%** | 5 year loan rate:   - 8%<br>$31,729 earns:   + <u>10%</u><br>Loan average:   **+ 2%** | 5 year loan rate:   - 0%<br>$18,288 earns:   + <u>5%</u><br>Loan average:   **+ 5%** |
| Loan payment:   $184.17<br>**$20,971 earns 2%:**   <u>-34.95</u><br>Monthly payment:   **$149.22** | Loan payment:   $193.33<br>**$22,148 earns 3%:**   <u>-55.37</u><br>Monthly payment:   **$137.96** | Car payment:   $506.91<br>**$31,729 earns 10%:** <u>-264.40</u><br>Monthly payment:   **$242.51** | Loan payment:   $250.00<br>**$18,288 earns:**   <u>-72.60</u><br>Monthly payment:   **$177.40** |
| **Money continues to grow throughout the years:**<br><u>*Rule of 72: 2% = 36 years</u><br>Age  35.......... $20,971<br>Age  71.......... $41,942<br>Age 107.......... Pushing Daisies | **Money continues to grow throughout the years:**<br><u>*Rule of 72: 3% = 24 years</u><br>Age  35........... $ 22,148<br>Age  59........... $ 40,531<br>Age  83........... $ 74,172<br>Age 107.......... Bub-Bye | **Money continues to grow throughout the years:**<br><u>*Rule of 72: 10% = 7.2 yrs</u><br>Age 35........... $    31,729<br>Age 42........... $    63,458<br>Age 49........... $  126,916<br>Age 56........... $  253,832<br>Age 63........... $  507,664<br>Age 70........... $1,015,328 | **Cash value continues to grow throughout the yrs:**<br><u>Rule of 72: Does not apply</u><br>Age 35........... $   18,288<br>Age 45........... $   27,113<br>Age 55........... $   39,561<br>Age 65........... $   55,590<br>Age 75........... $   74,799<br>Age 85........... $   95,251<br>Age 95........... $ 140,998 |

*For explanation of the rule of 72, see **page 139**.

# SECRET FORMULA = INTEREST WORKS HARDER

The **Rule of 72** is a formula for approximating the time it will take for a given amount of money to double at a given compound interest rate. The formula is simply 72 divided by the interest rate.

**Example:** 18 year old deposits $100 into savings account that pays 2% at credit union. Formula: 72 ÷ 2% = 36 years. Thus, $100 doubles to $200 by the time teenager ages to 54.

| 2% = 36 Years Deposit $1,000 | Currently Earn ___% Life Savings $_____ | 10% = 7.2 Years Deposit $1,000 |
|---|---|---|
| 1,000 at age 20 | $ _____ age _____ | 1,000 at age 20 |
| 2,000 at age 56 | $ _____ age _____ | 2,000 27 |
| 4,000 at age 92 | $ _____ age _____ | 4,000 34 |
| 8,000 at age 128 | $ _____ age _____ | 8,000 at age 41 |
| 16,000 at age 164 | $ _____ age _____ | 16,000 48 |
| | | 32,000 55 |
| | | 64,000 at age 62 |
| | | 128,000 69 |
| | | 256,000 76 |
| | | 512,000 at age 83 |
| | | 1,024,000 90 |
| | | 2,048,000 97 |
| | | 4,096,000 at age 104 |

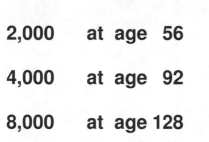 $100 earning 1%...

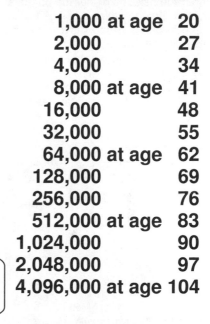 ...will double to $200 in 72 years.

## INTEREST CHART: HOW SOON WILL YOUR MONEY DOUBLE?

| Rate | Years | Rate | Years |
|---|---|---|---|
| 1% | = 72 | 8% | = 9 |
| 1.5% | = 48 | 8.5% | = 8.5 |
| 2% | = 36 | 9% | = 8 |
| 2.5% | = 28.8 | 10% | = 7.2 |
| 3% | = 24 | 10.5% | = 6.9 |
| 3.5% | = 20.6 | 11% | = 6.5 |
| 4% | = 18 | 11.5% | = 6.3 |
| 4.5% | = 16 | 12% | = 6 |
| 5% | = 14.4 | 12.5% | = 5.8 |
| 5.5% | = 13.1 | 13% | = 5.5 |
| 6% | = 12 | 13.5% | = 5.3 |
| 6.5% | = 11.1 | 14% | = 5.1 |
| 7% | = 10.3 | 14.5% | = 5 |
| 7.5% | = 9.6 | 15% | = 4.8 |

**For Current Interest Rates, Visit:**
www.bankrate.com
www.marketwatch.com
www.interest.com
www.moneycafe.com

When you (finally) earn more than you spend, it's time to strongly consider saving and investing money for your future. Begin by asking yourself:

- **What are my goals?**
- **What is my period?**
- **How much risk can I tolerate?**

Let's talk about risk. In the world of finance, risk is the uncertainty that the investment will grow per your expectation. In other words, the real risk is that you will not achieve your financial objective. The thing to remember is that the higher the risk, the greater the chance of loss. The most important thing to know about risk, however, is the higher the risk, the higher the potential return. **Risk equals reward**. Doing nothing is a risk. Putting your money in an insured savings account is low risk, but low return, especially when inflation is factored in. Gambling in Las Vegas is a big risk, but there will be a few big winners. Knowing how much risk you can stand is a crucial first step in developing a saving or investment plan to reach your goals. Risk can be shown as a pyramid:

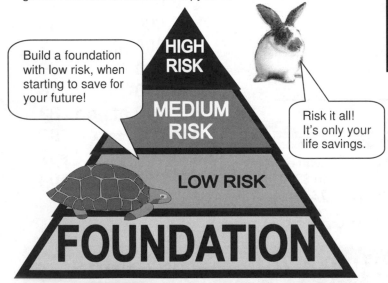

Build a foundation with low risk, when starting to save for your future!

Risk it all! It's only your life savings.

**FOUNDATION:** The bottom layer of the pyramid: This is safe, where your money earns interest only. The important thing about this foundation is that the principal cannot be lost. The money here is used to pay bills. It is your emergency fund, enough money to pay 3-6 months of expenses should you lose your job, car breaks down, or you have a medical emergency which is not covered by insurance. Foundation products: Checking and savings accounts, CDs, Savings Bonds, and SIRPs.

**LOW RISK:** This is your home. It is money saved for short-term goals like a vacation next year, a new car in two years. If your child begins college in a few years, your savings and investments should be low-risk. If you don't need the money for three years or more, invest in the stock market through index mutual funds, also, consider mortgage bond funds.

**MEDIUM RISK:** Longer-term goals and retirement savings such as IRAs should shoulder more risk because the money will not be needed. It has plenty of time to grow. I consider the stock market to be a medium risk, just make sure your portfolio is diversified. Real Estate Investment Trusts are lower in risk than the purchase of investment property, but both can be considered.

**HIGH RISK:** I'm a conservative investor and believe only a small percentage of your assets, if any at all, should be invested in high-risk things like options, futures and foreign currencies. Gambling fits into this category, just don't risk more than you can afford to lose.

**March 3, 2009**

**Nasdaq: - 73.8% | S&P 500: - 55.2% | Dow: - 52.3%**

# For investors, 'bloodbath' reflects fear

**Belief in markets shaken as Dow hits 12-year low and closes under 6,800**

By Adam Shell
USA TODAY

NEW YORK— If there ever was a symbol of investors' lack of confidence in the government's ability to stem the financial crises, it was the Dow Jones industrials plunging below 7000 Monday and closing at levels not seen since April 1997.

**Adjusting your risk by age:**

- **Age 18-30:** Your focal point should be targeted toward developing a foundation and low-risk plan of action.
**Recommended distribution:** Put 60%-80% of your funds in foundation and 20%-40% in low-risk levels.
- **Age 30-45:** If you've built your foundation, you can start looking into higher levels of risk.
**Recommended distribution:** Put 20%-40% in the foundation level, 30%-45% in the low-risk level, 10%-20% in medium-risk and 10% in high-risk levels.
- **Age 45-60:** Time to make sure your foundation will still be rock solid in the future, especially when you're no longer working and collecting a paycheck.
**Recommended distribution:** Put 5%-20% in foundation, 45%-60% in low-risk, 15%-25% in medium-risk, and 10-15% (assuming your risk tolerance) in high-risk levels.
- **Age 60+:** Adjusting to a more solid foundation is crucial for conservation of your money for the long haul.
**Recommended allocation:** Put 40%-60% in foundation and low-risk levels, 10%-20% in medium-risk, and 5% possibly in high-risk levels.

Bubble, bubble, toil and trouble...

Article by: Bill Stanley a fee-only Financial Planner in Colorado Springs, CO. Bill can be reached at **MoneyCoachBill@aol.com**

Normally, people save and invest for financial security, retirement, children's college education, etc. In today's financial market place, there is a variety of products to choose. Risk has its rewards, but it can also cause you a lot of misery, as you can see from the 2001 chart below. By the way, 1997, 2000, 2002 and 2008 were bad years too.

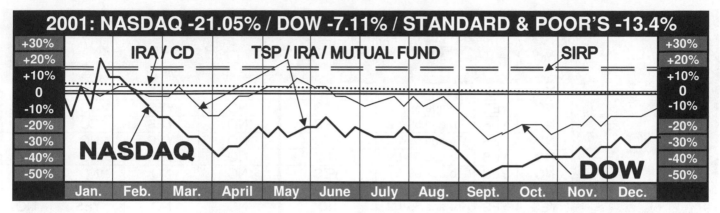

When it comes to saving and investing money, some people can handle high-risk and others only low-risk. The information and examples below will help you to understand the volatility between different savings, investments and supplements. **Important tip:** Never put all your eggs (money) in one basket (investment).

**Fixed dollar savings, investments & supplements:** Principal and / or income that is contractually set in advance, offers greater security of principal, but modest rates of return.

Savings Accounts
NOW Accounts
Money Market Accounts
Certificates of Deposit
Treasury Notes and Bills
Bonds: Savings, Treasury, Corporate, Municipals
Life Insurance Cash Value / Fund (Side Fund)
Tax-Deferred Annuities

**Variable dollar savings, investments & supplements:** Neither principal nor income is contractually set in advance. Higher risk of loss, but can earn higher rate of return.

Common Stock
Mutual Funds
Variable Annuities / Variable Life Insurance
Real Estate
Commodities
Futures
Fine Arts
Precious Metals

**Example: $1,200** lump sum deposited yearly into a hypothetical tax-deferred, fixed dollar fund that pays 7% annually.

**Example: $1,200** lump sum deposited yearly into a hypothetical tax-deferred, aggressive growth variable fund.

| Year | Deposit | Interest | Account | Year | Deposit | Interest | Account |
|------|---------|----------|---------|------|---------|----------|---------|
| 1 | 1,200 | 7% | $ 1,284 | 1 | 1,200 | 54.57% | $ 1,855 |
| 2 | 1,200 | 7% | 2,658 | 2 | 1,200 | 3.99% | 3,177 |
| 3 | 1,200 | 7% | 4,128 | 3 | 1,200 | 12.81% | 4,937 |
| 4 | 1,200 | 7% | 5,701 | 4 | 1,200 | –(4.62)% | 5,854 |
| 5 | 1,200 | 7% | 7,384 | 5 | 1,200 | 48.92% | 10,505 |
| 6 | 1,200 | 7% | 9,185 | 6 | 1,200 | 4.17% | 12,193 |
| 7 | 1,200 | 7% | 11,112 | 7 | 1,200 | 9.17% | 14,621 |
| 8 | 1,200 | 7% | 13,174 | 8 | 1,200 | 9.91% | 17,389 |
| 9 | 1,200 | 7% | 15,380 | 9 | 1,200 | 32.41% | 24,614 |
| 10 | 1,200 | 7% | **$17,740** | 10 | 1,200 | –(31.70)% | **$17,631** |

**Slow and easy:** Even with a modest rate of return, fixed dollar savings can offer wealth with less risk, especially if the individual starts socking money away early in life or individual has already acquired wealth and would like to continue earning interest with less risk.

**Not for squeamish or faint of heart:** The variable fund above shows just how volatile the market can be, therefore, make sure you diversify your investments. **Note:** As a rule of thumb, financial advisors state that it takes up to three years to recoup losses in an investment.

Someone once asked Albert Einstein, what was the most amazing discovery he had encountered? Without hesitation, he replied, *"Compound interest."* Of course, you don't have to be a scientific genius to appreciate the *miracle of compounding*. The ability of money to grow over time has benefited anyone who has ever saved for a goal or retirement. Unfortunately, a taxable account can erode compound interest, stealing much of your profits. Therefore, what can one do to keep gains? Use products that defer taxes, and you'll pay either none or until earnings are withdrawn (see tax-deferred products below).

## Qualified Tax-deferred Products: What tax-deferred products work best for you?

| Products | Positives: NO / Negatives: YES | | | | Positives: YES / Negatives: NO | | | |
|---|---|---|---|---|---|---|---|---|
| | Income Limits | Fees | Withdrawal Penalties End | Subject to Income Tax | Guaranteed Interest | Loans or Collateral | Job-to-Job Portable | Cash Value |
| Bonds EE, HH, I | NO | NO | 5 -Years | Interest Only | NO | NO | YES | NO |
| 401 k | NO | YES | To age 59-1/2 | YES | *NO | YES | **NO | NO |
| 403 b | NO | YES | To age 59-1/2 | YES | *NO | YES | **NO | NO |
| Thrift Savings Plan | NO | YES | To age 59-1/2 | YES | NO | YES | **NO | NO |
| Keogh Plans | NO | YES | To age 59-1/2 | YES | *NO | YES | **NO | NO |
| SEP IRA | NO | YES | To age 59-1/2 | YES | *NO | NO | **NO | NO |
| Traditional IRA | YES | YES | To age 59-1/2 | YES | *NO | NO | YES | NO |
| Roth IRA | YES | YES | To age 59-1/2 | NO | *NO | NO | YES | NO |
| SIRP | NO | YES | NONE*** | Interest Only | YES | YES | YES | YES |
| Whole Life | NO | YES | 10-Years | NO on loans | YES | YES | YES | YES |
| Universal Life | NO | YES | 10-Years | NO on loans | YES | YES | YES | YES |
| Variable Life | NO | YES | To age 59-1/2 | NO on loans | YES | YES | YES | YES |
| Annuity | NO | YES | To age 59-1/2 | Interest Only | YES | NO | YES | NO |

**\* Guaranteed interest:** If funds are in 5-year CD.   **\*\* Job change:** Can no longer contribute, but can be rolled into IRA or other eligible plans.
**\*\*\* Early withdrawal Penalties:** None for Servicemembers' & their spouses. Penalties may apply for the general public (check with ins. Rep).

Let's see how *tax-deferred vs. taxable* compound interest works, when depositing a lump sum of $1,200 yearly into an account that will average 10% up to age 65 (taxable account: 15% tax bracket). **NOTE:** Your tax bracket may be higher.

| AGE / YEAR WHEN 65 | TOTAL DEPOSITS | 10% TAX-DEFERRED | TOTAL AFTER TAX | INTEREST EARNED | 15% TAX BRACKET |
|---|---|---|---|---|---|
| 20 / 45th Yr | $45,000 | $948,954 | $586,591 | $54,064 | $8,110 |
| 21 / 44th Yr | $44,000 | $861,486 | $539,436 | $49,718 | $7,458 |
| 22 / 43rd Yr | $43,000 | $781,969 | $495,976 | $45,712 | $6,856 |
| 23 / 42nd Yr | $42,000 | $709,681 | $455,921 | $42,020 | $6,303 |
| 24 / 41st Yr | $41,000 | $643,964 | $419,004 | $38,618 | $5,793 |
| 25 / 40th Yr | $40,000 | $584,222 | $384,979 | $35,482 | $5,322 |
| 26 / 39th Yr | $39,000 | $529,911 | $353,619 | $32,592 | $4,889 |
| 27 / 38th Yr | $38,000 | $480,537 | $324,716 | $29,928 | $4,489 |
| 28 / 37th Yr | $37,000 | $435,652 | $298,078 | $27,473 | $4,121 |
| 29 / 36th Yr | $36,000 | $394,847 | $273,526 | $25,210 | $3,781 |
| 30 / 35th Yr | $35,000 | $357,752 | $250,898 | $23,124 | $3,469 |
| 31 / 34th Yr | $34,000 | $324,029 | $230,042 | $21,202 | $3,180 |
| 32 / 33rd Yr | $33,000 | $293,372 | $210,820 | $19,430 | $2,915 |
| 33 / 32nd Yr | $32,000 | $265,502 | $193,104 | $17,798 | $2,670 |
| 34 / 31st Yr | $31,000 | $240,165 | $176,776 | $16,293 | $2,444 |
| 35 / 30th Yr | $30,000 | $217,132 | $161,728 | $14,906 | $2,236 |
| 36 / 29th Yr | $29,000 | $196,193 | $147,858 | $13,627 | $2,044 |
| 37 / 28th Yr | $28,000 | $177,157 | $135,074 | $12,449 | $1,867 |
| 38 / 27th Yr | $27,000 | $159,852 | $123,292 | $11,363 | $1,705 |
| 39 / 26th Yr | $26,000 | $144,120 | $112,434 | $10,363 | $1,554 |
| 40 / 25th Yr | $25,000 | $129,818 | $102,425 | $ 9,440 | $1,416 |
| 41 / 24th Yr | $24,000 | $116,816 | $ 93,201 | $ 8,590 | $1,289 |
| 42 / 23rd Yr | $23,000 | $104,997 | $ 84,700 | $ 7,806 | $1,171 |
| 43 / 22nd Yr | $22,000 | $ 94,252 | $ 76,864 | $ 7,084 | $1,063 |
| 44 / 21st Yr | $21,000 | $ 84,483 | $ 69,643 | $ 6,419 | $ 963 |
| 45 / 20th Yr | $20,000 | $ 75,603 | $ 62,987 | $ 5,805 | $ 871 |

**FACT:** It costs money to do business when saving or investing. The information below will assist you to compare and choose programs that perform well at lowest cost.

■ **UP-FRONT COSTS:** The average domestic equity fund has a load of 2.2%. There are several fees to consider when investing such as reimbursement fees, transaction fees, *low-account-balance fees*, and *low-activity fees*. In addition, *no-transaction-fee-funds* are not free. Usually, you will pay a higher *expense ratio* for these. **EXAMPLE:** $5,000 deposit with a 5% front load would leave $4,750 balance in fund.

■ **EXPENSE RATIOS:** Within a funds prospectus, you will find their *expense ratio*. Expense ratios cover management and 12(b)-1-distribution fees, and other costs related with doing business. The average *expense ratio* today is 1.4%. **EXAMPLE:** $1 million in a fund with a 1.4% *expense ratio* would cost $14,000 for the year.

■ **TRADING COSTS:** When a fund buys or sells a stock for its shareholders, it usually pays a broker a commission. Furthermore, there may be an impact cost, which applies when a fund's own trade causes a stock's price to move unfavorably as the trade unfolds. Also, there may be a delay cost, or penalty of a stock's price moving negatively while a large order is executed over days or weeks. Then there are missed-trade costs, which occur when a manager sets an overly stingy limit order and misses a trade. Experts estimate that the average per-trade total of these costs range from 1.4% (index funds), 1.6% (large-cap growth funds) to 3.1% (small-cap growth funds). **EXAMPLE:** Large-cap growth fund making a $1 million trade, might incur 1.6% in costs. If fund buys and sells equivalent of its entire portfolio in a year (many do), *annual transaction* costs will be 1.6%, or 3.2% of total assets.

■ **INSURANCE PREMIUMS:** Insurance companies charge premiums for insurance coverage, which encompass management fees, agent commissions, and all other costs associated with doing business. Some premiums, build cash value over time. **EXAMPLE:** Insurance premiums total $16,920 over a span of 45 years. Cash value in the policy builds to $7,128.

■ **FINALLY:** Compare the examples on right between an IRA and SIRP (forty-year period). Both have fees.

## IRA
**Interest Track Record:** 11%
**Load:** None
**Expense Ratio:** 1.4%
**Taxes:** None / Tax-Deferred
**Monthly Deposit:** $250

| Accumulation | | Expenses | |
|---|---|---|---|
| 1. $ | 3,283 | $ | 47 |
| 2. | 6,874 | | 100 |
| 3. | 10,797 | | 163 |
| 4. | 15,080 | | 234 |
| 5. | 19,752 | | 317 |
| 6. | 24,848 | | 407 |
| 7. | 30,405 | | 507 |
| 8. | 36,460 | | 619 |
| 9. | 43,052 | | 749 |
| 10. | 50,218 | | 900 |
| | | | **$4,043** |
| 11. | 58,003 | | 1,069 |
| 12. | 66,454 | | 1,259 |
| 13. | 75,613 | | 1,480 |
| 14. | 85,533 | | 1,728 |
| 15. | 96,267 | | 2,005 |
| 16. | 107,872 | | 2,314 |
| 17. | 120,410 | | 2,658 |
| 18. | 133,930 | | 3,055 |
| 19. | 148,512 | | 3,481 |
| 20. | 164,209 | | 3,969 |
| | | | **$27,061** |
| 21. | 181,129 | | 4,473 |
| 22. | 199,295 | | 5,089 |
| 23. | 218,799 | | 5,748 |
| 24. | 239,721 | | 6,475 |
| 25. | 262,119 | | 7,301 |
| 26. | 286,072 | | 8,210 |
| 27. | 311,629 | | 9,241 |
| 28. | 338,900 | | 10,337 |
| 29. | 367,935 | | 11,575 |
| 30. | 398,809 | | 12,929 |
| | | | **$108,339** |
| 31. | 431,557 | | 14,451 |
| 32. | 466,296 | | 16,063 |
| 33. | 503,051 | | 17,868 |
| 34. | 541,832 | | 19,885 |
| 35. | 582,750 | | 22,013 |
| 36. | 625,801 | | 24,382 |
| 37. | 671,027 | | 26,942 |
| 38. | 718,393 | | 29,777 |
| 39. | 768,637 | | 32,110 |
| 40. | 820,372 | | 36,145 |

**Total Expenses: $348,075**

(3% yearly inflation rate included)
Yearly expense average: **$8,702**

## SIRP
**Interest Track Record:** 11%
**Load:** Insurance Premiums
**Expense Ratio:** None
**Taxes:** None / Tax-Deferred
**Monthly Deposit:** $250

| Accumulation | | Expenses |
|---|---|---|
| 1. $ | 1,110 | $2,000 |
| 2. | 3,801 | 667 |
| 3. | 6,787 | 667 |
| 4. | 10,103 | 667 |
| 5. | 13,782 | 667 |
| 6. | 17,867 | 667 |
| 7. | 22,401 | 667 |
| 8. | 27,434 | 667 |
| 9. | 33,020 | 667 |
| 10. | 39,221 | 667 |
| | | **$8,003** |
| 11. | 46,104 | 667 |
| 12. | 53,744 | 667 |
| 13. | 62,224 | 667 |
| 14. | 71,638 | 667 |
| 15. | 82,086 | 667 |
| 16. | 93,684 | 667 |
| 17. | 106,558 | 667 |
| 18. | 120,848 | 667 |
| 19. | 136,710 | 667 |
| 20. | 154,317 | 667 |
| | | **$14,673** |
| 21. | 173,860 | 667 |
| 22. | 195,554 | 667 |
| 23. | 219,633 | 667 |
| 24. | 246,361 | 667 |
| 25. | 276,030 | 667 |
| 26. | 308,961 | 667 |
| 27. | 345,516 | 667 |
| 28. | 386,091 | 667 |
| 29. | 431,130 | 667 |
| 30. | 481,123 | 667 |
| | | **$21,343** |
| 31. | 536,615 | 667 |
| 32. | 598,211 | 667 |
| 33. | 666,583 | 667 |
| 34. | 742,475 | 667 |
| 35. | 826,716 | 667 |
| 36. | 920,224 | 667 |
| 37. | 1,024,017 | 667 |
| 38. | 1,139,228 | 667 |
| 39. | 1,267,111 | 667 |
| 40. | 1,409,062 | 667 |

**Total Expenses:** $28,013
**Cash Value:** - 13,074
**Final Expenses:** 14,308
Yearly expense average: $  358

Use worksheet to determine and then list your financial portfolio guidelines to assist your coach or financial advisor, so they can give the proper recommendations necessary to help you succeed.

Disposable income you're willing to save each month: $ _____

1. *Type of saving or investment:*
   □ Fixed (contractual agreement)
   □ Variable (no contractual agreement)

2. *Risk tolerance:*
   □ Foundation (guaranteed interest)
   □ Low
   □ Medium
   □ High

3. *Interest track record required:*
   □ 1 year
   □ 5 Years
   □ 10 Years
   □ 20 Years or longer

4. *Taxes:*
   □ Tax-deferred
   □ Taxed

5. *Cost / Fees willing to accept:*
   □ Front Load          (2.2% average)
   □ Expense ratio       (1.5% average)
   □ Trading costs       (2.0% average)
   □ Insurance premiums (with cash value)
   □ Other _____

6. *Early withdrawal penalties:*
   □ End after 10 Years
   □ End age 59-1/2

7. *Options:*
   □ Insurance benefit
   □ Collateral benefit
   □ Probate free benefit
   □ Portable from job to job

8. *Retirement option:*
   □ After 10 Years
   □ 59-1/2

**NOTE: For hypothetical projections, see page 145 (SIRP insurance and cash value formulas at bottom)**

9. *Payment options:*
   □ Flexible
   □ Each paycheck
   □ Monthly
   □ Minimum $_____

10. *Other options(s) or Recommendations:* _____

_____

**HOW TO USE:** **EXAMPLE:** $200 saved monthly in account x 12 months = $2,400
In 20 years: $2,400 ($ 48,000 total principle saved) x  63.0025 (10% table) = $ 151,206
In 45 years: $2,400 ($108,000 total principle saved) x 790.7953 (10% table) = $1,897,909

Saving monthly: $_____
Interest earned: _____%
Years Saved: _____

**C-10**

## COMPOUND INTEREST TABLE: ONE DOLLAR PER ANUM: Results $

| YEAR | 2% | 3% | 4% | 5% | 6% | 7% | 8% | 9% | 10% | 11% |
|---|---|---|---|---|---|---|---|---|---|---|
| 1 | 1.0200 | 1.0300 | 1.0400 | 1.0500 | 1.0600 | 1.0700 | 1.0800 | 1.0900 | 1.1000 | 1.1100 |
| 2 | 2.0604 | 2.0909 | 2.1216 | 2.1525 | 2.1836 | 2.2149 | 2.2464 | 2.2781 | 2.3100 | 2.3421 |
| 3 | 3.1216 | 3.1836 | 3.2465 | 3.3101 | 3.3746 | 3.4399 | 3.5061 | 3.5731 | 3.6410 | 3.7097 |
| 4 | 4.2040 | 4.3091 | 4.4163 | 4.5256 | 4.6371 | 4.7507 | 4.8666 | 4.9847 | 5.1051 | 5.2278 |
| 5 | 5.3081 | 5.4684 | 5.6330 | 5.8019 | 5.9753 | 6.1533 | 6.3359 | 6.5233 | 6.7156 | 6.9129 |
| 6 | 6.4343 | 6.6625 | 6.8983 | 7.1420 | 7.3938 | 7.6540 | 7.9228 | 8.2004 | 8.4872 | 8.7833 |
| 7 | 7.5830 | 7.8923 | 8.2142 | 8.5491 | 8.8975 | 9.2598 | 9.6366 | 10.0285 | 10.4359 | 10.8594 |
| 8 | 8.7546 | 9.1591 | 9.5828 | 10.0266 | 10.4913 | 10.9780 | 11.4876 | 12.0210 | 12.5795 | 13.1640 |
| 9 | 9.9497 | 10.4639 | 11.0061 | 11.5779 | 12.1808 | 12.8164 | 13.4866 | 14.1929 | 14.9374 | 15.7220 |
| 10 | 11.1687 | 11.8078 | 12.4864 | 13.2068 | 13.9716 | 14.7836 | 15.6455 | 16.5603 | 17.5312 | 18.5614 |
| 11 | 12.4121 | 13.1920 | 14.0268 | 14.9171 | 15.8699 | 16.8885 | 17.9771 | 19.1407 | 20.3843 | 21.7132 |
| 12 | 13.6803 | 14.6178 | 15.6268 | 16.7130 | 17.8821 | 19.1406 | 20.4953 | 21.9534 | 23.5227 | 25.2116 |
| 13 | 14.9739 | 16.0863 | 17.2919 | 18.5986 | 20.0151 | 21.5505 | 23.2149 | 25.0192 | 26.9750 | 29.0949 |
| 14 | 16.2934 | 17.5989 | 19.0236 | 20.5786 | 22.2760 | 24.1290 | 26.1521 | 28.3609 | 30.7725 | 33.4054 |
| 15 | 17.6393 | 19.1569 | 20.8245 | 22.6575 | 24.6725 | 26.8881 | 29.3243 | 32.0034 | 34.9497 | 38.1899 |
| 16 | 19.0121 | 20.7616 | 22.6975 | 24.8404 | 27.2129 | 29.8402 | 32.7502 | 35.9737 | 39.5447 | 43.5008 |
| 17 | 20.4123 | 22.4144 | 24.6454 | 27.1324 | 29.9057 | 32.9990 | 36.4502 | 40.3013 | 44.5992 | 49.3959 |
| 18 | 21.8406 | 24.1169 | 26.6712 | 29.5390 | 32.7600 | 36.3790 | 40.4463 | 45.0185 | 50.1591 | 55.9395 |
| 19 | 23.2974 | 25.8704 | 28.7781 | 32.0660 | 35.7856 | 39.9955 | 44.7620 | 50.1601 | 56.2750 | 63.2028 |
| 20 | 24.7833 | 27.6765 | 30.9692 | 34.7193 | 38.9927 | 43.8652 | 49.4229 | 55.7645 | 63.0025 | 71.2651 |
| 21 | 26.2990 | 29.5368 | 33.2480 | 37.5052 | 42.3923 | 48.0057 | 54.4568 | 61.8733 | 70.4027 | 80.2143 |
| 22 | 27.8450 | 31.4529 | 35.6179 | 40.4305 | 45.9958 | 52.4361 | 59.8933 | 68.5319 | 78.5430 | 90.1479 |
| 23 | 29.4219 | 33.4265 | 38.0826 | 43.5020 | 49.8156 | 57.1767 | 65.7648 | 75.7898 | 87.4973 | 101.1742 |
| 24 | 31.0303 | 35.4593 | 40.6459 | 46.7271 | 53.8645 | 62.2490 | 72.1059 | 83.7009 | 97.3471 | 113.4133 |
| 25 | 32.6709 | 37.5530 | 43.3117 | 50.1135 | 58.1564 | 67.6765 | 78.9544 | 92.3240 | 108.1818 | 126.9988 |
| 26 | 34.3443 | 39.7096 | 46.0842 | 53.6691 | 62.7058 | 73.4838 | 86.3508 | 101.7231 | 120.0999 | 142.0786 |
| 27 | 36.0512 | 41.9309 | 48.9676 | 57.4026 | 67.5281 | 79.6977 | 94.3388 | 111.9682 | 133.2099 | 158.8173 |
| 28 | 37.7922 | 44.2189 | 51.9663 | 61.3227 | 72.6398 | 86.3465 | 102.9659 | 123.1354 | 147.6309 | 177.3972 |
| 29 | 39.5681 | 46.5754 | 55.0849 | 65.4388 | 78.0582 | 93.4608 | 112.2832 | 135.3075 | 163.4940 | 198.0209 |
| 30 | 41.3794 | 49.0027 | 58.3283 | 69.7608 | 83.8017 | 101.0730 | 122.3459 | 148.5752 | 180.9434 | 220.9132 |
| 31 | 43.2270 | 51.5028 | 61.7015 | 74.2988 | 89.8898 | 109.2182 | 133.2135 | 163.0370 | 200.1378 | 246.3236 |
| 32 | 45.1116 | 54.0778 | 65.2095 | 79.0638 | 96.3432 | 117.9334 | 144.9506 | 178.8003 | 221.2515 | 274.5292 |
| 33 | 47.0338 | 56.7302 | 68.8579 | 84.0670 | 103.1838 | 127.2588 | 157.6267 | 195.9823 | 244.4767 | 305.8374 |
| 34 | 48.9945 | 59.4621 | 72.6522 | 89.3203 | 110.4348 | 137.2369 | 171.3168 | 214.7108 | 270.0244 | 340.5896 |
| 35 | 50.9944 | 62.2759 | 76.5983 | 94.6363 | 118.1209 | 147.9135 | 186.1021 | 235.1247 | 298.1268 | 379.1644 |
| 36 | 53.0343 | 65.1742 | 80.7022 | 100.6281 | 126.2681 | 159.3374 | 202.0703 | 257.3759 | 329.0395 | 421.9825 |
| 37 | 55.1149 | 68.1594 | 84.9703 | 106.7095 | 134.9042 | 171.5610 | 219.3159 | 281.6298 | 363.0434 | 469.5106 |
| 38 | 57.2372 | 71.2342 | 89.4091 | 113.0950 | 144.0585 | 184.6403 | 237.9412 | 308.0665 | 400.4478 | 522.2667 |
| 39 | 59.4020 | 74.4013 | 94.0255 | 119.7998 | 153.7620 | 198.6351 | 258.0565 | 336.8824 | 441.5926 | 580.8261 |
| 40 | 61.6100 | 77.6633 | 98.8265 | 126.8398 | 164.0477 | 213.6096 | 279.7810 | 368.2919 | 486.8518 | 645.8269 |
| 41 | 63.8622 | 81.0232 | 103.8196 | 134.2318 | 174.9505 | 229.6322 | 303.2435 | 402.5281 | 536.6370 | 717.9779 |
| 42 | 66.1595 | 84.4839 | 109.0124 | 141.9933 | 186.5076 | 246.7765 | 328.5830 | 439.8457 | 591.4007 | 798.0655 |
| 43 | 68.5027 | 88.0484 | 114.4129 | 150.1430 | 198.7580 | 265.1209 | 355.9496 | 480.5218 | 651.6408 | 886.9627 |
| 44 | 70.8927 | 91.7199 | 120.0294 | 158.7002 | 211.7435 | 284.7493 | 385.5056 | 524.8587 | 717.9048 | 985.6386 |
| 45 | 73.3306 | 95.5015 | 125.8706 | 167.6852 | 225.5081 | 305.7518 | 417.4261 | 573.1860 | 790.7953 | 1095.1688 |
| 46 | 75.8172 | 99.3965 | 131.9454 | 177.1194 | 240.0986 | 328.2244 | 451.9002 | 625.8628 | 870.9749 | 1216.7474 |
| 47 | 78.3535 | 103.4084 | 138.2632 | 187.0254 | 255.5645 | 352.2701 | 489.1322 | 683.2804 | 959.1723 | 1351.6996 |
| 48 | 80.9406 | 107.5406 | 144.8337 | 197.4267 | 271.9584 | 377.9990 | 529.3427 | 745.8656 | 1050.1090 | 1501.4965 |
| 49 | 83.5794 | 111.7969 | 151.6671 | 208.3480 | 289.0359 | 405.5289 | 572.7702 | 814.0836 | 1162.9085 | 1667.7712 |
| 50 | 86.2110 | 116.1808 | 158.7738 | 219.8154 | 307.7651 | 434.9860 | 619.6718 | 888.4411 | 1280.2994 | 1852.3360 |

**SIRP: AGE (FACTOR) x PREMIUM = INS. COVERAGE**

| 18-20 (433.34) | 27-29 (333.34) | 37-40 (233.34) |
|---|---|---|
| 21-22 (400.00) | 30-32 (300.00) | 41-44 (200.00) |
| 23-26 (366.67) | 33-36 (266.67) | 45-48 (166.67) |

Example: Age 25 (366.67) x Premium ($120) = $44,000

**\*SIRP: ESTIMATED CASH VALUE (CV)**

TOTAL PREMUIM (TP) x 10 YEARS (.2486) = \*CV
TOTAL PREMUIM (TP) x 20 YEARS (.3797) = \*CV
TOTAL PREMUIM (TP) x AGE 65   (.4809) = \*CV
Example: TP $5,760 x 10 YRS (.2486) = $1,432 \*CV

In 1973, I made $5 per hour. However, that hourly wage allowed me to afford an apartment, car payment, utilities, etc. Yet, I still had money left over to save each month. Sadly, if I were still making $5 per hour today, I'd probably have to live in a cardboard box, because my hourly wage wouldn't have kept pace with today's prices due to inflation. To beat inflation, you must save and invest at a higher rate of return than the going rate of inflation.

## Example: Return on savings & investments 5% - 2% inflation = +3% above inflation.

If you'd like to retire someday and stay retired, start planning your war against inflation today, before inflation gets the best of your future retirement. Then again, if money gets tight in the future; you're still in good health and have the skill level, and then you might be able to come out of retirement and work for a while.

The chart below reflects the price of items from the past, present and possible future at an inflation rate of 5%.

| ITEMS | 1990 | 2000 | 2010 | 2020 | 2030 | 2040 | 2050 | 2060 |
|---|---|---|---|---|---|---|---|---|
| Stamps | .20 | .33 | .54 | .88 | 1.43 | 2.32 | 3.78 | 6.16 |
| Gallon of gas | 1.38 | 1.79 | 2.92 | 4.76 | 7.75 | 12.62 | 20.56 | 33.48 |
| 1-gallon of milk | 2.47 | 3.29 | 5.36 | 8.73 | 14.22 | 23.16 | 37.73 | 61.45 |
| Loaf of bread | 1.02 | 1.99 | 3.24 | 5.28 | 8.60 | 14.01 | 22.82 | 37.17 |
| Burger King whopper | 1.79 | 2.39 | 3.89 | 6.34 | 10.33 | 16.83 | 27.41 | 44.66 |
| Movie ticket | 4.50 | 7.50 | 12.25 | 20.00 | 32.50 | 53.00 | 86.00 | 140.00 |
| Groceries | 150 | 200 | 326 | 531 | 864 | 1,408 | 2,293 | 3,736 |
| Hospital room | 337 | 485 | 790 | 1,287 | 2,096 | 3,414 | 5,562 | 9,059 |
| Toyota Camry CE 4-dr | 12,375 | 16,500 | 20,158 | 32,835 | 53,484 | 87,120 | 141,909 | 231,155 |
| Mortgage-anywhere USA | 75,000 | 100,000 | 162,889 | 265,330 | 432,194 | 703,999 | 1,147M | 1.868 M |

## What you must earn to maintain (break even) your money's purchasing power

Your tax rate today: _____% + Inflation rate: _____% = You must earn _____% to keep up with inflation.

| | Inflation Rate: If inflation is 5% and you pay 15% in taxes, your investments must earn 5.9% to break even | | | | | | | | | | |
|---|---|---|---|---|---|---|---|---|---|---|---|
| TAX | 2% | 3% | 4% | 5% | 6% | 7% | 8% | 9% | 10% | 11% | 12% |
| 15% | 2.4 | 3.5 | 4.7 | 5.9 | 7.1 | 8.2 | 9.4 | 10.6 | 11.8 | 12.9 | 14.1 |
| 30% | 2.9 | 4.3 | 5.7 | 7.1 | 8.6 | 10.0 | 11.4 | 12.9 | 14.3 | 15.7 | 17.1 |
| 40% | 3.3 | 5.0 | 6.7 | 8.3 | 10.0 | 11.7 | 13.3 | 15.0 | 16.7 | 18.3 | 20.0 |

## 4-STEPS TO HELP INFLATION PROOF YOUR BILLS AND MONEY

1.) _LOANS_: Use low interest secured loans from savings through credit union(s) or utilize collateral loans from accounts / funds through commercial bank(s), etc.
2.) _CARS_: Pay with cash (no payments) or keep monthly payments the same or close throughout the years.
3.) _HOUSES_: Purchase homes with 15 year mortgages.
4.) _MONEY_: Put money into tax-deferred plans that can:
   A. Beat inflation
   B. Be used as collateral
   C. Be used for retirement

SAVINGS / COLLATERAL

YOU ARE BORN

PRIME EARNING YEARS

TOTAL DEBT

05  10  15  20  25  30  35  40  45  50  55  60  65  70

146

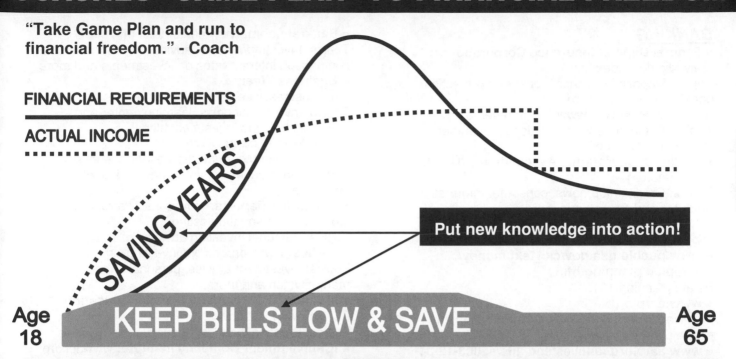

"Take Game Plan and run to financial freedom." - Coach

**FINANCIAL REQUIREMENTS**

**ACTUAL INCOME**

SAVING YEARS

**Put new knowledge into action!**

**KEEP BILLS LOW & SAVE**

Age 18

Age 65

C-10

1. <u>Save & don't procrastinate</u> (page 8).

2. <u>Seek financial guidance</u> through financial coaches or planners (page 14).

3. <u>Pay yourself first!</u> Save 20% or more of your income monthly (10% retirement & 10% for emergencies. See page 15).

4. <u>Establish</u> or <u>re-establish credit</u> through credit union by securing loan against savings account (page 22).

5. <u>Secure 2% to 3% loans</u> through credit union (page 23).

6. <u>Keep Finances Balanced</u> (page 32).

7. <u>Budget monthly</u> (page 153).

8. <u>Save $300 - $400 a month</u> in collateral accounts to finance future cars (page 74).

9. <u>Buy cars through auctions</u> (pages 80-83).

10. <u>Spend smart</u>, by timing purchases when things are on sale (page 85).

11. <u>Purchase multiplex</u> through VA home or state loan program (OPM) (page 110).

12. <u>Save pay raises throughout years</u> (page 120).

13. <u>Stop giving government free loans</u> by saving deduction(s) monthly (page 121).

14. <u>Build financial foundation</u> (page 130).

15. <u>Save comfortably</u> (page 131).

16. <u>Set financial goals</u> (page 132).

17. <u>Life insurance:</u> Use to protect your loved ones (pages 133 -136).

18. <u>Collateral:</u> Use it and not lose it. Keep money growing (page 138).

19. <u>Rule of 72:</u> Use rule and double your money (see page 139).

20. <u>Greater security:</u> Use fixed dollar plans with contractual agreements (page 141).

21. <u>Use tax-deferred saving plans</u> (page 142).

22. <u>Look for costly fees</u> within your retirement plans (page 143).

23. <u>Choose, plan & implement portfolio</u> (page 144 & 145).

24. <u>Beat inflation</u> (page 146).

25. <u>Stay financially ready</u> (Chapter 11).

## BANKING

- **Federal Deposit Insurance Corporation:**
www.fdic.gov/index.html
Topics: Deposit insurance, consumer protection, banking news and more.
- **Federal Reserve:** www.federalreserve.gov
Topics: Banking news, regulations, consumer information and more.
- **Credit Union National Association (CUNA):**
www.cuna.org
Topics: Credit union news, consumer information, products and service and more.

## ESTATE PLANNING

- **www.pueblo.gsa.gov/cic_text/money/ estateplan/planning.htm**
Estate planning 101.
- **www.aarp.org**
This website offers free, useful information on estate planning.
- **www.aarp.org/families/end_life/a2003-12-04- endoflife-will.html**
A free will preparation worksheet can be downloaded from site above.
- **www.irs.gov**
Internal Revenue Service website has up-to-date state tax information
- **www.abanet.org**
Website of American Bar Association (ABA) offers information on finding and using an estate planning attorney. The ABA does not make referrals.
Find Legal Help at **www.abanet.org/legalservices/ findlegalhelp/home.cfm.** The ABA Commission on Law and Aging offers a free tool kit for advance planning / medical directives. It can be downloaded at: **www.abanet.org/aging/publications/docs/ consumer_tool_kit_bk.pdf**

## INSURANCE

- **Insurance information institute:** www.iii.org
Topics: Life insurance and financial planning.
- **Insurance guide 101:**
www.insuranceguide101.com
Topics: All aspects of insurance.
- **Insure.com:** www.insure.com/articles
Topics: Insurance articles, quotes

## INVESTING & RETIREMENT PLANNING

- **About.com:**
http://beginnersinvest.about.com
Topics: Investing for beginners, investment essentials, articles and more.
- **AOL Money & Finance:**
http://money.aol.com/investing
Topics: Investment news, finance center, market coverage, Investing basics and more.
- **ARRP.org:** www.aarp.org/money/financial_ planning/sessionsix/investing.html
Topics: Financial planning, retirement, investing and more.

- **Bankrate.com:** www.bankrate.com
Topics: Investment news, advice, calculators, comparison interest rates on investments and more.
- **Business Week:**
www.businessweek.com/investor
Topics: Investment news, learning center and financial tools and investment blogs.
- **CNN Money.com:**
http://money.cnn.com/magazines/fortune/investing
Topics: Financial news, investing, market watch and more.
- **Consumer Reports:** www.consumerreports.org
cro/money/personal-investing
Topics: Personal investing advice.
- **Forbes:** www.forbes.com/investing
Topics: Investment articles, personal finance, market watch and more.
- **Institute of Consumer Financial Education (ICFE):** www.icfe.com
Topics: Personal finance, financial tools, & more.
- **ICI-Investment Company Institute:** www.ici.org
Topics: Investing in mutual funds, research/ statistics, investor education and more.
- **Investopedia:**
www.investopedia.com/university/beginner
Topics: Investing 101 (8-parts).
- **Kiplinger:** www.kiplinger.com/investing
Topics: Investment news, investment basics, advice, retirement planning, consumer awareness, market watch, and more.
- **The Motley Fool:** www.fool.com/investing.htm
Topics: Investing, personal finance, retirement, discussion boards and more.
- **MSN Money:**
http://moneycentral.msn.com/investor/home.asp
Topics: Investment news, personal finance center, advice, brokers, market summaries & more.
- **MyMoney.gov:** www.mymoney.gov
Topics: Government website with financial and investment tips and more.
- **Reuters:** www.reuters.com/finance
Topics: Financial articles, personal finance, investments, world market coverage and more.
- **SmartMoney.com:** www.smartmoney.com
Topics: Financial news, personal finance, investing, market watch and more.
- **U.S. Securities and Exchange Commission:**
www.sec.gov/investor/pubs/inws.htm
www.sec.gov/investor/pubs/inwsmf.htm
Fees: www.sec.gov/investor/tools/mfcc/mfcc-int.htm
Topics: Great investment advice.
- **Yahoo Finance:**
http://finance.yahoo.com/marketupdate?u
Topics: Investment news, personal finance, advice, investment tools, market coverage & more.

## FREE ADVICE

- **www.freeadvice.com**
Topics: Free, comprehensive, easy-to-understand information.

"Hey congratulations, you finished, Einstein! But, before you break your arm patting yourself on the back, snatch the $100 bill off my shoulder! Try it again! Hmm, just as I thought, you're still a 'grasshopper.' When you can snatch the $100 bill away from me, it will be time for you to stop reading this book, so remember, practice makes perfect. Now, I'm going to give you fair warning, don't come running up to me someday all weepy-eyed, bawling; 'Why didn't you *make* me plan my financial future?' I'm not your daddy or mommy, so get that through your thick skull, but I will give you one last pep talk. If you procrastinate, you might end up like 96% of the population at 65. **_BROKE!_** If on the other hand, you'd like to end up in the top 4%, then you must implement what we've been discussing. Don't lolly gag until next week, next month or next year; start this minute and continue to do everything in your power to act on this while my words are still ringing in your ears. You have one last assignment. Complete your *'pre-deployment and estate planning forms,'* then our financial journey together will come to an end. Now, sprint to the finishline; complete your last assignment and never look back. Fight the good fight and make me proud (sniff, sniff). If you ever need a good kick in the…attitude, then come and see me anytime. I'm always here, ready to give you a piece of my mind. Finally, I'd like to say, It's been a real pleasure knowing you. NOW MOOOOVE IT, Tweetle Dumb!"

**YOU DID IT, CHAMP!**

**PLANNING**

**FINANCIAL**

**START**

**FINISH**

## PRE-DEPLOYMENT & ESTATE PLANNING
## PART 1: PERSONAL INFORMATION

Use worksheet to create a checklist of personal information on you and family members (keep updated). In general, the information will be useful for future referencing purposes, and later, to settle your estate. In addition, do not leave checklist lying around where others may see it (store in safety deposit box, fireproof safe, etc.). **NOTE:** If you have more personal information to list than available space, make copies, fill-out and attach to checklist.

### PERSONAL INFORMATION: YOU AND SPOUSE

■ NAME (FULL): _____

ADDRESS: _____

PERMANENT: _____

CELL PH: _____ HOME: _____

DOB: _____ PLACE OF BIRTH: _____

SOCIAL SECURITY #: _____

DRIVERS LICENSE: _____

IDENTIFYING MARK(S): _____

MEDICAL CONDITION: _____

_____ BLOOD TYPE: _____

EMPLOYER: _____

ADDRESS: _____

PHONE: _____ EXT: _____

SUPERVISOR: _____

OTHER: _____

■ SPOUSE (FULL): _____

ADDRESS: _____

PERMANENT: _____

CELL PH: _____ HOME: _____

DOB: _____ PLACE OF BIRTH: _____

SOCIAL SECURITY #: _____

DRIVERS LICENSE: _____

IDENTIFYING MARK(S): _____

MEDICAL CONDITION: _____

_____ BLOOD TYPE: _____

EMPLOYER: _____

ADDRESS: _____

PHONE: _____ EXT: _____

SUPERVISOR: _____

OTHER: _____

### PERSONAL INFORMATION: DEPENDENTS

■ NAME (FULL): _____

RELATIONSHIP: _____

SOCIAL SECURITY #: _____

DOB: _____ PLACE OF BIRTH: _____

IDENTIFYING MARK(S): _____

MEDICAL CONDITION: _____

_____ BLOOD TYPE: _____

■ NAME (FULL): _____

RELATIONSHIP: _____

SOCIAL SECURITY #: _____

DOB: _____ PLACE OF BIRTH: _____

IDENTIFYING MARK(S): _____

MEDICAL CONDITION: _____

_____ BLOOD TYPE: _____

### PERSONAL INFORMATION: MILITARY

SERVICE #: _____

DATE ENTERED SERVICE: _____

ENLISTMENT DATE: _____

COMMISSION DATE: _____

DUTY STATUS: _____ ACTIVE _____ RESERVE

PRESENT RANK: _____

FLYING STATUS: _____

PAY DATE(S): _____ AND _____

OTHER: _____

### PROMOTION DATES

NEW RANK: _____ DATE: _____

NEW RANK: _____ DATE: _____

NEW RANK: _____ DATE: _____

NEW RANK: _____ DATE: _____

### DATES OF SERVICE TOURS

FROM: _____ TO: _____

FROM: _____ TO: _____

### COMMENTS

_____

_____

_____

# PRE-DEPLOYMENT & ESTATE PLANNING PART 2: RELATIVES AND IMPORTANT PEOPLE

Use worksheet to create a checklist of relatives and individuals that play a significant part in your life (keep list updated). In addition, do not leave checklist lying around where others may see it (store in safety deposit box, fireproof safe, etc.).
**NOTE:** If you have more to list than available space, make copies, fill-out and attach to checklist.

## REALATIVES

■ YOUR FATHER: _____

CELL PH: _____ HOME: _____

ADDRESS: _____

MOTHER: _____

CELL PH: _____ HOME: _____

ADDRESS: _____

BROTHER/SISTER: _____

CELL PH: _____ HOME: _____

ADDRESS: _____

OTHER: _____

CELL PH: _____ HOME: _____

ADDRESS: _____

■ SPOUSE'S FATHER: _____

CELL PH: _____ HOME: _____

ADDRESS: _____

MOTHER: _____

CELL PH: _____ HOME: _____

ADDRESS: _____

BROTHER/SISTER: _____

CELL PH: _____ HOME: _____

ADDRESS: _____

OTHER: _____

CELL PH: _____ HOME: _____

ADDRESS: _____

■ GUARDIAN: _____

CELL PH: _____ HOME: _____

ADDRESS: _____

■ MARRIED CHILD: _____

CELL PH: _____ HOME: _____

ADDRESS: _____

■ MARRIED CHILD: _____

CELL PH: _____ HOME: _____

ADDRESS: _____

## IMPORTANT PEOPLE

■ YOUR DOCTOR: _____

PHONE: _____ PHONE: _____

ADDRESS: _____

■ SPOUSE'S DOCTOR: _____

PHONE: _____ PHONE: _____

ADDRESS: _____

■ CHILDRENS DOCTOR: _____

PHONE: _____ PHONE: _____

ADDRESS: _____

■ VETERINARIAN: _____

PHONE: _____ PHONE: _____

ADDRESS: _____

■ LAWYER: _____

CELL PH: _____ PHONE: _____

ADDRESS: _____

■ TAX ADVISOR: _____

CELL PH: _____ PHONE: _____

ADDRESS: _____

■ ACCOUNTANT: _____

CELL PH: _____ PHONE: _____

ADDRESS: _____

■ CLERGYMAN: _____

CELL PH: _____ PHONE: _____

ADDRESS: _____

■ INSURANCE AGENT: _____

CELL PH: _____ PHONE: _____

ADDRESS: _____

■ EXECUTOR: _____

CELL PH: _____ PHONE: _____

ADDRESS: _____

■ SPOUSE'S EXECUTOR: _____

CELL PH: _____ PHONE: _____

ADDRESS: _____

Use worksheet to list assets you own and liabilities owed to others. After filling in, subtract liabilities from assets, this will then provide you with your personal net worth. In addition, it's important to update checklist whenever possible. Furthermore, do not leave checklists or documents lying around where others may see them (store in safety deposit box, fireproof safe, etc.). **NOTE:** If you have more items to list than available space, make copies, fill-out and attach to checklist.

| BALANCE CHART CHECKLIST: NET WORTH | | | |
|---|---|---|---|
| **ASSETS (ITEMS YOU OWN)** | **$** | **LIABILITIES (OWED TO OTHERS)** | **$** |
| *CASH ON HAND* | | *OWE ON MORTGAGES* | |
| HIDDEN CASH: | | 1st MORTGAGE: | |
| PIGGY BANK: | | 2nd MORTGAGE: | |
| *CHECKING ACCOUNT(S)* | | | |
| ACCOUNT # | | *CAR LOANS* | |
| ACCOUNT # | | ACCOUNT# | |
| *SAVING ACCOUNT(S)* | | ACCOUNT# | |
| ACCOUNT # | | ACCOUNT# | |
| ACCOUNT # | | *BANK LOANS* | |
| *LIFE INSURANCE CASH VALUE* | | ACCOUNT# | |
| POLICY # | | ACCOUNT# | |
| POLICY # | | ACCOUNT# | |
| POLICY # | | ACCOUNT# | |
| *BONDS OWNED* | | *CREDIT CARD DEBT* | |
| BOND TYPE: | | ACCOUNT# | |
| BOND TYPE: | | ACCOUNT# | |
| BOND TYPE: | | ACCOUNT# | |
| *STOCK OWNED* | | ACCOUNT# | |
| STOCK: | | ACCOUNT# | |
| STOCK: | | ACCOUNT# | |
| *MUTUAL FUNDS OWNED* | | ACCOUNT# | |
| FUND: | | *CHARGE CARD DEBT* | |
| FUND: | | ACCOUNT# | |
| *IRA* | | ACCOUNT# | |
| TRADITIONAL: | | ACCOUNT# | |
| ROTH: | | ACCOUNT# | |
| *TSP, 401K,403B, ETC.* | | ACCOUNT# | |
| | | ACCOUNT# | |
| | | *FINANCE LOANS* | |
| | | ACCOUNT# | |
| *ANNUITIES* | | ACCOUNT# | |
| | | *PERSONAL LOANS* | |
| | | ACCOUNT# | |
| *BUSINESS INTERESTS* | | ACCOUNT# | |
| | | *INSURANCE LOANS* | |
| *OTHER INVESTMENTS* | | ACCOUNT# | |
| | | ACCOUNT# | |
| | | *TAXES OWED* | |
| *FAIR MARKET VALUE: REAL ESTATE* | | FEDERAL: | |
| PERSONAL RESIDENCE(S): | | STATE: | |
| RENTAL PROPERTY: | | PROPERTY: | |
| UNDEVELOPED LAND: | | BUSINESS: | |
| *FAIR MARKET VALUE: CAR(S)* | | *OTHER DEBTS* | |
| CAR: | | | |
| CAR: | | | |
| CAR: | | | |
| *FAIR MARKET VALUE: OTHER ASSETS* | | | |
| FURNITURE: | | *TOTAL LIABILITIES* | |
| JEWELRY: | | | |
| RARE COINS: | | *TOTAL ASSETS* | |
| COLLECTIONS: | | | |
| OTHER: | | *(MINUS) TOTAL LIABILITIES* | |
| OTHER: | | | |
| ***TOTAL ASSETS*** | **$** | ***NET WORTH*** | **$** |

**61% of Americans either do not have a household budget or have difficulty sticking to a budget.**
(Source: Finlaw.com survey)

**57% of marriages fail over financial matters.**
(Source: Citibank survey)

The worksheet on this page will assist you in establishing a budget and help keep finances balanced. In addition, maintaining a monthly budget will give you less to worry about when an emergency or sudden deployment arises. **NOTE:** Furthermore, a budget will lend a hand in accomplishing goals you want to attain.

**Monthly living expenses:** Try to reduce your expenses by finding cheaper sources or give up bad habits.

## BUDGET WORKSHEET PART A: INCOME

| Income Source | Month: |
|---|---|
| Base Pay | $ |
| BAH | |
| BAS | |
| Hazard Pay | |
| | |
| Part Time Job | |
| Spouse Income | |
| Business Income | |
| EITC | |
| Child Support | |
| Alimony | |
| Social Security | |
| DIC | |
| Dividends | |
| Investment Income | |
| Pension(s) | |
| SBP | |
| | |
| | |
| | |
| **TOTAL INCOME** | $ |

## BUDGET WORKSHEET PART B: EXPENSES

| Expense Source | Month: |
|---|---|
| Federal Income Tax | $ |
| Social Security (FICA) | |
| Medicare | |
| State Withholding Tax | |
| SGLI & USSH:          AFAF / CFC: | |
| Allotment A:          B:          C: | |
| Direct Dep. A:          B:          C: | |
| Mortgage:          Rent: | |
| Storage A:          B: | |
| Elect:          Gas:          Water: | |
| Trash:          Sewage: | |
| Phone A:          B:          C: | |
| Internet | |
| Cable:          Satellite: | |
| Car Payment A:          B: | |
| Gasoline:          Oil / Lube Job: | |
| Auto Repairs:          Tune-ups: | |
| Auto Insurance A:          B: | |
| Bus:          Taxi:          Other: | |
| Parking:          Auto Tags: | |
| Medical:          Dental: | |
| Prescriptions A:          B:          C: | |
| Glasses:          Contacts: | |
| Groceries:          Pet Food: | |
| Lunches:          Snacks: | |
| Restaurants:          Fast Food: | |
| Entertainment:          Movies: | |
| Hobbies:          Interests: | |
| Subscriptions A:          B:          C: | |
| Barber:          Beauty Salon: | |
| Cosmetics:          Toiletries: | |
| Gifts:          Cards:          Postage: | |
| Dues:          Allowances: | |
| Charities:          Church: | |
| Pet A:          B:          C: | |
| Education:          Loans: | |
| Laundry:          Dry Cleaning: | |
| New Clothing A:          B:          C: | |
| Child Care A:          B:          C: | |
| Child Support:          Alimony: | |
| Credit card A:          B:          C: | |
| Charge card A:          B:          C: | |
| Loan A:          B:          C: | |
| Bank Fees A:          B:          C: | |
| Other Fees A:          B:          C: | |
| Life Insurance A:          B:          C: | |
| Savings A:          B:          C: | |
| Investment A:          B:          C: | |
| | |
| | |
| **TOTAL EXPENSES** | $ |

## WHAT CAUSES MONEY PROBLEMS:

■ **INSUFFICIENT FUNDS:** Writing checks on an account where funds may not yet be on deposit or not checking a Leave and Earning Statement to ensure the proper amount of funds deposited. Furthermore, more than one person writing checks off the same account, not annotating those checks, not reconciling check registry after each check or against the bank statement and finally, not deducting monthly service charges.

■ **OVEREXTENDING CREDIT:** Not considering the extra cost of accruing interest and payments due, exceed income. Treating credit as *"extra income,"* thinking that an individual purchase *"isn't very much money"* without considering that purchase made by credit. In addition, using credit cards like cash instead of only when needed during an emergency.

■ **IMPULSE SPENDING:** Buying something because someone else has one like it, not being able to resist displays or advertisements for an item or considering whether, or not you need that item to survive.

■ **NO BUDGET:** Spending without a purchasing plan. Not saving money for emergencies or changing spending habits when a lifestyle change happens. Finally, believing that a budget is not necessary.

## BUDGET SUMMARY

| | |
|---|---|
| Total Income | |
| Total Expenses | |
| **TOTAL DISPOSABLE INCOME** | $ |

**NOTE:** If disposable income is negative, go back to Chapter 4 and work toward getting financially balanced.

This section provides a life insurance needs worksheet, along with a checklist that will help you organize all your insurance policies in one place. Furthermore, it's important to update checklist whenever possible. In addition, do not leave checklist, statements or documents lying around where others may see them (store documents in safety deposit box, fireproof safe, etc.). **NOTE:** If you have more policies to list than available space, make copies, fill-out and attach to checklist.

## INSURANCE NEEDS WORKSHEET: IN FOUR STEPS

### 1. What is your net worth:

| In case of my death: My net worth | Amount |
|---|---|
| Cash in checking and savings accounts | |
| Money market funds | |
| Certificates of deposit | |
| Current value of government savings bonds | |
| Cash surrender value on insurance policies | |
| Equity in military / other pensions | |
| Equity in profit sharing plans | |
| Company sponsored savings plans | |
| Current value of annuities | |
| Loans owed you | |
| IRA's, SIRP, other retirement plans | |
| Keogh Account | |
| Tax refunds due | |
| Equity in your business | |
| Bonds | |
| Stocks | |
| Mutual Funds | |
| Investment trusts | |
| Equity in home and other real estate | |
| Automobiles | |
| Furniture and appliances | |
| Other: Jewelry, antiques, art, etc.) | |
| Other assets | |
| **TOTAL assets:** | $ |

### 3. Monthly Income needed for my family:

| Monthly income flow from: | Income |
|---|---|
| Surviving spouse monthly income | |
| Survivor Benefit Plan Payments (SBP) | |
| Dependency Indemnity Compensation (DIC) | |
| Social Security for spouse, children, parents | |
| Pensions and other company plans | |
| Investments and other retirement plans | |
| Other income from: | |
| Other income from: | |
| **My Family's Total Monthly Income** | $ |

| My Family's Monthly Expenses | Payments |
|---|---|
| Mortgage / Rent payment | |
| Utilities | |
| Telecommunication payments | |
| Food | |
| Clothing | |
| Transportation | |
| Child care | |
| Entertainment | |
| Loan Payments | |
| Other expenses | |
| **TOTAL family monthly expenses** | |
| **TOTAL family monthly income: Above** | |
| **Excess monthly income + or ( - )** | $ |

### 2. What I currently owe:

| In case of my death: What I owe | Amount |
|---|---|
| Mortgage debt and other real estate | |
| Second Mortgage | |
| Taxes due | |
| Child support / Alimony | |
| Automobile | |
| Furniture | |
| Appliances | |
| Medical and dental bills | |
| Other bills | |
| Personal loans | |
| Other loans (student, insurance, etc.) | |
| Credit cards, Charge cards, Gas cards | |
| Other | |
| **My TOTAL liabilities #2:** | $ |
| **My TOTAL assets #1:** | $ |
| **Lump sum excess income: + or ( - )** | $ |

### 4. Insurance coverage:

| My current insurance coverage | Coverage |
|---|---|
| SGLI / VGLI | |
| FEGLI | |
| Company Insurance Policy | |
| Term Insurance | |
| Whole Life Insurance | |
| Universal Insurance | |
| Supplemental Insurance Retirement Policy | |
| Variable Life Insurance | |
| Other | |
| **TOTAL Insurance coverage #4:** | $ |
| **Lump sum excess income #2: + or ( - )** | $ |
| **Excess will generate an income of:** | $ |
| **Excess monthly income #3: + or ( - )** | $ |
| **TOTAL monthly income for my family** | $ |
| If your calculations show that your survivors will not have enough monthly income, increase your insurance coverage. | |

## Insurance polices in force

**Document(s) Location:**

| Policy # | Insurance Company | Phone | Password | Type of Ins. | Beneficiary | Insurance Value |
|---|---|---|---|---|---|---|
| | | | | | | $ |
| | | | | | | $ |
| | | | | | | $ |
| | | | | | | $ |
| | | | | | | $ |
| | | | | | **Total Coverage In Force** | $ |

# PRE-DEPLOYMENT & ESTATE PLANNING PART 6: SAVINGS AND INVESTMENTS

This section provides a financial checklist that will help you organize all your financial information in one place. Furthermore, it's important to update checklist whenever possible. In addition, do not leave checklist, statements or documents lying around where others may see them (store documents in safety deposit box, fireproof safe, etc.).
**NOTE:** If you have more items to list than available space, make copies, fill-out and attach to checklist.

## Tax-Deferred Products
Document(s) Location:

| Name of company or institution | Phone number | Password | Purchase date | Monthly deposit | Maturity date | Estimated maturity value |
|---|---|---|---|---|---|---|
| | | | | | | |
| | | | | | | |
| | | | | | | |
| | | | | | | |
| | | | | | | |

## U.S. Treasury Bonds
Document(s) Location:

| Name of institution purchased from | Phone number | Password | Purchase date | Purchase price | Maturity date | Maturity value |
|---|---|---|---|---|---|---|
| | | | | | | |
| | | | | | | |
| | | | | | | |
| | | | | | | |
| | | | | | | |

## Funds: Mutual, Money Market, Etc.
Document(s) Location:

| Name of institution or fund | Phone number | Password | Purchase date | Number of shares | Unit / Share price | Total Investment |
|---|---|---|---|---|---|---|
| | | | | | | |
| | | | | | | |
| | | | | | | |
| | | | | | | |
| | | | | | | |

## Corporate Bonds / Municipal Bonds
Document(s) Location:

| Name of corporation / Municipality / coupon rate | Phone number | Password | Purchase date | Bond(s) number(s) | Unit cost | Total cost |
|---|---|---|---|---|---|---|
| | | | | | | |
| | | | | | | |
| | | | | | | |
| | | | | | | |
| | | | | | | |

## Corporate Stocks
Document(s) Location:

| Name of corporation | Phone number | Password | Purchase date | Number of shares | Unit cost | Total cost |
|---|---|---|---|---|---|---|
| | | | | | | |
| | | | | | | |
| | | | | | | |
| | | | | | | |
| | | | | | | |

## Other Savings/Investments/Supplements
Document(s) Location:

| Description | Phone number | Password | Purchase date | Amount of units | Unit cost | Total cost |
|---|---|---|---|---|---|---|
| | | | | | | |
| | | | | | | |

Do not leave checklist or documents lying around where others may see them (store documents in safety deposit box, fireproof safe, etc.).

**NOTE:** If you have more items to list than available space, make copies, fill-out and attach to checklist.

### WILL(S)

■ WILL FOR: _____

ATTORNEY: _____

■ WILL FOR: _____

ATTORNEY: _____

■ LIVING WILL FOR: _____

ATTORNEY: _____

■ LIVING WILL FOR: _____

ATTORNEY: _____

DL: _____ DATE: _____

### POWER OF ATTORNEY (POA)

■ POA FOR: _____

POA GIVEN TO: _____

■ POA FOR: _____

POA GIVEN TO: _____

■ POA FOR: _____

POA GIVEN TO: _____

DL: _____ DATE: _____

### MARRIAGE CERTIFICATE (MC)

■ MC FOR: _____

CERTIFICATE #: _____

■ MC FOR: _____

CERTIFICATE #: _____

DL: _____ DATE: _____

How long is this going to take, Sweetie?

It won't take long. Let's do this together, Pumpkin.

I'll get the pens.

### ADOPTION PAPERS (AP)

■ AP FOR: _____

CERTIFICATE #: _____

DL: _____ DATE: _____

### DIVORCE PAPERS (DP)

■ DP FOR: _____

CERTIFICATE #: _____

DL: _____ DATE: _____

### BIRTH CERTIFICATES (BC)

■ BC FOR: _____

CERTIFICATE #: _____

■ BC FOR: _____

CERTIFICATE #: _____

■ BC FOR: _____

CERTIFICATE #: _____

■ BC FOR: _____

CERTIFICATE #: _____

DL: _____ DATE: _____

### CITIZENSHIP (CP) / NATURALIZATION PAPERS (NP)

■ CP/NP FOR: _____

CERTIFICATE #: _____

■ CP/NP FOR: _____

CERTIFICATE #: _____

DL: _____ DATE: _____

### MILITARY RECORDS (MR)

■ MR FOR: _____

CERTIFICATE #: _____

■ MR FOR: _____

CERTIFICATE #: _____

■ MR FOR: _____

CERTIFICATE #: _____

DL: _____ DATE: _____

### SOCIAL SECURITY RECORDS (SSR)

■ SSR FOR: _____

SS#: _____

DL: _____ DATE: _____

## BURIAL INSTRUCTIONS (BI)

■ BI FOR: _____

PRE-PAID SERVICES, PLOT, ETC.: _____

■ BI FOR: _____

PRE-PAID SERVICES, PLOT, ETC.: _____

DL: _____ DATE: _____

## DEATH CERTIFICATES (DC)

■ DC FOR: _____

CERTIFICATE #: _____

DL: _____ DATE: _____

## PASSPORTS, VISAS

■ FOR: _____

■ FOR: _____

■ FOR: _____

■ FOR: _____

■ FOR: _____

DL: _____ DATE: _____

## SOCIAL SECURITY CARDS

■ DL: _____ DATE: _____

## COPY OF EMERGENCY DATA CARD (DD FORM 93)

■ DL: _____ DATE: _____

## COURT ORDERS / PENDING LEGAL ACTIONS

■ LEGAL ACTION: _____

CASE #: _____

■ LEGAL ACTION: _____

CASE #: _____

■ LEGAL ACTION: _____

CASE #: _____

■ LEGAL ACTION: _____

CASE #: _____

DL: _____ DATE: _____

## INCOME TAX RETURNS

____ FEDERAL TAXES (LAST 5 YEARS):

_____, _____, _____, _____, _____

DL: _____ DATE: _____

____ STATE TAXES ( LAST 5 YEARS):

_____, _____, _____, _____, _____

DL: _____ DATE: _____

____ PENDING TAXES YEARS: _____, _____, _____

DL: _____ DATE: _____

## CHURCH RECORDS (CR)

■ CR FOR: _____

CR: _____

■ CR FOR: _____

CR: _____

DL: _____ DATE: _____

## REAL ESTATE (RE) RECORDS

■ RE ADDRESS: _____

DEED/RECORD: _____

■ RE ADDRESS: _____

DEED/RECORD: _____

■ RE ADDRESS: _____

DEED/RECORD: _____

■ RE ADDRESS: _____

DEED/RECORD: _____

DL & KEYS: _____ DATE: _____

## VEHICLES & RECREATIONAL TITLES

■ YEAR/MAKE/MODEL: _____

REGISTRATION #: _____ STATE: ____

TITLE #: _____ LICENSE #: _____

■ YEAR/MAKE/MODEL: _____

REGISTRATION #: _____ STATE: ____

TITLE #: _____ LICENSE #: _____

■ YEAR/MAKE/MODEL: _____

REGISTRATION #: _____ STATE: ____

TITLE #: _____ LICENSE #: _____

DL & KEY(S): _____ DATE: _____

## BUSINESS OR PARTNERSHIP AGREEMENTS (PA)

■ BUSINESS / PA: _____

■ FEDERAL TAX ID: _____

■ STATE TAX ID: _____

DL: _____ DATE: _____

## CONTRACTS: LEASE, RENTAL, LOANS, ETC.

■ COMPANY: _____ PHONE: _____

STATE : _____ ACCOUNT #: _____

■ COMPANY: _____ PHONE: _____

STATE : _____ ACCOUNT #: _____

DL: _____ DATE: _____

## OUTSTANDING LOANS (OWED YOU OR BY YOU)

- LOAN TO OR FROM: _____

ACCOUNT #: _____ PHONE: _____

- LOAN TO OR FROM: _____

ACCOUNT #: _____ PHONE: _____

DL: _____ DATE: _____

## CREDIT CARDS & CHARGE CARDS (CC)

- CC COMPANY: _____ PH: _____

ACCOUNT #: _____ BALANCE: _____

- CC COMPANY: _____ PH: _____

ACCOUNT #: _____ BALANCE: _____

- CC COMPANY: _____ PH: _____

ACCOUNT #: _____ BALANCE: _____

- CC COMPANY: _____ PH: _____

ACCOUNT #: _____ BALANCE: _____

- CC COMPANY: _____ PH: _____

ACCOUNT #: _____ BALANCE: _____

DL: _____ DATE: _____

## STORAGE UNITS(S)

- STORAGE CO: _____ PH: _____

ADDRESS: _____

STORAGE #: _____ PASSWORD / CODE: _____

- STORAGE CO: _____ PH: _____

ADDRESS: _____

STORAGE #: _____ PASSWORD / CODE: _____

DL & KEYS: _____ DATE: _____

You're awesome! Keep planning!

## TELECOMMUNICATIONS

- FOR: _____ DATE: _____

CELL PHONE CARRIER: _____

ACCOUNT #: _____ PASSWORD: _____

WEBSITE: _____ PH: _____

- FOR: _____ DATE: _____

CELL PHONE CARRIER: _____

ACCOUNT #: _____ PASSWORD: _____

WEBSITE: _____ PH: _____

- HOME PH SERVICE: _____

ACCOUNT #: _____ PASSWORD: _____

WEBSITE: _____ PH: _____

- INTERNET PROVIDER: _____

ACCOUNT #: _____ PASSWORD: _____

WEBSITE: _____ PH: _____

- SATELLITE CO: _____ DATE: _____

ACCOUNT #: _____ PASSWORD: _____

WEBSITE: _____ PH: _____

- CABLE CO: _____ DATE: _____

ACCOUNT #: _____ PASSWORD: _____

WEBSITE: _____ PH: _____

DL: _____ DATE: _____

## UTILITIES

- ELECTRIC PH: _____ PASSWORD: _____

- GAS PHONE: _____ PASSWORD: _____

- PROPANE PH: _____ PASSWORD: _____

- WATER PH: _____ PASSWORD: _____

- GARBAGE PH: _____ PASSWORD: _____

DL: _____ DATE: _____

## INSURANCE INFORMATION REVIEW & UPDATE

- COMPANY: _____ PH: _____

WEBSITE: _____

AUTO INS POLICYS: _____

_____

_____

- COMPANY: _____

MORTGAGE POLICY #: _____ PH: _____

- COMPANY: _____ PH: _____

PROPERTY & CASUALTY POLICY #: _____

DL: _____ DATE: _____

158

## PROPERTY REVIEW & INVENTORY

■ PHOTOGRAPH CONDITIONS OF YOUR PROPERTY:

_____

DL: _____ DATE: _____

■ VIDEO TAPE CONDITIONS OF YOUR PROPERTY:

_____

DL: _____ DATE: _____

■ ADD SERIAL NUMBERS TO PROPERTY INVENTORY:

DL: _____ DATE: _____

## ROAD SERVICE

■ ROAD SERVICE CO: _____

POLICY #: _____ PH: _____

DL: _____ DATE: _____

## BANK / CREDIT UNION CHECKING ACCOUNT

■ INSTITUTION: _____

CHECK ACC #: _____ PASSWORD: _____

WEBSITE: _____ PH: _____

LOCATION: _____ DATE: _____

■ INSTITUTION: _____

CHECK ACC #: _____ PASSWORD: _____

WEBSITE: _____ PH: _____

LOCATION: _____ DATE: _____

DL: _____ DATE: _____

## BANK / CREDIT UNION SAVINGS ACCOUNT

■ INSTITUTION: _____

SAVE ACC #: _____ PASSWORD: _____

WEBSITE: _____ PH: _____

LOCATION: _____ DATE: _____

■ INSTITUTION: _____

SAVE ACC #: _____ PASSWORD: _____

WEBSITE: _____ PH: _____

LOCATION: _____ DATE: _____

DL: _____ DATE: _____

## SAFETY DEPOSIT BOX

■ INSTITUTION: _____

REGISTERED UNDER: _____

BOX #: _____ KEYS AT: _____

DL: _____ DATE: _____

## MEDICAL INFORMATION

■ HEALTH CARE PROVIDER: _____

PERSONAL ID #: _____ PH: _____

■ LONG TERM CARE POLICY: _____

PERSONAL ID #: _____ PH: _____

■ HEALTH CARE PROXY: _____

■ ORGAN DONOR INFORMATION: _____

■ MEDICAL RECORDS: FAMILY (SHOTS, ETC.):

■ DENTAL RECORDS: FAMILY

■ MEDICAL RECORDS: PETS (VET., CLINIC, SHOTS, ETC.):

■ MEDICAL POA FOR: _____

DL: _____ DATE: _____

## OTHER DOCUMENTS & RECORDS

■ FOR: _____

COPIES OF ORDERS (TDY, PCS, ETC: _____

■ FOR: _____

COPY OF SGLI ELECTION FORM & DOCUMENTS:

■ FOR: _____

DRIVERS LICENSE: _____

■ WARRANTIES & GUARANTEES: CAR, APPLIANCES, ETC.

■ ALL PASSWORDS & CODES:

■ SCHOOL REGISTRATION DOCUMENTS, FORMS, ETC.

DL: _____ DATE: _____

## ALLOTMENTS (UPDATE)

■ FOR: _____ DATE: _____

■ FOR: _____ DATE: _____

■ FOR: _____ DATE: _____

DL: _____ DATE: _____

Honey, I got you a puppy dog to protect and keep you company until I get back from my deployment. His name is Happy! Can we keep him? Isn't he cute and lovable?

159

## DIRECT DEPOSITS (UPDATE)

- FOR: _____ DATE: _____
- FOR: _____ DATE: _____
- FOR: _____ DATE: _____

DL: _____ DATE: _____

## MILITARY ID's (UPDATE)

- FOR: _____ DATE: _____
- FOR: _____ DATE: _____
- FOR: _____ DATE: _____
- FOR: _____ DATE: _____

DL: _____ DATE: _____

## DEERS ENROLLMENT (UPDATE)

DATE: _____

## TRICARE STATUS (UPDATE)

DATE: _____

## FAMILY & IMMEDIATE RELATIVES (UPDATE LIST)

DATE: _____

## IMPORTANT PEOPLE (UPDATE LIST)

DATE: _____

## FINANCIAL RECORD KEEPING

____ Set up folder(s) to hold financial and legal documents and receipts in your absence (together with spouse)

## LEGAL CHECKLIST: REVIEW WITH SPOUSE

____ Prepare will(s) (spouse included). **NOTE:** Consider living will(s) (for both you and spouse)

____ Power of attorney(s) reviewed (with spouse). Consult with a legal advisor

____ Next of kin (including spouses) informed of rights, benefits, assistance available, wills and location of important documents

____ Parents informed how to make contact in case of emergency

____ Renew military ID card if it expires within three months before deployment

____ Emergency Data Card Updated

## FINANCIAL CHECKLIST: REVIEW WITH SPOUSE

____ Budget(s) reviewed and prepared for home and deployment expenses

____ Register all accounts (bills, savings, investments, etc.) to access online

____ Establish automatic payment plan (with spouse) to have (bills, savings, investments, etc.) paid

____ Contact financial advisor to discuss improving or help with financial situation before deployment

____ Review life insurance coverage for you (and family)

____ Review property and casualty insurance

____ Review financial needs. Take out loan if needed; ensure that loan is completed before deployment

____ Review investment options and tax-deferred plans

____ Plan for unexpected repairs on home and car(s) or bill(s) that come in higher due to weather (heating, etc.), medical, inflation, etc.

____ Bank and/or credit union accounts in both names with an **"or"** rather than an **"and"** between names (all accounts) or better yet, consider opening separate accounts to avoid overdrafts

____ Consider putting extra funds in checking account(s) or open special account just for emergencies

____ Factor in surplus income to budget from combat zone non-taxable income. **NOTE:** If deployed to combat zone, you may exclude taxes from some of your pay. Income not taxable in combat zone: Active duty pay, imminent danger/hostile-fire pay, reenlistment bonus, if it occurs in a month while you served in combat zone, pay you earned for meals provided by the service while in combat zone, and monetary awards for suggestions you made when serving in combat zone

____ Extend filing income taxes and IRA contributions if needed. NOTE: The IRS usually grants combat zone extensions for filing income taxes and IRA contributions. To learn more, visit **www.irs.gov**

____ If you want spouse to use AAFES Deferred Payment Plan (DPP), you must list spouse as an authorized user or give spouse Power of Attorney

____ Spouse has password to myPay to view LES

____ See if creditors will give you discounts for deployment

____ Contact credit card provider(s) if you intend to take card(s) on deployment (ask if they can reduce rate)

____ See if you qualify for the Servicemembers' Civil Relief Act for this deployment (for more see **page 34**)

____ If deployment is international, contact long distance provider and put family on international calling plan

## MEDICAL CHECKLIST

____ Make sure spouse understands the Family Member Dental Plan

____ Review TRICARE procedures with spouse

____ Review prescriptions for status of refills and expiration dates with spouse

____ Consider medical power of attorney for health care reasons in the event of injury

____ Names, phone numbers and addresses of family physician(s), Dentist/orthodontist and eye care specialist (include veterinarian information)

Take a 10 min walk through your home (if married, take spouse in tow). Carry this checklist to help you really see your home. The idea behind this exercise is to spot fire hazards and other potential dangers and eliminate them before they become
a disaster. If you're thinking you don't have any hazards, perhaps this list will change your mind.

### HOME IN GENERAL                    YES–NO

If you have children, is home childproofed?  _____

Are the furnace, water heater, heater, vents and chimneys inspected and serviced regularly?  _____

Are there dry leaves under porches, wooden chairs, in windowsills, garage or elsewhere?  _____

Does house have a smoke detector and is it Working? Put fresh battery in before shipping out  _____

### KITCHEN                            YES–NO

Are curtains, dishtowels, or paper items kept away from stove?  _____

Is stove's exhaust hood and ductwork clean of grease?  _____

Do you have working fire extinguisher close by?  _____

Are harmful cleansers lying around or in reach of children?  _____

Are sharp objects lying around or in reach of children?  _____

Are electrical devices in reach of children?  _____

### LIVING, DINING, BED & BATHROOMS    YES–NO

Is fireplace spark screen always closed?  _____

Is electrical wiring, circuits and outlets adequate to handle load?  _____

Is there sufficient space for air circulation around TV or other electrical devices?  _____

If smoking is allowed in home, are ashtrays available?  _____

Are matches and lighters out of reach of children?  _____

Does tub/shower have a rubber mat to prevent slipping while showering?  _____

Medicine cabinets locked?  _____

### GARAGE, UTILITY ROOM, WORKSHOP     YES–NO

Is dryer lint trap and vent (kept) clean?  _____

Are fuses the proper size for circuits they protect?  _____

Are combustible materials kept away from heat?  _____

Is paint thinners, paints and solvents kept in their original containers for easy identification?  _____

Is gasoline for lawn mower stored in safety can?  _____

Are oil-soaked rags in tight metal container to prevent combustion?  _____

Are trash, papers and cardboard boxes lying around on garage floor?  _____

### SELF-CHECK                         YES–NO

Do you use starter fluids (not gasoline) for barbeque fires and are barbeque mitts ember-proof?  _____

Are you using nonflammable liquids?  _____

Do you (and spouse) know the correct wattage bulbs for light fixtures (If not, now is a good time to check, also, don't forget outside light fixtures)?  _____

Do you (and spouse) know where the electrical box (fuse/circuit box) is and how to replace fuses?  _____

Do you (and spouse) know the location and procedure of shutting off water, gas, propane tank valves in case of broken or leaking pipes?  _____

Do you inspect electrical cords to make sure they're in good condition?  _____

Do you use extension cords for temporary convenience, but never permanently?  _____

Do you and family avoid using hairspray near open flames or while smoking?  _____

Do you unplug electrical devices that are around water after using?  _____

Does everyone in family know how to call the fire department?  _____

Does each phone have emergency numbers close by?  _____

Does your family have a fire escape plan and has your family done drills?  _____

Is your family familiar with alternate exits they can use in case of other emergencies?  _____

Do you make it a point not to leave your children (and their play friends) unattended and instruct baby sitters about emergency procedures?  _____

Do you have a policy of not smoking in the bedroom or in the house?  _____

Are fire extinguishers fully charged and in good working order?  _____

Do family members know where fire extinguishers are and how to use them?  _____

Does spouse and older children know how to contact police, fire dept., ambulance, poison center and locate family members by phone?  _____

Now it's time to add up your answers: If you answered **NO** to 2 or less, your home is safe. However, just one can cause a tragedy! If you answered 3 to 6 **NO's**, you are risking safety of your family. If you answered more than 7 **NO's**, you're asking for trouble. **TAKE ACTION NOW!!!**

C-11

## OTHER HOUSING PROJECTS

____ Replace filters (with spouse) on air conditioner and heating systems

____ If repairs are needed to house, especially roof, electrical, gas or water related, fix them now

____ If not done already, label fuses and circuit breakers and teach family how to use them

____ If no home security, arrange to have protection system installed

____ If you have a home security system, make sure it's in working condition

____ Leave instructions with trusted neighbor or friend should alarm activate

____ Make maintenance schedule for filter replacement and other regular maintenance

____ If you have sprinkler watering system, teach spouse how to work system and shut off

____ If you have a pool, teach spouse how to use cleaning equipment, maintenance filter, add chemicals, etc.

____ Consider home warranty protection program

____ Name and phone number of:

    ____ Plumber: _____

    ____ Electrician: _____

    ____ Handyman: _____

    ____ Housing office: _____

____ Military or police (local) crime prevention survey for your residence has been done

____ Your home or apartment has front door peephole and adequate locks on all doors and windows

## HOME TOOL KIT FOR EMERGENCIES & REPAIRS

____ Flashlights (for each family member)
____ Extra batteries
____ Fire extinguisher(s)
____ Assorted nails, screws and tacks
____ Masking tape
____ Duct tape
____ Electrical tape
____ Pliers
____ Hammer
____ Screwdrivers (assorted)
____ Scissors
____ Knife
____ Extra bulbs (correct wattage for light fixtures)
____ Extra heating & cooling filters
____ Well stocked first aid kit
____ Bottled water (one week)
____ Candles (2 dozen)
____ Matches and lighter
____ Food for a week

## IF LEAVING YOUR DWELLING UNATTENDED

____ Complete temporary change of address at post office

____ If you are renting your dwelling let your property owner know that you will be gone

____ Cancel subscriptions to residence

____ Secure weapons you have in home

____ Make arrangements with trusted family member or friend to secure and protect personal property. As an alternative, store property in a storage unit that is military friendly (discount)

____ Place high value items in a safety deposit box

## VEHICLE(S)

____ If storing car in storage while away, contact your auto insurance company to lower rate

____ Make sure your auto insurance, base decal, car license plates and inspection sticker are up to date

____ If car needs renewal while deployed, make schedule:

Inspection date: _____

Registration Date: _____

Renew base decal date: _____

Spouse drivers license renewal date: _____

____ Consider paying for roadside assistance

____ If car is in need of repair(s), fix now

____ Have car serviced (oil change, tune up, etc.)

____ List of trusted repair facilities (include tire, oil change shops & body shops)

162

____ Spouse checklist: Make maintenance schedule for oil, tires, etc. and brands used for car

____ Type of gasoline used for car: _____

____ Mileage at last tune up: _____

____ Mileage for next tune up: _____

____ Mileage at last tire rotation: _____

____ Mileage for next tire rotation: _____

____ Will tires need to be replaced while deployed? If so, when, what size, type & brand should be bought?

____ Mileage at last oil change: _____

____ Mileage for next oil change: _____

____ Grade of oil used for car: _____

____ Mileage at last lube job: _____

____ Mileage for next lube job: _____

____ Mileage at last: _____: _____

____ Mileage for next: _____: _____

____ Mileage at last: _____: _____

____ Mileage for next: _____: _____

____ Brand and size of battery (if needed) and post polarity (positive right or left?)

## EMERGENCY KIT FOR VEHICLE(S)

____ Flares
____ Spare tire (correct inflation)
____ Tire changing jack (make sure set is complete)
____ Jumper cables
____ Maps
____ First aid kit
____ Ice scraper
____ Flashlight
____ Batteries
____ Duct tape
____ Candle(s) and 2 small bowls (for heating)
____ Lighter and matches
____ Blankets
____ Bottled water
____ Call for help: coinage, calling card or cell phone
____ Camera for taking pictures of accident(s)
____ Dried food

## IT'S THE LITTLE THINGS THAT COUNT

____ Ensure children understand the separation

____ Encourage children to speak up, ask questions, express feelings and emotions

____ Notify children's school(s) of your deployment

____ Make fun videos with family before departure

____ Record bedtime stories for your children

____ Ensure that you know how to contact your family while deployed and vice versa

____ Plan separate communication time with spouse and each child

____ Have new family portrait taken, frame and hang in place for all to see

____ Make arrangement for access to base agencies (if needed). Provide list of those agencies with names (if possible), phone numbers and addresses

____ Be sure to take spare set of contact lenses and/or eyeglasses

## FAMILY: CHILDREN LEFT AT HOME

____ Discuss feelings and emotions with family members

____ Keep your normal routines with children (mealtimes, bedtimes, sport activities, etc)

____ Keep house rules intact. Don't let kids rule you

____ Let children participate in household chores. Praise them, and let them know how much it helps

____ Talk about deployed spouse in daily conversations with children to make them feel connected

____ Inspire children to write letters, e-mails, send taped messages, photos, artwork, etc.

____ Check with children's teachers to see how they are adjusting at school

## FAMILY: SPOUSE TIME

____ To help pass the time, start a hobby or volunteer time to help others

____ Be sure to set time aside for conversations with deployed spouse (e-mail or write on regular basis)

____ Be creative and fun when writing letters or e-mails to deployed spouse

____ Exercise, walk, ride a bike, etc., to pass time

____ Ensure that you set aside time for yourself

## OTHER PRE-DEPLOYMENT INFORMATION

**Military wide information:** www.militaryonesource.com
**AF Crossroads:** www.afcrossroads.com/famseparation/pre_dep_resources.cfm
**Deployment info:** www.pdhealth.mil/dcs/pre_deploy.a

Hmm!

Is there something wrong?

You don't have much time left.

Just a few minutes more and you're done

Tell it to me straight, Doc. How much time do I have left?

## IMPORTANT PHONE NUMBERS: TOP 12

POLICE: _____

FIRE DEPT: _____

POISON CONTROL: _____

AMBULANCE: _____

HOSPITAL: _____

DOCTOR: _____

PEDIATRICIAN: _____

DENTIST: _____

SCHOOL: _____

VETERINARIAN: _____

TRUSTED NEIGHBOR: _____

TRUSTED FRIEND: _____

## IMPORTANT PHONE NUMBERS: INSTALLATION

CHAPLAIN: _____

COMMANDER'S OFFICE: _____

COMPANY/
SQUADRON: _____

FAMILY CENTER: _____

FAMILY SUPPORT: _____

JAG LAWYER/AID: _____

OMBUDSMAN: _____

FAMILY READINESS: _____

YOUTH CENTER: _____

## IMPORTANT PHONE NUMBERS: FINANCIAL

BANK: _____

CREDIT UNION: _____

MORTGAGE CO: _____

ACCOUNTANT/
TAX SERVICE: _____

INVESTMENT FIRM: _____

CREDIT CARD(s): _____

LOANS: _____

STORAGE UNIT: _____

## IMPORTANT PHONE NUMBERS: INSURANCE

AUTO INS: _____

LIFE INS: _____

TRICARE: _____

DENTAL INS: _____

DWELLING: _____

## IMPORTANT PH. NUMBERS: REPAIR & OTHERS

REPAIR PERSON: _____

PLUMBER: _____

ELECTRICIAN: _____

HEATING: _____

COOLING: _____

GAS/ELECTRIC: _____

HOME SECURITY: _____

CABLE/SATELLITE: _____

PHONE CO: _____

INTERNET PROVIDER: _____

COMPUTER TECH.: _____

OTHER: _____

OTHER: _____

OTHER: _____

## FIRST AID: CHOKING

The illustration below shows the proper hand placement during the Heimlich maneuver. This maneuver is effective in dislodging small to moderate airway obstructions. If you are the only bystander on the scene, CALL 911 FIRST! If other bystanders are present, yell for someone to CALL 911.

STEP 1: For a conscious person who is sitting or standing, position yourself behind the person and reach your arms around his or her waist.

STEP 2: Place your fist, thumb side in, just above the person's navel and grab the fist tightly with your other hand.

STEP 3: Pull your fist abruptly upward and inward to increase airway pressure behind the obstructing object with quick thrusts and force it from the windpipe.
 If the person is conscious and lying on his or her back, straddle the person facing the head. Push your grasped fist upward and inward in a maneuver similar to the one above. You may need to repeat the procedure several times before the object is dislodged. If repeated attempts do not free the airway, an emergency cut in the windpipe (tracheotomy or cricothyrotomy) may be necessary.